STRATE STRUCTURE OF JAPANESE ENTERPRISES

Toyohiro Kono

Professor of Business Administration, Gakushuin University, Tokyo

Foreword by
Malcolm Falkus

The London School of Economics and Political Science

MACMILLAN

First published 1984 by
THE MACMILLAN PRESS LTD
London and Basingstoke
Companies and representatives
throughout the world

ISBN 0 333 33428 0 (hardcover)
ISBN 0 333 38273 0 (paperback)

Printed in Hong Kong

To Mizu

Contents

Foreword

Japan's sustained economic boom, the evident success achieved by so many Japanese enterprises in capturing world markets, and the speed with which Japanese businessmen have been able to introduce and develop new technologies, have all focused attention on the nature of Japan's business corporations. The Schumpeterian emphasis on entrepreneurship and on business inventiveness and initiative is once more coming into fashion as a major factor in explaining different patterns of growth between nations.

Professor Kono's major study is a welcome addition to the expanding literature on the modern Japanese economy. First and foremost, it is a study based on detailed original research into the structure and behaviour of many Japanese enterprises. In an area where conjecture and generalization often substitute for concrete information, especially in English-language studies, Professor Kono has given us a great deal of valuable information. Furthermore, the comparative approach adopted in this study is also particularly welcome. Detailed comparisons of Japanese enterprises with their counterparts in the USA, the United Kingdom and elsewhere illuminate not only the significant differences in corporate strategy and structure but also the similarities. Indeed, one of the most important contributions of this study is to stress the similarities in economic climate and response found in Japan and Western countries. Professor Kono demonstrates this not only through his analysis of national enterprises but also by examining the performances of Japanese subsidiaries abroad.

The author emphasizes throughout that many factors underlying Japan's success are by no means unique to Japan, rooted deep in Japanese history, but are in fact recent and rational innovations often readily transferable to other countries.

The study does much to increase our knowledge and understanding of Japanese business enterprises, and in questioning many traditional assumptions about Japan's economic success Professor Kono has given us a thought-provoking and challenging book.

MALCOLM FALKUS

Preface

In this book I analyze the product-market strategy, organizational structure and strategic decisions of Japanese corporations, focusing particularly on the strategic aspects of Japanese management.

The aim of this book is comparable with that in Rumelt's *Strategy and Structure and Economic Performance of American Corporations*, Channon's *Strategy and Structure of British Enterprise*, Dyas and Thanheiser's *The Emerging European Enterprise – Strategy and Structure in French and German Industry*; however, I analyze a wider aspect of strategy than the above three books.

I have analyzed the practices of relatively large and successful Japanese corporations. These practices are different from those of unsuccessful Japanese companies, and I have therefore tried to find the success factors or causal relations of business strategies. At the same time, the differences between the strategies of relatively successful companies are also analyzed to find the relationships among the sub-systems of management.

These Japanese company practices are both similar to and different from those of American and European companies. I emphasize the differences more than the similarities, but the methods of some successful foreign companies do have much in common with the practices of successful Japanese corporations. This suggests that there are universal principles behind corporate strategies. The international comparison of similarities and differences also makes clear what are the key elements for the performance of the organization.

There are four characteristics of the management practices of successful Japanese corporations. First, successful Japanese corporations are *innovative*. The goals of organization are long-term-oriented and growth-oriented. The top management is independent of the owners. The corporations are aggressive in new-product development and use formal long-range planning systems for making strategic decisions (Chapters 2, 3, 8 and 9).

Second, successful Japanese corporations are *competition-oriented*.

They compete with one another, and, to survive the competition, their product-mix is of a more specialized or technology-related rather than conglomerate type. Vertical grouping or quasi-vertical integration is also used. Multinational investment is increasing to expand the market, and is transplanting the Japanese style of management (Chapters 4, 5, 6 and 7).

Third, successful Japanese corporations are *centralized* and *soft* organizations. The head office is large, the research laboratories are centralized, and the product divisions, if they are used, are not delegated with overall functions as independent units. These centralizations are convenient for making large strategic moves. The organization is soft and organismic, jobs are ambiguously defined, and group decisions are used at each level of the hierarchy (Chapter 10).

Fourth, successful Japanese corporations *respect their workers*. They provide more opportunities for promotion and wage increases, and do not make any discrimination between blue-collar and white-collar workers (Chapter 11).

This book focuses on the first three characteristics. I have tried to locate these characteristics in typologies of management in each area, stressing the successful combination of various management features.

Most of these features were deliberately and rationally shaped after the Second World War. It is a misconception to believe that they are solely rooted in (the unique) Japanese culture. The separation of ownership from management, management committees, quasi-vertical integration, long-range planning systems, lifetime employment, ambiguously defined jobs, promotions and wage increases by length of service and merit, respect for workers – all these characteristics were formed after 1945 as a result of rational decision, though some of the systems were practised to some extent by some companies before the war.

There are a number of criticisms levelled against the universality of the Japanese style of management. The popular one is that, since Japanese culture is unique, Japanese management is also unique. As I have already stated, this is a misconception. Another criticism is that there are many weaknesses in Japanese enterprises. For example, Japanese businesses have not been original or inventive in the past. This criticism is just. However, in this book I analyze mostly only the favourable characteristics of successful Japanese companies – although I do also raise problems at the end of each chapter. Lastly, the Japanese style of management may experience difficulty in a slow-growth economy. The Japanese economy has now been moving in low gear since 1973, but many Japanese corporations have shown they can survive in a slow economy. It is obvious, however, that Japanese management will have to undergo some modification to take account of slower growth in the future. These problems are again analyzed at the end of each chapter.

I have been studying corporate strategy and strategic management decisions for many years and have written a number of books on the subject in Japanese. This book is partly the result of those studies and, in addition, of a good deal of empirical research. Data from 102 large manufacturing corporations were collected and analyzed. More than five mail questionnaire surveys were conducted, one of which was circulated in the USA and in the United Kingdom. I also visited a number of companies and interviewed many managers.

My stay as a Fulbright Visiting Scholar at the Graduate School of Management, UCLA, in 1975, arranged by Professor George Steiner, and my time as a Visiting Professor at the London Graduate School of Business Studies in 1980, arranged by Professor John Stopford, were both very beneficial for making comparative analyses. I wish to extend my thanks to Professors Steiner and Stopford not only for making the arrangements for me but also for sharing their thoughts with me.

In Japan I also owe ideas to many corporate planners, and to academic friends, especially to those in the Academy of Organizational Science and to colleagues in my own university. Professors Kuniyoshi Urabe, Kenichi Yasumuro, Kozo Nishida, Takashi Uchino and Tatsuhiko Kawashima read parts of the manuscript and gave me valuable comments. Professor Akihiro Koyama helped me in the computer processing of data. Misses Masami Akiyama, Kumi Miki and Kazue Watanabe helped me to analyze the materials and did a great deal of typing for me. Mrs Sheila Gibb devoted hours to correcting the English of the manuscript, and my wife Mizu spent many days typing, and always encouraged me. Miss Anne-Lucie Norton of the Macmillan Press has given me much help in the publication of this book. I wish to extend my hearty gratitude to all of these people.

TOYOHIRO KONO

1 Introduction

1.1 THE SUBJECT OF ANALYSIS

Much of the literature on the analysis of Japanese management systems in comparison with US or European management practices places stress on such characteristics as lifetime employment, promotion and wage increase by length of service, group decision with 'bottom-up' approach, ambiguous responsibility of individuals and company-wide unions. These analyses are more concerned with operational decisions, motivation and leadership (Vogel, 1979; Pascale and Athos, 1981; Ouchi, 1981).

This book is more concerned with the strategy, structure and strategic decisions. The framework of analysis is indicated in Figure 1.1. There are six sub-systems: (i) top management, (ii) goals of the organization, (iii) product–market strategy, (iv) capability structure, (v) operations, and (vi) the decision-making process. (Similar models are in Koontz and O'Donnel, 1972; Farmer and Richman, 1965; Negandi and Prasad, 1971.)

These six sub-systems have precedent and subordinate relationships, as the arrow shows. This is a simplified model, however. There are reverse arrows and fitting and mismatching relationships. For example, top management makes decisions on product–market strategy, but the new product mix may change the key skill for the company and the managers who hold the key skill will be promoted to top management. When both sub-systems change in dynamic fitting relations as the environment changes, then the performance will be good.

The ability and value system of top management are affected by the environment and in turn affect the product–market strategy. The goals of the organization also affect the product–market strategy, and conversely the product–market strategy affects the goals of organization.

The product–market strategy is the choice of domain where the

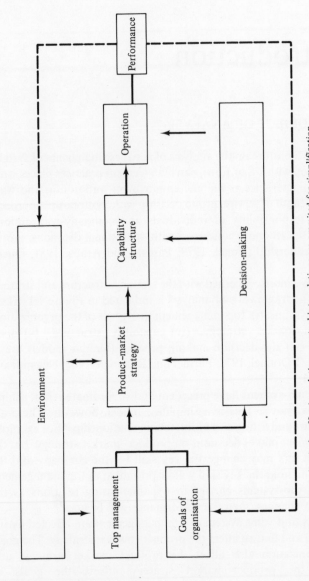

FIGURE 1.1 Framework of analysis

Note: the arrows indicate the affecting relations; mutual interrelations are ommited for simplification.

organization's activities will take place. It is comprised of the diversification of product or product mix, the vertical integration, the multinational management and the competition strategy. It affects the organizational structure, and it needs a fitting relationship with the capability structure. In order for the operation to be carried out efficiently and the performance of the organization to be high, the product–market strategy has to respond to the needs of the market, and also has to be supported by the capability structure.

The capability structure is the organizational structure, the management system, the fixed assets and the personnel capability. This can be called the resource structure. The capability structure has four key areas: strategy integration capability (top management and planning staff), development capability (development department), production capability (production department) and marketing capability (marketing department). The capability structure is different from the organizational structure, but the latter is one factor of the former.

Decision-making is one of the processes of management – that is, the planning, organizing and controlling process. Here we emphasize the planning process. With the change of environment, top management perceives the new opportunity, and finds that, by using the existing capability plus some change, they can make use of the new opportunity. They also perceive that there will be a gap of goals if they do not make use of the opportunity. Thus the product–market strategy is changed, and this affects other sub-systems. The capability cannot be changed instantly; there needs to be continuity. So this year's capability puts constraint on the next year's product–market strategy. This is one of the phases of the synergy (for the concept of synergy, see Ansoff, 1965).

Thus we assume that the perception by top management of opportunity outside and inside the organization is the starting-point or the independent variable, as the arrow of Figure 1.1 shows. This is the reason why we start by analysing top management first.

Why then do we put emphasis on the analysis of the product–market strategy? It is because the performance of the corporation is greatly affected by the product–market strategy. In a number of surveys in Japan about the opinions of top management as to which were the most important factors affecting performance, four items appeared every time: new-product development, competitive strength, strengthening of capability structure, and rationalization.

The subject of this book is similar to Rumelt's *Strategy, Structure and Economic Performance* (1974), Channon's *The Strategy and Structure of British Enterprise* (1973), and Dyas and Thanheiser's, *The Emerging*

European Enterprise (1976). It differs, however, in that it deals with the decision-making process.

We are not interested in which factors most affect the organizational structure. The organizational structure may be affected by technology, whether the product is made to order or mass produced (Woodward, 1965). It may be affected by uncertainty (Perrow, 1970; Lawrence and Lorsch, 1967), or by size and other multiple factors (Pugh *et al.*, 1969). We are interested in product–market strategy more than in the structure itself, because it affects the performance to a greater extent.

1.2 CORPORATIONS SELECTED

The research is concentrated on 102 large manufacturing corporations (summarized in Appendix 4.1) that are relatively successful. 'Relatively successful' means that corporations with bad performances were excluded. The analysis of product–market strategy in Chapters 4, 5, 6 and 7 concentrates on these 102 companies. The data base of other chapters is taken mostly from these 102 companies, but sometimes from other companies, making use of published research.

Out of these 102 companies, 4 companies were selected for intensive analysis. They are Toyota Motor, Hitachi, Matsushita Electric and Canon. They range from specialized to diversified companies.

Sources of information are (i) published material, especially annual reports, (ii) a number of visits to the companies, (iii) mailed questionnaire surveys, (iv) books on companies, in particular 100 books on Japanese corporations by the Asahi Sonorama Company.

The author stayed at the Graduate School of Management, UCLA, for one year in 1975–6, and seven months at the London Graduate School of Business Studies in 1980–1. These opportunities were convenient for collecting the information on US and British enterprises, and for international comparison.

1.3 THE APPROACH FOR INTERNATIONAL COMPARISON

This book tries to find the similarities and differences in practice in strategy, structure and decision-making processes, and causal relationships between these sub-systems. The analysis is concentrated on the important factors that affect the performance. In order to find these significant factors, the differences between successful companies and unsuccessful companies in Japan are analysed, and the practices of the successful companies are described. These practices are then compared with business practices in the USA, the UK and in other developed countries. The author tries to find the differences more than the similarities, and believes, however, that different practices are transferable to a great extent. When the same cause–effect relationships work in different countries, the different practices in one country can be transferred to another. Japanese business learned much from US and European theories, and improved its own business practice. The same can be said about the principle found in Japan; it too is transferable to a great extent.

There are similarities and differences in the environment of business. If the differences of environment are not critical to the management, or if no strong fit exists between the environmental sub-systems and the management system, or if the environment can be changed, then the theory found in Japanese enterprises can be applied to Western enterprises, and conversely US business theory can be applied to Japanese business.

There is a misconception that Japanese management is unique, based on a unique cultural background, and that it is not universal, and not transferable. Most of the characteristics of Japanese management style were formed after the Second World War as a result of rational thinking, and many theories and business practices (e.g. management committee, quality control) were transplanted from the USA or Europe. A visitor to Japanese businesses once said 'there was no new fish, but the method of cooking was better' or 'the same basic principle was implemented thoroughly here'.

Management systems must have a good fit with environmental systems such as political, educational, social and economic systems, and internal management sub-systems must also fit one another, so there are some limitations on the transferability of any management system from one country to another. However, the author finds that there are more universal principles than different, contingent principles.

In order to demonstrate what kind of Japanese management styles are universal, and what is transferable to other countries and what is not, we can use two methods. One is to observe the practices of Japanese subsidiaries in foreign countries. This is discussed in Chapter 6 of this book. Another method is to look at the practices of well-managed companies in several different countries and try to find the similarities between them. Here the author wishes to examine the case of ICI.

ICI is undoubtedly a well-managed company, and there are many similarities between the management style of ICI and that of successful Japanese companies. At ICI corporate philosophy is clearly stated, missions and philosophies are openly declared. ICI stresses increased growth and share of the market as its goals. At the top level, there is a management committee that meets once a week and discusses strategic issues. Five out of twelve full-time directors are technology or science graduates. The product mix is technology-related diversification. It has a long-range plan that integrates the strategic projects. It carries out aggressive research (spending £164 million, 3.6 per cent on sales in 1978), aggressive capital investment (£701 million, 16 per cent on sales in 1978). Even in the paint division, there is a good research laboratory, and the production facilities are on a large scale.

Jobs are firmly structured, but job enlargement and job rotations are tried among similar jobs after training. ICI has only two centralized negotiation units – a joint negotiation committee for weekly paid workers and one for monthly paid staff. Wage contract is thus centralized. There are works committees at corporate level, division level, works level and plant level. At plant level, the committee (managers and shops stewards) meets once a month and discusses all problems other than wages. The business and investment committee is another form of joint consultation and it deals with strategic problems.

ICI respects people. Managers and supervisors are encouraged to spend more than 20 per cent of their time on personnel management. There is no time recorder on the paint division, for example. The number of employees has been reduced continuously, by long-range plan, by natural turnover, not by sudden redundancy. It has a profit-sharing system. There are many job grades – seven grades under the supervisor grade – thus increasing opportunities for promotion. Job grading and wage scales are standardized throughout the company without regard to union membership.

These features are not exactly the same as those of Japanese systems, but there are many similarities and we can see that Japanese systems are not particularly unusual. The author's purpose is to find the differences between the practices of Japanese corporations and foreign enterprises, in order to discover the causes of the differences in performance; but the characteristics of Japanese management style can be found in many of the successful US or UK enterprises. For the basis of this statement, the author makes two assumptions: first, that there are more similarities among successful Japanese companies, and more variations among foreign companies; second, that the characteristics of Japanese management style are not rooted in the unique culture, but were shaped by rational thinking after the Second World War. The approaches of comparative study are explained in Appendix 1.1.

1.4 THE ENVIRONMENT – STRUCTURE AND BEHAVIOUR

It is dangerous to overemphasize the differences in environment, for there are more similarities between environments in Japan and in Western countries than there are differences. Largely speaking, the educational system of Japan is very similar to that of the USA and the political system of Japan is similar to that of the UK. Japan imported these systems from these countries.

There is a difference, however, between business environments. Even in this case, if the mutual interaction between business and environment is weak, the same management system can succeed. This can be stated as a universal principle. In this section, we will look at differences of environment. The interaction may be weak or strong, and the management system may or may not be transferable.

1.4.1 Sociological System

The population of Japan numbers 117 million, and is approximately twice the population of the UK, West Germany and France. Living standards are about the same as in these countries. The Japanese home market is large enough to ensure that successful new products that survive the competition in Japan have enough competitive power to survive in the world market.

One might suspect that many Japanese would die immediately after retirement, because they work too hard. However, the life expectancy at birth of the Japanese male is 73.3 years – longer than that of any other large developed country. The British male lives about 69.6 years on average. (In 1921–5 life expectancy for a male in Japan was 42 years.) This long life expectancy is one of the indicators of development but it will bring about an increase in the number of old people. Consequently the wage increase and promotion by length of service system will need some modification in the future.

Most Japanese live in city areas, so one might imagine that the crime rate is high. The statistics in 1979 are shown in Table 1.1.

In 1981 there were 446 universities (excluding 517 two-year colleges that have 0.7 million students) and 1.8 million students. Approximately

TABLE 1.1 Crime rate per 100 000 inhabitants

	Homicide	Forcible rape	Robbery
USA	9.7	34.5	212.1
UK	2.5	10.1	25.4
Japan	1.6	2.4	1.8
Arrest rate in Japan	97.5%	89.3%	76.3%

Source: National Police Agency, Japan.

300 000 out of 400 000 university graduates are supplied every year to various organizations, the balance being mostly the female graduates. It is not unusual for university graduates to account for more than 20 per cent of total employees in high-technology-product companies. The percentage of young people in higher education in Japan is 38 per cent, while it is 45 per cent in the USA, 22 per cent in the UK and 22 per cent in West Germany among the same age group (Ministry of Education, 1980). The increase in the number of university students was provided mostly by the expansion of private universities.

During the six years in elementary school, three years in junior high school and three years in senior high school, a structured education with a uniform curriculum for every pupil is stressed, all students being considered of equal capability. The equal treatment and group training has a very important effect in elementary and junior education, because of the homogeneity of the Japanese people. Up to junior-high-school level, a morning meeting is held every day, and the school head gives a speech. So the morning meeting in business enterprises is nothing new to Japanese workers. School excursions are compulsory. Many schools have school mottos and school songs. Group spirit rather than individualism is emphasized in such an educational system.

The author brought three children to Santa Monica while staying as a visiting scholar at UCLA. In the elementary school there was no morning meeting, and in the classroom children at each table studied different things depending upon their ability. In the high school the same year students seldom met together, but attended different classes according to their ability. Thus this system was different from the Japanese junior-education system.

Generally speaking, however, the total educational system in Japan is similar to the US system, especially in higher education. There are public and private universities and this system is flexible enough to meet the demands of the society.

One of the characteristics of the Japanese value system is organization-orientedness. Devotion to organization is a fundamental value of Japanese people. Workers will select one formal organization, and devote themselves to that alone. The ethos that requires respect for the independence of the individual, freedom of the individual, and more hours for leisure has not traditionally had the highest value for the Japanese people. Organization-orientedness comes from traditional culture.

The Japan Broadcasting Authority (Nihon Hoso Kyokai – NHK) recently conducted a survey on the value system of the Japanese (NHK, 1979). Asked whether the employee would sacrifice his private life to devote himself to the organization, the response was as follows: 'Do you devote yourself to the organization at the sacrifice of your private life?'

Yes – 25 per cent; Possibly yes – 44 per cent; No – 28 per cent. (The sample included every level of worker, from ordinary workers to managers.)

Another survey conducted concerned the importance of the job as the source of value in life. The result was another indication of organization-

TABLE 1.2 Value of life – an international survey

| | *'Which is the more important source for the value of life?'* | |
	Job %	*Life outside job* %
Japan		
Young	38	48
Adult	65	27
USA		
Young	25	63
Adult	34	51
UK		
Young	23	68
Adult	27	60

Notes
[1] The number indicates the percentage of respondents who selected each item.
[2] The ages of the young are between 18 and 24, the age of adults is over 35.
[3] Survey by Prime Minister's Office 1978, sample was 1500 young and adult workers in Japan, in the USA and in the UK.
[4] Prime Minister's Office: The attitude of young workers in the organizations, 1978. The table is only a part of the analysis of many questions and answers.

orientation. As Table 1.2 shows, many Japanese workers select their job rather than their life outside the job as the source of value of life. The percentage is higher than that of the US or UK workers. The importance of job value increases as the age of the workers increases. The other survey by NHK (Japan Broadcasting Authority) also shows that there is a tendency to rate the job more highly among older workers, but this becomes less significant as the years pass. The average age of Japanese workers is increasing. The future situation can be forecast by these three factors.

1.4.2 Political System

Since the end of war, there has been the continuous dominance of the conservative party (Liberal Democrats). The Socialist Party has never obtained a majority except once (in 1949). This has enabled a long-term economic policy to be worked out. There are many factions in the Liberal Democratic Party: they compete with and criticize one another, and these small groups help the party to be viable.

In 1981 Liberal Democrats occupied 288 out of 511 seats in the lower house (House of Representatives); the Socialist Party members accounted for only 104. There is, however, an increasing number of members from 'middle of the road' organizations such as Komeito, Democratic Socialists and the New Liberal Club, occupying about 80 seats altogether. In the future there is the possibility that the Liberal Democrats will lose their majority and will have to form a mixed Cabinet with these middle-of-the-road parties. This change will end the long-lived political stability in Japan.

The Liberal Democratic Party is financially supported by business, but is voted for by people from every section of the community – even by members of the labour unions. The Socialist Party is financially supported by labour unions, and is voted for mostly by union members.

The civil service in Japan is competent, and plays a very important role in government, in collecting information, in enacting laws and in the operation of the government. Japanese politicians rely on the civil service to a much greater extent than occurs in the USA or the UK. In the USA, the politicians depend on lobbies for information; in the UK the civil service plays a less significant role because of the more frequent changes in government.

The MITI (Ministry of International Trade and Industry) plays an important role co-ordinating business activity, although the role is overemphasized by foreigners. The MITI does not have strong legal powers but through fragmental powers to issue permits and licences, and through persuasion, it has influential power. For example, when there was overcapacity in the shipbuilding industry, MITI formed a committee from all the shipbuilding companies and encouraged it to work out plans to curtail the capacity.

The Economic Planning Agency under the authority of the Prime Minister's Office set up long-range economic plans in 1955, 1960, 1965, 1967, 1970, 1973, 1976 and 1979. These long-range plans gave a stimulus to business, became guidelines for business long-range planning, and encouraged management in long-term thinking.

Unlike big business in the USA, business in Japan is not antagonistic to the government. Unlike its counterpart in the UK, the government is not preoccupied with rescuing ailing public enterprises. It is more concerned with positive changes of industrial structure.

Japanese government is not an expensive organization. The government expenditure is 10 per cent of gross national product, as compared with 18 per cent in the USA and 20 per cent in the UK. The numbers employed in the civil service amount to 10 per cent of all the employed population, but it is 21 per cent in the USA and 24 per cent in the UK.

The labour unions make up another political organization. The union members accounted for 31 per cent of about 40 million employed workers in 1980 (35 per cent in 1970). This unionization rate is a little higher than in the USA (23 per cent in 1978), and lower than in the UK (57 per cent in 1978). The unions are organized on a company basis, and during the last ten years the days lost in labour disputes were fewer than in the USA and the UK, but more than in West Germany.

There is good co-operation between complementary organizations, and strong competition among similar-function organizations. The relations between political parties and government bureaucrats, business and government, business and unions, business and universities, and business and homes are co-operative; however, businesses in the same line are in severe competition.

Therefore, what are the conditions for co-operation between complementary organizations? First, each organization tends to recognize the mission of the organization, and tries to see its role in the wider environment. This is the organization-orientedness of the organization; for example, in the case of the railway strike, the union leader was very anxious to end the strike because it was against the interests of the public. Second, there are plural organizations with the same functions. There are not only public and private business enterprises, but there are public and private universities, more than two labour federations, and sometimes two unions in the same profession in one company. They tend to be flexible and competitive. In order to solicit more members, each organization has to improve performance. Third, the government plays an important role as a co-ordinator. Fourth, the daily newspapers are centralized and powerful in Japan. There are three major national daily papers and two minor national daily papers. The *Asahi* is the number two paper and its circulation is 7.5 million a day. The quality level of these major papers is high compared with the *Daily Mirror* or *Los Angeles Times*. (We do not compare with the *New York Times* or *The Times* because the circulation numbers are quite different.) These newspapers are powerful and function as a means of social feedback to ensure the legitimacy of business organizations' operations. When pollution became a problem, the newspapers reported the facts every day and criticized the activity of business, and as a result the level of pollution control in Japan became one of the highest in the world.

1.4.3 The Economy

The performance of the Japanese economy in the past has been good. The real growth rate after 1959 until the oil crisis in 1973 was more than 10 per cent, and even after that it was approximately 5 per cent. The gross national product of Japan in 1950 was only 4 per cent of that of the USA, but in 1980 it was 40 per cent of that in the USA. Japanese steel, cars and electrical home appliances are penetrating world markets.

There are many weak sectors, however. The labour productivity in agriculture is one-tenth that in the USA; the productivity in retail industry is one-half that in the USA. The chemical industry and the paper and pulp industry have high labour productivity, but the profit margin is low. The pharmaceutical industry is not very competitive. Japan is behind the USA in atomic energy production technology and in the airplane industry. The industries that are affected by the price of resources (for example, the petrochemical industry) are weak. The large-system products that are supported by the defence budget (for example, airplane manufacture) are also weak.

Japanese industry is strong in mass-produced products in large organizations, where the co-operation of the worker is essential; also, in high-technology products where high-level skills are required. It was fortunate that these technology-intensive products, such as steel and electrical home appliances, were in growing demand in world markets.

The high growth rate of the economy was achieved by reallocating human resources. Even in 1950, 48 per cent of all workers were employed in primary industry, but in 1978 this was reduced to 11 per cent. In the manufacturing industry, which employs 35 per cent of the workforce now, the structure has changed. The major industry before the war was the textile industry, but it is now heavy industry; that is, the metallurgical, machinery and chemical industry: these three account for 50 per cent of the manufacturing workers.

The savings rate of Japanese households is very high. Household saving as a percentage of disposable income was about 20 per cent over the last twenty years, while it was 7–10 per cent in the USA and in the UK (OECD, 1979). This high savings ratio could support the high growth rate. There are several reasons for the high savings rate. The large bonus payment in summer and in winter that accounts for about 40 per cent of salary is one reason, the trust in political stability is another. This large-scale saving went mostly to the banks, the banks loaned the money to industries directly, not through securities, with the result that most of the capital of the corporations is loan capital from banks. The net worth ratio (equity ratio) of Japanese corporations is only 20 per cent on average (421 large manufacturing companies in 1978 (Mitsubishi Soken, 1978)). However, the banks have a longer-term view than the shareholders: to let the companies grow to ensure an increase in the demand for loans. The banks do not intervene in management unless the companies suffer from serious deficits.

1.4.4 The Research System

Research is conducted by universities, public research institutions and by private companies. These institutions respectively spend about 22 per cent, 13 per cent and 65 per cent of total research expenditure (Science and Technology Agency, 1980). These ratios are almost the same in the USA and in the UK. The distribution of the source of cost – or of who pays for the research – is different. In Japan the distribution of the source of cost is almost the same as the distribution of activity. In other words, each research organization is self-supporting, with the exception of the public universities. Government spending was only 34 per cent of all research expenditure in 1977, but in the USA and in the UK government spending was over 50 per cent in 1977. Basic research was difficult in this situation. There were only three Nobel prize-winners in science. The ratio of payment for imported technology over receipts for exported technology was five to one in Japan, while it is one to ten in the USA and almost the same in the UK.

Japanese industry was strong in the application of imported technology and the development of new products; but there was little original breakthrough. The capacity for such application is one of the strengths of Japanese industry, because the final economic products are important for the economic welfare. The importing of technology is becoming difficult, however, and Japan has to improve her own creative ability.

What, then, is the future perspective on the research capability of Japan? First, research expenditure is increasing. The ratio of research expenditure to gross national product was about 2.2 per cent in 1980, and this ratio is almost the same as in the USA, the UK, West Germany and France. This means that the actual amount is twice as large as that of European countries. On the industry level, the percentage of research expenditure on sales is increasing, especially in technology-intensive industry. The ratio in the electrical machinery industry was 3.71 per cent in 1980 for example (Statistics Bureau, 1981). As the size of the company grows, the amount of research expenditure increases.

Second, the number of people engaged in research is large – approximately 310 000 in Japan in 1980, 630 000 in the USA, 80 000 in the UK and 100 000 in West Germany (Science and Technology Agency, 1980). This means that Japan has three times as many researchers compared with the UK and other European countries. In addition, the number of students who major in engineering and natural science and who are graduating from universities every year is approximately 100 000 in Japan, 200 000 in the USA and 30 000 in the UK, West Germany and France. If the same percentage of Japanese graduates as those of other countries goes into research, then the advantage in numbers engaged in research will continue, assuming that the quality of education is the same. There are more universities in Japan and more university students than in European countries, although the quality of education is somewhat inferior.

On the industry level, the percentage of researchers among total employees is high, especially in technology-intensive industries – 5.5 per cent in electrical machinery and 4.0 per cent in fine machinery for example (in 1980).

Whether Japanese-style working conditions such as lifetime employment, promotion and wage increase by length of service and respect for people promote or hinder creative activity is debatable. This will be studied in later chapters. There are merits and demerits in the Japanese system. One advantage is that with the lifetime employment system, research can be conducted under long-range plans and an accumulation of knowledge is possible. The disadvantage is that it is hard to start the risky, unstable venture business or independent research groups, because under the lifetime employment system few competent researchers enter unstable organizations.

1.5 SUMMARY

This book seeks to analyse the strategy, structure and strategic decisions of Japanese corporations. The framework of analysis is shown in Figure 1.1.

The analysis is on the practice of successful Japanese corporations, as compared with unsuccessful Japanese corporations. This volume analyses also the similarities and differences of management practices as compared with US or UK corporate practices, with more emphasis on differences. By looking at the differences we can uncover the hidden key factors. As the Japanese themselves imported many management theories and practices, so the Japanese system can also be transferable, within certain limitations.

Some of the practices considered as characteristic of Japanese management can be seen in some successful US or UK enterprises. This means the Japanese style is universal in one sense.

Why are there similarities of management practice between Japanese enterprises and some US enterprises, at the same time as there are differences? The author assumes that Japanese management practices are more similar among successful Japanese companies, and that there are more variations among US or UK companies. The author assumes also that most of the characteristics of Japanese management style were shaped after the war by rational thinking, and not deeply rooted in the culture of Japan.

There are two important factors in the environment of business in Japan. One is that Japan is an adaptive society. It was able to make use of modern technology and to override a number of economic crises. There are more than 440 universities, public and private, which put much emphasis on technology and science and provide the business organizations with a large number of highly educated people.

Long-range economic planning and other consistent public policies were made possible because of the long period in office of the Liberal Democrat Party, which was supported by a competent civil service. There is good co-operation between complementary organizations: for example, between business and university, business and government, business and labour unions. There is, however, severe competition between organizations with the same function. The high savings rate provided the funds for aggressive investment at low interest rates. Most of the important new technology was positively imported and development research was emphasized. These factors all contributed to Japan's adaptability and, as a result, to the high economic growth after the war.

The second important characteristic is the organization-orientation of the people. Devotion to formal organizations is a fundamental value of the Japanese people; they will select one organization and will devote themselves to that organization for their lifetime.

These factors underlie the characteristics of Japanese management. But it is a misconception to say that the features of Japanese management are solely rooted in Japanese culture. On the contrary, most of the features were shaped after the war by rational judgement.

1.5.1 Problems

The environmental conditions that fostered the high growth rate after the war could change in the future.

1.5.1.1 Political stability

The number of seats obtained by the Liberal Democrats shows a long-term trend to decline in both the House of Representatives (511 members) and the House of Councillors (252 members). In several recent elections, Liberal Democrats won by a very thin margin. The Socialist Party is also losing seats and three middle-of-the-road parties are making gains. If the Liberal Democrats lose their majority, then the present political stability will decline.

In the UK the alternate dominance of two opposing political parties has been a most serious obstacle to growth, because it has hampered co-operation between the government and business, and made it impossible to establish a long-term policy. Japan may find herself in a similar situation in the future.

1.5.1.2 Value system of the workers

As the living standards of the people rise, their value system changes. Although the organization-orientation of Japanese people is rooted in their traditional values, the recent change of lifestyle is beyond precedence. The survey shows the long-term decline of organization-orientation and the value of the job. Young people are more in-dividualistic and leisure-oriented.

1.5.1.3 International constraints

The degree of Japan's dependency on foreign trade is not very high. The figure for exports divided by gross national product is about 13 per cent, as against 9 per cent in the USA, 22 per cent in the UK and 23 per cent in West Germany (Bank of Japan, 1981). However, Japan's share of exports in the free world trade market is about 7 per cent, which is comparable to that of the USA and other countries. The exporting goods are technology-intensive ones that the importing countries, especially the developing countries, want to produce. The export market of Japan is highly diversified, but if the constraints against imports are strengthened by the importing countries, then funds to buy natural resources will fall short. Japan will have to make efforts to find new high-technology products and to increase her investment in multinational management in foreign countries to replace the exports.

APPENDIX 1.1: THE APPROACHES OF INTERNATIONAL COMPARATIVE STUDY

The six approaches are indicated in Table 1.3. The universal approach assumes that there is only one theory (cell one), or a group of universal theories (cell 3). A group of universal theories means that the countries are grouped by develop-

TABLE 1.3 Contingency theory matrix

Countries	Universal approach	Contingency approach	Emphasis on difference
In one country	(1) Universal theory	(2) (National) Contingency theory	(X) 'It all depends.'
In more than one country	(3) Universal theory (or international grouping of universal theory) (or convergence theory)	(4) International grouping of contingency theory	(Y) Emphasis on differences

ment stage, and universal theories are found in each stage. This is sometimes called the convergency theory.

If a fitting relationship is found between more than two sub-systems of the organization and the environment, this supports a contingency theory. For example, if it is found that a technology-related diversification with many technology-major top managers has a good performance, this supports a kind of contingency theory, because the fitting of more than two sub-systems and performance is analysed (cell 2).

If the researcher tries to find only the differences of practices and causal relations, the approach is cell X and cell Y, and he assumes that there is no theory – it all depends on other sub-systems. If the researcher assumes that although there are differences there are more similarities of practice among well-managed successful companies in advanced countries, then he is applying an international universal theory (cell 3). If we can say that in every country the successful companies have high security of employment, and this seems to be the reason for high performance, then this supports an international universal theory (cell 3). If we can say that in every country the job security in technology-intensive companies brings about a good performance, but that job security in labour-intensive companies brings about a bad performance, then this supports an international contingency theory (cell 4). If we can say that in developed countries job security leads to good performance, but that in less-developed countries severe discipline improves the performance, then this supports a kind of international contingency theory (cell 4). If it is apparent that the less-developed countries will progress and become developed countries, and the same principle can be applied to management at the same development stage, this supports the convergency theory (cell 3).

By using an equation, we can express the above four as follows:
performance $(P) = F$ (one   organizational   sub-system (X),   other organizational sub-system (Y), country sub-system (Z))

(1) $P = F(X, Y^*, Z^*)$ – universal theory
(2) $P = F(X, Y, Z^*)$ – contingency theory
(3) $P = F(X, Y^*, Z)$ – international grouping of universal theory
(4) $P = F(X, Y, Z)$ – international grouping of contingency theory
The asterisk ($*$) indicates fixed value, because it is an unimportant variable.

If Z is in orderly progress, then (3) can be called the convergency theory.

What, then, is the approach of this book? This is hard to categorize, because the author does not like to be constricted by strict methodology. As far as possible, it has been attempted to find an international universal theory (cell 3) and, to a lesser extent, an international contingency theory (cell 4). If it is stated that these are the characteristics of Japanese management that are different from those of the majority of foreign enterprises, but that these characteristics are found in a few successful companies in foreign countries, then this is an international universal theory. (On contingency theory, see Kast and Rosenzweig, 1973; Woodward, 1965; Lawrence and Lorsch, 1967; Fiedler, 1967. On international comparison, see Farmer and Richman, 1965; Negandi and Prasad, 1971; Schollhammer, 1969.)

REFERENCES

Bank of Japan (1981) *Comparative International Statistics*, Tokyo, Bank of Japan.

Kono, T. (1974) *Keiei Senryaku no Kaimei* (Analysis of Corporate Strategy), Tokyo, Diamond Sha.

Ministry of Education (1980) *Statistical Abstract of Education, Science and Culture*, Tokyo, Ministry of Education.

Mitsubishi Soken (1978) *Kigyo Keiei no Bunseki* (Financial Analysis of Business), Tokyo, Mitsubishi Soken.

NHK (National Broadcasting System) (1979) *Nihonjin no Shokugyokan* (Attitudes of Japanese Workers), Tokyo, NHK.

Nihon Hoso Kyokai (1978) *Nihonjin no Shokugyo Kan* (Views on the Jobs by the Japanese), Tokyo, Nohon Hoso Shuppan.

Prime Minister's Office (1978) *Soshiki de Hataraku Seishonen no Ishiki* (Attitude of Young Workers in the Organizations), Tokyo, Prime Minister's Office.

Science and Technology Agency (1980) *Kagaku Gijitsu Hakusho* (The White Paper on Science and Technology), Tokyo, Science and Technology Agency.

Statistics Bureau (1981) *Report on the Survey of Research and Development*, Tokyo, Statistics Bureau.

Ansoff, H. I. (1965) *Corporate Strategy*, New York, McGraw-Hill.

Chandler, A. D. (1962) *Strategy and Structure: Chapters in the History of the Industrial Enterprise*, Mass., MIT Press.

Channon, D. F. (1973) *The Strategy and Structure of British Enterprise*, London, Macmillan.

Dyas, G. P. and Thanheiser, H. T. (1976) *The Emerging European Enterprise: Strategy and Structure in French and German Industry*, London, Macmillan.

Farmer, R. N. and Richman, B. A. (1965) *Comparative Management and Economic Progress*, Ill., Richard D. Irwin.

Fielder, F. E. (1967) *A Theory of Leadership Effectiveness*, New York, McGraw-Hill.

Gort, M. (1962) *Diversification and Integration in American Industry*, Princeton, Princeton University Press.

Greiner, L. (1972) 'Evolution and Revolution as Organization Grows', *Harvard Business Review*, July–Aug.

Kast, F. E. and Rosenzweig, J. E. (1973) *Contingency Views of Organization and Management*, Chicago, Science Research Associates.

Koontz, H. and O'Donnel, C. (1972) *Management: A Systems Analysis of Managerial Functions*, New York, McGraw-Hill.

Lawrence, P. R. and Lorsch, J. W. (1967) *Organization and Environment*, Mass., Harvard University Press.

Miles, R. and Snow, C. (1978) *Organizational Strategy, Structure and Process*, New York, McGraw-Hill.

Negandi, A. R. and Prasad, S. B. (1971) *Comparative Management*, New York, Appleton-Century-Crofts.

OECD (1979) *National Accounts of OECD Countries*, Paris, OECD.

Ouchi, W. (1981) *Theory Z*, Mass., Addison-Wesley.

Pascale, R. T. and Athos, A. G. (1981) *The Art of Japanese Management*, New York, Simon & Schuster.

Perrow, C. (1970) *Organizational Analysis*, Calif, Wadsworth.

Pugh, Hickson, Hinings and Turner (1969) 'The Context of Organizations', *Administrative Science Quarterly*, vol. 14.

Rumelt, R. P. (1974) *Stragegy, Structure and Economic Performance*, Mass., Harvard University Press.

Schollhammer, H. (1969) 'The Comparative Management Theory Jungle', *Academy of Management Journal*, vol. 12.

Steiner and Miner (1977) *Management Policy and Strategy*, New York, Macmillan.

Stopford, J. M. and Wells, L. T. (1972) *Managing the Multinational Enterprise*, New York, Basic Books.

Thompson, J. (1967) *Organizations in Action*, New York, McGraw-Hill.

Vogel, E. F. (1979) *Japan as Number One*, Mass., Harvard University Press.

Woodward, J. (1965) *Industrial Organization, Theory and Practice*, London, Oxford University Press.

2 Top Management

There are four levels of management: trusteeship management, general management, departmental management and field management (Holden, Fish and Smith, 1941). We will call the first two levels top management, and will investigate its general pattern in Japan.

Top management is expected to perform several functions. First, it is expected to define the value system and the goal of the organization, taking into consideration the demands of shareholders and other stakeholders. Second, it is expected to define the relationship between the organization and the environment, or to make decisions on product–market strategy. Third, it is expected to organize, that is, to formulate the organizational structure and select the key personnel (Katz and Kahn, 1966). Thus strategy, structure and performance are greatly influenced by top management.

On the other hand, the strategy defines the central key expertise, and influences the promotion of top executives. The technology-related diversified companies require technological knowledge and technological experts in control; the marketing-related diversifier requires to have a marketing man in top management. The strategy has to have continuity, and if there is a good fit between the strategy and the technical skill of the top executives the strategy can be successful.

2.1 BOARD OF DIRECTORS

At the trusteeship level of corporation, there are two organs, the board of directors and the auditor. The auditor is a formal organ of the company according to Japanese company law. These two organs do not function effectively. The board of directors in the Japanese corporation is not the sovereign organ; it is only a formality. It meets less than once a month, and makes decisions only on legally required minimum matters: long-range plans are seldom submitted to the board for authorization. Only 13 per cent of Japanese companies submit long-range plans to the

21

board for authorization, while 35 per cent of US corporations and 64 per cent of UK corporations do so (see Table 9.3).

There are several reasons why the board is not the actual governing body. The important ones are (i) the extent of divorce of management from ownership is advanced in Japan, (ii) most of the directors are full-time company members, and (iii) the management committee of full-time senior directors functions effectively. These reasons are mutually interrelated.

Separation of management from ownership not only affects the decline of the board's power, but also the goals of the corporation. Before the war a handful of families (Zaibatsu, Mitsui, Mitsubishi, Sumitomo and so on) owned the majority of the stock of large corporation in key industries. Most of the large corporations were controlled by the owners.

After the war the holding companies of these Zaibatsu families were dissolved, and all stocks were sold to the public. Now the extent of separation of management from ownership of large corporations is the highest among the advanced countries, though it is a fallacy to say that all Japanese corporations have divorced management from ownership; most of the small businesses are controlled by their owners and there are also some large corporations where there are owners in control. Kagono investigated 189 large corporations in 1971 (Kagono's paper in Urabe, 1975) and found the distribution given in Table 2.1.

The board is expected to represent the interests of stockowners, and should include a shareholders' representative, but because of the separation of management from ownership, there is no representation of the shareholders on the board, and there is almost no voice among the

TABLE 2.1. Distribution of ownership types of 189 large corporations

	Companies	%
Private ownership	0	0
Majority ownership	3	2
Minority control	17	8
Management control	169	90
Total	189	100

Notes:
[1] Control is measured by ultimate control.
[2] Minority control means actual control with the control group holding more than 10% and less than 50% share of stock.

owners. This separation also affects the goals of the corporation; the short-term profit is not considered important; earnings per share is seldom used as the goal.

There are few outside members on the board. This is an important cause of its weak function. The number of directors varies from company to company depending upon the size of the company, but the average in large corporations is sixteen persons (Furukawa, 1973, 134 companies), and the average number of outside members is only 1.6. The same survey shows that 34 per cent of large corporations do not have outside members. Toyota and Canon do not have any outside director for example. There is no committee under the board, either.

In the USA and UK the percentage of outside members on boards of directors is about 40 per cent, and inside members (former officers and present officers) account for approximately 60 per cent (Koontz, 1967). Because of this the US board is performing, in addition to legal functions, such functions as giving advice on financing, monitoring the decisions of officers, and authorizing long-range plans.

The reasons for the low percentage of outside directors in Japanese corporations are as follows. There is more separation of management from ownership. This has already been mentioned. As a concept, the corporation is considered as an organization of employees like a community organization, or *Gemeinschaft* (Tönnies, 1887) and outside members are not welcome in positions of authority. The meaning of director is different from that in the USA or in the UK, with high prestige value being attached to the title of 'director'. There is no such position as vice president. The title of director holds higher prestige value than just the title of head of department. If one man is entitled to become a member of the board while remaining as head of a department, his status changes and there is a high possibility of his being promoted to a further higher position. The directors thus comprise the chairman, the president, the general top management and the higher position of head of department. Such precious titles cannot be given to outside members.

There are both merits and demerits in the decline of the board's powers. Full-time top management who have been promoted from within the company can have the highest authority; and can be sealed off from outside power, especially from the pressure of ownership. The organization can aim at long-term growth for the benefit of the employees at the sacrifice of short-term profit, and this can result in the increase of profit in the long run.

The demerit is that there is nobody to check the power of the president, the chief executive officer. The president can be all-powerful.

If there is no group decision-making body at the general management level, this drawback can be serious, but in Japan, as analysed later, management committees are popular.

The decline of the board's powers can be seen in the USA and in the UK, but in Japan the extent of the board's ineffectiveness is much more remarkable.

2.2 MANAGEMENT COMMITTEE AT GENERAL MANAGEMENT LEVEL

In Japan the management committee of senior full-time directors is the most important decision-making body at the top. Holden, Fish and Smith classified the types of general management level into four: one chief executive, management committee (council of general executives), assembly of department heads (chief executive and council of divisional executives), and the board of directors working as general management (Holden, Fish and Smith, 1941). In Japan the management committee as a group decision-making body was created during the 1950s in most of the large corporations; the rate of diffusion is very high. There are a number of surveys on the management committee (Furukawa, 1973, 134 companies; Kansai Branch, Japan Productivity Centre, 1976, 490 companies). According to these surveys, 87 per cent or 86 per cent of the large corporations have management committees. Even in 1960 a survey on 229 companies showed that 70 per cent of them already had management committees (Doyukai, 1960).

We will neglect the case of medium-sized companies. If we include the medium-sized companies, we see a different percentage. The 1978 survey made by MITI on 344 large manufacturing corporations and 197 medium-sized manufacturing corporations shows a slightly different trend. According to this survey, the top management organization of 197 medium-sized companies was classified as follows. Some 42 per cent of companies had management committees, 50 per cent of companies had a board of directors as the top organ of management, 7 per cent had a meeting of department heads as top management and the one-man type was not listed as a classification. In the case of medium-sized companies the number of directors is not so large and there are almost no outside directors, so the board of directors can work not only as a legal organ but also as a general management organization.

We will here analyse the case of large corporations where the number of board members is too large, and the management committee is comprised of selected higher-status members of the board. The average number on the management committee is approximately ten, and usually includes the chairman, the president and the chief executive officer, and four to six executive directors. This means that ten senior directors out of sixteen directors constitute the management committee. These ten directors each have a broad responsibility for corporate decisions covering several departments, receiving reports from these departments, and giving advice to them. They are not identical to department heads; their major responsibilities are the general management – although sometimes some executive directors are department heads. In the case of Canon, six out of nine members of the management committee are department heads.´ In such cases, the management committee is a mixture of council of general management and council of divisional executives. It is supposed, however, that the department head will act as part of general management, and will not represent the interests of the department.

The management committee meets once a week, Tuesday morning or Monday afternoon. The clerical office of the management committee is the planning department in most cases, which will arrange the topics and materials.

The management committee is not an advisory committee to the president, nor an information dissemination meeting, but a decision-making body. According to the survey conducted by the Kansai Branch of Japan Productivity Centre, 34 per cent of the responding companies say it is a decision-making body, and 44 per cent say it is an advisory organ to the president but in reality a decision-making body.

The power of the president in the management committee varies from company to company. At one extreme the committee is a one-man show. At the other extreme the president only listens to the discussion and rarely extends his opinion, but in cases where there is a wide conflict of opinion, or where the issue in his judgement is too critical, he may take action. The majority of cases are between these two extremes.

There is a tendency that the longer the tenure of the president, the larger the difference in competence, and the stronger the leadership of the president. The president of a specialized company tends to have stronger powers than the president of a diversified company, because he knows more.

In the USA or UK, this kind of management committee is not necessarily popular. Recently in the USA, however, there has been a growing tendency towards having a group at the top as a group decision-making body. The name of this body may be the president's office, management committee, senior executive committee, planning committee or some other name. There are usually three to five committee members. In the case of a diversified newspaper company, the members are the chairman (chief executive officer), vice chairman and president; in the case of a diversified electric appliances company, the 'office of chief executive' comprises the chief executive officer, the president, the vice president in administration, vice president in finance, and former chief executive office. They meet more than once a week, and make decisions as a group. Such a spread of the president's office in large corporations seems to be a recent development. The reason for it may be that the rapidly changing environments impose on top management a heavy burden of difficult strategic decisions; also that the tendency towards diversification and multinational management make the decisions more difficult.

There are some differences between management committees in Japanese corporations and those in US or UK corporations. First, the members of Japanese committees have a broader responsibility; most of them are not heads of department. In the USA or the UK, the responsibility of each member is usually clear. Second, management committees have fewer members in the USA than in Japan. According to my survey, the management committee at IBM has four, at Northrop four, at Goodyear six, at Fluor eight and at GE nine members. Because of this, it is not unusual for the head of the product department to confront top management to discuss long-range plans separately, and the top management committee will spend day after day discussing long-range plans in the USA. The process of decision-making is a kind of one-to-one confrontation process and it is not frequently used in Japan, where long-range plans will be discussed by the management committee, one of whom will represent any product division. Third, the diffusion of management committee is wider in Japan than in the USA or in the UK. Group decisions at every level of management is popular in Japan.

Recently in Japan there has appeared a tendency to strengthen the top ranks of the group decision-making body. In addition to the ordinary management committee, many companies have created another body – the senior management committee. This is composed of the chairman, president and a few senior executive directors, in all between five and eight members. The 'senior management committee' discusses only the strategic problems and refers the issues to the management committee for a final decision. The senior committee is a free discussion or brainstorming body for strategic issues. In other cases the issues are divided into two; the strategic issues are discussed and decided by the senior management committee and operational issues are discussed and decided by the ordinary management committee.

This two-group system emerged for two reasons. The constituent of management committees is supposed to be concerned with the general management, but it came to represent the interests of the departments concerned because the senior director was responsible to some area of the function or the product, though the responsibility was very broad. Another problem is that management committees tend to show more interest in operational issues than strategic issues, because the former is clearer and less risky. The committee might willingly spend a long time deciding the location of the company resort house, but will not decide the new policy on multinational management.

A dual top group system is one of the means to cope with these problems, but there is also another approach. Hitachi has a policy committee meeting once a month to make decisions on strategic issues, but the members of the policy committee are exactly the same as those of the management committee (sixteen members) held once a week. Sumitomo Electric holds a policy committee meeting twice a month on strategic issues, and a management committee meeting once a week on operational issues, but the members on the two committees are exactly the same.

According to my survey of twenty-five large manufacturing companies, about two-fifths have two-group systems, one-fifth have two kinds of meeting but one management committee, and the remaining two-fifths have one management committee.

Specialized companies tend to have only one management committee and diversified companies tend to have a two-group system, because in the latter case the issues tend to be more divergent and to be uncertain.

In addition to these general management committees, many companies have meetings of department heads for exchange of information, and functional committees on research and development, marketing and production, in order to co-ordinate the functional activities of diversified divisions.

The group decision-making at various levels of the management hierarchy is one of the characteristics of Japanese management. The history of this style of management is not clear. Even as early as about 1700, when the Mitsui family ran a large-scale business financing and retailing cloth, it had a group decision-making body at the top called 'O-moto-kata' which consisted of the members of eleven families and about the same number of professional managers, and met twice a month. This may indicate that there is a traditional attitude on group decision-making. There is a long tradition of thought that decisions should be made by consensus. In 604, Prince Shotoku, in the Constitution for government, emphasized the concept of harmony among the people and also stressed that decisions should be made after discussions with the people.

It is, however, an oversimplification to say that group decision comes only from Japanese tradition. The management committee is a device that developed after the war, especially from about 1950, as a result of rational decisions and by introducing American management practices (Noda, 1960).

The effects of group decisions at the top seem to be as follows:

1. The group decision takes the greater degree of risk. It has been said that group decision tends to be conservative and mediocre. Under certain conditions it can be the opposite. R. D. Clark indicates three reasons for the group to shift to risk-taking (Clark, 1971). Through group discussion much more information becomes available and uncertainty is reduced, and with more information the committee members become willing to take risks. Second, group decision frees each individual from full responsibility, since he perceives that the decision has been shaped by the group. And lastly, in group discussion the risk-taking opinion tends to have higher value than the conservative opinion, and the relatively cautious member will eventually follow the moderately risky opinion. This shift of value towards risk is observed when the consequences of failure are not severe. In Japanese corporations, the group decision is used at every level of organization, and this is one of the reasons why Japanese corporations have been innovative.

2. In order to persuade many members towards a group decision, information has to be collected and provided and this results in rational decision-making. This situation is different where one responsible person as an individual makes a decision based on less information, or based on intuition. Also in a group decision, diverse information is available when the group members all represent various fields of knowledge.

3. The member of the group can be a linking pin with the group on a lower level, and thus the decision can be conveyed to the lower levels effectively. (The concept of linking pin comes from Likert, 1967.) The senior executive is usually responsible for several departments, and the decision at the top can make use of information and ideas from lower levels and can be easily implemented. The group decision can thus be used as a means of participation.

There are several preconditions where the group decision is successful and innovative. The necessary information has to be collected beforehand, several alternatives have to be provided, problems and effects have to be prepared by the staff. This kind of job is usually performed by the planning department with five to ten staff members or by the respective departments concerned. The participants are encouraged to present their opinions, and there should be an atmosphere of freedom of expression. This is possible when minority opinions are welcome, and when the president (usually the chief executive officer) is willing to listen to these opinions instead of forcing his own.

However, when the issue is very important and risky, and when the majority is against it but when the president thinks the issue is critical to the survival of the company, he has to take more action. He has to persuade the other members, and has to make the final decision by himself.

In order for the decision of the management committee to be effective, the team members should be well informed of the issue before the meeting starts, and the materials either sent to the members beforehand or an oral explanation delivered to key personnel. This oral communication is sometimes called 'Nemawashi' (originally meaning to dig round the root of a tree), or lobbying or log rolling. This process is necessary for group decision-making, and this is part of the process of group decision-making. It is not a political manipulation, as it is sometimes misunderstood to be. When this communication is well done, the discussion in the management committee may be short, and may look like a mere formality, but this does not mean that the decision of the management committee is only one of formality. For group decision Nemawashi is necessary, and the total decision process is still a group decision-making process.

2.3 THE TOP MANAGERS

2.3.1 The Meaning of Directors

The majority of the directors on the board are full-time inside members, and the directors have a special meaning as top manager in Japan. They include the chairman (only one-third of all companies has this post), the president and the chief executive officer, senior executive directors and executive directors in charge of several departments, and ordinary directors who are usually the heads of important departments. Many department heads, however, are not directors. For example, at Hitachi in 1980 there were twenty-five directors, and one of them was an outside part-timer. Twelve of the members included the chairman, president, senior executive directors and executive directors who were all in charge of general management. The remaining twelve members were ordinary directors and they were heads of department. At Hitachi there are nineteen staff departments, thirteen divisions, four training centres, six research laboratories, eleven sales offices and two hospitals – fifty-five departments in all. Only twelve out of fifty-five are directors. To study the directors is thus to study the general management and selected key departmental managers. In American terms, they may correspond to chairman, president, executive vice presidents and selected key vice presidents.

2.3.2 Selection of Directors

2.3.2.1 Stock ownership

Directors are not selected to represent the stockholders, but are chosen for their particular abilities. They own few of the shares in the company. The author computed the stock owned by 2200 directors of 102 large manufacturing corporations, and the total ownership in 1978 accounted for only 1.42 per cent of all stocks outstanding.

2.3.2.2 Age of directors

There is a misconception that under the length of service system, promotion is slow and Japanese executives are all aged. The MITI survey in 1978 of 344 large manufacturing corporations indicated that the average age of directors was at that time 57.7 years (MITI, 1978). According to my survey, the average age of 2200 directors of the 102 largest manufacturing corporations was 56.4 years (in 1978): this age is approximately the same as the average age of vice presidents in large US corporations. Another survey in 1981 by the economic journal *Diamond* (11 July 1981) on the age distribution of 1522 newly selected directors of 656 large corporations in all business areas showed that the average age was 53. New directors between the ages of 50 and 56 account for 66 per cent of promotion. This average age of promotion is consistent with the average age of existing directors. The percentage of directors promoted under the age of 50 is only 13 per cent. This means that promotion is very slow and there are very few special promotions of younger men.

Under the lifetime employment system and the promotion by merit and length of service system, too early promotion of one outstanding person will discourage ninety-nine persons, and it will also disrupt later promotion because such a person will not leave the company for quite some time. One or two companies have tried to set up a 'fast track' system for outstanding people, but it did not work well. For Japanese corporations team work is all important; outstanding people tend to be more individualistic and less co-operative with colleagues.

2.3.2.3 Age of the president (chief executive officer)

In Japan, the president is usually the chief executive officer, and the chairman is rarely so. The MITI survey of 344 large manufacturing corporations in 1978 showed that the average age of the president was 63.3 years (MITI, 1978). According to my survey, the average age of the presidents in 102 manufacturing companies was 63.8 in 1978. This is a little older than the average age of 59 among 800 of the US chief executive officers (survey by Arthur Young Associates in 1980).

The length of tenure of the president in office varies from company to company, but a survey by one newspaper, *Nihon Keizai Shinbun*, on the length of service as president of seventy past presidents of twenty-five large manufacturing companies, shows that it averages just eight years (standard deviation, 5.1 years).

2.3.2.4 Promotion from within

The *Diamond* survey shows that out of 1522 promotions 80 per cent are from within the company, 13 per cent are from the parent company or from a subsidiary, and only 7 per cent from complete outsiders. Looking at several companies in detail, even in such fast-growing companies as Canon and Honda, there is no single director who did not come straight from university to the company. Hitachi and Matsushita have only two or three who are not direct from school. Sony is different; it has recruited many talented people from outside, and seven out of twenty-three full-time directors have been in the company for less than fifteen years. Sony is considered unusual and this policy was necessary because of its extremely fast growth and technology-intensiveness. In Japan, promotion from within encourages the middle managers to work harder to stay longer in one company.

2.3.2.5 Key technical skills

Generally speaking, holding of the resource is the source of power, and whoever holds the key resources for the organization will have the power. He will either be promoted to top management or will have the power to exercise control even when he stays outside the organization.

Top managers need to have three skills – conceptual skill, human skill and technical skill (Katz and Kahn, 1966), and the first two are the most important, though general managers must have some specialized skill until they are promoted to the top. The skills the promoted managers have must be the key skills, and by looking at the various departments whose managers are promoted to the top we can identify those skills that are considered particularly important in Japanese corporations, and can identify which departments are most influential. (An interesting analysis on the relationship between strategy and key skills is stated in Miles and Snow, 1978.) Table 2.2 is the survey on the departments from which the directors are promoted. Directors are top managers in Japanese corporations. Table 2.2 shows that there are four key areas – research and production, marketing, personnel and general management. (One-fourth of the sample companies are trade and finance firms, so there is a high percentage from marketing departments.) Each department has its own knowledge and behaviour pattern, and will influence the behaviour of the company as a whole.

Managers from research and production tend to be sensitive to technological development, and tend to make judgements on a rational basis. Sometimes they are more narrowly involved with engineering matters, and inclined to forget economic performance. The more top managers there are from this department, the more sensitive to technological innovation the company will be. The managers from marketing departments tend to be sensitive to the market, but they also tend to take a short-term view. The managers from personnel departments are skilled in human management. The managers from finance departments are more concerned with economic performance, but they tend to be insensitive to changes in the outside environment, and tend to put emphasis on short-term profit.

It is impressive that there is a high percentage of managers from research and production and marketing departments: this may result in top management showing high sensitivity to the environment. There is also a high percentage of managers promoted from personnel departments, which demonstrates that personnel management is considered important in Japanese corporations.

TABLE 2.2   Departments from which managers are
promoted to directors (656 large companies)

	%
Research and development	8.7
Production	6.5
Plant manager	9.6
Sub-total	24.8
Marketing and export	18.2
Sales branch office manager	7.6
Sub-total	25.8
Personnel	12.1
Finance and accounting	4.8
Material	1.8
Sub-total	18.8
Planning	5.8
Division managers	9.9
Regional branch managers	8.3
Sub-total	24.0
Others (general management)	6.7
Total	100.0
	(1195 persons)

Notes:
[1] Adapted from *Diamond* (July 1981) vol. 11.
[2] 1195 directors promoted from within the company.

Unlike US or UK corporations there are not so many top managers
from finance departments in Japanese corporations. It is sometimes said
that in the USA, many graduate students in business schools who major
in finance and accounting become top managers and this orients the
corporations towards short-term profits.

To support the reliability of Table 2.2, let us look at a different survey.
According to a survey by MITI (Ministry of International Trade and
Industry) on the management systems of Japanese large manufacturing
corporations, the specialities of the top ten managers of 344 large
corporations in 1978 were as follows: research and production – 3.7
persons; marketing – 3.0 persons; finance and accounting – 1.9 persons;

personnel and planning – 1.8 persons; total, – 10.4 persons (MITI, 1978).

This survey of the expertise of existing top managers also shows that there is a very high percentage of top managers whose most important expertise is in research and production. The next most important skill is marketing, and then comes finance and personnel. Finance has a little higher percentage in this survey. Personnel skill is also considered important.

The specialities of top managers will disclose what key resources the company needs. They will also characterize the strengthes and weaknesses of the corporation and its behaviour patterns.

A recent survey by Japan Association of Top Managers (Nikkeiren) on the careers of 6121 directors of 313 large corporations in 1981 disclosed that 16.2 per cent of them had been the officer of the labour union. This suggests that skill in personnel management is one of the key skills, and that there is a good co-operative relationship between the corporation and the union.

2.3.3 Educational Background and Typical Career

The general ability of top managers can be measured by their educational background. Aonuma has studied the change in the educational background of the top managers of large corporations since 1900 (Aonuma, 1965). University graduates (including graduates from three-year colleges) in 1900 accounted for 5 per cent (of 420 top managers), in 1926 for 60 per cent (of 500 top managers), and in 1962 for 90 per cent (of 1500 top managers). This shows that from 1926 a very high percentage of top managers have been university graduates. Aonuma's study also revealed that 16.5 per cent majored in law, 13 per cent in economics, 22 per cent in commerce, and 23 per cent in engineering in 1962.

The author investigated the educational background of about 2200 directors of 102 large manufacturing corporations, and this yielded the following data in 1978: university graduates – 93.8 per cent (social science – 49.6 per cent, engineering and natural science – 44.2 per cent); others – 6.2 per cent. (Note: The university includes the three-year college where students are enrolled after five-year middle school, in the pre-war educational system.) These surveys show that the educational background of Japanese top managers is high compared with that of European top managers, and that a very high percentage of top managers majored in engineering and natural science. The percentage of engineers is even higher – up to 50 per cent – in technology-related product companies. (This will be analysed in Chapter 4.) For example, in Hitachi seventeen out of twenty-five directors, in Matsushita twelve out of thirty-two full-time directors (including three non-graduates), in Canon ten out of sixteen directors are engineering and natural science graduates.

In this respect, Japanese top executives are different from UK executives. One survey shows that in Britain only 40 per cent of the chief executives are university graduates. Since 40 per cent of all university graduates are from engineering and science faculties; this means that only 16 per cent of British management has an engineering and science background (Hall *et al.*, 1969).

In Japan the best students from the universities enter the big companies. Before the war the civil service used to attract the best students, but it is not so now. Unlike the USA or the UK, the lawyer, accountant, or teaching professions do not have the highest prestige. The corporation provides the more challenging job; it offers more opportunity for promotion, higher prestige, and more colleagues to work with.

Once he enters the corporation, he will stay for life. Most of the present top executives have been working in one corporation for more than thirty years. He will be transferred from one department to another, within a certain range. For instance, an engineer may move from technical designing to production and to general manager of the plant, and sometimes even to the marketing department. He holds a certain core expertise but he also has wide experience. He will not move from company to company as a specialized professional.

The graduates from social science departments will experience marketing, accounting and personnel jobs. None of these jobs is considered as jobs for professionals. Again, he has no experience of any other company, but he has a wide experience within his own company. He has a core expertise, but he has a wider view and a wider human communication network than if he had moved, as a professional, from one company to another.

2.4 REMUNERATION

Before the war, the top managers of Japanese corporations used to receive about 5–10 per cent of company profit as a bonus. If this was distributed to ten managers, the amount for each was easily 100 times the salary of young employees. At that time the director could frequently entertain his subordinates at first-class restaurants at his own expense. Now the difference of pay between the top and the average worker has narrowed. The average total salary for the president is approximately 35 million yen per year (divided by 250 yen makes 140 000 dollars) which is about eleven times the wage of the average worker. It is estimated that the average pay for the US chief executive officer is around 440 000 dollars per year, which is about thirty times the average wage of the workers. The difference between the highest executive pay and the average worker's pay is narrower in Japan. The Japanese chief executive gets only one-third of the pay of his US counterpart, while the average worker in both countries gets approximately the same amount.

The average income of the directors is about 20 million yen per year (80 000 dollars, if divided by 250 yen), and it is about seven times the wage of ordinary workers. It is comprised of a monthly salary that accounts for 80 per cent of income, and distribution of corporate profit, which is about 20 per cent of the directors' income. Distributed profit is only a fraction of corporate profit, usually less than 0.5 per cent, and the total amount is almost the same in each of the companies, unless the corporation loses money. In other words, the financial incentive is lacking for top managers because the bonus is not linked to the profit; though no bonus is paid when the company cannot make a profit.

The fringe benefits are not so large. A company car plus driver service (not the car itself) is provided by the company. The cost for entertainment of company guests is allocated but this cannot be a regular allowance. Housing is not usually provided. The stock option is rarely used, because the company cannot hold capital stock of its own.

The payment differential between top management and the average worker narrowed dramatically after the war; this is partly because of demand and supply at each level of skills, and partly because of post-war ideas of equality. Money is not an important motivation. What is important for motivating Japanese top management is the job itself, and the social prestige of the position, both of which are derived by the success of the corporation. As measurements of success, the growth rate, the size of the firm and profit rates on sales are considered important, and top managers work hard for this purpose.

2.5 REQUIRED MANAGERIAL SKILLS FOR TOP MANAGERS – CONCEPTUAL AND HUMAN SKILLS

For top managers, conceptual skills and human skills are more important than technical skills. We have already discussed the technical skill, and here we are concerned with more important skills.

The *Nihon Keizai Shimbun* newspaper conducted a series of interviews with the presidents of large manufacturing companies. Asked what were the important personal characteristics of the president, the presidents responded as in Table 2.3. Although the qualities in question are those of the president, we think that the response can be applied generally to all top executives.

The conceptual skill is the ability to perceive the relationship between the organization and the environment, and to see the total system of the

TABLE 2.3 Required skills and behaviours for the president (opinions stated by presidents of forty-one large manufacturing companies)

Conceptual skill	
1. Broad vision, international vision	12 (29%)
2. Long-range vision and flexibility	14 (34%)
3. Aggressive initiative and decision, appropriate decision under risk	17 (42%)
4. Hard work and hard study	4 (10%)
Sub-total	47
Human skill	
1. Clear statement of goals and guidelines	7 (17%)
2. Willingness to listen to other's opinion	9 (22%)
3.(a) Impartiality, unselfishness and faithfulness	12 (29%)
3.(b) Ability to use employees' capacity fully by right allocation and by fair sanction	10 (24%)
4.a Attractive personality	9 (22%)
4.b Ability to build up a team and create harmony	8 (20%)
Sub-total	55
Health	
1. Health	19 (46%)
Sub-total	19

Notes:
[1] The percentage indicates the number of items stated, divided by the number of presidents. Total percentage is over 100 because of overlapping.
[2] From a series of articles entitled 'Top Management' which appeared in the newspaper *Nihon Keizai Shimbun* throughout 1980 and 1981.

organization. Broad vision is the opposite of narrow, specialized perspective, and the top manager is expected to see the key areas that provide opportunity, or threat, to the organization. One president states that top managers should see the relationship between the organization and society, and think what can be done for society. Top management should be able to know the real needs of the consumer. When the activity of the organization is expanding world-wide, top management needs to have world-wide vision.

Long-range vision is the ability to see into the future, and to discover what should be done now to prepare for the future. Managers tend to be concerned with today's problems, but in order to prepare for the future they have to take a long-range view. They must be able to forecast the future development of technology, as well as being aware of the present stage, in order to find new opportunities. Such future vision is arriyed at by a kind of flash of intuition after the analysis of information. Great flexibility is necessary to be creative in this way – to see the new approach, new applications and methods that are quite different from today's products and process.

The president has to make decision with an element of risk, and cannot wait until everything is clear. When the issue is a new and important one without any antecedent, there remains a high degree of uncertainty; and when the opinion of the top managers is divided, and even when the majority is against him, he has to have the courage to run a risk. This aggressive decision-making has to be supported by enough information and accumulation of knowledge, but the top managers also need to make decisions when the future is still unclear.

Human skill is the ability to motivate people, to let the common man perform the unusual jobs. The top managers have to communicate the basic policy to let the follower know any new direction of the organization, and to let them know any important information or ideas.

Listening to others' opinions is stressed in order to develop flexible thinking, and to encourage subordinates to think and formulate creative ideas. The opposite of this is to force the ideas of top managers on their subordinates. Top managers listen to the opinions of subordinates with an open mind, do not stick to the traditional view and can have flexible opinions.

Unselfishness and impartiality are required in decision-making in every area, and can be a source of power. They are especially important in deciding the promotion of a subordinate to a key position, in order to have the best fit between the personnel and the job. To promote people from the same clique is contrary to this principle. To allocate the right people to the right job, top management has to be able to exercise impartial judgement to find real capability.

Both fair reward and fair punishment have to be given to subordinates at times, and the top managers have to be able to stand resentment occasionally. Impartial evaluation is very difficult, and the final decision on personal matters is often a lonely one.

The ability to build a team spirit and to be loved by subordinates is another requirement. It is possible to acquire this ability by being unselfish, impartial and by having deep concern for subordinates. Openmindedness and understanding attract people; faithfulness to one's word creates an atmosphere of trust. With these qualities a good manager can encourage team work, and can build good human relations. Students with exceptionally high grades at school and university tend to lack this ability, and are not usually chosen as top managers in Japanese corporations.

From these interviews, we find that there are two main characteristics recommended for Japanese top management behaviour. One is aggressive decision-making supported by far-sightedness. (Conservative deliberateness is not stressed.) That trait is evidenced in the actual behaviour of Japanese enterprises. The second one is the emphasis on human skill and this is the characteristic of Japanese corporations. In all Japanese corporations group activity is very important and group decision-making is used widely at each level of the organization; therefore the ability to build a good team is very necessary.

In order to understand the meaning of the desirable behaviour patterns of top management exhibited in Table 2.3, it is useful to locate it in the different types of top management behaviour. The behaviour patterns of top management are exhibited in Table 2.4. (To build this model, ideas of Mintzberg, 1973 – both references – and Steiner and Miner, 1977, were referred to.) These behaviour patterns can be classified into four types of managers:

1. The innovative and analytical type is an aggressive innovator and at the same time a good organizer.
2. The innovative and intuitive type is an aggressive but authoritarian type.
3. The conservative and analytical type is a theorist, interested in perfection, and does not take risks.
4. The conservative and intuitive type sticks to traditional methods.

The type shown in Table 2.3 apparently corresponds to the innovative and analytical type of Table 2.4. It is a debatable problem whether the

TABLE 2.4 Patterns of executive behaviour

Patterns / Elements	(a) Innovative and analytical	(b) Innovative and intuitive	(c) Conservative and analytical	(d) Conservative and intuitive
Value and decision-Making	1.1 Devoted	Selfish	Theoretically consistent	Selfish
	1.2 Aggressive and innovative	Aggressive and innovative	Idealistic and perfectionist	Conservative and tradition-oriented
	2.1 Sensitive to new information and new ideas	Sensitive to new opportunity by intuition	Sticking to principle, theoretical	Sticking to past experience
	2.2 Flexible in ideas, with many alternatives	Intuitive in ideas, with few alternatives	Suboptimizing and incremental	Inflexible
	3. Able to make quick decision and good integration	Tending to make quick decisions without enough consideration of resources	Reluctant to make decisions until sure of enough information and recources	Tending to delay decisions until serious gaps discovered
Leadership	1. Clear in setting out goals and guidelines	Tending to implement by himself, rather than setting out goals	(miscellaneous)	Lacking in goals
	2. Ready to listen to others' opinions	Ready to enforce his opinion, feared by others		Requiring obedience or allowing freedom
	3. Tolerant of failure	Critical of failure		Punishing deviation or applying no sanction (either authoritative or weak leadership)
	(participative)	(authoritative)		

Japanese top managers' desired pattern of behaviour is the actual pattern of behaviour. It is my estimation that there are more 'innovative and analytical types' and some 'innovative and intuitive types' in Japan.

How can these two skills be developed? Through rotation among many departments, a broad outlook can be cultivated. Under lifetime employment, the manager gains experience in many areas during more than thirty years of service.

Although the manager stays in one organization, the competition in the environment is severe and thus he has to learn to be aware of changes in the environment, and how important it is to be innovative in order to survive the competition. Long service in one company also encourages long-range thinking. Everybody has to be concerned with the prosperity of the company as a whole, and has to be concerned with the long-range future.

As a system, long-range planning encourages innovative and long-range thinking. More than 70 per cent of Japanese large corporations have had long-range planning systems for years. The success of long-range planning depends on the long-range orientation of top management, but the reverse relation exists.

Decisions have to be done by analytical process, by collecting enough information and enough ideas. This analytical skill is required to make decisions through the group decision-making process. In Japanese corporations, group decisions at every level from top to bottom are popular, and to persuade other people it is necessary to collect enough information.

Japanese corporations have a strong head office with competent middle managers. By making full use of middle management, top management can be analytical. Former experiences of top management in these staff departments encourage analytical thinking.

Lifetime employment is one of the important factors in developing human skills in Japanese organizations. In order to work for many years in one organization, one has to learn how to co-operate with others.

A leader has to state the goal clearly, otherwise the group cannot work effectively. It is a misconception that Japanese management is done by a bottom-up approach. Especially when it comes to strategic decisions, the leader has to find the opportunity and take the initiative to build the strategic policy. As a leader, he has to listen to others' ideas and this can motivate the activity of his subordinates. In the group decision-making process, it is very important that the manager learns through participative decisions and cannot force his opinion on others. It is also important in group decision-making, to persuade other people, to communicate beforehand, to log rolling or lobby or do Nemawashi. Through the preparatory stages of group decision-making the managers learn the importance of communication.

Extrinsic reward, too, is necessary to motivate the subordinate, in addition to intrinsic reward. Long-term evaluation is a characteristic of Japanese organizations; short-term evaluation does not motivate an employee to work for his lifetime. Tolerating failure and looking at positive performance are possible in a long-term evaluation system, and the manager learns this through long years of service.

Promotion is important as a reward and also as an allocation of human power. The small differentiation of promotion is effected even under the length of service system. This has to be decided by unselfish and impartial judgement. The managers know that over long years of service, unselfish and impartial treatment is the key to motivation and power.

These, then, are the conditions under which the top managers will become innovative and analytical. However, in the early stage of a company's establishment these conditions are lacking, so the pattern of behaviour then tends to be innovative and intuitive. However, as the company grows and diversifies, the pattern of behaviour evolves from (b) innovative and intuitive, to (a) innovative and analytical, and then as the company becomes older, it could become (c) conservative and analytical.

In the earlier stage when the company is small and the product mix is simple and specialized, the decisions are relatively simple, and intuitive decisions can be successful. However, as the company grows the situation changes, whether it becomes specialized or diversified. If the manager behaviour pattern does not evolve to analytical there is a danger of failure. The bankruptcies of Kojin and Fuji Sashi are examples of this. As the company becomes older, there is a danger that the behaviour pattern becomes (c) conservative and analytical. The cases of Mitsubishi Electric and Konishi-Roku demonstrate this. When the top managers of these companies were replaced, the behaviour pattern changed, with the result that there was a remarkable improvement in performance.

In Japan, we can assume that the change from (b) type to (a) type takes place quickly; (a) type is popular among successful large corporations. The diffusion of the system of long-range planning is evidence of this. The reasons for this popularity have already been mentioned, but most important of all is severe competition. Under intensive competition types other than (a) type can hardly survive. (The type (d), conservative and intuitive, is frequently seen in small family-owned businesses.) (This model is somewhat similar to Greiner, 1972.) The behaviour pattern affects the decision-making style of the corporation as a whole, and this will be studied in Chapter 8 (Table 8.10).

2.6 SUMMARY

There is separation of ownership and management, and top managers are selected by their ability and not by heritage. Most top managers have entered the company straight from university and have climbed to the top position. Length of service is important; there is no bullet-train track, but the top managers can survive the selection process because of competence.

Top management is a team, a mixture of marketing skill, technological skill and personnel management skill. The competition of the company in the market requires the organization to have strong competitive power, and marketing ability is one of the key resources. Finding the seeds of technological innovation is important in Japan because there has been a technology gap, and because the consumer is receptive to change. As a result, technological skill is one of the key resources, and by having a high percentage of engineering and natural science graduates in top management, innovation has been easily introduced. The philosophy of respecting everyone in the organization has made it necessary for management to have personnel management skills.

A management committee at the top is popular in Japan, and this functions as a group decision-making body. The group can make use of a mixture of the above key skills. Group decision-making can be innovative, because uncertainty is reduced. The group decision also needs enough information beforehand to persuade many people and this requires an analytical approach. These conditions explain why the behaviour of top managers can be innovative and analytical.

The typical Japanese top manager is as follows. He is a university graduate majoring in engineering or social science. He is likely to have joined a private company rather than a public organization, and not to have become an independent professional. He has worked in one company for at least thirty years. He was promoted slowly but steadily, and after some competition he was selected as a director. He worked hard because there was stability of status, and because there were chances of promotion. He frequently stays late in the evening at the company. He and his colleagues who entered the company at the same time have not competed much against one another, because everyone was promoted almost equally up to a certain level. He has his own speciality, but within a certain range he has been transferred from one department to another, from technical designing to production, or from marketing to personnel. Thus to some extent he has a broad outlook. He has a long-range outlook, because he has worked many years in one company and become accustomed to thinking on a long-range basis. He has identified himself with the company and has wanted the company to grow.

He is sensitive to human relations, and without this human skill he could not perform his job satisfactorily. In order to work for his lifetime, he has to be friendly to everybody. He has to work as a member of the team, his subordinates are competent, and he has to rely on these competent subordinates. To persuade others, he has had to have enough information, and he has had to be rational.

At the top level he works as a member of the top management committee and participates in innovative decision-making.

2.6.1 Problems

1. There are very few outside directors on the board. Once the president (chief executive officer) is in power, there is no countervailing power and no checking system, so the president can become a very strong director. The stockholders are scattered and are quite powerless.

There is a management committee at the top, and in theory the group decision-making system can control the extraordinary power of the president, but if the appointment of directors is in the hands of the president and if he chooses only yes-men, group decision-making does not work as a control. This happens sometimes. The president of Teijin Company, Ohya, was one such case and the financial performance of Teijin declined. Most of the companies that have gone bankrupt had either too strong a president or too weak top management.

The above problems can be avoided in most cases by the careful selection of the new president by the former president and by the chairman. Competition in the market is another checking force. Without the right strategic decisions the company cannot survive and group decision-making is useful in arriving at the right strategic decision.

2. There are too many conferences. In addition to the management committee at the top, many conferences are held before coming to a

decision. Top management spends a high percentage of its time holding conferences. It is rather hard for a top manager to have his own time to think creatively. In some cases he is not provided with his own office, but located in the corner of a large room. While this may improve communications, it deprives him of quiet thinking.

There are two solutions to this problem. One is to work longer hours; the top manager tends to stay late in his room every day. Another one is to have the staff to help him. The head office is strong in Japanese corporations and the planning department is active in helping him build his strategy.

3. There is little movement of executives between organizations. Since the length of service in one organization is the important element for promotion, the very competent cannot be promoted quickly, nor can they move to other organizations. There are merits and demerits in promotion from within the company. A system of promotion from inside can motivate the middle management, and can evaluate the employee on the basis of his long-term performance. On the other hand, by the recruitment of executives from outside, the company can strengthen the management in the short term, and can recruit able non-conformists like Watson, who moved from NCR to IBM.

REFERENCES

Aonuma, Y. (1965) *Nihon no Keieiso* (Japanese Top Management), Tokyo, Nihon Keizai Shimbun Sha.

Doyukai (1960) *Ishikettei no Jittai* (Practice on Management Decision Making), Tokyo, Doyukai.

Furukawa, E. (ed.) (1973) *Nihon no Kigyo Seicho* (The Growth of Japanese Enterprise), Tokyo, Chuokeizai Sha.

Kansai Branch, Japan Productivity Centre (1976) *Keiei Soshiki no Shin Doko* (New Trend of Business Organization), Osaka, Kansai Branch, Japan Productivity Centre.

Keizai Doyukai (1965) *Waga Kuni Dai Kigyo ni okeru Top Management no Kozo to Jitai* (Structure and State of Top Management of Japanese Large Enterprise), Tokyo, Keizai Doyukai.

Kono, T. (1978) *Keiei Gaku Genron* (Principles of Management), Tokyo, Hakuto Shobo.

Mito, K., Masaki, H. and Haruyama H. (1973) *Dai Kigyo ni okeru Shoyu to Shihai* (Ownership and Control in Large Corporations), Tokyo, Mirai-sha.

Nakagawa, K. (1972) *Keiei Rinen* (Business Philosophy), Tokyo, Diamond Sha.

Noda, K. (1960) *Nihon no Juyaku* (Japanese Top Management), Tokyo, Diamond Sha.

Okumura, A. (1981) *Nihon no Top Management* (Japanese Top Management), Tokyo, Diamond Sha.

Urabe, K. (1975) *Shin Keieisha Ron* (New Top Management), Tokyo, Diamond Sha.

MITI (Ministry of International Trade and Industry) (1976, 1977, 1978, 1980) *Atarashii Keieiryoku Shihyo* (New Indices on Managerial Capability), Tokyo.

Berle, A. A. and Means, G. C. (1932/1967) *The Modern Corporation and Private Property*, New York, Harcourt, Brace & World.

Channon, D. F. (1973) *The Strategy and Structure of British Enterprise*, London, Macmillan.

Clark III, R. D. (1971) 'Group-induced Shift Toward Risk, A Critical Appraisal', *Psychological Bulletin*, vol. 76, no. 4.

Drucker, P. (1974) *Management; Tasks, Responsibilities, Practices*, New York, Harper & Row.

Galbraith, J. K. (1967) *The New Industrial State*, Boston, Houghton Mifflin.

Granick, D. (1962) *The European Executive*, Doubleday.

Greiner, L. E. (1972) 'Evolution and Revolution as Organizations Grow', *Harvard Business Review*, July–Aug 1972.

Hall, D. J. *et al.* 'The European Business Elite', *European Business*, 23 October 1969.

Holden, P. E. Fish, L. S. and Smith, H. L. (1941) *Top Management Organization and Control*, Calif, Stanford University Press.

Katz, D. and Kahn, R. L. (1966) *Social Psychology of Organization*, New York, John Wiley.

Koontz, H. (1967) *The Board of Directors and Effective Management*, New York, McGraw-Hill.

Likert, R. (1967) *The Human Organization*, New York, McGraw-Hill.

McGivering, I., Matthews, D. and Scott, W. H. (1960) *Management in Britain*, Liverpool, Liverpool University Press.

Miles, R. E. and Snow, C. C. (1978) *Organizational Strategy, Structure and Process*, New York, McGraw-Hill.

Mintzberg, H. (1973) 'Strategy-making in Three Modes', *California Management Review*, Winter.

Mintzberg, H. (1973) *The Nature of Managerial Work*, New York, Harper & Row.

Steiner, G. and Miner, J. B. (1977) *Management Policy and Strategy*, New York, Macmillan.

Tönnies, F. (1887) *Gemeinschaft und Gesellschaft*.

Yoshino, Y. (1969) *Japan's Managerial System, Tradition and Innovation*, Cambridge, Mass., MIT Press.

3 Organizational Goals

3.1 CONCEPT OF GOALS

The goal of an organization is the direction in which the activity of the organization should be aimed. The goal can be called objective, purpose and end interchangeably.

The goal of an organization is formulated by those who have the key resources for the organization, and by the value system of the resource holders. Top management is one of the key resources, so the value system of top management affects the goal structure. But the man at the top cannot enforce his philosophy; he has to integrate the values of employees and stockholders.

Basic goals and basic policies affect the product–market strategy, which in turn affects the structure and operation, as Figure 3.1 shows. There is a hierarchy of goals and this system is the same as the system of planning. The goal is thus an 'outline of the plan'. Figure 3.1 indicates four levels of goals.

Drucker postulates seven key areas (Drucker, 1954), and these seven areas can be grouped under four levels:

1. Profitability ⎫
2. Productivity ⎬ basic goals and basic policies
3. Public responsibility – social responsibility
4. Innovation ⎫
5. Market standing ⎬ product–market strategy
6. Physical and financial resources ⎫
7. Manager performance and attitude ⎬ structure

The goal is explicitly stated or it is implicitly conceived, and is exposed as a pattern of behaviour. This is called the atmosphere of the corporation, or implied philosophy. Examples of brief namings of implied behaviour patterns are as follows: Matsushita Electric is a 'merchant', Hitachi is a 'country knight', Mitsubishi Electric is a 'lord', Toshiba is a 'gentleman' and Sony is a 'guinea pig'. The corporate atmosphere is a decision-

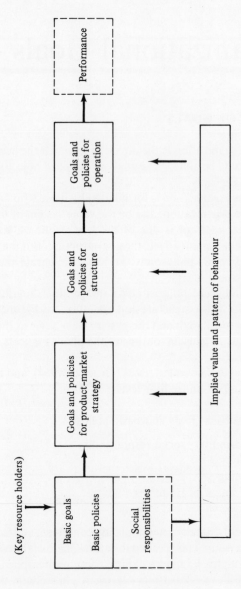

FIGURE 3.1 System of goals

making style and affects the company performance greatly. This atmosphere does not grow by itself, but is formulated gradually by the stated business creed and the corporate strategy, the behaviour of top management, and the system of sanctions. It is not changed by simple 'organizational development' training.

This chapter deals with the basic goals and basic policies. These are set out in (i) the business creed, (ii) occasional statements of top management, (iii) stated long-range goals and policies. They are also indoctrinated through the morning meeting, company magazine, company slogan, official training and so on. This indoctrination is considered important in Japanese corporations as a means of heightening the sense of identification with the organizaticn.

3.1.1 Case of Matsushita Electric Products Company

Figure 3.2 is an example of the system of goals of Matsushita Electric Company. The basic goals are comprised of the business creed and long-range goals and policies. The business creed usually states the mission, that is, the role the company wants to play in the society, the basic goals and code of behaviour of the employees. Figure 3.2 indicates that Matsushita wants to improve the quality of life through supplying the society with electric home appliances as cheaply as a water supply. This is a statement of the mission of the company.

This mission is supported by five principles. The first is the principle of mutual benefit between the company and the consumer, and this results in the growth of the company. The second is the principle of profit, which is attained through the contribution to society. The third is the principle of fair competition. This is the condition that the profit is the result of the contribution to the society. The fourth is the principle of benefit between the company and the stakeholder. The fifth is the principle of management by participation. This comes from the principle of respect for people. Thus the growth, profit, fair relation with the stakeholder and respect for people are the goals of the company, and how these goals are attained is briefly stated in the creed.

Seven spirits are the code of behaviour for the employee to follow in making decisions on product–market strategy and on internal matters. It should be recognized that these seven spirits not only govern internal behaviour but also control external behaviour.

The creed is followed by the long-range goals and policies. In Matsushita's case, growth rate, rate of return on sales and share of market are important goals.

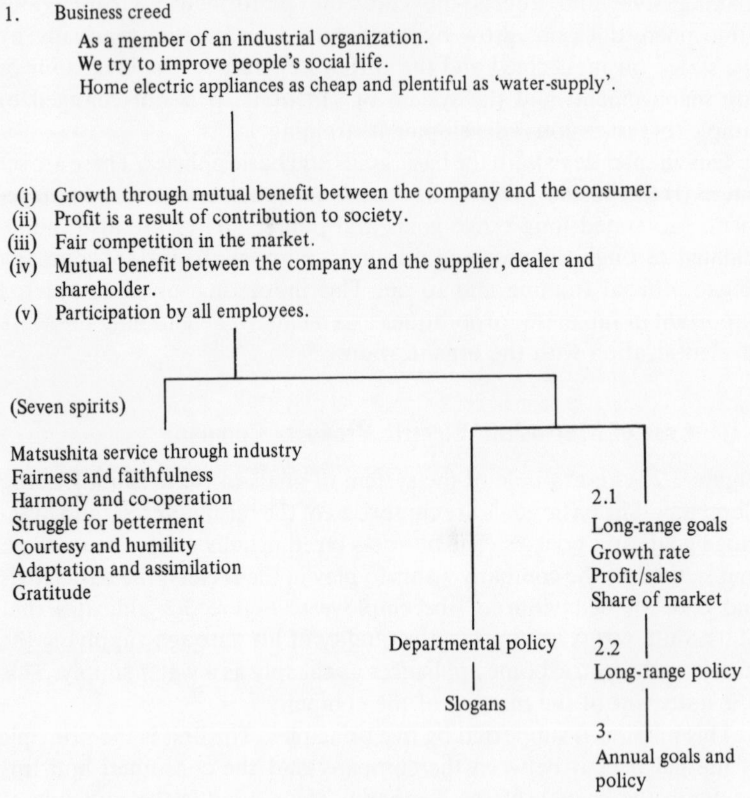

1.   Business creed
        As a member of an industrial organization.
        We try to improve people's social life.
        Home electric appliances as cheap and plentiful as 'water-supply'.

   (i)   Growth through mutual benefit between the company and the consumer.
  (ii)   Profit is a result of contribution to society.
 (iii)   Fair competition in the market.
  (iv)   Mutual benefit between the company and the supplier, dealer and
         shareholder.
   (v)   Participation by all employees.

(Seven spirits)

Matsushita service through industry
Fairness and faithfulness
Harmony and co-operation   2.1
Struggle for betterment   Long-range goals
Courtesy and humility   Growth rate
Adaptation and assimilation   Profit/sales
Gratitude   Share of market

                        Departmental policy   2.2
                                                      Long-range policy
                             Slogans
                                                      3.
                                                      Annual goals and
                                                      policy

FIGURE 3.2 Basic goals and policies of Matsushita Electric Products Company.

3.2 EMPHASIS ON MISSION AND CONCERN FOR PUBLIC INTEREST

The successful Japanese corporations try to look at the role they are playing in the larger environment, and try to make a contribution to the outer world. Matsushita emphasizes its social role, as Figure 3.2 shows.

Table 3.1 is the analysis of the business creeds of 269 Japanese corporations, and we notice that the aim of contribution to society has a high frequency ((1.1.1.) and (1.1.2) of Table 3.1). The analysis of the creed may seem to be merely superficial observation – the creeds of US corporations include similar principles – and the published principle may be different from actual behaviour, but in Japan there is more effort

TABLE 3.1 Frequency of items in business creed (269 companies)

1. Basic goal		
1.1.1	Good product at reasonable price. Quality first	131 (49%)
1.1.2	Contribution to the nation, to society. Mutual prosperity	149 (55%)
1.1.3	Prosperity of the corporation	13 (5%)
1.2	Fair profit	9 (3%)
1.3	Steady progress, gaining trust	39 (15%)
1.4	Welfare of employee, respect for employee	34 (13%)
2. General policy		
2.1	Progressiveness, activeness, creativity	119 (45%)
2.2	Analytical, scientific attitude	44 (17%)
2.3	High productivity	32 (12%)
2.4	Progress of corporate technology	78 (39%)
3. Code of behaviour		
3.1	Attitude towards company	
3.1.1	Faithfulness	81 (31%)
3.1.2	Thankfulness	22 (8%)
3.2 Attitude towards work		
3.2.1	Effort	33 (15%).
3.2.2	Responsibility, fulfilling duty	56 (21%)
3.2.3	Thrift, cleanliness, endurance	50 (19%)
3.2.4	Pride in work	13 (5%)
3.3 Attitude towards seniors, colleagues and subordinates		
3.3.1	Co-operation	145 (55%)
3.3.2	Love and courtesy	55 (21%)
3.4 Attitude towards self		
3.4.1	Health	28 (11%)
3.4.2	Diligence	15 (6%)
3.4.3	Cheerfulness	26 (10%)
3.4.4	Strict morality	47 (18%)

Notes:
[1] Arranged and computed by the author, from Oyama (1964).
[2] Number indicates the frequency, percentage was derived from number of item divided by number of companies.

to indoctrinate the philosophy, and there is more probability that the expressed principle will become the real principle.

The opposite of respect for the public interest is not to disregard the public interest; but to seek only the individual goal, to seek the profit of the company and expect the profit-making to result in the welfare of society. Respect for public interest is to see directly the effects of corporate behaviour on society. It is the 'larger-organization-orientedness of the individual organization'.

As proof of the implementation of this philosophy, there is good co-operation between the complementary organizations in Japan. There is good co-operation between business and government, between management and union, between buyer and parts manufacturers and between business and the educational institutions. There is thus good co-operation between organizations in complementary relationships but strong competition between organizations with the same functions. This is apparently characteristic of the Japanese social system, and it is the result of the tendency of each organization to try to see the role it is playing in the large environment.

This philosophy, influenced by Confucianism which stresses faithfulness, is a tradition of Japanese organizations. During the industrialization after the 1868 restoration, the government emphasized the need for a 'strong economy and strong military force', and the business leaders responded to this demand. After the First World War, respect for public interest was in conflict with the welfare of labour. The strong labour movement forced management to realize the problem, and since management was afraid of the increased power of the socialist movement, the welfare of employees came to be seen as an important value (Yoshino, 1968; Nakagawa, 1977).

After the Second World War, the reconstruction of the economy was the most important task, and the business leaders took it as an important mission, rather than just a search for profit. Until recently, Japan was a less developed country, and the national goal was clear because the advanced level of developed countries was the target. This is one of the causes of the public-orientedness of Japanese corporations, an attitude similar to the sentiment of nationalism.

As management is progressively separated from ownership, pressure to seek the short-term profit weakens; the executives want to perform a worthwhile task and tend to relate the function of the company to the benefit of society. They become more organization-oriented and society-oriented. Furthermore, by declaring that the company is devoting itself to society, management motivates the employee who is devoted to the organization and who is going to work there for life.

The author is saying that the Japanese corporation tries to devote itself to society and tries to determine its effects on society, and that it believes its contribution will bring about the profit. This belief tends to encourage innovation by the corporation. Hitachi, for example, wanted to replace imported electrical equipment by national products, so it made efforts to develop its own technology. Toyota and Canon did the same thing. Matsushita wants to serve the consumer. This results in market-orientedness, and Mastushita has developed a number of successful new products.

If the company is predominantly concerned with profit, it will restrict competition rather than innovation; it will acquire other companies to increase its earnings per share.

This respect for public interest is not identical with the goals of the organization, but it is a way of thinking that harmony between the public interest and the growth and profit of the company is possible. Nor is it identical with social responsibility. Social responsibility is the readiness to respond to society at the sacrifice of short-range profit. To prevent pollution, to help build hospitals and schools, to maintain unseen quality are the subject of social responsibility. To provide society with useful goods is not a social responsibility, because it brings about corporation growth and profit. The mission is the role of company which is in harmony with growth and profit.

3.3 CHARACTERISTICS OF GOALS

3.2.1 Growth-orientedness

The goals of the corporation are formulated by the holders of the key resources of the organization, and by the values of the holders. They can be divided into two – the system goals and the participants' goals. The system goals are the common denominators of the expectations of the resource holders, because they are the prerequisite for satisfaction. The growth of sales, the profit and stability of the organization are the system goals. The participants' goals are the direct desires of the resource holders which are in conflict with one another. The protection of employment and the dividend are the participants' goals. (Kono, 1977, and Perrow, 1970, show a different scheme.)

Growth is one of the system goals, and has high priority for Japanese corporations. Table 3.1 shows the frequency of business creed; (1.1.1), (1.1.2) and (1.1.3) have high frequency and they are all related to growth.

The author conducted a survey on long-range planning systems in Japan, in the UK and in the USA, which included a questionnaire about long-range goals. Table 3.2 shows the result of this questionnaire. In all three countries, sales, growth, profit and market share are important.

TABLE 3.2 Goals of long-range planning

'In what specific terms are the goals and policies of your long-range plans started? (Please tick as many as necessary.)'

	UK	Japan	USA
	(74 co.)	(327 co.)	(23 co.)
	%	%	%
1. Basic goals			
1. Sales	51	88*	63
2. Rate of growth (sales or profit)	59	64	65
3. Profit			
(a) Amount of profit	53	87*	57
(b) Profit ratio to total capital (or total assets)	59	42*	52
(c) Profit ratio to equity capital	18	27	57
(d) Profit ratio to sales	37	61*	44
(e) Standard deviation of profit (or limit of profit in the worst case)	0	16*	9
(f) Earning per share	37	18*	52
4. Market share	50	41	48
5. Capital structure	41	32	71
6. Dividend	30	43	39
7. Share price	8	2	26
8. Employee compensation	8	39*	17
9. Quality level of products	32	13*	17
10. Basic policy of growth	49	50	70
11. Basic policy of stability	14	34*	30
12. Basic policy on profit	47	51	61
13. Basic policy on social responsibility	16	19	13
2. Operational issues (productivity goals)			
1. Target value added	15	31*	4
2. Investment per employee	10	11	9
3. Target productivity of labour	37	46	13
4. Ratio of assets turnover	30	30	39
5. Policy for cost reduction	54	35*	44
6. NA	33	—	—

Notes:
[1] The asterisk (*) indicates the level of significance is 10 %, comparison is between UK and Japan only.
[2] For method of survey, see Appendix 9.1.
[3] The number shows the percentage of companies that use these items.

There are several differences, however. As Table 3.2 shows, sales, growth and profit amount are more important for Japanese corporations, and these are all indicators of growth.

As a measurement of growth, the sales amount is the most popular, because it is a recognized prestige scale, and it shows the amount of resources the company is processing. The consolidated sales amount is increasing in importance as the area of activity expands throughout the world, but at present the unconsolidated amount is more important. Other measurements like the market value of the stock (or the 'wealth'), the book value of the assets and the net worth are not so commonly used to indicate growth.

The reasons for the importance of growth are as follows. In a growth economy the growth of the company is necessary to protect its market position; and in order to maintain its relative competitive power, it has to grow at the same rate as the national economy, at the very least.

Since there is a separation of management from ownership, top management is more concerned with the growth of sales, rather than the earning per share. This is because it expands the amount of resources dealt with, and is an important symbol of success.

The employee has a high sense of identification with the organization and has the will to work for a lifetime. Growth provides the possibility of wage increases, which is supported by the natural increase in productivity; it also expands the number of jobs and positions for promotion. Since the employee does not move to other companies to obtain promotion, an increase in the number of positions is important. One president of a hotel business, explaining to the author his reason for expansion, said that the most important motive is to increase the number of positions for the employees.

Growth-oriented companies are sensitive to innovation and are competition-oriented, rather than protection-minded. They invest funds for the expansion of facilities aggressively, without worrying about the source of the funds. They will borrow money from the banks to increase their share of the market.

These companies will introduce new products by internal development or by licensing agreement, but they will not acquire other companies in order to diversify, because even if it increases the earnings per share the acquisition will not increase the number of jobs for employees.

3.3.2 Employees as Partners

Employees are respected as partners of the organization. They are not considered interchangeable elements for production. Lifetime employment is one of the results of this way of thinking. In times of depression employment levels are kept at the sacrifice of dividend and profit. American corporations tend to lay off the employee to maintain the dividend, and tend to regard the employee as an interchangeable element.

Tönnies put forward the concept of *Gemeinschaft* (community organization) and *Gesellschaft* (association) (Tönnies, 1887). *Gemeinschaft* is like a family or a church whose members are united by mutual love. Getting together is itself a source of joy. People love each other, share good luck and bad luck alike, help each other, trust each other and understand each other.

Gesellschaft is like a pure profit-making economic organization. People exchange each other, and will not work if there is no reward. There is no spiritual unity. People join together by contract, but they are apart and in tension. They work by division of labour, within the strict limit of the job; they each become one of the atoms of the organization.

Japanese organization is somewhat similar to *Gemeinschaft*, because the company respects the welfare of its employees giving them equal treatment, and in turn the employees devote themselves willingly to the organization. There is a good deal of evidence that the Japanese corporation is concerned with employee welfare like a *Gemeinschaft*. One instance is the lifetime employment system. The company does not lay off or discharge its employees. Promotion and wage increase by length of service is another example. All employees are treated equally as far as possible. Generous employee welfare facilities are another example.

In the business creed of Matsushita Electric (Figure 3.2) great stress is laid on the 'seven spirits' as a code of behaviour: they are repeated everyday in the morning meeting. The company wants good behaviour because it expects much from its employees, and because it respects the welfare of its employees.

In the survey of business creed shown in Table 3.1, the code of behaviour has high frequency. This comes from the concern for the employee; the company expects the employee to behave appropriately as a family member.

Long-range goals are shown in Table 3.2, and we find that employee compensation, target value added, and productivity of labour have a high frequency in Japan. This is further evidence of people-orientedness.

Employee-orientedness affects other goals. It embraces the concern for public interest and promotes growth-orientedness, and thus it affects the strategic decisions and helps to make the company more aggressive and innovative. In order to increase wages and to provide opportunities for promotion, the company has to grow, and in order to grow the company has be innovative. The most important effect of this way of thinking is that there is less resistance to changes at work; there is instead an attitude of encouragement towards modernization among the workforce – because employment is informally guaranteed, it is easy for the company to introduce new technology and labour-saving machines. The displaced employee will be transferred to other departments needing more people because of growth of sales.

This company attitude also improves the morale of the employees, making them willing to work hard, present new ideas, participate in the various campaigns of the company, including QC circle movement, and thus it enhances the quality level of products and reduces the costs.

This philosophy has several origins. The homogeneous population and culture throughout the Japanese islands is the basic reason. Devotion to formal organizations has been a traditional value in Japan for a long time, owing much to Confucian influence. Concern for people is a response to this philosophy.

Historically speaking, however, the concern for people was strengthened only after The Second World War. During 300 years of feudalism until 1868, the devotion to organization was encouraged, but respect for people was not a popular value. During the rapid industrialization after 1900, labour was not a key resource, and young female workers in particular had to work hard for many hours a day. With the growth of heavy industry skilled workers became important resources, and to protect the company from the active movement of labour organizers, the family concept was introduced into company thinking, to encourage co-operation between management and labour. The heavy industries (chemical products, steel, machinery, electric machinery, shipbuilding) needed skilled labourers, and they increased the voice.

After the Second World War the industrial structure changed still further, with heavy industry increasing its share. As the demand for skilled workers increased, their co-operation became essential for the company, and thus respect for people became an important goal. The development of technology-intensive industry further promoted this attitude which at the same time was being encouraged by the democratic movement and an escalation in the level of education. But the most important reason was that the employees had become the key resources.

On the other hand, capital was abundant because of the high rate of savings which accounted for over 20 per cent of income; and banks were a more important source of funds than the stock market, because most of the savings went to the banks. Thus stockholders had less power and less voice in the formation of goals.

3.3.3 Balancing Multiple Goals

Profitability and stability are also important system goals for Japanese corporations along with the growth rate. The problem is how to balance the multiple goals.

In measuring profitability, the return on total capital (or total assets) before interest and tax should be the most important consideration in Japan, as elsewhere. Table 3.2 indicates that it is important, but just as important is the profit ratio to sales. The reason for the use of return on sales, which does not reflect the turnover of assets, may largely be a matter of convenience. The return on sales is easier to compute, for each product, for each department, and for each company. The efficiency of assets is measured separately. The problem is that it is hard to set a standard for return of sales, because fair return depends upon the turnover of the assets.

For the goal of stability, the market share and the capital structure are important and the standard deviation of profit is used to some extent. Japanese companies are heavy users of loan capital, and a large part of capital investment is financed through borrowing from banks with the resulting equity ratio of about 20 per cent on average. For Japanese corporations, growth is more important, and to ensure stability the share of the market is more important than the high equity ratio.

For participants' goals, employee welfare has a higher priority than the dividend. Earnings per share is not so important. The desirable levels for participants' goals are not explicitly stated in many cases, and probably there is no set level of aspiration. For system goals, target values are set for growth, profitability and stability, and stress is laid in a balanced attainment of multiple goals. Many large corporations use a computer simulation to forecast the future of goal values, and to compare the forecast value with the desired value.

To establish the desired levels of goal value, the competitive approach is important because Japanese corporations are competition-oriented. To set the desired target sales amount or growth rate, return on investment, or market share, the targets values of competitors in the home country – and increasingly those in the USA and in Europe – are referred to, rather than the standards set by theoretical estimation.

This competitive attitude with respect to sales, growth rate and share of the market, at the sacrifice of short-range profit and equity ratio, has resulted in aggressive investment in equipment for expansion and for modernization, and in tremendous efforts to improve the quality and to lower the cost of the product. This in turn has resulted in actual competitive power in the world market.

Long-range planning and budgeting are extensively used, as tools for attaining a balanced achievement of multiple goals.

3.4 TIME HORIZON OF GOALS

For any organization the balancing of short-term performance and long-term performance is a problem, but a balance has to be attained. Some organizations, however, put more emphasis on short-term profit, and some put more emphasis on long-term performance. If the company invests a large amount of money in advertising and little in research and development, present sales will increase, but future sales will decline. If the company does not modernize its facilities, it may increase immediate profits but equipment will deteriorate and eventually profit and sales will decline. If the company does not put time and money into employee training, the future capability and morale of its employees will suffer. If the company does not develop new products, its future performance will be poor. The Japanese corporation is more long-term-oriented with respect to product–market strategy, to capability building and to performance.

There is a lot of evidence for this. For example, there is a high diffusion of long-range planning practices in Japan as far as the large corporation is concerned. Recent research indicates that approximately 70–80 per cent of large Japanese corporations have some kind of long-range planning systems. MITI's (Ministry of International Trade and Industry) yearly surveys on the corporate capability of about 540 corporations in 1973–80 found that 73 per cent in 1974, 71 per cent in 1975, 64 per cent in 1976, 66 per cent in 1977, 67 per cent in 1978 and 74 per cent in 1980 had long-range plans, and the performance of those who had long-range planning was better than that of the non-planners.

The successful Japanese corporation has been aggressive in investing funds for facilities for modernization and expansion, at the sacrifice of short-range profit. According to other MITI surveys of large manufacturing corporations (Japanese 103 corporations), fixed asset to labour ratio (or labour–equipment ratio) tripled during the last ten years, but in the USA and West Germany it increased only slightly with the resulting difference in the improvement of labour productivity. The successful Japanese corporation is willing to spend money training the employee who intends to work for a lifetime in the company. It pays to train the employee in the long run.

When a Japanese corporation develops a new product, it is not unusual for the company not to expect immediate profit or seek to recover the loss in four or five years, if it is a strategic product. Hitachi had to make a strategic decision in 1970 whether to continue the development of the computer, or to discontinue it like GE (discontinued in 1969) or RCA (discontinued in 1970). Hitachi decided to compete with the giant IBM, because Hitachi believed that the computer was a growing business, and that computer technology had great synergy with other products of the company. Top management poured a huge amount of money into research and development, and the central laboratory and Kanagawa Plant co-operated with one another for its development. The profit from the home appliances division was very large at that time, and it was poured into computer development. Now Hitachi holds the number two share in computer sales in Japan and has world-wide competitive power.

It is, however, an exaggeration to say that Hitachi is long-term-oriented in every aspect. There are apparently conflicting philosophies in operation. Applying the self-help principle, Hitachi installed a profit-centre system for the manufacturing plant, which stresses the short-term profit. Because of the profit responsibility, the plant tends to be concerned with the short-term performance, whereas the strategic products are controlled by the head office, to be developed taking a long-term view.

The reasons for the long-term-orientedness of Japanese corporations are as follows. Because of separation of management from ownership, the power of the executive is strong, and the management wants to see a secure future. The executive's tenure may be six or seven years, but he wants the company to grow in perpetuity. Unlike US executives, he is not fired by the deficit in short-term profit. The employee is working for a lifetime, and he too wants to see a long-term future. The middle managers put strong pressure on top management to look far ahead, because they also remain in the company for many years. If they are to be fired by short-range performance, which is usually the case in the USA, they would be short-sighted.

The owners of shares in the large corporations are scattered, and none of the stockholders has controlling power. According to the recent statistics of 1400 companies listed on the Tokyo Stock Exchange, individuals own only 30 per cent, the financial institutions own 40 per cent, and the other non-financial companies own 30 per cent of the shares. The largest shareholders are usually banks and insurance companies, which, however, are not allowed to own more than 10 per cent of any one company by the anti-monopoly law. They hold stock to assure a long-term relationship with the company, to loan money rather than to get profit; they have no power to control, because there are many other banks owning a similar proportion of the stock of the same company. Ownership by investment funds or pension funds is negligible, and there is no pressure for short-term profit from these funds. The non-financial companies are mostly either companies in the group or companies that are important suppliers of, or buyers from, this company. They too want to have long-term trade relations, and hold stocks as a partner. In 1950 individual shareholders accounted for 60 per cent of stock ownership, but the percentage fell to 30 per cent in 1980. The issuing company would welcome the shareholding of financial institutions and non-financial institutions who do not want to have controlling power, and who, because they are stable shareholders, will not sell the stocks when there is a risk of possible takeover.

The bank loan is a much more important source of funds for the corporations. The bank is concerned with increased lending to the company, and tends to take a long-term view. The bank wants to see long and continuous growth of the company, because it results in increased demand for loans. In the USA, the institutional investor tends to put pressure on raising the short-term profit which is declared in the quarterly financial report.

There is very little risk of being acquired by other companies in Japan, so the management is not worried about any temporary decline in the stock price.

The effect of long-term-orientedness is somewhat similar to the effect of growth-orientedness. Successful Japanese companies are eager to improve the quality of their products through quality-control techniques and through quality circle movement, because improved quality has long-term effects on the company's competitive position. In the car industry, the motor-cycle industry and the watch industry, quality is emphasized, and this has proved to be a strong competitive factor in the world market.

Successful Japanese companies tend to relate to their parts suppliers and sales channels on a long-term basis. They do not like to buy parts from the cheapest vendor and sell the products to the highest buyers on a short-term calculation. They try to see them as partners and try to formulate a quasi-vertical integration. This strategy is analysed in later chapters.

They have been aggressive in capital investment, evidenced by the steel industry and automobile industry. They are eager to train and improve the skills of their employees.

On the other hand, creative invention in the Japanese corporation has been less than in UK or US corporations, in spite of their long-term-orientedness. Japanese corporations have not spent a large amount on creative research, because, as late developers, it has been possible to buy licences. At present, however, Japanese corporations are increasing their research efforts.

3.5 COMMUNICATION AND INDOCTRINATION OF PHILOSOPHY AND GOALS

The clear communication of company missions and goals to the employees enhances their sense of identification with the organization. It also guides behaviour in the desired direction.

The case of Matsushita Electric is an interesting one. Matsushita has a clear statement of corporate philosophy, as is shown in Figure 3.2. This creed is repeated all the time. It is written in the booklet introducing the company to the new employee, and is explained in detail. The booklet explains the history of the company, the product, the organizational structure and the policy of each function. With this over-all knowledge of the company, it is expected that all employees will behave in the best way to attain the goal of the company, will perform their duties on their own initiative, even though there is no detailed job description.

Approximately eight months are spent training new employees to inspire them with the philosophy, goals and policies of the company along with the training on technical skills.

The morning meeting is held every day on every site, the company song is sung and the seven spirits are recited and one employee will give his or her opinion about the job to the assembly. The text of the seven spirits is hung on the wall, and the slogan for the current year is hung overhead throughout the plant.

On New Year's day approximately 7000 managers from all over the country are called together, and the chairman and the president declare the basic policy for the year. A long-range plan is worked out, and information about some of the new directions of strategy is delivered to all the employees through the company magazine.

These means of communication and indoctrination are practised not only in Japan, but also, with some modification, in subsidiaries abroad. When the author asked the plant manager what he considered the most important work motive for ordinary female employees, the manager replied that the satisfaction of the user of Matsushita products is one of the important motives.

The case of Matsushita may seem to be extreme, but it is not really so. The Seiko Group is said to be completely opposite and is considered a 'practical' company. The Seiko Group is the world's largest watch manufacturer, and it has had no stated business creed since it was established in 1892. However, it has a brochure that states the character of the company, and this is communicated to every employee. It holds a morning meeting every day to communicate the firm's policy. It also has a very active QC circle movement and almost every employee belongs to a group of six to ten members who meet to discuss QCDSH (quality, cost, delivery, safety and human relations). It has a very active suggestion system and each employee presents fifteen ideas a year on average. On the plant site, there is a slogan 'Trust of consumer I establish. From data I improve.' It has an atmosphere of encouraging challenge and welcoming new trial. Co-operative patterns of behaviour are formed through these movements and through practical experience.

Most of the successful Japanese corporations are much closer to Matsushita in practice. Toyota, Hitachi, Canon and Honda all have stated business creeds, and business goals are communicated in a number of ways. The means of such communications in many companies are as follows: business creed; guidance books for new employees that range from thirty to 150 pages; monthly or biweekly company magazine; slogans, campaigns; morning meetings; all kinds of training; New Year's message from the president; abstract of long-range planning and budget.

As already stated, there are two models of organization. One is community organization (*Gemeinschaft*) and the other is economic organization (*Gesellschaft*) (Tönnies, 1887). This classification is very similar to Theory Y and Theory X (MacGregor, 1960), Theory A and Theory Z (Ouchi, 1981), System IV and System I (Likert, 1967), or morale involvement and calculative involvement (Etzioni, 1961).

In community organization, the missions, goals and policies are clearly shown, and the company member identifies with these missions and thus with the organization. The employee is willing to do any related jobs, to present new ideas, to produce goods of quality in every detail, seen or unseen. It is not necessary to have a detailed job description. This model is similar to Japanese organization.

In the USA, the business policy is often made public, but business philosophy is not necessarily made clear, and there are fewer opportunities taken to communicate the company philosophy (Sutton emphasized the importance of business philosophy (Sutton *et al.*, 1965)). The employees' sense of identification is lower. They are motivated by economic rewards. They do only the ordered job, and since the turnover of employees is high, it is necessary to have detailed job descriptions. The company plan has to be allotted to each employee by MBO (management by objective). This is similar to *Gemeinschaft*.

In the UK, not so many corporations have company philosophies. It is impossible to see the business creed stated anywhere on plant sites in the UK. During my interview with many British executives, they gave two reasons for this. One is that the creeds are very similar from company to company, so it may not be very meaningful. Most of them simply state the company's responsibilities to society, to the consumer, to the supplier and to the employees. Another reason is that the values of employees in the UK are more individualistic than those of the Japanese. Employees have less sense of involvement with the organization so it does not work if the philosophy is publicly stated. (However, some successful British companies do have a stated philosophy, for example ICI and Marks & Spencer.)

Some Japanese corporations have failed because their philosophy was wrong, despite being clearly outlined. Eidai Company, the producer of laminated wood board and a fast-growing home constructor, had such a philosophy: 'Apply wisdom from the brain; those who do not have wisdom use sweat from the body; those who do not use wisdom or sweat leave the company quietly'. Eidai went bankrupt in 1978.

3.6 RELATIONSHIP BETWEEN PHILOSOPHY AND STRATEGY

The philosophy not only motivates the employee, but also gives direction to the strategy. The philosophy is roughly stated in the business creed. Its contents include an outline of the mission, the goal, the basic direction of strategy and structure, and the code of behaviour. Here we are concerned with the declared philosophy and the actual strategy and structure. Matsushita's business creed is shown in Figure 3.2. The mutual benefit is reflected in the basic policy of market-orientedness. The company is nicknamed a 'merchant' type. Mutual benefit is also reflected in the multinational management and the efforts of the company to make a contribution to the host country. It has faith in the meaning of profit, so it does not sell its products at dumped prices. It emphasizes participation and it developed its product division organization in 1933.

Hitachi's philosophy is called 'Odaira Spirit' following the name of an early leader, and is as follows: (i) devotion to society, quality products for the society, (ii) frontier spirit, self-help and aggressiveness, (iii) harmony and friendliness.

Hitachi's principal objective for founding the company in 1910 was to produce electrical equipment made by Japanese engineers to replace imports. This objective was very common at that time among many companies. It is expressed in (i) and (ii). The latter, especially, implied that the technology should be developed by Hitachi itself, and should rely on licensing as little as possible. Development of their own technology was the original aim and this policy was followed for many years. The nickname of 'country knight' may be derived from this principle. This changed after the war, and Hitachi began to buy licences aggressively, especially when it entered the home appliances market, in addition to accelerating research and development activity of its own. In the changed environment, the philosophy had to be modified.

This philosophy emphasized the national interest and technology orientation rather than a consumer and marketing orientation, which are characteristics of Matsushita Electric. This had some dysfunctional effects. The strategic move was steady but slow. Few of Hitachi's products have number one share of the market, because the company was slow to move. The starting time tends to be slow, but it has a strong technological accumulation, so its products are successful eventually.

The self-help principle extends to the profit centre system of every plant, not division, and each plant has profit responsibility. This practice also has dysfunctions, that is, the plant tends to be short-term profit-oriented, though the top management is long-term oriented.

The third principle, 'harmony and friendliness', does not mean quiet harmony, but rather the encouragement of discussion and participation. The company has an atmosphere of freedom of discussion without impairing the friendliness, and freedom to make mistakes if they come from genuine efforts. This principle has been useful in harnessing the innovative and creative ideas of the employees.

Toyota also emphasizes its business philosophy, and as a result 'management by planning' is their basic method of management. Toyota's business creed is composed of three parts: (i) Toyota as a world enterprise, (ii) good products, good thinking, (iii) cohesiveness, co-operation within the company, co-operation with parts manufacturers and sales channels.

Unlike other car manufacturers, Toyota entered the passenger car business early at a time when there was a much larger demand for freight trucks. The second item, good products, good thinking, was encouraged by the founder and is hung everywhere as a slogan on the plant sites. It is somewhat similar to the 'think' of IBM. This principle also lies behind the endless effort to improve the quality of their cars, to improve production methods, and make a steady reduction in price. An increased share of the market and lower prices were Toyota's important strategies.

The third principle is reflected in the strong co-operative grouping of 172 parts manufacturing companies into 'Kyoho-kai', and the equally strong exclusive sales channel of five lines, 320 stores, 2600 sales points, 33 000 salesmen in Japan.

The clearly stated philosophy can contribute to innovation in strategy, and to improvement in strategic decisions. There are several reasons for this. First, the business philosophy was, for the most part, formulated through the learning experience of the founder, and was modified by the experiences of succeeding executives. It is a statement of the principles of success. It is a specific key for that company and not necessarily applicable to other companies. The key principle changes as the environment changes, so the philosophy should change through the decades as was the case with Hitachi.

Second, the philosophy is usually innovative, especially in Japan. The company's 'contribution to society' can only be made through innovation. 'Good product, good thinking' is a direct statement encouraging innovation.

Another example is 'Sony Spirit', which reads as follows: 'Sony is a trail blazer, always a seeker of the unknown. Sony will never follow old trails, yet to be trod. Through this progress Sony wants to serve mankind.'

A further example is Honda's management policy: (i) proceed always with ambition and youthful spirit, (ii) respect sound theory, develop fresh ideas, and make the most effective use of time.

These examples, too, are direct statements that innovation is of value.

Third, the company philosophy makes clear the direction of the employee's effort, and the meaning of his work, and thus enhances his sense of identification and encourages innovation.

Stating the philosophy does not lead to success, however, if the above conditions are not satisfied. Eidai Sangyo's 'leave the company quietly' was not real learning from success, and did not emphasize devotion to innovation. Another example is Van Jacket, a company producing sporty suits for young people, which also went bankrupt. Its philosophy was 'enjoy the job, enjoy yourself'; the management style was fashion-oriented. The philosophy did not reflect any real learning from successful experience, and it did not encourage the installation of an appropriate management structure and system.

The above analysis is of the influence of the goals on the strategy. There is a reverse affecting relation also. The strategy affects the goals. There is a difference between the goals of the specialized company and the diversified company, as Table 3.3 shows. The specialized company puts more emphasis on profit. This difference originates in the difference in key resource holders and in the difference in value systems of them. The top management of a specialized company is more concerned with the growth of one product and its share of the market. This is also the key factor of profit and stability. In a diversified company, the profit is a common target for all products, and there is more concern for profit among the managers.

When the company increases its multinational investment, the consolidated value of sales and profit, rather than the unconsolidated value of the parent company, becomes more important. The scope of the managers expands, and the scope of the goal expands.

TABLE 3.3 Differences between goals of long-range planning according to difference of strategy

	Specialized nine companies %	Diversified eighteen companies %
Rate of growth	78	61
Profit ratio to total capital	33	56
Market share	89	56

Notes:
[1] The companies are selected from among the 102 companies in Table 4.1 and from among companies in Appendix 9.
[2] For method of survey, see Appendix 9.
[3] The number shows the ratio of companies using the goal items.

3.7 SUMMARY

Goals have a hierarchy (as is shown in Figure 3.1) and the corporate philosophy is the essence of the basic goals, goals for product–market strategy and structure, and the code of behaviour. In this chapter we have studied for the most part the basic goals and the goals of company strategy. The Japanese corporation puts emphasis on the public interest and its own mission in the environment. This has a tone of nationalism.

It also emphasizes the growth of the company rather than its short-term profit. It respects its workforce and looks on it as a community organization. It states its philosophy of management clearly, and indoctrinates its employees with this philosophy.

The reasons for these characteristics are as follows. The goals are set by those who hold the key resources and by their values. There is a clear separation of management from ownership; the management has stronger power and the values of management are public- and growth-oriented. Their employees want to work for life and they require top management to take a long-term view. The business philosophy is clearly stated, because the management wants the company to prosper indefinitely and because the employee wants to identify with his lifetime source of employment. The employee is organization-oriented and wants to know the mission and goals of the organization, and a clear statement of goals and policies in turn encourages the organization-orientedness. Thus there is a mutually reinforcing relationship.

These characteristics lead to aggressive strategies and innovative decisions. With these characteristics the successful Japanese corporation can be classified as an innovative *Gemeinschaft* (community organization). The other type of organization is the conservative *Gesellschaft*, where short-range profit and economic performance are important, and managers and workers are viewed as interchangeable parts, and where they are motivated not by the mission but by the economic rewards. The leader behaviour pattern may be conservative analytical or conservative intuitive, as shown in Table 1.3.

There are some dysfunctions connected with clearly stated philosophies and goals. It is sometimes better to be practical, opportunistic and flexible. There can be a conflict between the principles; there is a danger of clinging to obsolete philosophy.

3.7.1 Problems

There are also some problems inherent in the above characteristics. Orientation towards the public is on a national rather than a world-wide basis. The replacement of imports by made-in-Japan products was the important motive, but it was protected by tariffs. In times of depression, the company drives to increase its exports to maintain employment in its own company, with the resulting trade conflict in foreign countries. The values of top management with respect to the range of public interest have to be expanded.

The growth rate of the Japanese economy is decreasing, from 10 per cent to less than 5 per cent, and uncertainty about the future is increasing. Growth is the aspiration of both top management and the employees, but profit and stability will have to be more emphasized. For the satisficing principle the goal level has to be lowered, and for the maximizing principle, the weight for growth has to be changed.

With the improved level of income, individuality and private life are becoming more important values for young people than dedication to the organization. People no longer care to be part, as it were, of a Swiss-roll with the same pattern wherever it is cut, and as a result indoctrination becomes more difficult.

Creativity is different from innovativeness, and creativity is not impeded by clear goals, if the company philosophy encourages new ideas in addition to innovation. Many creative US companies, such as IBM, Hewlet Packard and Eli Lilly, have a clearly stated philosophy.

REFERENCES

Kono, T. (1966) *Keiei Keikaku no Riron* (Theory of Business Planning), Tokyo, Diamond Sha.
Kono, T. (1971) *Keiei Hoshin Ron* (Business Policy), Tokyo, Hakuto Shobo.
Kono, T. (1977) *Keieigaku Genron* (Principles of Management), Tokyo, Diamond Sha.
Nakagawa, K. (ed.) (1977) *Nihon teki Keiei* (Japanese Management), Tokyo, Nihon Keizai Shinbun.
Oyama, Y. (1964) *Shaze Shakun* (Business Creed), Tokyo.
Tsuchiya, H. (1964, 1967) *Nihon Keiei Rinen Shi* (History of Japanese Business Creed), Tokyo.
Yamashito, S. (1967) *Gendai no keiei Rinen* (Modern Business Creed), Tokyo, Hakuto Shobo.
Ansoff, H. I. (1965) *Corporate Strategy*, New York, McGraw-Hill.
Channon, D. F. (1973) *The Strategy and Structure of British Enterprise*, London, Macmillan.
Cyert, R. M. and March, J. G. (1963) *A Behavioral Theory of the Firm*, New Jersey, Prentice-Hall.
Drucker, P. F. (1954) *The Practice of Management*, New York, Harper & Brothers.
Etzioni, A. A. (1961) *A Comparative Analysis of Complex Organizations*, New

York, Free Press of Glencoe.

Galbraith, J. K. (1967) *The New Industrial State*, Boston, Houghton Mifflin.

Guth, W. D. and Tagiuri, R. (1965) 'Personal Values and Corporate Strategies', *Harvard Business Review*, Sep–Oct.

Koontz, H. and O'Donnel, C. J. (1959) *Principles of Management.*, New York, McGraw-Hill.

Likert, R. (1967) *The Human Organization*, New York, McGraw-Hill.

MacGregor, D. (1960) *The Human Side of Enterprise*, New York, McGraw-Hill.

March, J. G. and Simon, H. A. (1958) *Organizations*, New York, John Wiley.

Miles, R. and Show, C. (1978) *Organizational Strategy, Structure and Process*, New York, McGraw-Hill.

Ouchi, W. (1981) *Theory Z*, Philippines, Addison-Wesley.

Perrow, C. (1970) *Organizational Analysis: A Sociological View*, London, Tavistock Publications.

Richard, M. D. (1978) *Organizational Goal Structures*, Minnesota, West Publishing.

Steiner, G. A. (1969) *Top Management Planning*, New York, Macmillan.

Sutton, F. *et al.* (1956), *The American Business Creed*, Mass., Harvard University Press.

Tönnies, F. (1887) *Gemeinschaft und Gesellschaft.*

Yoshino, M. Y. (1968) *Japan's Managerial System*, Cambridge, Mass., MIT Press.

4 Product Mix and Diversification

4.1 FOUR PRODUCT–MARKET STRATEGIES

The product–market strategy is a strategy to select the environment, to determine the relationship between the company and the environment, to mark out the domain of the company activity. There are four areas for product–market strategy, as shown in Figure 4.1.

The product mix is the selection of the market – that is, the convenience or utility that the company proposes to provide for the customer. Vertical integration fixes the boundary between the system of the company and the market: the extent of control by the company over the process of production. Multinational management is the operation of production activity in other countries by transferring superior management and technical skills. Competition strategy is action taken to hold or increase the company's share of the market.

These four strategies are complementary to some extent, but beyond a certain level they are independent and compete for the resources.

The product–market strategy affects company performance a great deal. When demand for the product is declining, growth is impossible – no matter what kind of sophisticated organizational structure is set up.

The objectives of Chapters 4, 5, 6 and 7 are threefold. First, we will classify the strategies and make clear the concepts behind them. Second, we will investigate the empirical effects of these strategies on performances and try to find out the principles governing strategies and performances in Japan. Third, we will try to discover the characteristics of the strategies of Japanese enterprises.

There have been several similar studies in this area. Gort carried out pioneer research on diversification and integration of US companies (Gort, 1962). His approach is economic, and there is no analysis of the interconnection between strategy and structure. Channon's research on

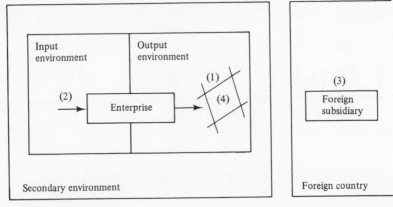

(1) Product-mix strategy
(2) Vertical integration
(3) Multinational management
(4) Competition strategy

FIGURE 4.1 Four product–market strategies

the strategy and structure of British enterprises and Rumelt's research on the strategy and structure of American enterprises are very similar to Gort's study (Channon, 1973; Rumelt, 1974). Rumelt's research, however, does not analyse vertical integration well, nor multinational management, and there is no analysis of the process of making strategic decisions. Channon's analysis is very narrative, and there is no analysis of the performance of each type of strategy. Research by Yoshihara and others on Japanese enterprises use Rumelt's concept. Their findings are enlightening, but they do not analyse vertical integration nor multinational management (Yoshihara *et al.*, 1979).

Analysis of strategy and structure has been conducted using other approaches. Woodward, Perrow and Thompson study the interconnection between technology and structure. They are not concerned with the marketing characteristics of the products, but with the characteristics of the production process, whether it is production to order, batch production or process production; and whether these processes are repetitive or not, capable of being analysed or not. We do not use this approach, because, although the technical process may affect the organization, it does not significantly affect the performance.

4.2 COMPANIES FOR INTENSIVE ANALYSIS

One hundred and two of the largest manufacturing companies were selected and intensively analysed. The industries they represent and the respective size of their sales are shown in Table 4.1. These companies are taken from among the largest 150 manufacturing companies, and the total sales come to more than 300 million dollars. At least two companies in the same industry were selected. These are all relatively successful companies with respect to return on investment, growth rate and stability, although there are differences in their respective performances.

The period of analysis is the eighteen years 1962–80. After the reconstruction of the national economy, the decade 1962–72 showed a high rate of growth, with a real growth rate of over 10 per cent on average. Following the oil crisis in 1973, the last eight years have been years of stable growth – about 5 per cent per year in real terms. During these eighteen years, many Japanese manufacturing companies gained com-

TABLE 4.1 Method of survey on 102 manufacturing companies

1. Sources of data:
     Data were collected from:
         Annual report, *Toyo-Keizai* quarterly report of companies, observation of company organization charts, *Diamond*'s who's who of company staff, mail questionnaire survey on research and development expenditures, multinational management and organizational structure, long-range planning and new product development.
2. Period of survey: 1962–80.
3. Companies classified by industry (in 1978):

(1) Food	11
(2) Fibre, pulp and paper	12
(3) Chemicals	16
(4) Petroleum, rubber, glass and cement	12
(5) Iron, steel and non-ferrous metals	11
(6) Machinery	8
(7) Electrical appliances	11
(8) Precision machine	8
(9) Transportation equipment and machinery	13
Total	102

4. Companies classified by size of sales (in 1978):

Over $10 000 million	0
$9999–$1000 million	46
$999–$333 "	48
$332–$100 "	8
Total	102

petitive power in world markets, but some also lost it – for example the petrochemical industries.

4.3 CONCEPT AND PRINCIPLES OF PRODUCT MIX AND DIVERSIFICATION

The product mix is the selection of growth products in such a way that the performance of the company is separated from the product life cycle (Gort, 1962). The demand for one product grows and declines. By changing the product mix the company separates its own fate from the fate of its products. If demand for one product continues to grow for many years, the company can specialize in that one product and can itself grow.

The single-product company (S in Table 4.2) is the company where sales of one product account for more than 95 per cent of total sales. For example, 95 per cent of Toyota's total sales are passenger cars, so it is classified as a single-product company.

The dominant-product company (D) is the company where one product accounts for less than 95 per cent but more than 70 per cent of total sales. For example, Kirin's sales of beer comprise up to 92 per cent, and soft drinks 8 per cent of sales, so it is classified as a dominant-product company. Teijin's sales of polyester fibre and nylon fibre comprise about 70 per cent of its total, so it is also classified as a dominant-product company.

The related-technology product company (RT) is a company where sales of one product account for less than 70 per cent, but where the sales

TABLE 4.2 Classification of product mix

Use Technology	Narrow		Wide Marketing, narrow	Marketing, wide
Narrow	S Single product-company	D Dominant-product company	RMT Related-marketing-and-technology product company	RT Related-technology product company
Wide			RM Related-marketing product company	U Unrelated-product company

of technologically related product groups account for more than 70 per cent of the total sales of the company. We should notice that the use or purpose of the products is varied.

The related-marketing product company (RM) is a company where sales of one product are less than 70 per cent and the sales of marketing-related products are more than 70 per cent of total sales of the company. We should notice again that the use or the purpose of the product is diverse. For example, Fujiya sells biscuits and operates restaurants and retail stores selling biscuits. All are marketing-related, but the technology is different and the use of product is not identical. Konishi-Roku produces photo film, cameras, and more recently photocopiers. These products are marketing-related, but the technologies and uses are different, so the product life cycle is also different.

The related-marketing-and-technology company (RMT) is one where sales of one product are less than 70 per cent, but the sales of marketing-related products and technically related products come to more than 70 per cent of total sales. Canon is classified as RMT, because cameras, photocopiers and calculators are mutually marketing- and technology-related, and the total sales of these products account for more than 70 per cent of all sales. (The marketing-related product group need not overlap exactly with the technology-related product group.)

The unrelated product company (U) sells less than 70 per cent marketing-related products and less than 70 per cent technology-related products. For example Ube Kosan was originally a coal-mining company, but it now produces fertilizers, plastics, cement and industrial machinery.

To find whether the two products are marketing-related or not the author used the number of Standard Product Classification. The Standard Product Classification, unlike Standard Industry Classification, classifies products by the similarity of their use and marketing. If the first two digits of SPC have the same number, they are marketing-related. For example the SPC number of beer is 07221, and that of soft drinks 0712, so they are marketing-related.

The SPC number of biscuits is 06481 and that of drugs 811–819, so they are not marketing-related. In addition to these numbers, the author also used subjective judgement.

To determine if the two products are technology-related, the author used the number of Standard Industry Classification, which classifies products by the similarity of their production technology. If the SIC numbers of the first two digits are the same, the two products are technology-related. For example the SIC number of fertilizer is 261 and that of plastics is 2637; they are technology-related. Again, the author used subjective judgement also.

It is also necessary to define the concept of 'the same product'. The term can be defined using the following criteria:

1. The number of Standard Product Classification (SPC). If the SPC number of the first three digits is the same for the two or more products, they are the same product. The SPC numbers of milk, dried milk and condensed milk are 01221, 01222, 01222 respectively, so they are the same product. The number of beer is 07221 and that of soft drinks is 07122, so they are different products.
2. Subjective judgement. When two products have the same use or purpose, and can be substituted (for example, milk, dried milk and condensed milk), they are the same product.
3. Joint products. For example, gasoline, heavy oil, kerosene and machine oil are jointly produced from crude oil. They have different uses, but they cannot be separated, so they are considered the same product.

The above classification is similar to Channon's and Rumelt's classification (Channon, 1973; Rumelt, 1974), but not exactly the same. Rumelt includes vertical integration as one of the elements of diversification, but vertical integration is a different concept from diversification. Diversification is related to the variety of uses of the products, and separates the performance of the company as a whole from the product life cycle. Rumelt also neglects the marketing-relatedness; he sees only the technological relationship. His concepts of 'constrained', meaning limited to one core technology, and of 'linked', meaning two or more core technologies, are complicated and inappropriate. Our concept is based on the mutual relationship of the products as a group.

In summary, the use or purpose is the key element of product mix, because the product life cycle differs according to the use. If the uses of the products of one company are limited, the company is a specialized company (S and D). If the uses of the products of one company are very varied, it is a diversified company. If the products have different uses, but if they are marketing- or technology-related, the company can have synergy effects, giving the company strong competitive power. The camera and the calculator have different uses and life cycles, but as products they are marketing-related and technology-related.

We should notice that the above classification is based on existing products, and does not refer to change of products. Ansoff's definition of diversification means the addition of new products, and differs from the

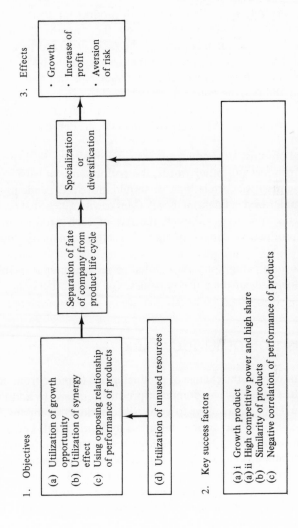

FIGURE 4.2 Objectives and success factors of product mix

concept of diversification in this chapter (Ansoff, 1965). The product mix is the state of the existing products. This is a broader concept and affects the performance to a greater extent than the addition of new products.

The objectives of specialization and diversification are indicated in Figure 4.2. The major objective of product-mix strategy is to utilize growth opportunity by selecting a growth product, or a product in an earlier stage of its life cycle. In order to grow, the company has to change the product mix; and for this purpose the product has to be a growth product, and the company's share of the market has to be high.

If its products have similar characteristics and can use the same research capabilities, the same production facilities and same marketing resources, then the diversified company can have high efficiency by using large-scale processing. (Synergy is explained in Penrose, 1959, and Ansoff, 1965.)

The third objective of product mix is to attain stability by diversifying the use of products; in other words, the performance of each product should have negative correlations, or should move independently. This aspect is emphasized in financial theory (Markowitz, 1959; Sharpe, 1970). To attain the objective, although the use of each product may be different, production capability and marketing capability must be similar.

The following paragraphs are devoted to testing these principles by analysing the cases of the 102 companies, and some others.

4.4 TRANSITION OF PRODUCT MIX

The general trend in the change of product mix is to move from being a single product company to a dominant-product company by adding new products, and from there move to a diversified-products company. Table 4.3 is a simplified model of the transition by Scott (Scott, 1971).

Japanese corporations roughly follow this pattern. The transition of the product mix and organizational structure of 102 Japanese corporations over the last eighteen years is shown in Table 4.4. During that time the number of specialized companies has decreased from forty-eight to thirty-seven. For comparison, the transition of product mix in the USA and UK is shown in Table 4.5.

In the USA and in the UK in 1950, specialized companies (the single-product companies and dominant-product companies) accounted for two-thirds of all companies, but over the next twenty years (by 1970) the

TABLE 4.3 Three-stage-model of product mix and organizational structure (simplified Scott model)

Stage Company characteristics	I Single product	II Dominant product	III Multiple products
1. Related strategies	(Not institutional, oriented by owner – manager)	Vertical integration	Vertical disintegration
		Increase of products Research for product improvement and process improvement	Acquisition and divestment Research for new products
2. Goals	Conflict between needs of owners versus needs of firm	Market share and cost	Return on investment, market share, growth
3. Organizational structure	Little formal structure	Functional organization	Product division

Source: Scott (1971).

number had decreased to about one-third. (In 1980 it was still one-third in the UK.)

In all three countries, Japan, the USA and the UK, there is a universal trend from specialized companies to diversified companies. Considering that the time span was only about twenty years, the change has been remarkable.

In Japan, however, the change has been less significant. In 1962 the percentage of specialized companies in Japan was lower than that in the other two countries (46 per cent versus 69 per cent and 75 per cent). At present, compared with US corporations, the level of diversification is low, and there are more specialized companies (S and D), more related diversified companies (RMT, RT, RM) and fewer unrelated companies (U). In addition, the products of the unrelated companies in Japan are not markedly unrelated, and in this the companies resemble technology-related companies (RT).

Why does Japan have more specialized companies, more related-products companies, and fewer unrelated companies? It is determined by three factors; (i) opportunities for growth products, (ii) gaps in the

TABLE 4.4 Transition of product–market strategy and structure
(102 companies)

		1962	1967	1972	1976	1980	Through the year
	S	18	18	16	14	14	16
	D	30	29	23	25	23	24
	Sub-total	(48)	(47)	(39)	(39)	(37)	(40)
Product–market Strategy	RMT	14	15	19	21	23	19
	RT	25	24	28	27	30	26
	RM	6	6	6	6	6	6
	U	9	10	10	9	6	11
	Sub-total	(54)	(55)	(63)	(63)	(65)	(62)
	Total	102	102	102	102	102	102
	F		55		46	43	
	F & Div.		7		11	13	
Structure			—		—	—	
			62		57	56	
	Div		40		45	46	

Note: For abbreviations, see Appendix 4.1.

TABLE 4.5 Transition of product mix and organizational structure in the USA and UK

	US		UK		
	1949 %	1969 %	1950 %	1970 %	1980 %
Single product	35	6	34	6	9
Dominant product	35	29	41	34	26
Sub-total	70	35	75	40	35
Related product	27	45	23	54	47
Unrelated product	3	20	2	6	18
Total	100	100	100	100	100
Product-division companies	24	78	13	72	—
Source	189 co. (Rumelt, 1974)	183 co.	92 co. (Channon, 1973)	100 co.	200 co. (Channon, 1982)

performance, or problems with existing products, (iii) attitudes of top management towards opportunity. (We have already stated that diversification has three objectives. These three determining factors are closely related to the goals, but the determining factors are expressed from different angles.)

The past twenty years has been a period of relatively high growth in the Japanese economy, and there have been abundant opportunities for growth without greatly changing the product mix. Toyota Motor Company and Bridgestone Tire and Rubber Company could both grow as specialized companies. The top management of Bridgestone tried to diversify into the conveyer belt business and foam rubber products, but since the demand for tyres increased and Bridgestone's share of the market increased, the company continued to be a dominant-product company, although in 1962 it had been a technology-related product company selling a lot of rubber-related consumer products. Its top management was aggressive and long-term oriented, but the environmental factors made it disadvantageous to diversify. The rate of return was high because the market share was the highest, so there were no gaps in performance.

Hitachi has continued to be a technology-related company. Its product mix in 1980 was heavy electrical equipment (31 per cent), home electrical appliances (22 per cent), electronics and communication products (23 per cent), industrial machinery (12 per cent), transportation equipment and components (12 per cent). It was more diversified than General Electric, but, since the acquisition of Utah International by GE, it is now a less diversified and more technology-related company than GE. As far as technology-related products go, however, Hitachi's products are changing. For example, nuclear power equipment, colour television sets, computers and LSI have become much more important products than they were in 1962. Thus it has been possible for Hitachi to find growth products within the same diversification category, and top management aggressively sought growth products to take in.

One reason for the low level of diversification and related diversification was the intensity of competition. As analysed in Chapter 7, competition is intense in most areas of Japanese industry, and in order to survive the competition the products have to have competitive superiority, either as a result of specialization or by synergy. If Hitachi produced ships like Litton Industries, it would certainly lose out in the competition. Also, because of the intense competition, the conglomerate is rare in Japan.

When there is a gap in the performance, or when the gap is foreseen, the company diversifies into different areas, and tries to hold on to its competitive power by pouring in enough resources. Mitsui Ship Building Company diversified from shipbuilding into industrial machinery and into steel structures to compensate for the fluctuation of demand for ships and to close the gap in stability. Some other shipbuilding companies, such as Hakodate Dock Company and Sasebo Heavy Industry Company, did not diversify, could not survive the fluctuations of demand, and are now on the border of bankruptcy, with zero net worth. In the same environment, the strategy on product mix has varied from company to company because of the difference in views of top management.

Nihon Kogyo (Nippon Mining) was a producer of copper and a specialized company in 1955, but it entered the oil refinery business and became an unrelated-product company; however, the growth rate of its oil products was so high that it became a dominant-products company. The growth rate over eighteen years was 17 per cent (nominal). Other non-ferrous metal companies, such as Mitsui Metal and Mitsubishi Metal, remained solely as non-ferrous metal companies, and their growth rate was much lower – about 13 per cent during the same period. This is another case where the attitude of the top management played an important role.

Canon and Nihon Kogaku are both in the camera industry, but Canon has diversified into office equipment and attained a higher growth rate (21 per cent over the last nine years) than Nihon Kogaku (14 per cent over the same period). Again the difference in attitude of top management has resulted in a different product mix though the environment was the same.

The author tried regression analysis on the causes behind changes of diversification level. The hypothesis is as follows:

change of diversification level $= f$ (gap in growth rate of existing products, gap in rate of return)

This assumes that if there are gaps in growth rate and rate of return, then the company will diversify. The estimated value of parameters is as follows:

$$\text{PMT·L} - \text{PMT·E} = 0.8556 - 0.078 \ (\text{BGT·E}) + 0.064 \ (\text{ROT·E})$$
$$\text{(24 cases)} \qquad\qquad (\sigma = 0.062) \qquad\qquad (\sigma = 0.077)$$

$$(R = 0.337)$$

PMT·L – diversification level, later period; PMT·E – diversification level, earlier period; BGT·E – business growth rate, earlier period; ROT·E – return on investment, earlier period; σ standard deviation).

The correlation is not very weak and the values of coefficients are somewhat meaningful. This equation suggests that when business growth rate is low the diversification level rises, and when the rate of return is high the diversification level becomes higher still. This finding does not endorse the above mentioned hypothesis; instead, the principle seems to be the following: change of diversification $= f$ (gap in growth rate of existing products, and slack from profit). This model is not yet convincing. The forces of diversification are more future-oriented (as in Figure 4.2), and the attitude of top management plays an important role.

It is necessary to look back over a longer history of diversification among Japanese corporations. Before the Second World War the Zaibatsu companies, such as Mitsubishi and Mitsui, diversified into a lot of industries and dominated the key ones. During the war period these companies had to diversify further to meet the demands for war products. There were frequent acquisitions and mergers to increase the productivity of scarce resources, and to diversify quickly to meet military needs. Thus, before the war, the level of diversification of Zaibatsu family companies was high, both at group level and at individual company level. The Zaibatsu companies looked for the growth opportunities. At the same time, management skills and funds for investment were scarce resources, so the diversification of large companies was necessary. The availability of resources is an important force for diversification of large companies in developing countries. (This factor is stressed by Penrose, 1956.)

After the war, the Zaibatsu family companies were dissolved, and the diversification level of each company suddenly went down. However, since then Japanese companies have gradually added new products by introducing new technology from the USA and from Europe, to attain the present level of diversification.

4.4.1 Seventy-year History of Hitachi

Hitachi belonged to Nissan Konzern (Zaibatsu) group, but Hitachi itself diversified into a number of products. A small plant for repairing motors used for copper-mining and refining plant was established at Hitachi in 1906; it was the origin of the present company. In 1912 it became an independent company. Unlike other electrical products companies,

Hitachi did not have any joint venture agreements with other advanced foreign companies such as General Electric, Westinghouse or Siemens. It put emphasis on original technology; and its products were motors and transformers. After the First World War it introduced generators and water wheels, pumps and non-electrical machines. In the meantime, the military demands increased, and to meet these demands Hitachi started to produce electric wire, communication equipment and vacuum bulbs. Many of these diversifications were carried out by acquisition of other companies in order to meet the demand quickly.

After the Second World War, the Zaibatsu were dissolved, and Hitachi had to divest itself of its wire manufacturing and shipbuilding business among others. Hitachi's management perceived that a new opportunity was developing for electrical products but the technology gap was large, so it discarded the policy of independent research. It bought licences on nuclear power generators from GE, and on computers and television technology from RCA, and many other patents from the USA. It hurriedly constructed distribution channels. Hitachi had gone into light electrical products before the war, and they became more important than heavy electric products after the war. For instance, Hitachi did not produce electric home appliances before the war, but these became one of the major products groups after 1945.

It now has five technology-elated products groups – heavy electrical industrial equipment, electrical home appliances, electronics and communication products, industrial machinery and transportation equipment.

Hitachi introduced the product division structure in 1960, after rearranging its production system so that one plant belonged to one product division. It now applies the product division structure, but the responsibility for profit rests on the plant, while the product division performs the planning, co-ordinating and sales functions. The plant is the actual product division with full responsibility for profit.

Hitchi's case shows the typical pattern of historical change of product mix in large Japanese corporations. Hitachi utilized the growth opportunity, but after the war the technology-relatedness was an important principle for diversification.

4.5 DIVERSIFICATION AND OTHER STRATEGIES

Hereafter we will mainly analyse the diversification strategy of 102 manufacturing companies after 1962.

4.5.1 Specialization and Multinational Management

We can assume that the specialized company has a higher multinational management level than diversified companies. (Multinational management level is measured by the percentage of production of over 25 per cent owned foreign subsidiary companies.) There are two reasons for this assumption. The specialized company can make a more productive use of its resources by expanding the geographical area for production, than by looking for opportunities for new-product development. In the USA, the automobile, computer and oil refinery companies have adopted this strategy. (In Japan, these industries are at a low level of multinational management as yet.) In Japan, some synthetic fibre companies (Toray and Teijin) and some ball-bearing companies (Nihon Seiko) are specialized and have a high multinational management level. Put conversely, the diversified company has more opportunities for growth at home by developing new products, so it has less incentive for going abroad.

This hypothesis cannot be verified by our survey, the results of which are shown in Table 4.6. The dominant-product company (D) has a higher level of multinational management, but the level of the single-product company is lower than the average. The combined level of multinational management of the single-product company and the dominant-product company is also lower than the average.

On the other hand, some of the related-marketing-and-technology

TABLE 4.6 Diversification and other product–market strategies

	No. of co.	MNM %	VER %	SHA	RAD %	SPR %	BGT %	EXP %
S	16	3.09	22.17	0.65	1.06	2.15*	14.84	14.39
D	24	6.60	22.35	0.62	1.72	5.14	13.47	15.88
RMT	19	7.03	23.55	0.58	2.83*	5.14	13.99	20.12
RT	26	5.27	25.89	0.64	2.61*	2.81	13.31	19.71
RM	6	8.70	22.18	0.62	1.27	11.05*	11.10*	14.50
U	11	3.31	24.80	0.69	1.26	1.02*	13.65	14.82
Average		5.56	23.70	0.63	1.97	3.98	13.62	17.22
s.d.		7.25	6.40	0.29	1.57	5.26	2.50	14.67

Notes:
[1] MNM – multinational management; VER – vertical integration; SHA – share of market; RAD – research and development; SPR – sales promotion; BGT – business growth rate; EXP – export.
[2] For other abbreviations, see Appendix 4.1
[3] The asterick (*) indicates the level of significance is 10 %.
[4] For values of sixty-four high performers, see Table 4.14 in Appendix 4.1.

product companies, such as Matsushita, Sony and Sanyo, have a high level of foreign investment. Some diversified companies want to expand their market by multinational management, in order to reap the advantages of large-scale production and marketing. This is possible if the product has competitive power.

4.5.2 Specialization and Vertical Integration

There is an assumption that the specialized company (especially the dominant-product company) has a high level of vertical integration (Gort, 1962; Scott, 1971; Wrigley, 1970). The reason for this assumption is, in the author's opinion, that the specialized company has a straight-line process of production, and it requires large quantities of a few items of raw materials and components, so it is economical to integrate these processes. Brewing companies, oil refineries and the steel industry are included in this category. Also, with the downstream process, it is profitable to integrate the downward process and the sales channel because the number of products is limited.

According to our survey, however, there is no significant difference between the levels of vertical integration of each category of diversification, as seen in Table 4.6. Here the level of vertical integration is measured by value added divided by sales minus profit rate. This measurement is a proxy variable and, furthermore, it does not represent the quasi-vertical integration.

Technology-related product companies (RT) have a slightly higher level of vertical integration (25.89 per cent). They include Hitachi, Toshiba, NEC, Nihon Kokan Steel and Mitsui Shipbuilding. These companies have higher vertical integration observed by other detailed analyses. These high-technology companies, with high research and development ratios, have to compete by quality, so it is more advantageous to produce the key components within the company. Hitachi produces LSI, cable and electric motors, and since after-sales service is important for sales, the sales channel is also integrated.

Thus, there is no clear evidence that the specialized company has a higher level of vertical integration than the diversified company.

4.5.3 Diversification and Share of Market

One might assume that the specialized company has a large share of the market, because it can have a stronger competitive power as a result of specialization. Our empirical study denies this assumption. There is no relationship between the types of diversification and the share of market, as can be seen in Table 4.6. (The relative share was measured by giving the second largest share 1.0, and by weighting the number by the percentage of sales mix when the company is marketing more than one product.)

This is an important finding. It is possible for the diversified company to hold a large share of the market (or production). Hitachi, Matsushita, Sony and Canon are diversified companies, and have a large share of the market in each product area. Large market share is related to profitability, so one of the key success factors for the diversified company is to hold a large share of the market.

4.5.4 Diversification and Research and Development Expenditure

The technology-related products company (RMT and RT) has a higher than average ratio of research and development expenditure (to sales). This is shown in Table 4.6. The related-technology-and-marketing product company (RMT) has 2.83 per cent, and the technology-related company (RT) has 2.61 per cent, both of which are much higher than the average. This is because these technology-related diversifiers are selling technology-intensive products. This may seem self-evident, but it is an important factor in success.

4.5.5 Diversification and Sales Promotion

The ratio of sales promotion expenditure to sales is related to the nature of the product. If the products are consumer goods, the ratio is high. Related-marketing-and-technology product companies (RMT) and related-marketing product companies (RM) have a high ratio. Among them food, cosmetics, drugs, and electrical appliances all have a higher than average ratio of sales promotion to sales.

4.5.6 Diversification and Export

Exports can be a substitute for diversification, so it is possible to imagine that the export ratio of the specialized company is high. This assumption is not supported by the evidence. Table 4.6 shows that diversified companies (RMT and RT) have a slightly higher than average ratio of exports, and that technology-intensiveness is related to exports. Among specialized companies, those in the automobile, steel and watch industries have a high export ratio, and among diversified companies, those in shipbuilding, electric home appliances and camera industries have a high export ratio.

TWO CASES OF STRATEGY MIX

Toyota

Toyota and Isuzu were almost identical companies before the war, but Toyota's return on investment over the last eighteen years has been three times as high as Isuzu's (17.7 per cent versus 6.61), and Toyota's growth rate is 1.5 times as high as Isuzu's growth in the same period. Toyota specialized in passenger cars, because they were seen as a growth product, but Isuzu produced freight trucks as well as passenger cars, and did not allocate enough resources to the development of the latter. Toyota's basic product–market strategy was specialization, but also full-line policy for passenger cars. Toyota did not go multinational; its foreign production in 1980 was only 2.4 per cent of total production. Its exports, however, account for 44 per cent of sales. It will have to increase its foreign production. The vertical integration ratio is not high – in fact, somewhat lower than other companies. The strategy for integration was quasi-vertical integration, by controlling and helping the 172 components manufacturers. They form a group called 'Kyoho-kai', and supply components to Toyota exclusively. Some 320 dealers with 33 000 salesmen are exclusive distributors of Toyota cars. Toyota's share of the market in 1980 was the largest for all sizes of car, though its position has been constantly threatened by Nissan. Its research and development has about 3 per cent ratio to sales, costing 400 million dollars in 1980, and employing 2500 people in three laboratories. This percentage is higher than other companies in the same business. The sales efforts were made by the sales company, which was a strong and independent subsidiary, and which put pressure on Toyota to be more customer-oriented. Its slogan was 'the user first, the dealer second and the maker third'. This sales company merged with the manufacturing company in 1982.

Hitachi

Hitachi is a diversified company – a technology-related product company. Its product mix ranges from large power-generating equipment to colour television and to super LSI. Hitachi's production by the foreign subsidiaries is only 5.1 per cent of home production, but the export ratio was about 25 per cent in 1980. The export ratios of the five product lines are almost the same. Its vertical integration is higher than other companies; it produces its own key parts and sells the products through its own sales channels. The sales channel for consumer products is, however, quasi-integrated. The share of the market of every line of products is not the largest, but usually second or third. The company's top management says that because of diversification it is hard to hold the top market share in every product, but business commentators say Hitachi is playing safe, and enters the market as the second runner. Its research expenditure was about 5 per cent of sales, or 500 million dollars, in 1980, and it employed about 9000 research people in eight laboratories and on some plant sites at that time. Its research policy was to conduct original research, but after the war it introduced American and European technology. Recently, however, it has succeeded in developing a number of original inventions. The sales promotion expenditure is less than 1 per cent of sales, and is much lower than the other five big electrical equipment manufacturers. It emphasizes technology, and is pouring resources into electronics. Its slogan is 'electronics and energy'.

Both Toyota and Hitachi are successful cases of strategy mix. We will investigate types of successful strategy mix and unsuccessful strategy mix further in the following sections, but we will here tentatively state the following hypotheses that have been formed partly by observing the difference of performance between various types of diversification, and by comparing the strategy mix of sixty-four high-performance companies out of the 102 companies with the strategy mix of all 102 companies. The strategy mix of the sixty-four high performers is shown in Table 4.14 in the Appendix.

Successful Strategy Mix

For specialized companies, the growth rate of the product is high and the size of the market of the main product is large. For diversified companies, the growth rate of the products is high, and the products are similar with a resulting synergic effect on company performance.

For both specialized and diversified companies, the market share is high, if not the highest. In order to attain this high share, either research expenditure or sales promotion expenditure must also be high. For technology-intensive product companies, research expenditure is large and sales promotion expenditure is low. For marketing-intensive products, the sales promotion is high.

The key process is vertically integrated, but the level of integration is not high, and quasi-vertical integration is used to a great extent. The multinational management level is not related to performance, but the ratio of exports is high.

Unsuccessful Strategy Mix

The growth rate of the products is low. For diversified companies, the synergy effect is lacking, and the level of diversification is higher. The share of the market is low, because both the research expenditure and sales promotion expenditure are low. Unsuccessful companies tend to use quasi-vertical integration to a lesser extent than successful companies. The export ratio is low. We will investigate these hypotheses in the following sections.

4.6 DIVERSIFICATION AND PERFORMANCE

We will start here by simply comparing the performance of each category of specialization and diversification, and then will add other strategies and will investigate the performance of different strategy-mix companies.

4.6.1 Measurement of Performance

As measurements of performance, we used the following five items:

1. Growth rate. The growth rate of nominal sales (GRT) was used. We did not use the growth rate of value-added or the profit or the profit per share, because the growth of sales is considered the most important value by Japanese corporations.
2. Profit. It is measured by rate of return on total assets (ROT). It is the ratio of profit before tax and interest divided by total assets. This is the most meaningful yardstick. The equity ratio of Japanese corporations is low, so the net profit after tax and interest divided by net worth, or net profit divided by total assets, are only partial ratios.
3. Stability. We used two scales: the standard deviation of return on investment (DEV) and the equity ratio (EQU). The smaller the standard deviation, and the greater the equity ratio, the more stable the company is. (This is not the place to begin a complicated discussion on the concept of company stability, but a few words are necessary. The stability of the company can be measured by the probability of loss; this can be computed by rate of return after interest and tax divided by the standard deviation of rate of return (Kono, 1974; stability index $= [\mathrm{ROT} - \text{interest rate } (1 - \mathrm{EQU})] \div \mathrm{DEV})$. Then we should state that stability is affected by three factors, ROT, DEV and EQU, but here we have used only two.)

4. The total performance. The total performance is measured by combining the above three factors:

$SOG = ROT - DEV + GRT + EQU \times 1/3$ This model assumes one utility unit for each item, and one-third utility for equity ratio.

4.6.2 Types of Diversification and the Performance

We investigated the relationship between the different types of diversification and the performance of 102 manufacturing companies over a period of eighteen years. The result is shown in Table 4.7(a). The type of diversification of one company changes over the years, so the company is classified by the type of longest duration. Through the analysis of performance, we can verify the following statements:

TABLE 4.7(a) Diversification and performance

Types	No. of co.	(1) ROT 1962–80 %	(2) DEV 1962–80 %	(3) GRT 1962–80 %	(4) EQU 1967 and 1980 %	(5) SOG (1)−(2)+(3) +(4) × 1/3
S	16	8.90 (2.93)	2.48 (0.80)	14.90* (3.78)	25.08 (10.95)	29.69 (7.47)
D	24	9.38 (2.64)	2.65* (1.21)	12.43 (3.12)	28.57 (8.35)	28.69 (6.24)
RMT	19	10.69** (3.16)	2.59 (1.17)	15.01* (2.98)	29.59* (12.51)	32.97** (7.75)
RT	26	8.39 (2.41)	1.92* (1.10)	13.85 (2.44)	25.29 (11.07)	28.74 (6.13)
RM	6	8.33 (2.28)	2.62 (1.30)	11.42 (6.56)	25.42 (7.67)	25.60 (9.48)
U	11	7.55* (1.91)	1.47** (0.69)	15.33* (1.91)	18.46* (8.81)	27.57 (4.19)
Total	102					
Average s.d.		9.04 2.76	2.29 1.13	13.91 3.37	26.10 10.63	29.35 6.87

Notes:
[1] ( ) = standard deviation among companies.
[2] * . . . level of significance is 10%. ** . . . the level is 5%.
[3] For abbreviations, see Appendix 4.1.

TABLE 4.7(b) Diversification and performance

(1) ROT = 1.730 + 2.631 (MMT) − 0.662 (PMT)^2 + 0.275 (BGT) + 2.479 (SHA)
         (σ = 0.893)   (σ = 0.295)   (σ = 0.104)   (σ = 0.893) (R = 0.427)

(2) DEV   – – – (No meaningful correlation)

(3) GRT   – – – (No meaningful correlation)

(4) EQU = 8.144 + 10.628 (PMT) − 2.732 (PMT)^2 + 0.322 (BGT) + 9.244 (SHA)
         (σ = 5.623)   (σ = 1.160)   (σ = 0.408)   (σ = 3.515) (R = 0.382)

(5) SOG = 4.567 + 6.144 (RMT) − 1.360 (PMT)^2 + 1.66 (BGT) + 5.063 (SHA)
         (σ = 3.460˙)   (σ = 0.714)   (σ = 0.251)   (σ = 2.163) (R = 0.475)

Notes:
[1] σ = standard deviation.
[2] For abbreviations, see Appendix 4.1.

1.1 The rate of return on total investment changes with convex curve (mountain-shape), as the level of diversification increases.

1.2 Among the diversified companies, the related-technology-and-marketing product company (RMT) has the highest return by synergy.

As the level of diversification increases, the rate of return increases and then decreases, showing a convex curve. Over eighteen years the record for best performance is held by related-marketing-and-technology product companies (RMT). Sony and Matsushita belong to this group. The dominant-product company (D) comes next, and then follows the single-product company (S). Nissan and Toyota belong to S, and Teijin and Bridgestone Tire belong to D. The unrelated company shows the lowest rate of return. The same trend is seen in equity ratio (EQU). This convex curve cannot be seen in the standard deviation of rate of return over eighteen years (DEV), nor in growth rate (GRT).

Then we tried the regression analysis, using numbers as follows:

$$S = 1, D = 1.3, RMT = 2, RT = 2.8, RM = 3, U = 4$$

These numbers are represented by PMT variable. The results of regression analysis are shown in Table 4.7(b). In this analysis two variables, business growth rate (BGT) and share of market (SHA), are added and the influence of these two factors is separated, because these two variables have a large impact on the performance. The analysis shows that the rate of return changes as a second-grade parabola curve, and the values of parameter are meaningful (measured by t value).

Among the diversifiers, the RMT has the highest return and the unrelated (U) has the lowest return. This seems to show that the effect of synergy is important. The common use of research capability, shared use of production facilities, result in the advantage of scale of production. Furthermore, the common use of the marketing channel, of buyers and consumers, of marketing systems and of the same company image bring about the advantages of scale of marketing. The unrelated (U) has the lowest effect of synergy, so the rate of return is the lowest. The related-technology (RT) and the related-marketing (RM) have partial synergy, so the return is medium. Thus we can support the above 1.2 statement.

2.1 The standard deviation of rate of return decreases as the level of diversification increases.

2.2 Among the diversified companies, companies that have dispersed markets (RT and U) have less standard deviation of rate of return.

The standard deviation of rate of return of each company over eighteen years is one of the measurements of stability. Table 4.7(a) shows that the deviation (DEV) is highest in the dominant-product companies (D), and becomes lower as the level of diversification rises, and is lowest in the unrelated-product company (U). Both the related-technology company (RT) and the unrelated (U) have lower deviation, because the product use (or purpose) and the market are scattered. This shows that diversification stabilizes profit under certain conditions. However, the marketing-related diversifiers (RMT and RM) have a high standard deviation. This is because the market is similar and the sales and profit vary in similar directions.

3. There is no consistent relation between the growth rate and the type of diversification.

Table 4.7(a) shows that there are three peaks. The growth rates of S, RMT and U are high. These companies have selected growth areas. We should notice that the unrelated (U) has the highest growth rate.

4. The equity ratio shows a convex curve in relation to the level of diversification.

The equity ratio has a similar trend to that of the rate of return. Table 4.7(a) shows that RMT has the peak ratio and Table 4.7(b) shows that there is a second-degree parabola relationship when the influences of business growth rate and share of market are separated.

5. Over-all performance is best in the related-technology-and-marketing product companies.

The over-all performance (SOG) is computed by the following: $SOG = ROT - DEV + GRT + EQU \times 1/3$. As seen in Table 4.7(a), SOG of RMT is the best.

4.6.3 Types of Diversification, the Growth Rate of Business and the Share of Market

It is generally accepted that not only the types of diversification, but the growth rate of business and the share of market, have a great impact on performance. The latter two are much more emphasized by the BCG model or growth-share matrix model (Schoeffler *et al.*, 1974; Buzzell *et al.*, 1975; Hofer and Schendel, 1978). In order to analyse the effect of diversification types, and growth rate of the business, plus share of the market, we conducted a multi-variables regression analysis, using dummy variables for the types of diversification.

The objective of the analysis is twofold. On the one hand it is to investigate the effect on performance of the types of diversification, by separating the effects of the growth and the market share of the product. On the other hand it is to discover the effects of the growth rate of business and the share of the product on performance.

The equation is as follows: $Y = a_0 + a_1(S) + a_2(D) + a_3(RMT) + a_4(RT) + a_5(RM) + a_6(U) + a_7(SHA) + a_8(BGT)$. (The notation of variables is explained in Appendix 4.1.) For analysis, in the case of a single-product company, $S = 1$, and $D = 0$, $RMT = 0$, $RT = 0$, $RM = 0$, $U = 0$, and values of (SHA) and (BGT) are input. A similar method is used for other types of diversification.

The results of the analysis are shown in Table 4.7(c). In the case of

TABLE 4.7(c) Diversification and performance (Regression analysis using dummy variable)

Independent variable \ Dependent variable	ROT	DEV	GRT	EQU	SOG
Constant	3.12	1.76	3.89	14.25	10.76
S		−0.25			−0.72
		(0.35)			(1.79)
D	0.97		−1.45	3.40	
	(0.64)		(0.88)	(2.86)	
RMT	2.23	−0.08	0.72	4.56	3.85
	(0.69)	(0.33)	(0.91)	(3.07)	(1.65)
RT		−0.72			
		(0.31)			
RM	0.57		−0.66		
	(1.12)		(1.35)		
U	−1.09	−1.20	1.35	−7.45	−1.76
	(0.84)	(0.39)	(1.05)	(3.64)	(2.04)
SHA	2.60	0.16	−0.39	9.49	5.22
(av. = 0.63)	(0.87)	(0.38)	(0.94)	(3.55)	(2.14)
BGT	0.27	0.06	0.76	0.37	1.10
(av. = 13.62)	(0.11)	(0.05)	(0.11)	(0.43)	(0.26)
Correlation ($R =$)	0.49	0.38	0.65	0.40	0.51

Notes:
[1] The equation is: dependent variable = $a_0 + a_1(S) + a_2(D) + a_3(RMT) + a_4(RT) + a_5(RM) + a_6(U) + a_7(SHA) + a_8(BGT)$.

[2] For abbreviations, see Appendix 4.1.

[3] Stepwise regression was applied for analysis. Empty spaces show that the values are not meaningful.

[4] ( ) shows standard deviation of coefficient.

regression analysis using the dummy variable, the rank order by the value of the coefficient (or parameter) of the independent variable is important; the higher the value, the larger the effect on the dependent variable. In other words, the rank order of value of the coefficient shows the rank order of importance of the independent variable on the effect to the dependent variable. When we look at the ROT column, the value of the coefficient of RMT is the largest, and the rank order by value of coefficient is, RMT, D, RM and U. The value of U is the smallest. This order is exactly the same as the order of performance of Table 4.7(a). This means that the order of performance in Table 4.7(a) is valid, if we separate the effects of the business growth rate and the company's share of market. On the DEV (the standard deviation of ROT), the rank order of value of coefficient in Table 4.7(c) is the same as the order of Table 4.7(a). The U has the least DEV, and then RT comes next. RM and RMT have a larger deviation. The growth rate is highest for U followed by RMT in Table 4.7(c), and this order is the same as in Table 4.7(a). The equity ratio (EQU) is best for RMT, followed by D, and worst for U. This order is the same as in Table 4.7(a). Thus we can say that the simple comparison of performance in Table 4.7(a) is valid, with a few exceptions, even if we separate the effects of business growth rate and company share of the market.

Next, the analysis of Table 4.7(c) shows the impacts of business growth rate (BGT) and the share of market (SHA). Considering the absolute value of these two independent variables and the value of the coefficient, we find that the market share has a large impact on ROT and EQU, but does not affect DEV and GRT. The business growth rate affects ROT, GRT and EQU, but does not affect DEV. The impacts of these factors will be further analysed in the next section.

4.6.4 Product Mix by Growth-share Matrix

The product mix on the growth-share matrix could be a substitute for the classification of diversification by relatedness, as shown in Table 4.2. We wish to analyse this problem. The growth-share matrix model or BCG model assumes that the growth rate of the business and the company's market share have the most important impact on profit and liquidity. The simplified assumption is shown in Figure 4.3. The following principles of product mix are derived from this assumption:

1. A mixture of 'cat', 'star' and 'cow' products results in the best company performance – moderate profitability, good liquidity and long-range growth of sales and profit.

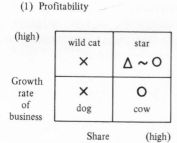

(1) Profitability

(2) Cash flow

Notes:
x-poor. △-medium. o-good. ⊚-excellent.

FIGURE 4.3 Assumptions of growth-share matrix

2. A mixture of 'cat' and 'star' results in unstable profitability and poor liquidity.
3. A mixture of 'cow' and 'dog' results in decline of sales and profitability.

We will here examine the assumptions of this model, indicated in Figure 4.3.

We first have to took at the analyses of Tables 4.7(b) and 4.7(c) again. We can see the effect of business growth rate (BGT) and share of market (SHA) on the performance. Tables 4.7(b) and 4.7(c) show that the share of the market has a large impact on the rate of return (ROT). The market share of the diversified company was computed by adding the share of each product multiplied by the ratio of the sales of each product to total sales of the company. The market share also affects the equity ratio. The larger the share, the higher the equity ratio. The impact of business growth rate on rate of return is greater than the impact of the market share ($0.275 \times 13.6\,2 > 2.479 \times 0.63$ in Table 4.7(b)). It also has some impact on equity ratio, but to a lesser extent than the share of market.

These analyses roughly confirm the assumption of Figure 4.3, but analysis shows that the 'star' product, not the 'cow' product, has the best performance, because the larger the share, and the higher the business growth rate, the better the profitability and the liquidity.

We need to conduct more detailed analyses to confirm the above findings. For this purpose, the author selected forty-seven relatively specialized companies in the twelve industries. We should use products for the analysis, but data on the performance of the products is not available, so we have to use the relatively specialized companies as a substitute.

We analysed the forty-seven manufacturing companies which overlap to a great extent with the 102 companies and investigated the relationship between the growth-share position and performance over the five years 1967–72, and the six years between 1972–8. The twelve industries are as follows:

Industries with less product differentiation – synthetic fibre; pulp and paper; rubber; cement; glass.
Industries with more product differentiation – confectionery; drugs; machine tool; automobile; camera; watch; musical instruments.

The results are shown in Figure 4.4. These results are not completely congruent with the assumptions of Figure 4.3. The findings are as follows:

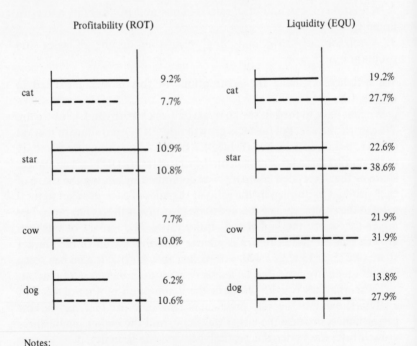

Notes:
1 ─────────── non-differentiated products.
   ─ ─ ─ ─ ─ ─ differentiated products.
2 Dividing line of real growth rate is 10% during 1967 and 1973,
   4% during 1973 and 1978.
3 Dividing line of share is 0.9 of relative share, the second
   largest share is given the number of 1.0.

FIGURE 4.4 Survey on twelve products of forty-seven companies

1. 'Star' products have the highest profitability and best liquidity. Undifferentiated products, especially 'star' products, show much better performance than 'cow' products. This differs from the BCG model. One of the reasons for this is that in Japan the product life cycle is shorter; the product advances quickly and reaches the decline stage in a shorter period.
2. In the case of differentiated products, the difference of performance between 'star', 'cow' and 'dog' product is slight. The performances of 'cow' and 'dog' are not low.
3. There are many products (actually companies) which are in the 'cow' and 'dog' area; improving the performance of these products is more important than taking negative action, such as harvesting or divesting.

The above findings have some implication for strategies that are different from the standard strategy of the BCG model.

First, the 'star' product has the best performance with respect to profitability and liquidity. The 'cash cow' does not have the best performance, as it does in the BCG model. So the company should try to have as many 'star' products as possible, whether the company is specialized or diversified.

Second, the company should have 'star' products as their central pillar, and should support other products with profits and by funds. If funds are short, the company can borrow money from the banks, because the 'star' has a high profitability and equity ratio.

Third, if the company can differentiate its product, it can improve profitability and liquidity, even if the product is a 'dog' product. Product differentiation becomes possible through research and advertisement, through good product designing, sales channels and services.

What is the relationship between growth-share matrix and the types of diversification shown in Table 4.2? The diversification model assumes that the relationship between the products is important, and that synergy is important and has an important impact on profitability and stability.

Market share is based on competitive power, and is also partly based on synergy; so to some extent the diversification model provides the basis for a growth-share matrix model.

The diversification model maintains that the performance is stabilized when the use of product is scattered, especially when the variations in performance of each product are negatively correlated, or are independent of each other. The growth-share matrix sees a stabilizing effect in the support from the 'cash cow' product, but it is possible that every product suffers from decline in demand if the uses of all products are the same.

It is more convenient to use the diversification model to analyse the interrelationship between strategy and structure. Specialized companies have different organizational characteristics from diversified companies; this will be analysed in the next section and in Chapter 10.

The product position in the growth-share matrix model can also interrelate with the organizational structure. This is analysed by the Arthur D. Little Company (Brown and O'Connor, 1974), and by Miles and Snow (1978), but the relationship is not very convincing.

The diversification model and the growth-share matrix model can complement each other, however. The specialized company can grow if the product is a growth product and if its market share is large. For any kind of diversification the products need to be high-growth products and the company to have a high market share in order to attain high performance.

CASES ON DIVERSIFICATION AND PERFORMANCE

Kojin Company (old name: Kokoku Rayon and Pulp Company)

Kojin was established in 1937 as a rayon and pulp company. In 1957 the company faced a crisis, because rayon and pulp were declining industries. Subsequently the top management was changed; the company decided to diversify to escape from the decline in business, and to enter a growth industry. It diversified into synthetic fibres, and recently it invested heavily in diversification into flame-resistant fibres, drugs (11 per cent of sales) and even more heavily in housing and land development (40 per cent of sales). Its sales reached 300 million yen at their peak in 1974. It went bankrupt, however, in 1975 because of heavy losses that were concealed for several years by modified financial statements. The direct cause of failure was the decline in the price of land after the oil crisis in 1973, most of the land having been bought at peak prices before the crisis, using borrowed money. The flame-resistant fibre was another problem product. A lot of money was invested in this new fibre without conducting sufficient market research. It turned out that there was almost no demand for this expensive fibre. The president, who came from an insurance company, favoured strong one-man leadership. He started to diversify from rayon and pulp in 1960 into the various products stated above, which were not very related. Kojin may be classified as an unrelated product company. There was little synergy between the products, nor, at the same time, was there any strong and profitable core product. Every product was low growth, low share and low profit. Moreover the fund for investment was largely financed from borrowed money, and the equity ratio was only 8 per cent. The president, Nishiyama, did not install any comprehensive long-range planning system; as well as being autocratic, his decisions tended to be intuitive, rather than analytical.

Konishi-Roku Company

Konishi-Roku was established in 1936, and was well known as a manufacturer of film and cameras before the war. These were the two major products until 1967, when the company suffered a heavy loss. The failure was partly due to defective colour film, but mostly due to the low share of the market, and the products were not very competitive. Top management were from the controlling family. Labour disputes were frequent; the personnel management emphasized punishment rather than reward, and decisions tended to be conservative. In 1967 the president from the controlling family retired, and a new management team was appointed. Following this, new successful products appeared one by one – new colour film, medium-sized dry copier 'Ubix', a small camera with a flash light mechanism, high-speed colour film (ASA 400), a small auto-focus camera; all of them proved to be highly successful. Company sales grew by 15.8 per cent over eighteen years to 200 billion yen in 1980, and the average rate of return during these years was 9 per cent. The company is classified as a marketing-related product company, because the technologies of film and of cameras and copying machines are different. The products do not have the highest share of the market, but they are very competitive. The major reason for the success was the aggressive development of growth products which had strong competitive power.

The reasons for this change of strategy were, first, that the president and top management team were changed. The new president·was prepared to take risks with development. Second, planning for new-product development became market-oriented, and management was encouraged to collect enough information about real needs before developing new products. For example, sufficient information was collected before developing the first auto-focus camera in the world, although the patent had been bought from Honeywell. Third, the personnel management was changed; the training, personnel selection and evaluation method were changed; the company's originally highly superior engineers were mobilized, and the abilities of all the employees were fully utilized. The reasons for the recovery of Konishi-Roku were a change of product mix by introducing successful new products. The slogan of the company is now 'challenge spirit'.

Summarizing this section, it was found that the related-marketing-and-technology product company (RMT) has the highest performance. It is evident that one of the success factors of diversification is synergy. The unrelated-product company has the lowest profitability. Second, the growth rate of business and the share of the company affect the profitability and the growth rate of the company. This is supported by the multiple regression analysis in Table 4.7(b) and Table 4.7(c). This principle is emphasized differently by the BCG model, where the 'cow' product has the best performance. Our findings show that the 'star' product has the best performance (Figure 4.4). We also found that if the product is differentiated, even low-growth and low-share products can have a reasonably high performance. Third, the diversified company can stabilize profits if the market is scattered. This is evidenced by the lower standard deviation of rate of return of diversified companies (RT and U) as compared with the specialized companies (S and D), as is seen in Table 4.7(a).

4.7 DIVERSIFICATION AND ORGANIZATIONAL STRUCTURE

The product mix affects the organizational structure and there is a fitting and mismatching relationship. Table 4.8 is a typical statement on the fitting relationship.

The assumptions of Table 4.8 are maintained by Scott, Greiner, Rumelt, Channon, Stopford and Miles and Snow (Scott, 1971; Greiner, 1972;

TABLE 4.8 Asumptions on fitting relationship between strategy and structure

	Specialized company	Diversified company
1. Top management	One man	Team
2. Research	Centralized	Decentralized
3. Head office	Large	Small
4. Departmental organization structure	Functional	Product division

Rumelt, 1974; Channon, 1973; Stopford, 1972; Miles and Snow, 1978).
We have to examine these assumptions.

4.7.1 Top Management

It is assumed that the specialized company has a simple product mix,
and a small number of members of top management have access to
enough strategic information, so that top management can be one man,
or a small number of top managers. On the other hand, it is assumed that
the diversified company needs complicated strategic information, so it
needs to have a team at the top.

According to our survey on the long-range planning process, this
difference was not found. Both the specialized and the diversified
company have management committees in Japan. There is some
difference in the level of expertise of top management, however. The
technology-related products companies (RMT and RT) have more
engineering or natural-science graduates at the top (see Table 4.9). The
marketing-related products companies (RM) have the smallest percentage of engineers at the top. These are both fitting relationships.
There is no difference in the ages of directors (Table 4.9).

The influential group was not studied by this research, but the
technology-intensive product companies recruit a high percentage of

TABLE 4.9 Diversification and top management

	No. of co.	AGD years	TEC %	AGE years
S	16	56.59	39.60	34.51
D	24	55.49	42.42	33.49
RMT	19	55.78	46.35	33.34
RT	26	57.56	50.67**	34.26
RM	6	55.10	28.18**	32.78
U	11	57.20	44.72	36.01
Total	(102)			
Average		56.41	44.22	34.05
s.d.		2.80	13.48	2.76

Notes:
[1] AGD – average age of directors (officers); TEC – ratio of directors who are graduates
from engineering or natural science departments; AGE – average age of employees. For
other abbreviations, see Appendix 4.1.
[2] Two asterisks (**) indicate the level of significance is 5%.

natural science or engineering graduates, and they tend to be respected. The percentage of such graduates among the top managers (directors) in technology-related products companies is even higher (see Table 4.9). For example, Hitachi recruited 564 university graduates and 1440 high-school students in 1980. Among the 564 university graduates, 464 were engineering and natural-science majors (234 had second degrees or master's degrees in science subjects). Hitachi's top management is composed of 64 per cent engineers and 36 per cent social-science graduates. Engineers tend to have greater influence and power in Hitachi, because technology is the key resource for that company.

4.7.2 Strategy-generating Departments – Planning Department, and Research and Development Department

4.7.2.1 Planning department

It is sometimes assumed that the specialized company has a large planning staff, and that the diversified company has fewer staff at the head office, and more in each division. According to the analysis of the survey on long-range planning conducted in 1979, there is no difference between them:

Nine specialized companies . . . 11.4 persons (standard deviation = 12.0 persons)
Eighteen diversified companies . . . 11.3 persons (standard deviation = 9.0 persons)

(This figure excludes the assistants. If assistants are included, the figures are 13.7 persons and 13.3 persons respectively.)

4.7.2.2 Research and development department

It is also sometimes assumed that the specialized company has a centralized laboratory and that the diversified company has both a central laboratory and a division laboratory. This is not the case with Japanese corporations. Even diversified companies have centralized laboratories. Hitachi is a diversified company and has eight laboratories, only two of which belong to a division, the rest being under head-office control. The division has a development section, but employees there are mostly engaged in designing. Matsushita is also a diversified company, but all nine of its research laboratories are centralized. Mitsubishi Heavy Industry Company is a very diversified company, but again all five research laboratories are directly controlled by the head office. Takeda is a diversified pharmaceutical company with a large central laboratory: its drug division does not have a research department, but the four minor product divisions each have their own research department. This is a rare case.

These examples show that Japanese diversified companies have centralized research laboratories. There are several advantages in centralizing research. Centralization makes it easier to concentrate the human resources, to co-ordinate research activity, especially with regard to large projects. The system products like computers and robots that utilize a variety of scientific disciplines are being produced in increasing numbers and co-ordination is becoming more important. Centralization makes it possible for the laboratory to make a longer view and to conduct more basic research, freed from the short-term profit responsibility of the divisions.

Technology-related diversifiers (RMT, RT) have higher research expenditures (Table 4.6), and their laboratories are larger. This is a simple fitting relationship.

4.7.3 Head Office

The head office in Japanese corporations is strong, irrespective of the level of diversification, and irrespective of the functional or divisional organizational structure. The author sent questionnaires relating to this to 102 companies, out of which 43 companies responded.

The results are shown in Table 4.10. The seventeen specialized companies have 1126 persons in their head offices, which accounts for

TABLE 4.10 Number of staff in the head office

	Average number	% of total employee
Specialized companies (S, D) (17 co.)	1126 persons ($\sigma = 1156$)	8.9 ($\sigma = 4.6$)
Diversified companies (R, U) (27 co.)	997 persons ($\sigma = 1037$)	9.1 ($\sigma = 5.1$)

Notes:
[1] Survey by mail questionnaire conducted in 1982.
[2] Sample is 44 manufacturing companies out of 102 companies.
[3] The head office includes the top management and people in the staff departments; excludes research laboratory and sales channels.
[4] σ in parentheses means standard deviation.

8.9 per cent of the total number of employees. The diversified company has 997 persons in the head office accounting for 9.1 per cent of all employees. The absolute number in diversified companies is as large as in the specialized companies, and the percentage is even higher.

Hitachi employs more than 2000 persons in its head office, for example. The head office of GE in the USA probably accommodates about 300 or 400, the head office of GEC in London has only about a hundred employees; ICI too has about a hundred employees in its London office. Specialized companies in the USA and in the UK, however, have a large number of personnel in their head offices. In the two head offices of Royal Dutch Shell it may come to more than 2000. The oil companies in the USA have large numbers of head office staff.

In the USA and UK there are differences in the numbers of personnel in the head offices, depending upon the level of diversification; on average, the number is lower than that of Japanese companies.

The reasons for and the effects of these large head office staffs will be analysed in Chapter 10, but here we will investigate a few points. Two effects are important. In a changing environment, large strategic moves, such as huge capital investments or large-scale development of new products, are necessary. These large moves cannot be delegated to the divisions. They have to be planned in the head office and decided by top management. In a competitive environment, marketing function and production function have to be strong, to ensure that the products are of high quality and low cost and strengthen the sales channel. These functions are more vigorous with strong centralized staff departments in the head office.

4.7.4 Departmental Organizational Structure

It is usually assumed that the specialized company uses a functional organization structure, while the diversified company uses a product division structure. In fact it goes further in the USA and in the UK. Even specialized companies use division structure, either product division or geographic division structure, to delegate authority.

Rumelt classifies departmental structure as follows: (i) functional, (ii) functional for major product; division structure for minor products, (iii) product division, (iv) geographical division, (v) holding company.

We have used the same classification in this research. Class (ii), functional for major product and division for minor product, was identified, but it was sometimes classified as functional, because the Japanese corporation has a strong head office, and the typical division structure is rare. Among the 102 companies there is only one geographical division, and no holding company type. Pure holding companies are not allowed by anti-monopoly law. Sony uses a subsidiary form for its plant and sales department, but the authority of these subsidiaries is limited, and the organization can hardly be described as a type of holding company.

The outline of results of the survey comparing the 102 companies with companies in two other countries is shown in Table 4.11. The number of division structures is increasing in the 102 Japanese corporations, as the product mix becomes more diversified, but the extent of diffusion of product division is far less than in the other two countries. In the USA, more than 80 per cent of companies have division structure (including holding company structure). Not only diversified companies, but also specialized companies use the division structure. Only 45 per cent of Japanese corporations use division structure, while there are more than 60 per cent diversified companies.

The matching of the diversification type and organization structure is indicated in Table 4.12. The strategy roughly matches the structure, but there are many 'mismatchings', that is, diversified companies (R) may use functional structure.

What are the reasons for this 'mismatching' in Japanese corporations? The division structure has several disadvantages, and this is made clear by the survey conducted by Kansai Productivity Centre (Kansai Seisansei Honbu, 1976). First, the functional capability, especially the marketing function, is weakened by division structure. To cope with a competitive environment, a strong marketing function is advantageous. Second, the division tends to take a short-term view and to suboptimize.

We investigated the difference in performance when strategy and structure were matched or 'mismatched'. The specialized company can take both functional structure and division structure, and there is no problem of 'mismatching'. When diversified companies adopt functional organization, this can be considered 'mismatching', so we investigated the difference in rates of return of diversified companies, whether functional organization companies or divisional organization companies. During the earlier period 1962–72 the difference in return on investment was as follows (F & Div. is included in F):

$$\{R, U\} \cap F \quad \dots \quad ROT \cdot E = 9.25$$
$$\text{(23 cases)} \qquad\qquad (\sigma = 2.69)$$
$$\{R, U\} \cap Div. \quad \dots \quad ROT \cdot E = 9.52$$
$$\text{(32 cases)} \qquad\qquad (\sigma = 3.50)$$

TABLE 4.11 International comparison of organizational structure

Organization structure \ Country year	USA 1949 189 co. %	USA 1969 183 co. %	UK 1950 92 co. %	UK 1970 96 co. %	Japan 1967 102 co. %	Japan 1976 102 co. %	Japan 1980 102 co. %
Functional	63 }76	11 }20	}57	}8	53 }60	45 }56	42 }55
Functional and product division	13	9			7	11	13
Product division	20	76	13 }...	}71	40	43	44
Geographic division	0	2	30		0	1	1
Holding company	4	2		21	0	0	0
Source	(Rumelt, 1974)		(Channon, 1973)		(Kono, 1980)		

TABLE 4.12 Diversification and organizational structure (102 companies)

	1967	1980
S and F	17	14
(F & Div.)	(0)	(3)
S and Div.	1	0
D and F	22	19
(F & Div.)	(3)	(5)
D and Div.	7	4
R and F	20	21
(F & Div.)	(3)	(5)
R and Div.	25	38
U and F	3	2
(F & Div.)	(1)	(0)
U and Div.	7	4
F	62	56
(F & Div.)	(7)	(13)
Div.	40	46

Notes:
[1] F – functional organization (including F & Div.); Div. – division structure; F & Div. – functional organization for major product, division structure for minor product.
[2] S – specialized-product company; D – dominant-product company; R – related-product company; U – unrelated product company.

There is no meaningful difference in rate of return between the functional organization structure and divisional organization structure.

During the later period (1972–80), the difference was as follows:

$\{R, U\} \cap F$ ... $ROT \cdot L = 8.54$
(23 cases) $(\sigma = 3.12)$
$\{R, U\} \cap Div.$ ... $ROT \cdot L = 8.03$
(42 cases) $(\sigma = 2.63)$

We could not find any meaningful difference in performance in either period.

4.8 SUMMARY

The top management of Japanese corporations is aggressive and the goal is long-range oriented. These characteristics might lead to high-level diversification, but it is not so in Japan. The level of diversification in Japanese corporations is lower than in the USA, and the diversification is more technology-related. The reason for the lower level of diversification is that there were many high-growth products like cars and tyres. The competition is severe and diversification is neither easy nor successful. Less use of acquisition or merger is another reason.

The performance is related to the product mix. The performance of the related-marketing-and-technology product company is the most successful. However, the specialized company can also show good performance if its product has significant growth and if the company's market share is high. The related-technology product company and unrelated product company show a lower deviation of rate of return, because the market is diversified.

The growth rate of the product and the market share is related to the performance in any kind of diversification. The low-growth product and low-share product, however, can produce a high return and high liquidity if the product is well differentiated. In this respect, research and development expenditure and sales promotion expenditure are important for high profitability.

The strategy affects the organizational structure; the specialized company has functional organizational structure and the diversified company has product division structure. However, in Japan the division structure is less popular, even for diversified companies, and authority is centralized, with a large number of staff in the head office. With such centralization large strategic moves are possible, and the functional capability of research, production and marketing tends to be strong.

The product mix and other related strategies of successful Japanese companies are shown in Table 4.13.

4.8.1 Problems

1. The effectiveness of classification of product mix. We analysed the characteristics of diversification types according to the synergy relationships. Even among the same types, however, there can be large differences in performance. In the same related-technology, the performances of Mitsui-Toatsu (fertilizers) and of Takeda (drugs) are quite different. The latter can differentiate its product, and the profit rate is very high. In the same single-product company group, the performances of Toyota and Toyokogyo are different – the latter having a lower share of the market and a much lower rate of return.

The growth-share matrix may be useful to classify product mix.

TABLE 4.13 Product mix and related strategies for success

	Specialized company (S and D)	Diversified company (R)
(a) Keys for success	(1) Growth product (2) High share	(1) Growth product (2) High share (3) Related products with synergy (4) Mutually independent move of performance
(b) Related strategies		
. R & D	} Either of the two is high	High R & D for RT and RMT
. Sales promotion		High sales promotion for RM
. Vertical integration	Quasi-vertical integration	Quasi-vertical integration
. Multinational management	Techlology-intensive product	Technology-intensive product
. Export	High	High
(c) Organizational structure		
. Top management	Management committee	Management committee
		More engineers for RT, RMT
. Head office	Large	Large
. Laboratory	Centralized	Centralized, some division laboratories
. Departmental organization	Funcational	Product division and functional

Classification by differentiated product or undifferentiated product may also be useful.

We admit that the growth-share matrix is a useful classification, and for every type of product mix the growth product and high market share are important factors in success. We can use this classification in addition to a synergy-related classification model.

The synergy-related classification model has several merits, and is widely used.

(a) Synergy is the basis for competitive power; thus it affects the share of market.
(b) The synergy-related classification model is relatively stable; the company tends to stay in the same type, compared with the growth-share matrix model.
(c) This model is also related to the organizational characteristics and other strategies. For example, technology-related diversification needs a high ratio of research expenditure.

There are many other classification models. In addition to the growth-share matrix model, there are such models as: differentiated product *v.* undifferentiated product; technology-intensive product–non-technology-intensive product; capital-intensive product *v.* labour-intensive product; consumer *v.* producer goods; mass-produced goods *v.* order-made goods.

The effectiveness of these classification models should be evaluated according to two factors – the impact on the performance and the impact on other management systems. The effectiveness of some of the above is analysed in Appendix 4.1.

2. Japan is entering a slow economic growth stage and, in order to sustain the growth rate, companies will have to diversify. However, whether the level of diversification will advance in the future in a slow-growth economy, or not, is unclear. In the past, exports have been a substitute for diversification (for example, cars and tyres), but this substitute will become more difficult to use. In Japan the needs of consumers will diversify as the level of consumption is already high; so a diversification strategy will become more advantageous than a specialization strategy.

3. Japanese corporations make much less use of division structure at present than US companies. An important decision for the future is whether decentralization will be advanced or not. With a division structure it would be easier to motivate employees. However, in order to

have strong functional capability, strong head office together with division structure may be the most effective.

4. A greater use of acquisition and merger will change the product mix. It will encourage diversification on the one hand, but on the other hand, it will make divestment easy, which will quickly decrease the number of products. Acquisition will accelerate the speed of change of product mix. The obstacle in the way of this strategy was the organization-orientedness of the employee, and it is debatable whether this strategy will become popular in the future.

Appendix 4.1: DEFINITION OF VARIABLES

1. S   Single-product firm
   D   Dominant-product firm
   RMT   Related products by marketing and technology firm
   RT   Related products by technology firm
   RM   Related products by marketing firm
   U   Unrelated-products firm

2. F   Functional organization structure
   Div.   Division organization structure
   F & Div.   Functional organization for major product, division structure for minor product

3. MNM   Multinational management level
   VER   Vertical integration level
   SHA   Share of market (sales)
   RAD   Research and development ratio
   SPR   Sales promotion ratio
   BGT   Business growth, total period
   EXP   Export ratio
   PMT   Diversification level, total period. Diversification level is computed by replacing $S = 1$, $D = 1.3$, $RMT = 2$, $RT = 2.8$, $RM = 3$, $U = 4$.
   PMT $\cdot$ E   Diversification level, earlier period
   PMT $\cdot$ L   Diversification level, later period

4. AGD   Average age of directors (= officers)
   TEC   Directors who are the graduates of natural science departments of universities, divided by all directors
   AGE   Average age of employees

5. ROT   Return on investment (on total assets) before interest and tax
   DEV   Standard deviation of ROT during eighteen years
   GRT   Sales growth rate per year, total period
   EQU   Equity ratio
   SOG $ROI - DEV + GRT + EQU \times 1/3$

6. Measurement

S	Sales of one product is over 95 per cent of total sales.
D	Sales of one product is over 70 per cent of total sales.
RMT	Sales of one product is less than 70 per cent and sales of marketing-related products is more than 70 per cent, and at the same time sales of technology related products is more than 70 per cent of total sales.
RT	Sales of one product is less than 70 per cent, and sales of technology-related products is more than 70 per cent of total sales.
RM	Sales of one product is less than 70 per cent, sales of marketing-related products is more than 70 per cent of toal sales.
U	Sales of marketing-related products is less than 70 per cent, and sales of technology-related products is less than 70 per cent.
MNM	Total production of subsidiaries in foreign countries, which are owned by more than 25 per cent, divided by the unconsolidated sales of the parent company.
VER	(Value added − profit after interest and tax) ÷ sales
SHA	The sales of the product of the second largest share is 1, and relative share is computed. This relative share is weighted by the percentage of sales of each product of a company.
RAD	Research and development expenditure divided by sales.
SPR	Sales commissions, advertisement and other sales promotion divided by sales. It excludes transportation cost and warehouse charge.
BGT	Nominal growth rate of the business to which the major product of the company belongs.
EXP	Export ÷ sales
PMT	S = 1, D = 1.3, RMT = 2, RT = 2.8, RM = 3, U = 4.

APPENDIX 4.2: PRODUCT DIFFERENTIATION AND PERFORMANCE

The product differentiation is measured not only by the sales promotion, but also by the research expenditure. By two measurements, the over-all product characteristics of the company can be classified into four, as is seen in Figure 4.5. The high-technology consumers' durable goods has the highest product differentiation. The high-technology producers' durable goods and fashionable goods come next. The raw material has the lowest product differentiation.

The performance is best in high-technology consumers' durable goods, the most differentiated products company, and is lowest in the least differentiated products, raw materials. The performances of the other two product categories fall between the above two. These findings are consistent with the findings of Figures 4.4. We find that product differentiation has an important impact on performance.

We should notice that this classification roughly corresponds to the classifi-

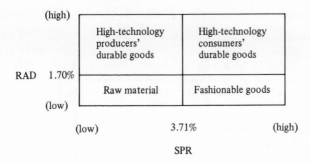

	102 companies	
	Av.	s.d.
1. ROT = 9.61 1. 11.40*	9.04	2.76
2. DEV = 2.06 2. 3.02*	2.29	1.13
3. GRT = 14.49 3. 14.78	13.91	3.37
4. EQU = 27.70 4. 34.98*	26.10	10.63
5. SOG = 31.33 5. 34.92*	29.35	6.87
(23 co.) (17 co.)		

1. 7.74*   1. 9.33
2. 1.90*   2. 2.94
3. 13.10   3. 12.68
4. 20.62*   4. 29.58
5. 26.49   5. 28.70
(45 co.)   (17 co.)

Note:
* Level of significance is 10%, comparison with the average.

FIGURE 4.5   Product differentiation and performance

cation of competition also. They are perfect competition (not indicated here), monopolistic competition (fashionable goods), oligopoly with differentiated products (two high-technology goods) and oligopoly without product differentiation (raw material).

TABLE 4.14 Diversification and other product–market strategies, sixty-four high performers

	No. of co.	MNM	VER	SHA	RAD	SPR	BGT	EXP
S	11	4.14	24.00	0.70	1.19	2.47	14.44	17.23
D	17	7.58	23.32	0.64	1.86	4.83	17.76**	17.39
RMT	15	7.98	23.29	0.55	3.43**	5.91	14.51	24.62*
RT	13	5.48	23.70	0.73	3.26*	4.31	13.33	18.32
RM	4	7.18	20.52	0.69	1.35	16.23**	12.35	13.85
U	4	1.10	25.22	0.63	1.25	0.93	13.60	12.13
	64							
Average (102 co.)		5.56	23.70	0.63	1.97	3.98	13.62	17.22
s.d. (102 co.)		7.25	6.40	0.29	1.57	5.26	2.50	14.67

Notes:
[1] The Rot of the above high performers is: ROT > 7.66 %.
[2] For RM, ROT > 7.19.
[3] * level of significance is 10 %, ** indicates that level is 5 %.

REFERENCES

Kono, T. (1974) *Keieisenryaku no Kaimei* (Analysis of Corporate Strategy), Tokyo, Diamond Sha.

Kono, T. (1977) *Keieigaku Genron* (Principles of Management), Tokyo, Hakuto Shobo.

Kono, T. (1980) *Senryaku Keieikeikaku no Tatekata* (Introduction to Strategic Planning), Tokyo, Diamond Sha.

Kansai Seisansei Honbu (1976) *Keiei Soshiki no Shin Doko* (New Trend of Organization Structure), Osaka, Kansai Seisansei Honbu.

Miyamoto, M. and Nakagawa, K. (1977) *Nihon Keieishi Koza* (Lecture on Japanese Business History), 5 vols, Tokyo, Nihon Keizai.

Yoshihara, E., Sakuma, A., Itami, K. and Kagono, T. (1979) *Nihon Kigyo no Takaku-ka Senryaku* (Diversification Strategy of Japanese Enterprise), Tokyo, Nihon Keizai.

Andrews, Kenneth R. (1971) *The Concept of Corporate Strategy*, Homewood, Ill., Dow Jones-Irwin.

Ansoff, H. I. (1965) *Corporate Strategy*, New York, McGraw-Hill.

Brown, J. K. and O'Connor, R. (1974) *Planning and the Corporate Planning Director*, New York, Conference Board.

Buzzell, R. D. *et al.* (1975) 'Market Share-Key to Profitability', *Harvard Business Review*, Jan–Feb.

Chandler, A. D. (1962) *Strategy and Structure*, Cambridge, Mass., MIT Press.

Channon, Derek F. (1973) *The Strategy and Structure of British Enterprise*, London, Macmillan.

Channon, D. F. (1982) 'Industrial Structure', *Long Range Planning*, London, Oct.

Dyas, G. P. and Thanheiser, H. T. (1976) *The Emerging European Enterprise, Strategy and Structure in French and German Industry*, London, Macmillan.

Galbraith, J. K. (1968) *The New Industrial State*, New York, Signet Books.

Galbraith, J. K. and Nathanson, D. A. (1978) *Strategy Implementation, Role of Structure and Process*, Los Angeles, West Publishing.

Gort, Michael (1962) *Diversification and Integration in American Industry*, Princeton, New Jersey, Princeton University Press.

Greiner, L. E. (1972) 'Evolution and Revolution as Organization Grows', *Harvard Business Review*, July–Aug.

Hofer, C. W. and Schendel, D. (1978) *Strategy Formulation, Analytical Concept*, Minnesota, West Publishing.

Kotler, P. (1976) *Marketing Management*, New Jersey, Prentice-Hall.

Markowitz, H. (1959) *Portfolio Selection*, New York, John Wiley.

Miles, R. E. and Snow, C. C. (1978) *Organizational Strategy, Structure and Process*, New York, McGraw-Hill.

Penrose, E. T. (1959) *The Theory of the Growth of the Firm*, Oxford, Basil Blackwell.

Perrow, C. (1970) *Organizational Analysis*, London, Tavistock Publications.

Richard, M. D. (1978) *Organizational Goal Structure*, Los Angeles, West Publishing.

Rumelt, Richard R. (1974) *Strategy, Strucure and Financial Performance*, Cambridge, Mass., Harvard University Press.

Schoeffler, S. *et al.* (1974) 'Impact of Strategic Planning on Profit Performance', *Harvard Business Review*, Mar–Apr.

Scott, B. R. (1971) *Stages of Corporate Development*, Boston, Harvard Business School.

Sharpe, W. F. (1970) *Portfolio Theory and Capital Markets*, New York, McGraw-Hill.

Steiner, G. (1969) *Top Management Planning*, New York, Macmillan.

Steiner, G. and Miner, J. B. (1977) *Management Policy and Strategy*, New York, Macmillan.

Stopford, John M. and Wells, Louis T. (1972) *Managing the Multinational Enterprise*, New York, Basic Books.

Thompson, J. (1967) *Organizations in Action*, New York, McGraw-Hill.

Woodward, J. (1965) *Industrial Organization, Theory and Practice*, London, Oxford University Press.

Wrigley, L. (1970) 'Divisional Autonomy and Diversification', unpublished doctoral thesis, Harvard Business School.

5 Vertical Integration

5.1 CONCEPT AND MEASUREMENT

Vertical integration is the practice whereby the market mechanism is replaced by internal transactions. It is the situation where a boundary line is drawn between the environment and the system of the company. It is also one of the product–market strategies that affects performance.

It is interesting to trace back the development of the Japanese watch industry, especially as represented by Seiko companies, in comparison with the Swiss watch industry. In Switzerland the component manufacturers are independent from the finished watch manufacturers who design and assemble the watch. In 1960 there were more than 500 finished watch manufacturers and more than 1000 independent component manufacturers. This was the basic reason why the introduction of electronics into the Swiss watch industry was delayed. A joint research laboratory was established in 1962, but it did not succeed in the development of the tuning-fork, nor of the quartz crystal watch.

On the other hand, Seiko companies produced all their major components within the company. The company was sufficiently large to integrate the production process to a high degree, which enabled it to develop the electronics components it required for the quartz crystal watch. Seiko was not originally strong in electronics, but its management perceived the needs, recruited the engineers and reinforced its capability in that area. Seiko not only makes the parts but also produces machines to manufacture the watch in its machine department and in a subsidiary company. It now produces liquid crystal, integrated circuits, crystal, and step motor, and these components are also sold as parts outside the company.

In Switzerland, the technological innovation was a source of conflict among the component makers, so they resisted the change. Seiko produced its own major parts, and had no difficulty in changing the technology. In addition, Seiko was the largest watch manufacturer in 1960; it could enjoy the advantage of large-scale production even when it integrated the production of components. With this innovation Seiko increased its share of the market and by 1980 was producing 10 per cent of the total world watch production. This example shows that vertical integration was the key success factor in the watch industry.

There is another story, however. The Hong Kong watch industry increased its share of production tremendously by producing cheap quartz crystal watches, assembled using electronics components imported from Japan. They were newcomers; they had not integrated the parts manufacturing process, so it was easy for them to introduce the new technology. It is hard to tell whether the Hong Kong manufacturers have the real key technologies to survive in the future, but this is a case where the disintegration was an advantageous policy, even if it is only a temporary one. There are a number of essential factors in successful vertical integration.

5.1.1 Basic Concept

Vertical integration is a situation where the stages of production and distribution are included in one hierarchical system. As Williamson expressed it, it is to replace the market mechanism with the internal transaction (Williamson, 1975).

Vertical integration is a situation where the company in the main or key process controls the company in the auxiliary but next-to-key process. The key process holder has power over and can control the supplementary process company. The car manufacturer can integrate the components manufacturing process, but an automatic transmission manufacturer cannot 'integrate' the car manufacturing process.

The integrated process should be an important successive process – as we call it, a 'next-to-key' process. It is meaningful for the car manufacturer to integrate the transmission production process, but it is meaningless to integrate the simple repairment work of building.

Vertical integration means integrating a process that could be an independent business – for instance, the watch manufacturer who produces LSI, which could be produced as an independent business. Gort says that if the company integrates a process whose four-digit SIC number differs from that of the main process, it is vertical integration. This is similar definition to ours. Thus we cannot say that agriculture, power generation and transmission and the domestic gas supply systems are vertically integrated businesses, because the partial processes of these businesses cannot be independent businesses.

5.1.1.1 *Backward and forward integration*

Vertical integration can be classified in three ways:

1. Backward integration. For example, the company produces its own components.

2. Forward integration of the production process. For example, the steel-maker produces steel structures for building.

3. Forward integration of distribution. For example, the company operates its own sales channel.

5.1.1.2 *Method of integration*

The above classification is concerned with the process or the stage at which integration takes place. The following classification is concerned with the method of integration:

1. Consolidated integration. This includes (i) the integrated process carried out by a department of the company, and (ii) the integrated process carried out by the subsidiary owing up to more than 50 per cent.

2. Quasi-integration, or grouping. This also divides into two: (i) Exclusive quasi-integration is the situation where the integrated process is carried out by an independent company, but one that is controlled by the key process company by means of a long-term contract and a variety of services provided by the controlling company. The integrated company is not owned by majority ownership, but it sells to, or buys from, one company only. The controlling company carries out the most important key process, so it has a controlling power. (ii) Selective quasi-integration. The key-process company controls the upstream or downstream company by means of long-term contracts and services, but neither the upstream nor the downstream company belongs to that one company, and they may sell to or buy from other companies. The relation is, however, a long-term one, and there is a controlling power on the side of the key-process company. Both these kinds of quasi-integration are widely used in Japan. Simple long-term contracts, however, and temporary contracts do not constitute vertical integration.

Vertical integration serves to unify the decision-making on and operation of several processes for a common purpose. To integrate, especially in quasi-vertical integration, some kind of power is necessary. It does not necessarily come from ownership, but from unequal transaction between the key-process company and the integrated companies.

5.1.2 Measurement of Integration Level

To measure the level, we have to define the major process and auxiliary process. The main process employs the largest number of people, or has the largest value added. In addition, the main process is a key process for competition and for profit; it holds the core of competitive strength. The supplementary process employs fewer people, has fewer assets and yields less value added, but it can be an independent business.

We have several alternatives as the measurements of the level of integration.

1. Number of personnel: (a) employment in the supplementary process ÷ total employment (this was used by Gort), (b) employment in the supplementary process including subsidiaries ÷ total employment including subsidiaries, (c) employment in the supplementary process plus qasi-integrated process ÷ total employment including quasi-integration.

2. Total assets, using the same combination as above, replacing employment with total assets.

3. Value added. Value added is closely related to vertical integration. As shown in Figure 5.1, if four companies are engaged in four stages, the

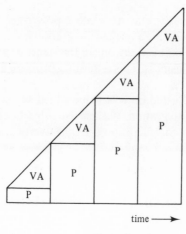

time ⟶

Stage of production

Note:
VA - value added; P - purchase from outside.

FIGURE 5.1 Stages of production and value added

ratio of value added to the sales in the earlier stage is higher than those of later stages. If one company produces all four stages, then the ratio of value added to sales is more than 80 per cent.

Value added includes profit, and the profit varies depending upon competitive power, so it is necessary to deduct the profit rate from the ratio of value added. Ratio of value added to sales − rate of net return on sales = adjusted ratio of value added.

The adjusted value added has several alternatives: (3a) adjusted ratio of value added of the company, unconsolidated, (3b) adjusted ratio of value added of the company, by consolidated financial statement, (3c) adjusted ratio of value added of the company, including the quasi-vertical integration.

This chapter uses the (3a) formula for computation. This is an incomplete measurement, because it does not include the data on subsidiary companies, nor on quasi-integrated companies. However it is not possible to collect further information. It is not feasible, for instance, to use employment data: even the data on value added cannot be collected from foreign companies. Gort collected these data (not the adjusted ratio) by some means and found that there was a high correlation between the percentage of employment (1(a)) and the ratio of value added (Gort, 1962). This suggests the usefulness of this ratio as a measurement.

We stated previously that an electric-power-generating company cannot be said to have a high vertical integration level even if the ratio of value added is high, because any one of the stages in production cannot be an independent business. This is another problem of the use of value added.

We use the the adjusted ratio of value added as one measurement of the level of vertical integration. We also use subjective judgement in this chapter, taking into consideration the quasi-vertical integration.

5.2 OBJECTIVES OF VERTICAL INTEGRATION AND CHARACTERISTICS OF VERTICAL INTEGRATION OF JAPANESE ENTERPRISES

Williamson lists many objectives of vertical integration (Williamson, 1975), and consolidating his and other authors' views, we can state four important objectives of vertical integration.

1. To avoid uncertainty. To ensure the supply of materials and

components, and to ensure the sales of the products by controlling the downstream process and the distribution process.

2. To restrict the competition by monopolizing the supply of raw materials and components, and by monopolizing the distribution channel. If not to monopolize, the company gains an advantageous competitive position by controlling the next-to-key processes.

3. To improve the quality and cost. When there is a synergic effect from the similarity of technology used in the main process and the integrated process, integration results in the advantages of mass production. For example by integrating the iron and steel manufacturing processes, the costs of energy, transport and inventory are saved, and, what is more important, the quality of steel is improved by controlling the process automatically by computer using the input data from the preceding stage. When similar technology is used in the production of components and assembly of the finished product, the quality of the components is improved and a merit of large-scale production can be attained.

4. To adapt to the change of technology quickly, by changing the range of processes on a planned basis.

Japanese companies put emphasis on objectives 3. and 4. by controlling a series of key processes that affect the quality and cost, the quality and cost of the finished product are improved and lowered respectively. By controlling the sales channel the company can provide a good after-sales service and can save distribution costs. In both cases, the key processes for profit are integrated, improving the quality and lowering cost.

By using integration the company can introduce new technology quickly. The case of Seiko, Toyota and Matsushita are examples. Also, by integrating the sales channel, the company can rapidly introduce the new product to the market.

Integration in Japanese corporations has the following three characteristics that help to attain these objectives.

1. The key processes are integrated, although the vertical integration measured by value added over sales is not high. For example, Seiko, Honda and YKK (Yoshida Kogyo Co.) all make the machine tools necessary for their products. Hitachi and NEC (Nihon Electric) produce IC and LSI, for their own use and for sale, but they do not produce the television cabinets nor simple plastic components. American companies tend to produce the raw materials and components to a greater extent, while they buy from outside in some key products. Japanese manufacturers are more selective. For example, Ford owns a large steel

manufacturing plant in the USA, and it produces wheels, radiators and seats for its own cars. According to an analysis by Small Business Administration, a Japanese car manufacturer buys 75 per cent of the parts from outside, most of them from quasi-integrated makers, but a US car manufacturer buys 52 per cent of the parts from independent outside manufacturers, and the rest are produced by thirteen component divisions (Small Business Administration, 1980). Consequently, value added (including profit) over sales of Toyota is about 16 per cent (in 1978), but those of Ford and General Motors are 34 per cent and 44 per cent respectively (in 1978).

2. Quasi-vertical integration is used with the formation of a co-operative group of companies. For example, Toyota has a Kyohokai of 172 component manufacturers, a Seihokai of twenty-one component manufacturers and an Eeihokai of thirty-six parts manufacturers. Nissan has a Takarakai of 158 parts manufacturers. The two finished car companies give long-term regular orders to these groups of companies, which helps to improve quality and cost control, and makes it possible to introduce new technology promptly. In the USA and UK, components manufacturers are independent; they do not like to join a controlled group.

3. The quasi-vertical integration is also a feature of their sales channels. For example, Toyota, Nissan and Matsushita have strong wholesale departments, and at the retail stage they have strong teams of exclusive or selective sales channels. Matsushita has 120 wholesalers that are fully controlled and 25 000 'National Shops' whose sales of Matsushita products account for more than 80 per cent of their total sales. Toyota controls 323 exclusive retail stores which have 2600 shops and employ 33 000 salesmen. These integrated sales channels make strong sales promotion and swift introduction of new products possible. In the USA and UK the sales channels want to be independent, and exclusive channels are used to a lesser extent – relationships are based on contract, not on formation of a group.

What effects can we expect to see from the Japanese style of vertical integration? First, it is possible to improve the quality of the products. The main process company is usually large and has an accumulation of technology, which it transfers to the group company. It pays to teach, because the relationship is exclusive and is on a long-term basis. The main process company teaches and monitors its own method of quality control, but does not inspect the incoming components. The main process company also gives advice on their system of general management, production management, long-range and short-range planning, and cost control. It also transfers technology to the sales channel.

Second, it is possible to raise planning to an even more detailed level to stabilize production and to reduce costs. Some companies maintain a continuous flow of production without any inventory of components by using detailed comprehensive planning. Toyota's 'Kanban' system, or 'just-in-time' system, is made possible by grouping the parts makers. With stabilized orders it is also possible for them to reduce their costs and to improve quality.

Third, it is possible to introduce new technology promptly. The extent of vertical integration in the large successful corporations is selective and wide-ranging if we include quasi-vertical integration. By integrating the key processes, a unified system is built up, and it is possible to develop new products in a shorter period of time. It has been said that the British motor-cycle producers could not control their parts manu-facturers; it took six months to obtain new components. On the other hand, Honda produces important parts and machines, and controls the parts manufacturers, so it can introduce the new products on a planned basis. Seiko could also introduce new products at an earlier time.

Fourth, by the use of quasi-integration, the main process company can save funds for investment and thus have greater flexibility. For example, Nihon Denso, in the Toyota group, is a maker of electrical components such as sparking plugs, car air conditioners and other electronic car parts. It is strong in electronic technology and has large financial resources, and is in a position to share in the technological development of car electronics with Toyota, who, by this means, can expand their own technological capability. Quasi-vertical integration has the advantage of division of labour and the benefits of integration at the same time. Group members can also finance their own investment for expansion and thus Toyota can save money for capital investment.

5.3 CASES OF VERTICAL INTEGRATION

5.3.1 The Case of Toyota Motor Company

The passenger car consists of about 5000 components, and it is impossible for the car manufacturer to produce them all. Such raw materials as steel, aluminium, copper and plastics have to be bought in from outside. Rubber tyres, window glass and batteries are bought from independent manufacturers since they need specialized technologies and large investments to produce. Standard parts such as bolts, nuts and wheels are brought in from outside, because they do not require any high technology.

Key components and processes that represent the differentiated high skill of the company, such as the production of engines, body pressing, final assembly and paint-spraying, are done within the company. The components that rank next in importance to the key process components are bought from subsidiaries or affiliated companies. These companies, approximately 230 in all, make up Kyohokai (literally meaning co-operation-Toyota-association) and two other groups. According to an estimate from Toyota's financial statement, about 60 per cent of expenditure for materials and parts are paid to these affiliated companies.

Control of the affiliated companies is not necessarily effected by majority ownership of stocks, but rather by minority ownership, by sending directors from Toyota who work as full-time directors, and by long-term contract. These affiliated companies produce crankshafts, piston pins, spring steel, castings, engine components, body components, automatic transmission, transmission, coolers, meters, radiators, exhaust pipes and filters, and supply Toyota with these components. They sell components to other car manufacturers and they diversify into other products, but the bulk of their sales is to Toyota. They are not Toyota's only suppliers for any one component, however. To avoid dependence on any one supplier Toyota selects two.

These companies build long-range plans and short-range plans in compliance with Toyota's plans. Toyota has expanded rapidly and is developing new cars all the time, so it is necessary to control and to have the co-operation of its suppliers in order to implement the expansion and to maintain secrecy on new products.

Toyota gives technical advice on production technology and on quality control in order to raise the technology level of these components, and to enhance the quality level and performance of Toyota cars. Toyota sends its own production technology staff to the affiliated company if requested, and they stay one month or two with the company to instruct them in production control methods.

Toyota's basic policy has been to reduce its costs and prices as much as possible to compete with other car manufacturers, and to implement this policy it was seen as necessary to give assistance in keeping down the cost of parts.

The Kanban system or just-in-time system, which in practice means delivery of parts every two hours to the Toyota plant, and no stocks, is one important means to reduce costs, and it is made possible by this co-operative relationship with the affiliated companies. The Kanban system is the result of detailed planning. The component company draws up a three-year plan, half-year plan, three-month plan and one-month plan, which are all integrated with Toyota's plans to ensure synchronized delivery of components every two hours. It is said that the supplier cannot be accused of falling short with parts in as far as the supply is carried out according to this planned schedule.

The transfer price of parts is based on cost plus profit, and also on a kind of bargaining. Toyota requests that the cost should be reduced all the time. The supplier perceives that Toyota's policy is 'not to kill, neither to keep alive easily'.

Toyota controls the affiliated parts manufacturers by giving them long-term contracts; it does not suspend the relationship easily even if there should be any trouble, as is the case for instance with some UK and US companies. The affiliated companies have grown rapidly and become well-managed companies as Toyota has grown.

Toyota also lends money to these companies and guarantees company borrowing, in addition to investing in the equity. The amount of financial aid is equal to about 10 per cent of the total payment to an affiliated company.

By doing this Toyota can save resources for investment. It makes use of the financial capability of the affiliated company, which is enhanced by grouping which itself saves financial cost by reduced risk. Toyota can avert the risk of concentration on parts production. The affiliated company is independent and self-supporting and can diversify to some extent, and can sell components to Toyota's competitiors.

The sales channel is also a strong cohesive group. The sales department (formerly a sales company) is in charge of wholesaling and exporting, and controls the multinational subsidiaries. The sales department controls five lines of 250 retailers which own 2850 sales points and employ 33 000 salesmen in Japan. These retailers are not owned by Toyota, but they provide exclusive channels for Toyota, and are controlled by long-term contracts, appointment of directors, and by dealer service provided by Toyota. This is different from the situation in the USA and the UK, where the dealers are independent and sell one company's cars selectively by contract, but still sell cars from other companies, and can, if they wish, switch contracts from one company to another.

Each sales company has its own territory and monopolizes the sales of one line of cars, but they compete with other Toyota retailers of other lines of cars in the same territory. Each sales company is assigned a quota, which is decided by Toyota's market research and by negotiation between the two. The salary of salesmen is divided between a fixed amount representing the larger part of the wage, and a minor part that is based on an incentive system. The dependence on Toyota, territory system and fixed salary are mutually related; the sales channel is a controlled system, not an independent organization.

Toyota provides a variety of services to retailers. It accepts promissory notes and open accounts of retailers to reduce their financial burdens. The salesman is trained at Toyota training centres. Toyota provides instruction in financial management and accounting, and training in technical service; and it gives guidance on long-range and short-range planning.

These exclusive sales channels are the source of Toyota's strong competitive power and can contribute to quick market penetration of new products. At the same time, they are legally independent entities, and self-supporting, so Toyota is freed from the financial and administrative burden of maintaining a direct sales channel. Quasi-vertical integration is a flexible system.

5.3.2 The Case of Matsushita Electric Products Company

Matsushita is one of the largest electrical home appliance manufacturers in Japan, employing 12 000 people.

It is not unusual for the makers of electrical equipment to produce key parts inside their own company. GE in the USA, and GEC and Plessey in the UK all produce their own key parts. Matsushita probably produces more of its own key parts, and it is more selective about the parts it produces. From outside it purchases standard raw materials such as steel plate, stainless-steel plate, aluminum and copper wire. It makes its own batteries, carbon bars, vacuum tubes, integrated circuits, switch-boards, condensers, transformers, speakers, tuners, print base, brown tubes, and magnetic heads. It also produces automated machines. These parts and machines are manufactured by some of its forty-five divisions, as well as by subsidiaries. It is estimated from their financial statement that the percentage of purchase from the subsidiaries amounts to about 80 per cent of all purchase of materials and components from outside sources. This is one way of measuring quasi-vertical integration.

The reason for producing their own parts and machines is to improve and maintain the quality of their products. Matsushita was established in 1918; it has a long history and accumulated capability to produce components. It also sells the components and machines, so the scale of production is large.

A particular characteristic of Matsushita is the quasi-vertical integration of its sales channel. It has 230 wholesalers which sell only Matsushita products. Under these wholesalers there are 25 000 'National Shops' whose sales of Matsushita products account for more than 80 per cent of total sales, and another 25 000 'National Stores' whose sales of Matsushita products come to more than 50 per cent of total sales. They are selective sales channels that promote the sales of Matsushita products by list price if possible. Matsushita does not own any shares in the equity of these retailers but controls them by long-term contracts and by a number of services to dealers. These services include special rebates, instruction on management, subsidies for redesigning of stores, training classes for new technology, shared advertising, training of store owners and salesmen. This is in line with Matsushita's philosophy of 'mutual prosperity'.

Matsushita owns the wholesale channels, most of which came into existence through mergers between independent wholesalers. They deal with the wholesaling and transporting of Matsushita goods. Matsushita has a strong marketing department in the head office with twenty-four district offices under it. It draws up the marketing plans and provides services to the retailers. The products go directly to retailers from the product divisions. This is a typical case of quasi-vertical integration of the sales channels of successful large corporations in Japan.

5.3.3 The Case of Casio

Casio is a producer of electronic calculators and digital watches. It has also diversified into personal computer products. Casio was one of only three who could survive the competition out of forty electronic calculator manufacturers. Casio waged a radical price war, supported by a large-scale production system outside the company. It has grown rapidly since the establishment of the company in 1951, to a half-billion-dollar company in 1980. Unlike Toyota or Matsushita, Casio does not produce any components; it purchases IC and LSI from outside manufacturers on long-term contracts. It is said that Hitachi has a special production line for Casio. Even the assembly process is done outside the company. Casio has two factories, but they are used for testing the large-scale production of new products, for testing durability, and for inspecting the finished products.

Casio recognizes two processes as key processes. The first is the development of a new product, and the designing of a new system of products. Casio pioneered the introduction of a mini-type high-performance calculator at a very low price and was one of the first to use IC and LSI. The reinforcement of its research and development capability was an important strategy for Casio.

The second key process is marketing. The company spends a large amount of money on advertising through television, plugging Casio's commercial song. It made use of stationery stores as the sales outlet for calculators, selecting 20 000 stationery stores and forming Casio-kai (Casio groups). This was a new sales channel developed by Casio. Casio selected one wholesaler in each prefecture. It also has forty-eight sales offices which distribute Casio products to watch stores.

Casio does not produce LSI itself, but it buys only from Hitachi and Nihon Electric, and by concentrating its orders on two companies it procures the components very cheaply.

The level of integration in Casio is low. The company considers that the key processes for Casio are new-product development and marketing. Production may be important, but the company believes that the design of the production process, not the production itself, is next in importance to the above two key processes. It makes efforts to strengthen the resources for the two key processes.

Casio procures components by long-term contract. Its competition strategy was to reduce the price rather than to enhance the quality; its price war, based on large-scale production, was waged on the assumption that price has a very great effect on the elasticity of demand. For this policy it was more advantageous to buy rather than to manufacture.

Casio has grown rapidly over the last thirty years, so it has been necessary to make use of outside resources. In this respect Casio differs from Matsushita, which has a seventy-year history, and from Seiko companies, which are 100 years old. However, its strategy does not differ in principle from that of Toyota and Matsushita, in the sense that the key processes are integrated and for the important process quasi-integration is used.

5.3.4 Cases of Failure

5.3.4.1 Failure of integration

Vertical integration acts against the principle of specialization, against the principle of large-scale production, and is sealed off from free competition. In order to be successful, vertical integration has to be able to overcome these problems.

A giant supermarket store chain Daiei acquired a television manufacturer, and started to make its own private brand colour television 'Bubu'. Daiei had no technical expertise, there was no synergy of technology, and they could hardly sell the 'Bubu' set. This vertical integration proved to be a failure.

YKK (Yoshida Kogyo) is the largest manufacturer of zip-fasteners in the world. It also entered the aluminium window-frame business, the sales of which are now larger than the zip-fastener sales. As a vertical integration, the company announced its plans to build an aluminium refining plant. Fortunately, this plan was not implemented; there was no synergy on technology, no merit for location in Japan.

Mandam, a medium-sized male cosmetics and toiletry manufacturer, established a direct distribution system to the retailers, to compete with other large cosmetics makers who usually have exclusive wholesale channels. The company soon found that the direct sales channel was too expensive compared with the use of independent wholesalers, so it discontinued them. For vertical integration to be economical, the volume of production and sales has to be large enough.

5.3.4.2 *Failure of low integration*

(i) *The case of Standard Kogyo Company.* Standard used to produce radios, tape-recorders and amplifiers. In 1970 its sales had grown to 10 billion yen, but it purchased all components from outside. The policy was to purchase the best parts at the lowest price. The company did not have a strong core technology, and was weak in new-product development; it was a follower of the new products developed by other companies.

Its competitive power in the home market was weak, so it exported the bulk of its products to other countries where it did not have its own sales channels but sold through foreign wholesalers. The company did not have strong resources in any process; it did not have competitive power; it could not make a profit. The company was sold to a US corporation, then to Phillips Lamps Holding. It continues to show a loss account.

The differences between Standard and Casio are as follows. Casio had the distinguished capability to develop and pioneer new products, such as the first relay calculator and the first mini-electronics calculator, which Standard lacked. Casio established a strong sales channel of stationery stores supported by powerful advertising, but Standard depended on foreign companies.

(ii) *The case of Japanese oil refining companies*. Japanese oil companies do not hold any interests in oil extraction companies, so their financial performance is heavily dependent on the price of crude oil, change in exchange rates, and supply and demand in oil products. Those oil companies in Japan that are affiliated with foreign major oil companies have shown a relatively stable performance, because of the higher vertical integration.

5.4 VERTICAL INTEGRATION AND PERFORMANCE: THE CONDITIONS FOR SUCCESS

When the level of vertical integration is measured by adjusted value added ratio, there is a weak negative correlation between vertical integration and performance. The correlation coefficients of 102 manufacturing companies are as follows:

> Return on investment (ROT) . . . (−) 0.145, standard deviation of return on investment (DEV) . . . (−) 0.096, growth rate (GRT) . . . (−) 0.214, equity ratio (EQU) . . . (−) 0.11

The reason for this correlation is not clear. The measurement of vertical integration does not include quasi-vertical integration, so the measurement is imperfect.

The problem is not the level of integration, but the way the process is integrated. What, then, are the key success factors? We have already discussed the cases of success and failure in earlier sections, so we can arrive at the principles.

Vertical integration, however, has disadvantages that the success factors have to overcome. These disadvantages are as follows: (i) it is against the principles of the division of labour, (ii) it is against the principles of large-scale production, (iii) it is against the principle of free competition.

The success factors are related to these limitations. From a number of cases described in previous pages, we can conclude the following factors for success. First, the key processes for profit and growth are integrated. For the finished car manufacturer, designing the car and building the engine are the key processes. They are done inside the company. The automatic transmission is the next-to-key process, so it is produced by a manufacturer in the group (quasi-vertical integration). The wheels and tyres are bought in from outside suppliers. Thus different approaches are applied for integration. The general-purpose equipment is bought from outside, but special-purpose equipment is produced inside. This policy has been followed by successful watch, camera, automobile and motorcycle manufacturers. Casio knows that designing, production planning and marketing are key processes.

Second, it is necessary for the main process company to have a highly competitive core of high-level technology. This high-level technology is transferred to the next-to-the-key process, which results in strong competitive power. There should also be a synergy relationship so that the transferred technology is useful in other spheres. For example, Hitachi and NEC have a high accumulation of technological skill in electronics, and there is a synergy on the production of finished products and the production of IC and LSI, so by integrating the LSI production process, not only can the companies produce high-quality parts, but they can also expand the basis of their technology.

Seiko was not strong in electronics, but it perceived the need for this technology and recruited young electronics graduates and strengthened its capability. It had to produce the small IC and LSI it required because there were no other manufacturers. Seiko's electronics technology is transferred to other new products, such as small printers for personal computers – and even to personal computers themselves.

The Hong Kong watch producers were late starters, but as there were electronics components already available on the market, and since these producers emphasize low-price watches, it was advantageous for them not to produce the parts themselves but to import them from Japanese electronics manufacturers. They had the technology to produce the pin-lever watch which could be applied in the production of cheap digital watches, but they probably did not have the core electronics technology. They adopted the right strategy under the circumstances.

Third, the integrated process should be supported by large-scale production. The scale of production of the main process should be such that its cost is at the bottom of average cost curve. This is made possible by selling a part of the production, but for this practice the size of production has to be large. Pioneer Company (large stereo-player manufacturer) started to produce its own LSI, but it changed its policy because the scale of production was not large enough, and it could not make full use of the expensive equipment. Mandam Company, as already stated, started to establish wholesale branches, but the company was not large enough to support direct sales, so it discontinued the vertical integration of the wholesale process.

For the success of quasi-vertical integration, the size of the main process company is also important, because power is needed to control the auxiliary process company, and this power comes from the imbalance of exchange that rests on the size of the company and its level of expertise. The integrated company in the group has to be able to make a profit as the sole supplier, or as the sole seller of the product of the main process company.

Any process that does not fit in with the above three conditions will be treated separately. For example, the simple cleaning of the plant, simple repair of the building, guard service, simple packaging of the product, and standard raw materials are all bought from outside the company.

5.5 VERTICAL INTEGRATION AND OTHER STRATEGIES

5.5.1 Diversification and Vertical Integration

Sometimes vertical integration is confused with diversification. The expression 'vertical diversification' is an example (Ansoff, 1965). We should make the difference clear. Vertical integration cannot change the product life cycle. Diversification is a situation where one company produces more than one product, and each product has a different use and a different life cycle. On the other hand, vertical integration changes the boundaries of the system but does not change the use of the product. If a paper manufacturer produces a cardboard box for packaging instead of selling the cardboard to the box maker, it is not a change in the ultimate use of the paper. The forward integration of the production process, not the sales process, is somewhat similar to diversification, but the change of life cycle of the company product is limited.

As was analysed in Chapter 4, no difference was found between the integration levels of different diversification types (see Table 4.6).

5.5.2 Multinational Management and Vertical Integration

Multinational management to ensure the procurement of raw materials is world-wide vertical integration. This is important for oil refinery companies, steel and other metal companies, pulp and paper companies, and chemical companies that consume a large amount of imported raw materials.

The establishment of component production centres in foreign countries is one aspect of international vertical integration. Investment in establishing a sales company is also part of international vertical integration, although we do not include it under the heading of multinational management. We define multinational management as the establishment of foreign subsidiaries for production.

Quantitative relationships between the multinational management level and the vertical integration level will be analysed in Chapter 6 (see Table 6.2).

5.6 VERTICAL INTEGRATION AND ORGANIZATIONAL STRUCTURE

Vertical integration internalizes the market mechanism, and it naturally results in the enlargement of organizational structure and more departmentation.

5.6.1 Consolidated Integration

The production of components and machines and the direct sale of products necessitate either department or division structure or subsidiary structure. For example, the semi-conductor division, the machine division, the subsidiary company for parts production are departments for backward integration, and the district sales office and wholesale companies are organizations for downstream integration.

The transfer price of the semi-finished products and finished products is usually the market price minus distribution costs. This practice is used by Hitachi and Matsushita. According to the survey on the division structure of twenty four Japanese manufacturing corporations conducted by Nakahashi in 1980, the method of establishing the cost of transfer between the divisions is as follows. The transfer price is based on: cost – 22 per cent, cost plus profit – 15 per cent, market price – 34 per cent, negotiation – 19 per cent, others – 10 per cent (Nakahashi, 1981). This distribution is almost the same as in the USA (Vancil, 1979). If the transfer price is fixed by market price, it is possible for a components division to be a self-supporting division whose efficiency is tested by the market price mechanism. If the transfer price is decided by the cost-plus method, then any inefficiency can be survived.

We understand, however, that the process department is not a division but rather a functional organization, because it is sealed off from the market and is protected from competition in the open market, even if the price is fixed by the market price.

Some companies make their component. departments and sales

departments legally independent subsidiary companies. Seiko and Sony use this policy extensively and Canon uses it to some extent. The reasons for this form are: first, to make the department self-supporting and make their responsibility clearer. The subsidiary's activity is under the control of the main process company, but relatively speaking, the subsidiary company is more independent and has to bear all overhead expenses itself. Second, to take advantage of the difference in wages, a union is organized for each company, so it is possible that the subsidiary company may have a lower wage level. This factor was utilized to a greater extent in the past, but it is disappearing because of the levelling of wage differences between large and small companies, and between the city company and the local company. Third, especially in the case of sales companies, the personnel management style of the subsidiary can be different from that of the parent company. The Japanese style of personnel management requires that everybody should be treated equally, and be given equal opportunity for promotion. The new recruit who enters the sales department may wish to be transferred to production or to the personnel department. If he is employed by the sales company, he will no longer be subject to such wide rotation, thus his dissatisfaction may be smaller.

5.6.2 Quasi-integration

The independent company in the quasi-vertical integration group is controlled by the main process company. The production department of the main process company gives a variety of services, and transfers technology and the management know-how to the upstream company. The sales department does the same for the sales company. These transfers of service and expertise are the sources of power.

The power originates in the holding of resources, and in the imbalance of exchange by the use of these resources. Assurance of long-term trade and transfer of management skill are two important sources of power, and the ownership of stock and sending of directors are the means for confirming the control. The integrated company can receive a number of services, and can improve the quality and bring down the cost of its products. Toyota's case is an example.

5.7 SUMMARY

The vertical integration in Japanese corporations has the following characteristics. First, it integrates the key processes. US companies tend to integrate the unimportant processes, and buy some important processes from outside. The extensive use of consultants may be one example. The successful Japanese company is more selective of the processes it integrates.

Second, the successful Japanese company makes use of quasi-vertical integration. Quasi-vertical integration covers both the upstream and the downstream process. The most important process is internally operated, or under consolidated integration, and the next-to-key processes are operated by quasi-integration. A number of services are provided for the quasi-integrated company. These transfers of skill are important sources of power.

What are the reasons for these characteristics? First, the successful Japanese company was sensitive to innovation. In order to introduce the new technology and to develop the new product, it found it necessary to produce the key parts itself, or buy them from a group company. It is too late to use parts that are already available in the market. The early utilization of semi-conductors for radio and TV by Sony and Hitachi is a case in point. The development of the small quartz crystal watch by Seiko is another example. Seiko started to produce IC, liquid crystal, small crystal forks and step-motors. For rapid growth it was necessary to utilize outside resources, and at the same time to carry out the prompt introduction of the new technology quasi-integration was a necessary means. Quasi-vertical integration has been used with companies making cars, electric products, fine machinery and steel. On the other hand, unimportant processes have not been integrated to make the most efficient use of limited resources for growth.

Second, the Japanese consumer puts more emphasis on the quality of products than on the price. The cheap Kodak camera and the pin-lever watch from Hong Kong have not obtained a large share of the Japanese market in comparison with the sophisticated Japanese camera and watch. Japanese companies would rather use good-quality parts of reliable quality – even if they are expensive – than buy cheap parts from outside, in order to produce reliable, high-quality finished goods. For this it is necessary to produce the key parts inside or have them produced by the group company.

At the same time, to supply good after-sales services, the formation of exclusive or selective distribution channels is necessary. These distribution channels were also necessary to conduct the sales promotion of newly developed products which appeared in large numbers after the war.

Third, the group orientation of Japanese people helps the system of quasi-integration. Japanese corporations compete intensively with companies in the same line of business, but they try to co-operate with companies in a complementary relationship. This is necessary to survive and to grow, and to ensure jobs for their lifetime employees. In the USA or UK, management prefers to be independent, and does not like to belong to a controlled group.

The effects of the Japanese style of vertical integration are as follows.

First, it makes it possible to carry out innovation promptly. Seiko companies are an example of how development and production of key parts within the group made the early introduction of new technology possible.

On the other hand, old processes in the integration become unnecessary because of technological change. For example, the production of shafts for cars ceases with the introduction of front engines. To prevent this inflexibility it is necessary to restrict integration to the key process. On the other hand, the use of quasi-integration increases flexibility. This flexibility is not attained by the easy breaking of relationships nor by divestment. If the integrated relationship can be broken as soon as there is a change of technology, the status of the company in the group becomes very unstable, and much harm will be done to the mutual trust and long-term prosperity of both sides.

Second, vertical integration facilitates the transfer of technology and accumulation of technology, and improves the quality. If the company develops the technology to produce super LSI, but production is ordered outside the company, then accumulation and expansion of the new technology can hardly be promoted.

Third, integration gives birth to high-level planning, and can enhance the efficiency of the system as a whole. Toyota's just-in-time system or Kanban system is made possible by quasi-integration.

Fourth, the strong sales channel makes it possible for new products to penetrate the market swiftly. The life cycle of the product in Japan tends to be short, and this is partly because of the strong quasi-vertical integration of sales channels.

5.7.1 Problems

Vertical integration has a number of problems, many of which have been analysed already. Here we will analyse the problems of Japanese-style vertical integration.

5.7.1.1 *Size of the parent company*

The analysis of vertical integration in this book has concentrated on large manufacturing corporations. The medium-sized company has to use a different policy – for example, Mandam and Pioneer, which extended integration but soon found that it was unprofitable and changed its policy. The medium-sized company has to be more selective in integration, and has to discover the real core of its competitive strength. The smaller companies have to choose whether to enter a group or remain independent. According to the survey by the Small Business Administration, about 60 per cent of small manufacturing business belongs to groups attached to large corporations. (The definition of small business is one where the number of employees is less than 300 (Small Business Administration, 1980).)

5.7.1.2 *The size of integrated retail stores*

Integrated retail stores tend to be small. The large electric home appliance stores and large supermarkets are increasing their share of sales. These big stores are independent and sell a wide range of brands; consumers thus have a large choice in such stores. The exclusive channel sells only one company's products and the choice is limited.

The large independent stores also offer goods at lower prices. Unlike department stores, they can discount the list price, because of lower overhead costs. Lower prices make them competitive with the exclusive channel stores, because of their mass sales.

After-sales service, which is one of the strengths of the integrated stores, is provided by the service stations of the production company, so the difference is small in this respect. In addition the number of maintenance-free products is increasing.

For all the above reasons the small stores are losing their share of sales, and the manufacturing company will have to change their strategy and use multi-channels.

5.7.1.3 *Flexible or inflexible*

We mentioned that adaptation to technological change can be swift when there is vertical integration, especially quasi-vertical integration, because the central company can plan and direct change. Seiko and Toyota are both good examples. On the other hand, if the investment is large, vertical integration results in inflexibility. A few years ago, the petrochemical industry in Japan was strongly competitive, and was proud of its scale of production, but since the price of oil rose from $3 per barrel to $35, it lost its competitive power. The petrochemical industry will have to change its strategy on what stage of process should be located in what country, and to change the location of production at the upstream stage. The methods of vertical integration need to alter according to the change of environment, and heavy investment is a constraint on this change.

The same thing can be seen in the automobile industry. The production of Japanese cars in the USA or Europe affects the parts manufacturers at home, and the greater the production abroad, the less the demand for components in Japan. This tends to obstruct the positive development of multinational management in establishing production centres in foreign countries. This is a kind of exit barrier.

The new trend is that component manufacturers who have gained enough competitive power in world markets by belonging to a group, and so benefiting from transfer of technology, are beginning to operate factories in the vicinity of the foreign plant of the main process company.

REFERENCES

Kibi, M. (1980) *Hitachi Seisakusho* (Hitachi Company), Tokyo, Asahi Sonorama.

Kono, T. (1974) *Keiei Senryaku no Kaimei* (Analysis of Corporate Strategy), Tokyo, Diamond Sha.

MITI (1980) *Wagakuni Kigyo no Kaigai Katsudo* (Multinational Management of Japanese Enterprises), Tokyo, MITI.

Nakagawa, K. (ed.) (1977) *Nihon-teki Keiei* (Japanese Management), Tokyo, Nihonkeizai.

Nakahashi, K. (1981) *Jigyobusei Kiyyo ni okeru Soshiki Sekkei (Organizational Design in Product Divisions)*, Tokyo, Otarer.

Okano, M. (1980) *Kashio Keisanki* (Casio Company), Tokyo, Asahi Sonorama.

Ono, R. (1980) *Seiko Group* (Seiko Group), Tokyo, Asahi Sonorama.

Small Business Administration (1980) *Chusho Kigyo Hakusho* (White Paper on Small Business), Tokyo, SBA.

Wakayama, F. and Sugimoto, T. (1978) *Toyota no Himitsu* (Secret on Toyota), Tokyo, Koshobo.

Ansoff, H. Igor (1965) *Corporate Strategy*, New York, McGraw-Hill.

Bain, J. S. (1968) *Industrial Organization*, New York, John Wiley.

Channon, D. F. (1973) *The Strategy and Structure of British Enterprise*, London, Macmillan.

Dryas, G. P. and Thanheiser, H. T. (1976) *The Emerging European Enterprise*, London, Macmillan.

Gort, M. (1962) *Diversification and Integration in American Industry*, Princeton, Princeton University Press.

Penrose, E. (1959) *The Theory of the Growth of the Firm*, Oxford, Basil Blackwell.

Porter, M. (1980) *Competition Strategy*, New York, Free Press.

Rumelt, R. P. (1974) *Strategy, Structure and Economic Performance*, Cambridge, Mass., Harvard University Press.

Schonberger, R. J. (1982) 'The Transfer of Japanese Manufacturing Management Approaches to U.S. Industry,' *Academy of Management Review*, July.

Williamson, O. E. (1975) *Market and Hierarchies; Analysis and Antitrust Implications*, New York, Free Press.

Vancil, R. F. (1979) *Decentralization: Managerial Ambiguity by Design*, Ill., Dow Jones-Irwin.

6 Multinational Management

In this chapter we will describe the status of multinational management in 102 manufacturing corporations, the principles derived from it, and the transferability of the Japanese style of management. The author visited more than twenty Japanese subsidiaries in the USA, the Philippines, Malaysia and the UK, and conducted interviews with Japanese managers and local managers. This chapter is based on these interviews, and on the analysis of statistical data.

6.1 CONCEPT, TYPES AND OBJECTIVES OF MULTINATIONAL MANAGEMENT

Multinational management is established in order to expand the area of production by transplanting superior management skills to foreign countries, and in order to build a production base in several areas, to increase the sales and profit, and stabilize the performance of the parent company. Companies can be classified into three types, seen from the international point of view:

6.1.1 Home Country-oriented Companies

Production and marketing are limited to within the home country. The company may import raw materials, but any alternative strategy is confined to the domestic market. We defined this type as the company whose export ratio (the exports divided by the sales) is less than 10 per cent and whose foreign production ratio (the foreign production divided by the sales of the parent company) is less than 10 per cent. As is shown in Table 6.1, thirty-four companies out of 102 are classified under this heading. Brewing, dairy products, pharmaceutical products, oil refining, pulp and paper and non-ferrous metal companies belong to this category, and, with the exception of pharmaceuticals, they are, generally speaking, low-technology industries.

142

TABLE 6.1 Classification of 102 companies by international orientation

1. Home country-oriented company	34 companies (EXP < 10%, MNM < 10%)
2. Export-oriented company	50 companies (EXP > 10%. MNM < 10%)
3. Multinational company	18 companies (MNM > 10%)

Notes:
EXP . . . export ÷ sales of parent company.
MNM . . . foreign production ÷ sales of parent company.

6.1.2 Export-oriented companies

The export ratio is more than 10 per cent but the foreign production ratio is less than 10 per cent; these are the features of the export-oriented company. Fifty companies out of the 102 manufacturing companies belong to this type (see Table 6.1). They include companies that manufacture chemicals, steel, heavy machinery, cars, ships and precision instruments. They are all technology-intensive. Either capital investment needed for production is very high (for example, steel), or transport costs are low (for example, cameras).

6.1.3 The multinational company

The author's definition is that if one company's foreign subsidiary production is more than 10 per cent of the production of the parent company, it is a multinational company. The company should also own more than 25 per cent shares of the subsidiary. The number 10 per cent is not very meaningful, but we think that our definition is not very different from other definitions, such as, the multinational corporation has subsidiaries in which it has a greater than 25 per cent share in more than six countries (for example, Stopford and Wells, 1972). As is seen in Table 6.1, there are 18 companies in this category out of 102. There are no transnational enterprises among the 102 companies. The transnational company is, like the Shell group, Unilever or IBM, a company whose management is completely international, whose shareholders are scattered over many countries, and whose manufacturing plants are located all over the world. (This definition is used by Dymza, 1972, and others.)

There is a hierarchy in the objectives of foreign operation and, as seen in Figure 6.1, the subsidiaries can be classified into four according to their direct objectives. The market-oriented subsidiary manufactures

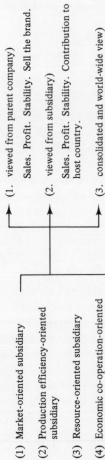

Intermediate goals

(1) Market-oriented subsidiary

(2) Production efficiency-oriented
subsidiary

(3) Resource-oriented subsidiary

(4) Economic co-operation-oriented
subsidiary

Final goals

(1. viewed from parent company)

   Sales. Profit. Stability. Sell the brand.

(2) viewed from subsidiary)

   Sales. Profit. Stability. Contribution to
   host country.

(3) consolidated and world-wide view)

   Sales. Profit. Stability. World-wide share.

Strategy and Structure of Japanese Enterprises

goods to replace exports to the host country. (According to the MITI survey, this accounts for about 78 per cent of subsidiaries of manufacturing companies (MITI, 1978); the sample of this survey was 3200 subsidiaries of 1250 parent companies.) The production efficiency-oriented subsidiary functions as the production centre and the manufactured goods are exported all over the world. (According to the MITI survey, this accounts for about 15 per cent of subsidiaries of manufacturing companies.) The distinction between the two is clear in developing countries. A subsidiary of Matsushita in Malaysia produces television sets for sale in Malaysia. The cost of production is slightly higher than the cost of production in Japan, including transport charges, but the tariff for imports is so high that the subsidiary can still make a profit. A subsidiary of NEC (Nippon Electric Company) in Malaysia produces integrated circuits, which it has to produce with lower costs than in Japan because IC is exported all over the world. However, the subsidiary of Matsushita in the UK which produces colour television sets has to have a competitive cost advantage because there is no protective tariff. It has to compete with all other brands, and has to export its products to other EEC countries.

The resource-oriented subsidiary aims at assuring the procurement of materials. (This accounts for about 6 per cent of subsidiaries of manufacturing companies, according to the MITI survey. The low percentage may be due to the fact that this kind of investment is shared by many companies, with an individual ownership of less than 25 per cent. The steel industry is one example.)

The economic co-operation of the host country has to be part of the objective of any foreign subsidiary, and sometimes, though very rarely, this is the main objective of foreign investment. For example, Nippon Steel established a steel plant with a capacity of 200 000 tons a year in Malaysia. The parent company sent ninety-two of its staff to Malaysia at the peak period for construction. Now there are only two Japanese managers. Despite the small capacity, the plant is making a profit, because all raw materials including charcoal from rubber trees are produced at home, and the product is low-quality steel rod for construction. Nippon Steel receives a small amount of dividend from its 16 per cent ownership and a low rate of remuneration for technical assistance. This factory functions, however, as a show window of technical assistance to developing countries.

As eventual objectives, the sales, profit and stability of the company are important. The problem is whether the contribution to the unconsolidated goals of the parent company are more important (see

Figure 6.1) than the effects on the consolidated performance of the company as a whole. For example, the dividend from the subsidiary is a contribution to the unconsolidated profit of the parent company, but it has a neutral effect on the consolidated performance of the whole company.

The three-goal distinction of Figure 6.1 may correspond to Perlmutter's classification of three attitudes, home country-oriented (or ethnocentric), host country-oriented (or polycentric) and world-oriented (or geocentric) (Perlmutter, 1969). The three distinctions are also similar to 9.1 style, 1.9 style and 9.9 style of leadership put forward by Blake and Mouton (1964).

What is the position of Japanese multinational companies with regard to Perlmutter's three types? The Japanese company is mostly concerned with the performance of the parent company, but the trend is towards the consolidated performance. Previously, Japanese companies did not consolidate the financial statement, but recently company law has been changed and they are required to publish consolidated statements. In addition, as the area of operation expands, the number of key resource holders for the company increases, and the expectations of the management and key staff-members have to be taken into account in the formation of corporate goals. As the area of operation expands, the area of expectation of the management of the parent company also expands, and the management comes to regard the consolidated sales as the measurement of the growth of the company.

Advertisement, 'selling the brand', is also an important item. The manufacturing plant in the host country may be producing only a small amount of goods, but by its very existence the name of the company becomes familiar to the host country; and as the brand penetrates, the company can sell other goods with less resistance. This has long-term effects on the sales and profit of the company.

6.2 SIZE OF MULTINATIONAL MANAGEMENT OF JAPANESE CORPORATIONS

The history of multinational management in Japanese corporations goes back some time before the Second World War when a lot of independent companies, subsidiaries and plants of the railway, mining, textile, metal and chemical industries were set up in Manchuria and in China. After the war, as the economy recovered, the management skill of Japanese corporations improved and exports increased, followed by

an upturn in foreign investment; however, the level of foreign investment is lower at present than that of the USA or the UK. In 1980 the
accumulated balance of foreign investment was 36 billion dollars which
accounted for about 2.5 per cent of GNP, as against 7.3 per cent in the
USA and 11 per cent in the UK. It is estimated that the production of
American manufacturing companies' foreign subsidiaries is 1.5 times
the exports, but the same ratio in Japanese manufacturing corporations
is less than one-third. This also can be seen in the case of the 102
manufacturing corporations. The amount of foreign investment is
increasing, however.

The areas of investment of manufacturing companies have been
heavily concentrated in developing countries, but are now spreading to
the USA and to EEC countries. The products of foreign subsidiaries are
also changing from labour-intensive products, such as textiles, to
technology-intensive products, such as electric home appliances. As yet,
however, Japanese marketing-intensive companies have not invested
overseas as marketing-intensive companies like Coca Cola, General
Foods, Unilever or BAT have done.

6.3 MULTINATIONAL MANAGEMENT AND OTHER STRATEGIES

6.3.1 Diversification, Vertical Integration and Multinational Management

The 102 manufacturing corporations are classified into four types,
according to the level of multinational management, and a number of
characteristics of their strategies and performances are exhibited and
analysed in Table 6.2.

MNM level (multinational management level) refers to foreign
production (from over 25 per cent owned subsidiaries) divided by sales
of the parent company; MMN (medium multinational) refers to
companies whose MNM level is 10–20 per cent; HMN (high multinational) refers to companies whose MNM level is over 20 per cent.

As shown in Table 6.2, there is no significant difference in diversification level (PMT) between the four levels of multinational management and the average. (Here the diversification level PMT is measured
as, $S = 1$, $D = 1.3$, $RMT = 2$, $RT = 2.8$, $RM = 3$ and $U = 4$.) We find
that it is possible to diversify and at the same time to engage in foreign
investment. For example, Matsushita and Sony are both related-

TABLE 6.2 Profile of companies at each level of multinational management

HMN ... MNM > 20 %   LMN ... MNM > 5 %
MMN ... MNM > 10 %   NMN ... MNM < 5 %
MNM (%) = foreign production ÷ parent company production

Level	HMN	MMN	HMN + MMN	LMN	NMN	Av.	s.d.
No. of companies	5	13	18	22	62	102	102
PMT. L	2.02	2.38	2.28			2.12	0.85
VER. L	23.05%	24.60	24.17			24.79	7.69
SHA. L	0.84	0.57	0.64			0.63	0.30
RAD. L	3.20%	2.14	2.43			2.26	1.96
SPR. L	1.85%	2.30	2.17			3.62	5.22
EXP. L	34.60%	22.42	25.81			22.04	19.84
BGT. L	9.34%	10.23	9.98			11.80	4.05
ROT. L	8.96%	8.32	8.50			8.33	2.95
DEV. L	2.10%	1.59	1.73			1.91	1.17
GRT. L	11.14%	10.42*	10.62*			12.72	4.97
EQU. L	35.10%	22.15	25.75			24.14	14.05
SOG. L	29.70	24.54	25.97			27.19	9.17
MNM	29.48%	13.75	18.12	6.94	1.42	5.56	7.25

Notes:
[1] For the meaning of variables, see Appendix 4.1.
[2] The values of variables are for the latter half of the period, 1970–80. L indicates this.
[3] Numbers in LMN and NMN are omitted, because they are similar to the average.

marketing-and-technology companies and both have a high level of foreign investment. (Table 4.6 also shows that the MNM levels of S and D are not so high.)

The vertical integration (VER) of the parent company is measured by the value added ratio minus net profit ratio, and again there is no significant difference between the four levels of multinational management (see Table 6.2).

Foreign investment is, however, a possible means of international vertical integration. The mining and steel companies make upstream investments in foreign countries to secure raw materials. Such investment is usually done as a joint venture with other companies, and subsidiaries in which one company owns more than 25 per cent are rather rare. In such a case the figure does not appear in our survey.

Ford Europe produces components in several European countries which are then transported to assembly plants in various countries. This is a case of international vertical integration, expanding the vertical integration of the home country to that of multinational territory. No Japanese manufacturing company has gone thus far in international operations. Some electrical product companies have established components manufacturing centres in developing countries, but only to a limited extent. On the contrary, the flow is rather in the opposite direction. Key parts are produced in Japan and sent to foreign subsidiaries for assembly. This is another type of vertical integration, a kind of 'downstream' vertical integration. But if the assembly process is transferred to a foreign country, it does not change the level of vertical integration; we cannot say that this kind of multinational management enhances the level of vertical integration.

The establishment in foreign countries of sales companies to promote exports and to sell the products manufactured in other foreign subsidiaries is widely practised. According to the MITI survey, about one in four of all subsidiaries of manufacturing companies is established for this purpose. We do not include such commercial-purpose subsidiaries under the heading of multinational management, but we see that Japanese companies emphasize a strong sales channel in foreign operations, and the channel is sometimes more important than the production base.

6.3.2 Research and Development and Sales Promotion of Parent Companies

Since multinational management involves the transplanting of superior technology, the ratio of research and development to the sales of parent companies should be high. This assumption is supported by the opinions of many others (Stopford and Wells, 1972; Kolde, 1974).

Table 6.2 shows the survey results, and we find that the ratio of R and D of high multinationals (HMN) is higher, but that of medium multinationals (MMN) is lower than the average. This is probably due to the fact that unsuccessful as well as successful investments are included. Foreign investment by synthetic fibre companies was not successful, for example. So the author divided the HMN and MMN companies into those with high performance and those with low performance. Table 6.3 shows the results. The dividing line is the 9 per cent rate of return on total assets of the parent company (we assume that the performance of subsidiaries affects the performance of the parent company). The high-performance multinational company has a much

TABLE 6.3 Profile of higher-return companies and lower-return companies among multinational companies

Level of MNM	HMN + MMN	
ROT	ROT ⩾ 9%	ROT < 9%
Number of companies	7	11
PMT. L	1.77	2.61
VER. L	25.31	23.44
SHA. L	0.72	0.59
RAD. L	3.49	1.76
SPR. L	2.18	2.17
EXP. L	35.62*	19.55
BGT. L	12.00	8.70

Note: 'L' indicates latter period, 1970–80.

higher R and D expenditure than the low performer, 3.49 per cent versus 1.76 per cent. This suggests that the technology-intensive company can be more successful in multinational investment, although the performance of the parent company is also affected by the home country activity.

Next we investigated the sales promotion expenditure. Many books on multinational management state that product differentiation by large expenditure on advertisement can be a cause of foreign production (Stopford and Wells, 1972; Kolde, 1974). Coca Cola and General Foods are cases in point. The Japanese multinationals (HMN and MMN) spend much less than the average on sales promotion (SRP), as is seen in Table 6.2. The sales promotion expenditures of high-performing multinationals and low-performing multinationals were compared and found to have no difference: both have lower ratios (see Table 6.3).

6.3.3 Relationship with Other International Strategy–Export

There are two problems. They are (i) whether multinational management increases or decreases exports, (ii) whether multinational management is an alternative to exports or not. They are different problems.

Logically thinking, multinational management should increase exports, because, in the case of market-oriented investment, branches are established overseas to overcome restrictions of imports or tariff barriers, and with foreign production the export of components or other materials will increase. In the case of production efficiency-oriented investment, costs will be reduced and exports from the production centre will increase. In the case of resources-oriented investment,

TABLE 6.4 Export ratio of multinational company

Industry	Companies with foreign subsidiaries %	All companies %
Textile	13.8	10.7
Chemistry	6.9	7.7
Electric machine	20.6	14.1
Transporation equipment	29.7	21.4

Source: MITI, 1975. (Companies with foreign subsidiaries in four businesses are selected from 780 companies in all industries.)

competitive power will increase by acquiring a source of cheap materials. Thus foreign investment has a favourable effect on exports.

According to our analysis, the multinational company has a slightly higher ratio of export (EXP) (see Table 6.2) but the difference is not significant. There are three measurements to analyse the relationship between exports and multinational management:

1. The export ratio after investment is compared with the situation where there was no multinational investment.
2. The export ratio of the multinational corporation is compared with that of the non-multinational.
3. The export ratio of the multinational corporation is compared with that of the non-multinational in the same industry.

Among the above three, 1. is the real measurement, but it is hard to make. Table 6.2 uses 2., and we could not find evidence that the multinational has a significantly higher export ratio. The survey by MITI uses 3. measurement (shown in Table 6.4). The 780 parent companies that have more than one foreign subsidiary have a higher export ratio than the total companies in the same industry, including multinationals. This can be seen as support for the logical assumption.

The next problem is how to select the alternatives, when both export and foreign production are feasible. To analyse this, we can classify the 102 manufacturing corporations into three major types. This is a reclassification of export-oriented companies and multinational companies in Table 6.1:

(a) Corporations selling products with little foreign investment and a high export ratio (export-oriented company in Table 6.1). The following are included in this category:

(a)(i) Small, high-technology product companies – high-quality watches and cameras.

(a)(ii) The products are medium-sized, but if foreign investment is to be done, the investment is too large – automobiles and steel.

(a)(iii) Large, order-made product companies – heavy electrical goods and shipbuilding.

Companies selling these products prefer export to foreign production because in (a)(i) transport costs are low; in (a)(ii) the risk of overseas investment is too great; and in (a)(iii) production control is difficult.

(b) Corporations with large foreign production and few exports.

(b)(i) Companies producing bulky goods – cement and plate glass.

(b)(ii) Companies producing bulky goods that use imported raw materials – paper and electric wire.

In (b)(i) the transport costs are large, and in (b)(ii) investment is made for resources procurement but the export of finished products is difficult.

(c) Corporations with large foreign production and a large amount of exports.

(c)(i) Companies selling medium-sized high-technology products – home appliances, rubber tyres.

(c)(ii) Companies producing synthetic fibres.

The (c)(i) products are the subject of successful foreign operations, but (c)(ii) products are losing the game, because companies producing them do not have world-competitive strength.

The above analyses are useful as a means of finding the business areas suitable for multinational management.

6.3.4 Relationship with Other International Strategy – Licensing and Plant Engineering

The export of technology is appropriate for the foreign company that already has high-related management skills thus making it suitable for advanced countries. Many authors state that it is appropriate when the market is small, or when the expanding company does not want to bear the risk (Kolde, 1974; Kindleberger, 1970), but these are not essential factors.

Japanese corporations have been importing patents for many years, and so far licensing from Japanese corporations has been small. However, it has been increasing recently, as the technology level of Japanese corporations rises.

World-wide joint-venture contracts to build world-wide production networks are closely related to licensing. Car manufacturers such as Nissan and Honda intend to build such a network. The car industry already has sufficient capacity, and the strong car companies are trying to build a world-wide network through licensing and through partial ownership.

Plant engineering is also a substitute for foreign investment. It involves the sale of services to construct high-technology plant, such as petrochemical and steel plant, and nuclear power stations. It is a transfer of a bulk of knowledge, and in that it resembles the multinational management operation. The company does not, however, operate the plant after construction, and thus does not bear the risk of operation. Plant engineering is appropriate for production that requires huge investment like steel plant, or for socialist countries who do not allow foreign ownership.

Summarising the above analyses, the areas fit for various international strategies are shown in Figure 6.2. Foreign production, export, licensing and plant engineering are mutually exclusive alternatives. Two elements are important in drawing the dividing line – the size of investment required and the cost of transport.

When the investment is very large, plant engineering or export is appropriate. Because of the high element of risk, foreign investment in one plant should be limited to the plant of below medium investment.

The size of the product is another element. Small-size high-technology products are appropriate for export, because the transport costs are low.

Small-size products with a medium level of technology, such as medium-quality cameras and watches, are suitable either for export or for foreign production. With medium-level technology, production control is easy, and such goods can be produced in developing countries.

Medium-sized high-technology products are also suitable for foreign production. Examples are electric home appliances and rubber tyres. Their high technology can be their competitive strength. Since they are relatively bulky the transport costs are high; however, mass production can be managed from a distance.

Heavy electrical equipment like electricity generators are not suitable for foreign production, because they are made to order and the production management is difficult from a distance. Such products are appropriate for export.

To assure a supply of raw materials foreign investment becomes necessary. It may be possible to import these materials but the exporting

154

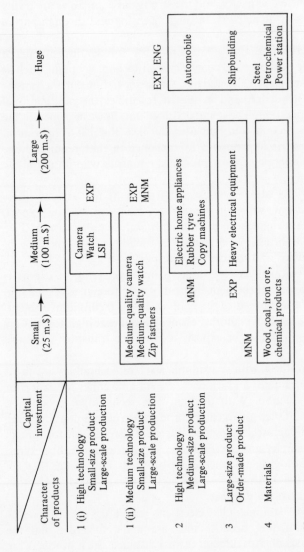

FIGURE 6.2 Areas for multinational management (assumption: the market is large enough and there is no restriction on imports)

Notes:
1 EXP – export, MNM – multinational management, ENG – plant engineering.
2 Dollar amount indicates approximate size of maximum capital investment.
3 Licensing is not indicated, because it depends on the capability of the receiving partner

country may request investment. If the investment is very large, joint ventures with other companies can be undertaken.

Food and textiles are fit neither for export nor foreign production, because the technology is low. If the brand is very well known, however, multinational management is feasible to some extent.

When one company diversifies, it should use different international strategies for different products. Hitachi, for example, uses foreign production for electric home appliances, but exports or licenses for heavy electrical equipment, and does plant engineering for power plant construction. The model shown in Figure 6.2 assumes (i) there is no restriction on imports, (ii) the market is large enough.

On a different model, if the market is small export is appropriate, if the market is medium licensing is appropriate, if the market is large foreign production is appropriate (Kindleberger, 1970; Kolde, 1974). However, this model is too simple.

Another model assumes that labour-intensive products are produced in developing countries, and technology-intensive products are produced in developed countries (Dymsza, 1972). This model is also too simple. The Japanese textile companies applied this principle and failed. It neglects to take into account that superiority in technology is essential for the success of foreign production.

6.4 THE EFFECT OF MULTINATIONAL MANAGEMENT ON THE PERFORMANCE OF THE COMPANY, AND KEY SUCCESS FACTORS OF THE SUBSIDIARIES

6.4.1 Multinational Management and the Performance of the Company

Multinational management affects the performance of the parent company and also the consolidated performance. The causal relations are shown in Figure 6.3.

The first analysis compares the performance of low multinationals with that of the medium and high multinational investment companies. Table 6.2 shows the differences in performance. The HMN and MMN companies have neither significantly better performance nor worse performance. Although the sample is not large enough, Table 6.2 suggests that the level of multinational management itself does not affect the performance. The problem is what are the key success factors of the subsidiaries that may improve the performance of the parent company and the consolidated group as a whole.

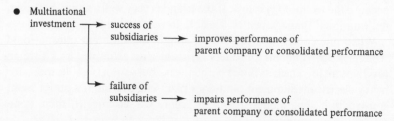

FIGURE 6.3 Impact of multinational investment on performance

'The success of the subsidiary' can be defined as the subsidiary contributing to the consolidated performance, and in order to see how the contribution is made, the performance is measured from three angles, as shown in Figure 6.4. It is necessary to have this breakdown to measure the contribution. We then established a model on the success factors, and this is also exhibited in Figure 6.4.

This model was formulated from a number of the author's direct and indirect observations. It assumes that the product is selected appropriately, satisfying the principle of Figure 6.2. The framework of this model is the same as that of this book: top management, goal, product–market strategy, structure, decision-making and performance.

Technological strength in the parent company is required for the subsidiary to have technological superiority and to produce high-quality goods. This is one of the two important keys. For example, the success of subsidiaries of Matsushita and Sony depends on the technological strength of the parent companies. The failure of the subsidiaries of textile companies and plywood board companies are due to the lack of technological strength in the parent companies.

The second important key is to transfer the Japanese management style to the subsidiary by way of the Japanese managers stationed at the subsidiary. The author found that when the management of the subsidiary is delegated to the local managers of the host country from the beginning (not in later years), the operation fails. This sometimes happens in the case of a joint venture. A subsidiary of Daiwaseiko (fishing rods and reel manufacturer) based in Scotland is one of the cases of failure. (This policy was changed afterwards.) It is necessary to transplant the philosophy of management and to practise the style of Japanese management; a mixture of hard discipline and warm treatment.

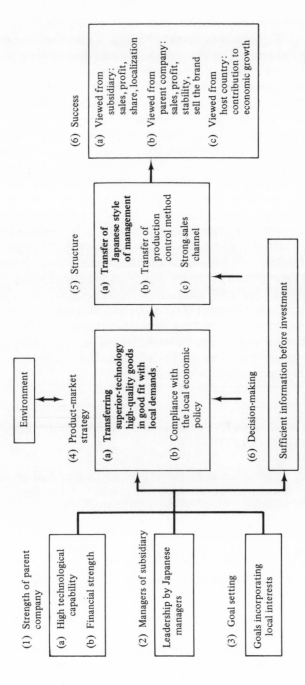

FIGURE 6.4 **Key factors of success** (assuming products are selected properly, following the principle of Figure 6.2)

This model was supported by other surveys. One survey was conducted in 1980 by Sanwa Bank's Foreign Trade and Investment Consulting Department on seventy subsidiaries. Fifty out of the seventy subsidiaries were successful, and twenty were unsuccessful, and the reasons for success were analysed by interview and by analyses of published papers. The left side of Table 6.5 shows the results. The items are the same as those in Figure 6.4. We find that superiority of technology (4)(a) and (5)(b) and transfer of Japanese style (5)(a) are important items.

The other survey is by the Association of Multinational Companies (Zaigai Kigyo Kyokai) on the reasons of divestment of fifty-eight subsidiaries. In 1979 the Association conducted interviews with the parent companies on eighteen cases, and analysed published materials on forty cases. The divestment consisted mostly of the sale of the assets or the company. A few cases represented sales of profitable subsidiaries, but these were a minority, so the survey shows the reasons for failure. The reasons for failure are the reverse side of the success factors. This survey shows that for superiority of technology (4)(a) and (5)(b) are important, but transplanting Japanese management systems (5)(a) is not emphasized. Environmental factors (4)(a) are considered equally important.

These two surveys show that the success factor model of Figure 6.4 is valid, and they indicate the relative importance of the items in this figure. The following three sections will be devoted to the analysis of success factors of high-performance companies.

6.5 THE ORGANIZATION OF THE PARENT COMPANY AND THE METHOD OF CONTROL

Appropriate organization of the parent company and method of control is necessary to transfer the technology successfully and to assure a fair return. They have an interconnecting relationship with the strategy.

6.5.1 The Organization of the Head Office

Many writers on the administrative organization of multinational management state that the stages of development are as follows:

1. The foreign subsidiary is set up under the production department or under the product division.
2. The international department is set up to control the subsidiaries.
3. The global organization. The product division or geographical

division controls both theforeign subsidiary and the plant in the home country; there is no separation of control between the foreign subsidiary and the plant in the home country.
4. The matrix organization, where both the product division and the geographical subsidiary company control the production subsidiary (Stopford and Wells, 1972; Robock and Simmonds, 1977; Kolde, 1974; Robinson, 1973).

The Japanese company roughly follows these stages, but there are differences. The typical pattern is as follows:

1. Subsidiaries under the production department or under the product division.
2. Subsidiaries under the export department.
3. Matrix organization, subsidiaries under the international department and under the production department or the product division.

Many companies start from type 1 of the above, and foreign sales are promoted by a separate sales company under the control of the export department. In cases of companies whose exports are very large, the production subsidiary is set up under the export department (type 2), but the production is controlled by the production department, so it becomes a kind of matrix organization. Toyota has examples of this type. As the amount of foreign investment increases, the international department is set up and controls both the production subsidiary and the sales subsidiary (type 3). In addition, the production department controls the subsidiary, so this type is actually a matrix organization. Matsushita, Sony, Hitachi and Ajinomoto use this type.

According to the survey by MITI in 1975, type 1 accounts for 24 per cent, type 2 accounts for 16 per cent, and type 3 accounts for 50 per cent of large corporations – corporations whose foreign investment is over 1 billion yen. The other recent survey by Okumura and others of 170 manufacturing companies shows that type 1 accounts for about 26 per cent, type 2 30 per cent and type 3 35 per cent (Okumura, 1981).

The international department is highly diffused, a result of the larger social distance between Japan and other Asian countries on the one hand and between Japan and Western countries on the other. Special administration by the international department is necessary to cope with this social distance. By contrast, the product division of a UK company may easily control its subsidiaries in EEC countries together with the home plant. The international department in Japan is usually responsible for controlling the subsidiary, for licensing, for exporting and for planning and control of international strategy.

TABLE 6.5 Success factors of fifty subsidiaries and reasons for divestment of fifty-eight subsidiaries

Success factors	(cases)	Reasons for divestment	(cases)
(1) Technological and financial capability of parent company		Deterioration of performance of parent company	14
		Change of multinational policy of parent company	9
		Financial difficulty	6
(2) Top management			
Quality of expatriate	3	Insufficient training of expatriate	1
(3) Goal setting			
Co-operation with partner	10	Conflict with local partner	13
		Conflict with Japanese partner	3
(4)(a) High-quality goods in good fit with local demands	10	Insufficient demand for products	29
Growth of demands of local market	3	Change of competitive condition (new entry, new substitutes)	18
International division of labour		Rising price of raw materials	12
		Falling price of products	9
(4)(b) Compliance with economic policy and favourable economic environment			
Localization	10	Rising wage cost	11
Favourable condition provided by local government	9	Rising cost of construction	5
		High interest rate	4
		Restriction in import of machine, material and component	9

(5)(a) Transfer of Japanese style of management		Devaluation of local currency	5
High consideration on personal management	15	Rising ratio of local procurement required	5
Japanese style of management	9	Lowered ratio of ownership	9
		Unstable political and social environment	10
(5)(b) Transfer of production technology		Problem on personnel management	3
High quality of equipment and production control	12		
Quality control	6	Problems on equipment and production technology	9
Reduction of production cost	7	Difficulty in procuring materials and components	7
		Problems on quality control	4
(5)(c) Strong sales channel			
Good marketing system	15	Problems on marketing	10
Stable customer	9		
After-sales service	2		
(6) Decision-making			
Sufficient information before investment	6	Insufficient marketing research and feasibility study	18
Timing of international operation	16		

Notes:
[1] Survey by Sanwa Bank in 1980, cases of fifty successful subsidiaries out of seventy cases.
[2] Survey by Association of Multinational Companies, fifty-eight cases of divestment.

6.5.2 Internationalization of the Head Office

IBM employs about a thousand foreigners in its head office and many directors and executives are foreigners. Royal Dutch Shell and Unilever have directors and executives from two countries. According to the survey, these cases are rather exceptional, and even US and European multinational companies have few foreigners at the top. A survey of eighty-six British multinational companies found that only 57 out of 1000 directors of multinational companies were foreigners (Robock and Simmonds, 1977). Japanese corporations do not have any foreigners at the top level nor at the middle management level, even in case of Sony, Matsushita or Toray which have a high level of multinational management. There are two reasons for this.

The foreign managers can rarely speak Japanese so there is a problem of communication. Second, the directors of Japanese corporations are mostly selected from inside; few directors come from outside the company. As was explained in Chapter 2, the name of director bears a high status value, so the position has to be reserved for the Japanese managers.

In the future, as the level of multinational management is enhanced, the number of foreigners at the top level will increase. Internationalization of the head office is needed for two reasons. One is to increase the number of opportunities for promotion of managers in the subsidiaries; the other is to increase the amount of international information.

6.5.3 Method of Control

The term 'control' is not liked by people working in the subsidiary, but the control is necessary to transfer the know-how and to divide the fruits of success fairly.

As means of control, stock ownership, holding of loan capital, sending directors, transfer of technology and control of sales channels are all available (Robinson, 1973). Stock ownership is the ultimate control power. The average percentage of stock in foreign subsidiaries held by Japanese corporations is lower than that of US and UK multinationals. The reasons are clear; Japanese corporations have more investment in developing countries. Japanese corporations would like 100 per cent ownership, but the Philippines and other developing countries restrict the level of ownership. The Philippines, for example, only allows, by its Investment Incentive Act, 100 per cent ownership for 'pioneering

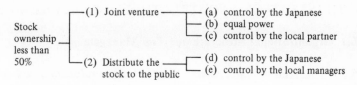

FIGURE 6.5 Types of control under minority ownership

enterprise', 50 per cent for 'preferred enterprise' and less than 30 per cent for other enterprises.

When the ownership is not more than 50 per cent, companies can be divided as shown in Figure 6.5.

According to the author's observation, the successful cases are (a) and (d) in Figure 6.5: other cases are not successful. One large textile subsidiary in Malaysia was not successful because the management was delegated to Chinese managers from Hong Kong, where the head office of the partner is located. The construction of the plant itself was unsatisfactory; there was a 20 per cent rejection rate for defective quality, efficiency was low and the subsidiary suffered from large losses. In order to revitalize the subsidiary, the Japanese parent company took over control, sent about a hundred managers and technicians, and transferred a Japanese production control system, quality control system, specifications and other management skills, and after a few years the subsidiary began to make a profit.

On the other hand, joint ventures in Japan are mostly managed by Japanese staff, and many of them are successful. Fuji-Zerox is one example. Even the 100 per cent owned Japan IBM is managed by Japanese.

The basic principles are the same. When there are differences in management skill between two companies or between two countries, the superior company or managers from the country with superior management skill should have greater control. This is further studied in the following section.

6.6 THE STRATEGY AND STRUCTURE OF THE SUBSIDIARY

6.6.1 Organizational Structure and Top Management

6.6.1.1 The relationship between the production subsidiary and sales subsidiary

In the first stage a sales company and sales channels are established, and then the production company is built. The integration between production and sales takes places through self-co-ordination. At a later stage the district company is established, and it then integrates the production and sales. Sony in the USA and UK, and Matsushita Electric in the USA use this structure.

In production efficiency-oriented subsidiaries, exports are taken care of by the export department (inside or outside the international department) of the parent company.

6.6.1.2 Top management

(i) *Board of directors.* Where there is about 50 per cent ownership, half of the directors are selected locally whether the company is of the joint-venture type or ownership-by-the-general-public type. This is a kind of localization. In Matsushita in Malaysia, six out of ten directors are Japanese and four out of six live in Tokyo, the remaining four are Malaysians. Such a high use of outside members is different from the management style of Japanese corporations in the home country.

Where the subsidiary is 100 per cent owned the majority of directors are Japanese, with some local office bearers. Sony UK has four directors: three are Japanese (two live in Tokyo) and one, the managing director of the company, is British. All are Sony people. Matsushita UK has five directors, of whom four are Japanese and one British, and they are all inside people.

(ii) *General management.* The majority of Japanese corporations in Japan have a management committee of selected full-time directors who make decisions as a group. This system is transferred to their foreign subsidiaries. In most cases, the top managers of the subsidiary form the management committee, meeting once a week or twice a month and making decisions as a group. In Matsushita in Malaysia, two Japanese and four locals, who are each responsible for one department, meet twice a month and make decisions as a group. Matsushita in the UK is a

100 per cent owned company; the management committee is comprised of four Japanese and three Britons, and it meets once a week. The management committees of Sony UK and of YKK UK, the majority of whose members are British, meet once a month. Thus the tradition of group decision-making at the top is transferred to the foreign subsidiary.

6.6.1.3 The number of Japanese managers

There are three types of management classified by the positions occupied by Japanese:

1. The president, the plant manager and managers of all departments are Japanese. This type is used by newly established companies or by production efficiency-oriented companies.
2. The plant manager and the managers of the finance department and technology department are Japanese. There is a large Japanese technological staff in the technology department. This type is seen in technology-intensive product companies.
3. The plant manager and the finance department manager are Japanese, and other Japanese have positions as assistants to heads of departments. This type is found in long-established subsidiaries.

Selection of the appropriate type depends on the following factors. First, number of years' experience since establishment: Matsushita in Malaysia shifted from type 1 to type 3. Second, technology-intensiveness. The higher the technology required, the more Japanese are stationed with the company. Third, the need for integration. The greater the need for integration, the more the company employs expatriates. Production centre subsidiaries belong to this category.

Generally speaking, there are said to be more Japanese in Japanese subsidiaries than the number of expatriates in US subsidiaries. According to MITI's survey, 42 per cent of all managers of manufacturing companies and 70 per cent of managers of trade companies are Japanese. In contrast, the number of expatriates in the US subsidiaries in Japan is rather low; sometimes there are no Americans.

The reasons for this general pattern has already been explained. It is necessary to transfer the Japanese management system for success, and many Japanese are needed for this transfer. The other reason is the need for communication in Japanese. It is hard to find local people who can write and speak Japanese fluently, and who at the same time are also competent in management skills. The success of subsidiaries in foreign countries is essential for the employees of the subsidiary and also for the benefit of the host country. This success is only attained by good management. The promotion of local people is not for the benefit of the host country, if the management of the subsidiary fails.

In the case of foreign subsidiaries in Japan, Japanese managers can speak and write English and, what is more important, they know how to practise the Japanese style of management, and this tends to bring about good performance. They know better how to implement quality control and how to operate the QC circle movement. The transfer of technology from the parent company is carried out by sending the Japanese managers to the parent company for refresher courses after the establishment of the subsidiary.

6.6.1.4 *The quality of Japanese managers and length of stay with the subsidiary*

Generally speaking, the local managers tend to criticize the expatriate managers saying that since top people from the parent company do not like to go abroad, second-class people are sent and placed in higher positions and overpaid (Dymza, 1972). This cannot be generalized. The Japanese managers, especially the president, the plant manager and other managers, are selected from among the most highly qualified personnel. This is the author's impression after many interviews.

Some companies stipulate that the length of stay will be three years for technical staff and five years for clerical staff. Actually the managers in higher positions, especially the president and many plant managers, stay for seven or eight years. This is often inconvenient for managers, especially where the education of their children is concerned, but it is desirable for the success of the subsidiary. The key factor is opportunity for promotion in the parent company after returning home. If they are treated favourably, competent people are willing to go abroad. (Concerning the satisfaction of Japanese managers sent abroad, see Yasumuro, 1982.)

6.6.2 Product–Market Strategy and Strategic Decisions

6.6.2.1 *The product mix and the level of technology*

The basic principle for appropriate production in the subsidiary has already been explained in Figure 6.2. The high level of technology embodied in the products is the most important key success factor. There have been a number of cases of failure where low-technology goods were produced. The production of sports shoes, sweaters, pencils, and umbrellas in Taiwan; the production of pyjamas and the construction of recreation grounds in the Philippines; the production of aluminium window frames and of plywood board in Malaysia; the production of plastic board in the UK – these are all cases of failure because of lack of competitive strength.

6.6.2.2 Specialization and diversification

The market-oriented subsidiary in the developing country tends to produce many goods. For example, Matsushita in the Philippines and in Malaysia makes television sets, refrigerators, stereo players, electric fans, battery and electric rice cookers in each company, all with less than 1000 employees. The operation is protected by tariff barriers in these countries, so even if the cost of production is slightly higher than in the home country, the company can still make a profit.

NEC in Malaysia, as a production centre, produces integrated circuits for export, and the company is specialized to produce only IC and transistors. Matsushita in the UK produces colour television sets and music centres. It is specialized to have competitive power, even if it is a market-oriented subsidiary. In developed countries, there is no difference in strategy between the export-substitute subsidiary and the production-centre subsidiary. The principle is as shown in Figure 6.6.

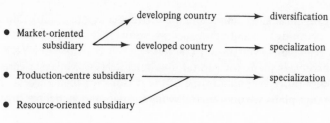

FIGURE 6.6 Specialization and diversification of subsidiaries

6.6.2.3 The procurement of machinery, components and raw materials

The subsidiary company needs to import key machinery, key components and materials from the home country for better product quality and lower cost. The parent company wants to export the above goods to increase its own exports. The host country wants the subsidiary to buy them in the local market and stipulates that a certain percentage of procurement of materials should be done in the host country. Here is the conflict.

According to the author's observation, the ratio of imports from the parent company is much higher than might be expected. In many cases the key machinery is produced by the parent company (YKK and Matsushita), and imported. This is an important means of technology transfer. Even in developed countries, YKK imports steel wire, aluminium wire, and slider, and Matsushita imports brown tubes and steel plates.

In developing countries, the subsidiary has to produce the key parts to heighten the ratio of procurement in the host country. Matsushita in Malaysia has a parts production department, and 60 per cent of materials are procured in that country.

The vertical integration of key parts production and the use of quasi-vertical integration of upstream and downstream process is characteristic of successful Japanese companies, and this strategy is followed as much as the environmental constraints allow: imports are one of the means of implementing this strategy.

Some companies try to organize a team of components suppliers in the host country. This is a quasi-vertical integration in the host country. Kawasaki in the USA, for example, has tried to form a team and to transfer its management system, based on long-term agreement.

6.6.2.4 *Long-range planning as a means of strategic decision-making*

Many Japanese subsidiaries and their parent companies think that long-range planning is essential for success. Sony UK has five-year plans and three-year plans, Matsushita UK has three-year plans, and YKK UK has three-year plans for capital investment. NEC Malaysia considers that long-range planning is one of the reasons for their success. These long-range plans are built up following formats and guidelines provided by the parent company and authorized by the parent company. The parent company controls the decisions of the subsidiary by this means.

The parent company controls strategic decisions by other means, such as the annual conference of the presidents, frequent visits of the expatriate managers to the parent company, authorization of annual budgets and monthly reports and financial statements to the parent company.

Okumura and others conducted research into multinational management of 170 manufacturing companies, and asked how company decisions were centralised and decentralised. The survey shows that the principles are the same as those for management in the home country.

The strategic decisions are centralised and operational decisions are delegated. Selection of top managers, decisions on product mix, new product development, capital investment and amount of production are all decided by the parent company's top management or by the joint decisions of the parent company and its subsidiary (Okumura, 1981).

6.6.3 Transfer of Business Philosophy and Goal Setting

It has been pointed out that US corporations enforced the American system too much in their subsidiaries and failed. The problem now arises as to whether the Japanese corporation is committing the same mistake. Richman maintains that the mountain shape model, the middle road between the local system and American system, shows the best performance (Richman and Copen, 1972). The same principle applies to the Japanese subsidiary. The problem is how to transfer the Japanese style of management.

6.6.3.1 *Transfer of business philosophy*

Successful Japanese companies emphasize their business philosophy stating their missions and goals. A clear business philosophy increases the employees' sense of identification and makes innovation easy. This was discussed in Chapter 3. Many successful US and UK companies also have clear statements of business philosophy: ICI and Marks & Spencer in the UK; IBM, Hewlet Packard, Johnson and Johnson in the USA. It is not strange then that successful subsidiaries should import the business philosophy of their parent companies.

Matsushita in the Philippines with the co-operation of its partner in the joint venture displays notice boards of 'the seven spirits', stating 'National service through Industry, Fairness, Harmony and co-operation'. Every day the morning meeting is held, the company song is sung and any one employee can give his or her opinion in turn. Matsuhita in Malaysia also displays 'the seven spirits', and holds morning meetings where the company song is sung and one employee states his opinion. In the UK, the core of the culture is different, and Matsushita does not display 'the seven spirits', nor do the employees sing the company song. However, everywhere in the plant there are boards saying 'Cleanliness and tidiness produce quality'; the basic idea that profit is the result of service to the society is emphasized; morning meetings are held; and on Wednesday morning all members of the plant meet together.

It may seem that Matsushita is an extreme case, but it is not so. Hitachi in the Philippines displays the Hitachi spirit throughout the plant, holds radio physical exercises every morning, and a morning meeting in every section. Sony UK instructs the new recruits in the Sony spirit; YKK UK emphasizes the 'cycle of goodness' all the time.

The philosophy of the Japanese corporation has three characteristics. It emphasizes (i) service to the society, (ii) mutual co-operation and harmony, and (iii) respect for people. The first point is to stress the need for innovation rather than short-term profit; the second is to emphasize the organismic organization rather than the mechanistic organization; the third one is to emphasize its organization as a community rather than an economic unit.

The ease with which these philosophies can be transferred depends on three factors:

1. Individualism or group orientation. The more individualistic the culture the more difficult the transferring becomes.
2. Pride in the superiority of the culture. The more pride, the more difficult the transferring is.
3. The prestige of the parent company. The higher the prestige, the easier the transfer.

The last factor is more important than the first two factors, and the difficulty of transferring company philosophy should not be over-emphasized.

6.6.3.2 Goals of the subsidiary

The goal of the company is part of its philosophy and is a concrete target for the company. According to the author's survey of goals over a number of visits, the following are the most typical items: (i) sales and growth rate, (ii) share of the market, (iii) profit, especially rate of return on total investment, (iv) localization and contribution to the host country. These goals are formulated by the expectations of the parent company and by the expectations of local managers. The Japanese parent company tends to put emphasis on long-term achievement of these goals. As an example, the goals of Ajinomoto Malaysia are growth of sales, rate of return on total assets and localization. The market share is not emphasized because the share is already 70 per cent. Localization involves, most importantly, the public distribution of stock to reduce the ownership of the parent company from 60 per cent to 30 per cent, and the promotion of local managers by training. The goals of Sony UK are sales and growth, rate of return on sales, share of the market and contribution to the host country. Important contributions are increased exports and increased procurement from local markets.

We should notice that localization is an important goal. Some companies consider it as a constraint, but many think of it as one of their goals and it derives directly from their philosophies. The typical items of localization are as follows: – the distribution of stock to the public in developing countries, promotion of local managers, more procurement from local markets, and contribution to the exports of the host country.

These items have trade-off relations with one another, and a balance is necessary. Localization may have a negative correlation with market share and growth, and in such cases a satisfactory level should be set in order to maintain a balance. This is no more, however, than the general approach of setting the goal levels of the organization at any time.

6.6.4 Organization Structure and Personnel Management of the Subsidiary

The social environment of the host country is different from that of Japan, so the transplanted Japanese style needs some modification. The Japanese managers perceive that the local people have the following characteristic of behaviour in both developed and developing countries:

(a) The organization tends to be mechanistic because of the following characteristics. People do only what is ordered. Punishment plays a more important role than reward. People do not acknowledge the mistakes they have made, and they do not try to learn from them. People specialize, and are specialist-oriented. People compete with one another and do not teach one another, because of the merit system. Communication between colleagues is not good.
(b) The organization tends to be economic. The sense of identification with the organization is low and staff turnover is high. People leave the company when they acquire a certain skill. The status of blue-collar workers is lower than that of white-collar workers. The hierarchical differences are larger, and there is much less equality.

With these social characteristics to contend with, it is rather strange that much of the Japanese management style can in fact be transferred, especially if it does not touch the core of the culture.

6.6.4.1 From mechanistic organization to organismic organization

The definition of the two organizational characteristics was made by

Burns and Stalker (Burns and Stalker, 1961). The mechanistic organization is a hard organization. It has clear job division, more specialization and more centralization of authority. The organismic organization and more decentralization of authority. Burns and Stalker stated
that in a stable environment the mechanistic organization is effective,
and in an unstable environment the organismic organization works
better. Apart from this viewpoint, the author finds that organization in
the USA and in the UK has more mechanistic characteristics and
Japanese organization is more organismic.

(i) *The labour union.* The labour union seems to be an uncontrollable
environment, but the company does have some choice. Unions in Japan
are organized as company-wide unions, so changing jobs to adapt to
changes in the environment is easy. On the other hand, unions in the UK
are organized as craft unions, so it frequently happens that one company
has members of six unions. As a result, job demarcation is strict, which
hampers job changing and innovation.

There is, however, a new trend in the UK whereby unions are
becoming open unions to protect themselves from the decrease in
membership brought about by changes in technology. TGWU
(Transportation and General Workers' Union), for example, welcomes
a number of jobs. Japanese companies utilize this trend, making
agreements with one union and thereafter having a closed shop
agreement to avoid having too many unions. Sony UK negotiates with
AUEW, Matsushita UK with GMWU, YKK with TGWU, to be freed
from the problem of job demarcation.

In the Philippines, there are national unions and company-wide
unions. Japanese subsidiaries in many cases have one company-wide
union.

In Malaysia, the unions are organized as industrial unions, as in the
USA. Japanese subsidiaries make contracts with one industrial union.
Negotiations between one company and one industrial union, which is
typical in the USA, present few problems of job demarcation. So by
selecting one union Japanese subsidiaries hope to have job flexibility.

(ii) *Job classification and the wage system.* In Japan, job classification is
very flexible and there are many opportunities for promotion and wage
increase; thus the incentive to work is strong. These are important traits
of the length of service system. With some limitations, these characteristics can be transferred. The system used by Japanese subsidiaries

has the following characteristics: (i) ambiguous job titles, but clear responsibility, (ii) many grades, (iii) wide rate range, (iv) no differentiation between blue-collar and white-collar workers.

Ajinomoto Malaysia has five grades for workers, and the names of jobs – such as operator, mechanic, electrician, clerk and so on – are ambiguous. The same job appears in more than one grade, so promotion by length of service is possible. The maximum pay rate is about twice the minimum rate.

Matsushita in Malaysia has a job rate system, and the job names are ambiguous. There are five grades of clerk, from clerk(V) to clerk(I), four grades of general worker from production staff(confirmed) and production staff(III) to production staff(I). The salary schedule is clearly stated, but the maximum rate is about 2.2 times the minimum rate.

Matsushita in the UK has seven grades under the foreman. Job names – such as assembler, senior assembler – are ambiguous. The rate range is wide; wage increases in the same grade are possible six times to the maximum. This is rather unusual in the UK where the wage system is very simple.

Thus there are more opportunities for promotion and wage increase, and job changes are easier, under these personnel systems. An ambiguous job name does not mean that the responsibility is not clear. It has to be clear, because people are more individualistic, less devoted to the organization. Both the job and the responsibility can be changed using the same job name. This is a flexible system.

There is no differentiation between blue-collar and white-collar workers. The wage system, the method of payment, which is usually a monthly payment, and the bonus system are the same. Everybody wears the same uniform, from the plant manager to the simple worker.

Promotion has to be selective. In Japanese corporations at home promotion is slow and equal with slight differences reflecting merit. In the UK and in other countries, this system has to be modified. Competent staff have to be promoted to higher positions rapidly, otherwise they will leave the organization.

(iii) *Participation.* Japanese companies at home use group decision-making at every level of the organization. This system can be transferred with some modification. In a country of individualists, a clear definition of authority and responsibility is necessary; and if the job name is too ambiguous, people feel frustration. Within this environment, staff participation and the positive presentation of employees' opinions are encouraged. The Japanese managers may ask many questions to encourage participation: 'What other alternatives are possible?' 'Did you ask the opinions of the related department?'

The Japanese managers try to ask the opinions of people on related jobs as much as possible, before arriving at any decisions. This is necessary especially when the managers are assistants to the head of the department.

On the other hand, the following methods are used to encourage mutual communication and participation. Managers use one large room instead of each having separate rooms. Morning meetings are held, where one employee is requested to present a speech. There are suggestion systems; large signboards encourage employees' suggestions. Small-group activity is encouraged; items of study are selected by the group for discussion. This group activity is implemented with limited popularity. Overtime allowances are paid for activities after working hours. Everyone wears the same uniform at the plant site, from the plant manager to the lower workers – whether they are white-collar workers or blue-collar workers; everybody uses the same cafeteria, which is useful for improving communication.

The above method is implemented more successfully in developing countries than in developed countries.

6.6.4.2 *From economic organization to community organization*

The Japanese organization is more like *Gemeinschaft* than *Gesellschaft*. This concept of two organizational characteristics originates in Tönnies (Tönnies, 1887). In the community organization, the belonging itself is a joy, members are united by mutual love and trust, and they help each other. In economic organizations, each member wants economic rewards for their contribution, and though joined by contract, they are essentially separate. Japanese corporations want to transfer the characteristics of the community organization to their subsidiaries.

(i) *Egalitarianism*. Equal treatment, with only a small differentiation to reflect merit, is one of the characteristics of Japanese management. The equal treatment of blue-collar workers and white-collar workers is one of the salient characteristics. Both wear the same uniform, use the same dining-room, and are paid on the same salary schedule by monthly payment.

This equal treatment does not mean absolute equality, but rather a fair difference of promotion and wage increase reflecting employees' performance. The recording of performance is carefully designed for this purpose.

(ii) *Recruitment and retirement.* In Japan, the new recruit is chosen from among the fresh graduates from university and high school, and the company tries to employ them for their lifetime. Subsidiaries recruit from high schools in the Philippines and in Malaysia, but not in the UK nor in the USA. There, introductions by present employees, advertisement, and direct visits by the applicants to the office are more usual methods of recruitment.

Worker's security of employment is a delicate problem. The lifetime employment of Japanese corporations in Japan is not a rigid contract. The subsidiary never makes contracts on lifetime employment. It tries to stabilize employment, and if a decrease in the number of employees is necessary, new recruitment is suspended and waits for natural retirement. This method has been used by YKK in the UK. In many cases, however, the growth rate of Japanese subsidiaries has been high, and the turnover of employees is generally higher than that in Japan, so lay-offs or discharges have not been necessary.

Less capable employees are kept on in Japanese corporations in Japan, the advantage of keeping them outweighing the disadvantage of firing. Subsidiaries in foreign countries do not keep on the obviously incompetent. If such workers were kept on it would be understood as excessive favouritism and result in defective morale. The subsidiary tries first to train the less capable employee, but those whose morale is too low or who are trouble-makers (who break rules about, for instance, smoking) are discharged. This discipline is sometimes stricter than in the local companies, and it is necessary if the community organization is to survive.

(iii) *Meetings to strengthen the group spirit.* Formal and informal meetings strengthen the cohesiveness of the group. The morning meeting and the small group activities are useful for this. Cultural education classes are held every week; athletic meetings, outings, Christmas and other parties, open house in the plant for the family of employees are all occasionally held and are paid for by the subsidiary. The simple invitation of the workers' family to the plant increases the concern of the family about the company and stimulates the cohesiveness of the company members.

6.6.4.3 Effects of the transfer of Japanese-style personnel management

What are the effects of Japanese-style management on the performance of the subsidiary and on the satisfaction of the employees? According to the author's direct observation on visits to more than twenty subsidiaries, the following results could be seen.

The performances of those subsidiaries whose managements were completely delegated to local managers from the beginning, and not in the later stages, were inferior, and the companies suffered losses. The fishing rod company in Scotland and the synthetic fibre company in Malaysia are examples of this.

The subsidiaries managed by the Japanese have a high reputation for the quality of their products. Absenteeism among the employees is low, usually less than 5 per cent. Employee turnover is less than 10 per cent in the Philippines and in Malaysia, but about 30 per cent in the UK. Some 30 per cent in the UK is a little higher than the average; the turnover rate in the paint division of ICI at Slough is said to be about 17 per cent.

On the other hand, there are many applicants registered on a waiting list for jobs with Sony UK at Bridgend. Sony employees are provided with uniforms, and they leave the plant wearing their uniforms because they are proud of being employed at Sony.

According to Thurley's comparative survey on the morale of employees, he found that employees of Japanese subsidiaries in the UK are more satisfied with the company, and with promotion, similarly satisfied with their seniors and peers, and less satisfied with their jobs and wages compared with employees of UK companies (Thurley *et al.*, 1980).

6.6.4.4 The transferability of Japanese-style personnel management

Generally speaking, most aspects of the Japanese personnel management system took shape after the war as a result of rational thinking rather than of the unique culture of Japan, so to a great extent they are transferable to other countries. The systems of successful US companies and UK companies have many similarities. Any system that originates in the core of the culture, however, is not transferable.

(i) *Non-transferable system.*

(a) Strong identification with the company. Where individualism is strong, identification with the company to the extent in Japan cannot be expected. Lifetime commitment and long overtime working cannot be transferred.

(b) Ambiguous job designation. It is possible to use an ambiguous title, but the job itself has to be clear. It is unfair to expect the employee to do any related job if the job definition is ambiguous. It is necessary to outline the authority and responsibility because the sense of identification is not high and there are also differences of capability between individual workers.

(c) Too much emphasis on length of service for wage increase and promotion. It is possible to use ambiguous job names, many grades and a limited rate range, but it is not possible to use too wide a rate range that reflects length of service and merit. It is hard to install a qualification status system that grades individuals by capability rather than by their jobs. The aspiration level of the employees on rate for the job is clear, so the Japanese system of wages for personal capability will result in a feeling of unfair treatment.

(ii) *Transferable system.* The following systems can be transferred:

(a) Systems that are congruent with the value of the society. One union in one company is advantageous both to the workforce and to the company. The craft-union system in the UK is nothing but the remains of an old system. Also, many opportunities for promotion and wage increase, stability of employment, and other systems that respect human rights are transferable.

(b) Systems that are related to conflicting values. The class system and egalitarianism are conflicting values, and both are still in existence. Equal treatment can be transferred and can be supported by a majority of the workforce. Examples of this are no differentiation between blue-collar and white-collar workers in the wearing of uniform.

(c) Unclear aspiration levels. A system of working in one large room, or one with frequent change of jobs, is transferable, because the aspiration levels on these matters are not clear.

Ueki conducted a survey on the transfer of Japanese management style to thirty Japanese subsidiaries in Brazil, and found that the subsidiaries that transferred the Japanese style of management performed better than those that did not. He asked the extent of the use of Japanese management style, and established ten scales. These are: use of business creed; lifetime employment; job flexibility; application of length of service to wage increase and promotion; use of consensus; use of large room for the office; extent of welfare system; transfer of general management skills; transfer of marketing skills; and transfer of production and quality-control skills. We should note that the last three are Japanese modifications of US management skills. He found that the fifteen majority-owned subsidiaries used the Japanese style to the greatest extent, seven subsidiaries that were joint Japanese–Brazilian ventures used it to a lesser extent, and the eight subsidiaries that were joint ventures with the government used it the least. He investigated the performance of all these groups, and found that the fifteen subsidiaries with majority Japanese ownership had the best performance, measured by the growth rate and rate of return (Ueki, 1982).

He also found that some Japanese management styles were not transferred. For example, over-high expectations of devotion to the organization, large-group conferences, unclear responsibility, suggestion systems, expectation of long-term service from trained highly skilled employees do not work well. The transfer was thus selective. He found that training and communication was important as a means of making the transfer acceptable to the local people. Ueki's findings that the selective transfer of Japanese management skills is effective for better performance coincides with our own.

6.7 SUMMARY

The direct objectives of multinational investment are; to replace exports, to manufacture where the cost of production is low, to secure raw materials and to contribute to the development of the local economy. The difference between the first two is decreasing.

The ultimate goal is the increase in sales and profit of the parent company. As the level of multinational management becomes higher, the company's horizons expand and the consolidated financial performance becomes more important.

The level of multinational management is not related to the level of diversification nor the level of vertical integration of the parent company. The high-performance multinational company has a high percentage of R and D expenditure, but has similar sales promotion expenditure to that of other companies.

Items that are fit for production in foreign countries have the following characteristics. They are products that incorporate high technology, are produced on a large scale, and can be mass produced, and can be managed by local people because of the repetitiveness involved. Electric home appliances are one example. Made-to-order production, such as shipbuilding, is not appropriate. It is also necessary that the production does not demand a huge investment. Steel plant needs too large an investment, so although it may be a good subject for plant engineering, it is not suitable for foreign investment.

Assuming that appropriate products are selected, the key success factors for multinational management are the transfer of high technology of the parent company, and the transfer of Japanese-style management. In order to do this, controlling power by the parent company and the employment of a certain number of Japanese staff in the subsidiary are necessary.

The subsidiaries display the characteristics of organismic organization. Job names are ambiguous and the rate range is large. Decisions are made by group discussion. The staff all work in one large room, and all employees wear the same uniform.

The subsidiaries display the characteristics of a community organization. They do not readily lay off their employees and, if any reduction in the workforce is necessary, it is done on a planned basis. Egalitarian ideas are emphasized. No differentiation is made between blue-collar and white-collar workers; both wear the same uniform and are paid on the same wage system. The morning meeting and small-group activities effectively help to form cohesive groups.

On the other hand, the personnel management is neither too soft nor too generous. Those who are considered trouble-makers, who disregard the rules, are discharged. The transfer of the Japanese style is by no means 'the home country-oriented management style' put forward by Perlmutter. It is modified in many respects to adapt to the different environment.

6.7.1 Problems

The author visited more than twenty subsidiaries in foreign countries, a number of indigenous companies and parent companies of the subsidiaries and found the following problems.

6.7.1.1 Criticism directed against the Japanese subsidiaries from the local people

1.(a) The price of components imported from the parent company is high, and the subsidiary is forced to contribute to the profit of the parent company. This criticism is frequent in developing countries where the exchange rate against the yen is constantly being devalued, and where the price of imports consequently has to be raised.

1.(b) The newest technology and equipment are not transferred. This criticism comes from partners in joint ventures in developing countries. The parent company is afraid of spill-over of the newest technology through the partner.

1.(c) The threat to existing producers in the same business. This is a problem in developed countries. YKK in the UK (zip-fasteners) and Hitachi in the UK (colour television) have met this problem. YKK has promised to buy a high percentage of materials in the UK, and Hitachi was forced into a joint venture with GEC, utilizing old factory facilities, which resulted in a burden to Hitachi.

The following problems are common to both developing and developed countries:

2.(a) The Japanese managers monopolize the key positions. The company does not promote local people. There are too many Japanese. The number of Japanese employees depends on the length of establishment and the level of technology required. As time elapses, local managers are trained and are promoted to key positions, excluding the positions of plant manager and finance manager. This is clearly seen in the changes in Matsushita Malaysia's organization chart in the last five years. To transfer the Japanese system, both technology and administration, it is necessary to have many Japanese staff members.

It is relatively difficult to promote indigenous people in production-centre subsidiaries because new confidential technologies are being transferred all the time.

2.(b) Over-high expectations of the identification of local work people with the company. Japanese managers ask them to work after 5 p.m. and to join in small-group activities. They ignore the difference in the value system.

3.(a) Japanese managers are always looking toward the parent company and are too concerned with their relationships with the staff of the parent company. They go to Tokyo at least once a month. Under the lifetime employment system, Japanese managers have to be promoted within the organization by the parent company.

3.(b) Japanese managers go back to Japan in three to five years, while local managers stay for life. They segregate themselves from the local people, and make friends only with their colleagues. Americans are similar in this respect, but they are more open. US managers are willing to spend time at management seminars or join the local rotary club, but Japanese managers are not.

6.7.1.2 Problems from the Japanese managers' viewpoint

1. Constraints on the import of materials and components. Imports of key components and key materials (e.g. steel) are essential for high-quality and low-cost products. Local governments may request that the ratio of local purchase on all material cost be more than 65 per cent for example.

2. Behavioural characteristics of the local people. The local people, whether in developing countries or developed countries, have different patterns of behaviour that come from different value systems, different religions, different educational systems and other social environments. These differences are perceived by the Japanese manager as inconvenient.

Typical problems have already been mentioned, and a few items will be repeated here. The local people do only what they are ordered to do, and do not do related jobs voluntarily. This is the most frequently cited problem everywhere in the USA, in the Philippines and in the UK. A similar problem is that the local people are specialized, and not interested in helping others.

Communication among the higher echelons of the staff is not very good. They compete against one another under the merit system. They do not teach their subordinates, nor communicate information to their colleagues.

The local people leave the company when they have acquired a certain skill, and they take advantage of any chance of getting higher pay.

3. The inconvenience in one's private life. The education of children is the most important problem. Parents want their children to go to Japanese universitites and be employed by Japanese companies and live in the same country as their parents in the future. In order to pass the entrance examination to Japanese universities, the children have to go to Japanese high schools. Thus many Japanese managers leave their high-school-age children in Japan with their mothers, and live alone in a foreign country for many years. The parents are also afraid that if their children stay with them too long in a foreign country, they will not be able to adapt to Japanese life again after returning.

In developing countries, moreover, life is not very comfortable, in that the climate is too hot and sometimes managers' lives are at risk.

6.7.1.3 Problems viewed from the parent company

The problems from the viewpoint of the subsidiary are part of the problems of the parent company. Additional problems are as follows:

1. The selection of strategies, new-product development or multinational investment. There are a number of alternative strategies: new-product development, additional vertical integration, strengthening competitive power, exporting, joint-venture agreements with foreign companies and foreign investment. These alternatives all compete for limited company resources. New-product development tends to have a higher priority than the others because it is a source of other strategies. The evaluation of foreign investment is not an easy matter because of the risks involved. Among its international strategies, companies put emphasis on exports rather than foreign investment.

2. Risks of foreign investment. According to financial theory, the reduction of risks of the company is more important than the absolute risk (Sharpe, 1970). It is rather difficult, however, to estimate the risk itself. One typical risk is that the national labour union will attack the Japanese subsidiary selectively and demand higher wages; labour productivity will be low; and the cost of quality of the product will be inferior to home-made products. In addition, there are political, economic and marketing risks.

REFERENCES

Kobayashi, N. (1980) *Nihon no Takokuseki Kigyo* (Japanese Multinational Corporations), Tokyo, Chuokeizai.

Kono, T. (1974) *Keiei Senryaku no Kaimei* (Analysis of Corporate Strategy), Tokyo, Diamond Sha.

Kono, T. (1977) *Keieigaku Genron* (Principles of Management), Tokyo, Diamond Sha.

Ministry of International Trade and Industry (MITI) (1975, 1978, 1980) *Waga Kuni Kigyo no Kaigai Katsudo* (Activities of Japanese Multinational Companies), Tokyo.

Nihon Rodokyokai (1975) *Waga Kuni Kaigai Shinshitsu Kigyo no Rodo Mondai, Philippine* (Labour Problems of Japanese Multinational Companies in the Philippines), Tokyo, Nihon Rodokyokai.

Nihon Rodokyokai (1975) (same series as the above), Malaysia.

Okumura, K. *et al.* (1981) *Wagakuni Keiei no Kakusaika ni kansuru Jisho Kenkyu* (Survey on Multinational Management), Yokohama, Yokohama Keiei Kenkyu.

Ueki, H. (1982) *Kokusai Keiei Itenron* (Transfer of Management Skill), Tokyo, Bunshindo.

Yasumuro, K. (1982) *Kokusai Keiei Kodoron* (Multinational Management), Tokyo, Moriyama.

Yoshihara, E. (1978) *Takokuseki Kigyoron* (Multinational Management), Tokyo, Maruzen.

Blake, R. R. and Mouton, J. S. (1964) *The Managerial Grid*, Texas, Gulf.

Brooke, M. Z. and Remmers, H. L. (1970) *The Strategy of Multinational Enterprise*, London, Longman.

Burns, T. and Stalker, G. M. (1961) *The Management of Innovation*, London, Tavistock Publications.

Dymsza, W. A. (1972) *Multinational Business Strategy*, New York, McGraw-Hill.

Farmer, R. N. and Richman, B. M. (1965) *Comparative Management and Economic Progress*, New York, R. D. Irwin.

Kindleberger, C. P. (ed.) (1970) *The International Corporation, A Symposium*, Mass., MIT Press.

Kolde, E. J. (1974) *The Multinational Company*, Mass., D. C. Heath & Co.

March, J. M. and Simon, H. A. (1958) *Organizations*, New York, John Wiley.

Perlmutter, H. V. (1969) 'The Tortuous Evolution of the Multinational Corporation', *Columbia Journal of World Business*, Jan–Feb.

Richman, B. and Copen, M. (1972) *International Management and Economic Development*, New York, McGraw-Hill.

Robock, S. H., Simmonds, K. and Zwick, J. (1977) *International Business and Multinational Enterprises*, Ill., Richard D. Irwin.

Robinson, R. D. (1973) *International Business Management*, New York, Holt, Rinehart & Winston.

Robinson, R. D. (1964) *International Business Policy*, New York, Holt, Rinehart & Winston.

Sharpe, W. F. (1970) *Portfolio Theory and Capital Markets*, New York, McGraw-Hill.

Skinner, W. (1968) *American Industry in Developing Economics*, New York, John Wiley.

Stopford, J. and Wells, L. T. (1972) *Managing the Multinational Enterprise*, New York, Basic Books.

Thurley, K. *et al.* (1980) *The Development of Personal Management in Japanese Enterprises in Great Britain*, London School of Economics.

Tönnies, F. (1887) *Gemeinschaft und Gesellschaft*.

Vernon, R. (1966) 'International Investment and International Trade in the Product Cycle', *Quarterly Journal of Economics*, vol. 80, no. 2.

7 Competition Strategy

Competition arises where many of the same or similar products are sold in the same market. Competition strategy is the strategy to increase or maintain the share of market, whether it is the share of old products or new ones.

7.1 A MODEL OF COMPETITION AND KEY SUCCESS FACTORS

The share of market is ruled by the following variables:

Share = F (share of previous period, comparative quality, comparative price, comparative sales promotion, comparative marketing channel strength)

Expressed simply, Share = F (previous share, Q, P, S, C)
Q = relative quality, P = relative price, S = share of sales promotion, C = share of channel strength
(the exact model is explained in Kono, 1974).

Quality in this equation means the design, the size and the quality level. It can include the product differentiation and segmentation. Porter emphasized cost leadership, product differentiation and segmentation as competition strategies (Porter, 1980). These are different angles from which to look at competition, and all three are clearly included in the above equation.

Competitive strength has five levels of hierarchy, as shown in Figure 7.1. At the second level, competitive strength has to be supported by three important capabilities, namely, development, production and marketing capabilities (see Figure 7.1). We will analyse the top two levels of Figure 7.1 in this chapter.

At the third level, the product–market strategy affects the competitive strength. For example, the Japanese shipbuilding industry has diversified into technology-related areas, and this has given synergic support to the

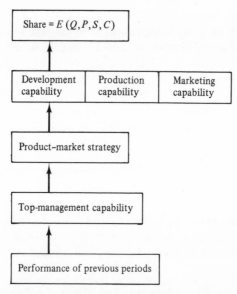

FIGURE 7.1 Hierarchy of competitive strength

competitiveness of their shipbuilding and has stabilized the sales of the company. At the fourth level, top management makes decisions on the above three levels of competitive strength. At the fifth level, performance, especially profit, is an important resource for competition. The more profit the more competitive power, and thus a positive circular relationship starts.

What are then the key factors for successful competition in the first level? Successful Japanese companies that are competitive in world markets are found in industries such as shipbuilding, camera, watch, motor-cycle and motor-vehicle manufacturing, and steel-making.

Companies in the following industries are not competitive in world markets, even if they have a comparatively high share of production in the home market: the textile, aluminium, petrochemical, pulp and paper, laminated wood board and aircraft industries.

From this analysis, we find that quality and price (or cost) are two important keys for success in world competition. Japanese companies are strong in world markets in high-technology, high-quality-labour-intensive assembly products. They are weak in world markets in low-technology products (such as textiles), because they do not have a comparative cost advantage. They are weak in process industries where the costs of raw materials are a predominant concern. Thus where the industry needs to have superiority in development capability and production capability, the Japanese companies are strong. The development and production capabilities are supported by a large number of university graduates, and a capable, well-trained labour force. Where the costs of simple labour and raw materials are important factors for success and where the level of technology is low and product differentiation is difficult, Japanese companies are weak.

7.2 CASES OF COMPETITIVE STRATEGY

In order to understand the factors behind some of Japanese companies' successful competition in the world market, we will analyse the competitive strategy of successful Japanese companies.

7.2.1 The Shipbuilding Industry: The Mitsui Engineering and Shipbuilding Company

Before the war the UK was the largest shipbuilding country; Japan, Germany and France each built only 20 per cent as many ships. After 1956, however, Japan was producing 1 750 000 tons a year, and thereafter became the largest shipbuilding country in the world. Japanese shipbuilders have been the most successful from the 1950s until 1980 at least, although the future prospect is not clear.

The Mitsui Shipbuilding Company is one of the five successful large shipbuilding companies in Japan. (The big five are Mitsubishi, Ishikawashima-Harima, Mitsui, Hitachi and Sumitomo.) The reasons for their success are as follows:

1. The development of large and economical ships. The demand structure of the world ship market changed after the 1950s. The production of oil, iron ore and coal increased and the demand for large, specialized bulk carriers increased. Ship owners requested low price with quick delivery. Ship owners in Greece and Norway, oil refining companies and mining companies became important buyers, and they ordered boats from any country so long as the boats were economical and quickly delivered. They did not stick to a policy of buying ships built in their home countries.

Mitsui and the other four successful companies responded to the new demands by developing large, economical and standard boats. To build boats of over 100 000 tons, Mitsui Shipbuilding constructed two new shipyards, Chiba shipyards in 1962 and Yura in 1974, in addition to reconstructing two existing shipyards. In Europe no company constructed large shipyards until 1965.

2. Innovation in production methods. (a) Computerized production planning. Mitsui has been using computers in every area for many years. The number of necessary parts and materials are calculated by computer and ordered from suppliers. The company has only one week's inventory of steel, while it is said that European shipbuilders hold three months' stock. One year is spent in designing and planning; six months are considered enough for construction. (b) Module construction system. With the conventional system, the steel plates were welded to the ship piece by piece; thus welding was dangerous and inefficient mostly done in the open space using high scaffolding. The module construction method made it possible to apply mass-production principles. Large steel blocks are erected in a large assembly shop to become a module. The module is rotated into optimum positions for welding, and welders can work from the easiest position. The module is then re-rotated and transported by a self-propelling system to be attached to the ship under construction. The introduction of this system resulted in welding precision and operating efficiency. (c) Automation. The steel plates are cut to parts thus minimizing waste of material. Designing for this is done with the use of computers. With instruction cards from the computer, the gas cutting machine, which has a 17-metre span, cuts several different-shaped plates at one time. Pipe fabrication is also fully automated under computer control. Transportation in the yard is either done by huge rail cranes or by self-propelling devices on rails. These are examples of automatic operations.

3. Diversification. The demand for ships fluctuates from year to year. To stabilize the sales and profit, successful shipbuilding companies diversified into technology-related areas such as steel structure, large diesel engines, heating or refrigerating plants and process plant construction. Sales from shipbuilding account for only 30 per cent of sales in the case of Mitsui, 20 per cent in Mitsubishi Heavy Industry and Ishikawashima-Harima Industries. Other companies that did not diversify (Kure, Fujinagata, Uraga, Sasebo, Hakodate) were either taken over or went bankrupt.

4. Human elements. The above innovations were possible because the top management was aggressive. Top management invested money in expanding and modernizing the equipment, with the resulting equity ratio of only 11 per cent (1980). Middle management was highly

competent, approximately 20 per cent of employees being university graduates.

In the case of UK shipbuilding companies, top management was conservative and did not modernize the shipyards, middle management was thin, and a number of labour unions were not co-operating in the modernization of plants. In 1980 British shipbuilders employed about 86 000 men to build about 1 million tons of shipping, but Mitsui employ only 12 000 in all divisions, to build not only about half a million tons of shipping but also to produce other machinery.

7.2.2 The Camera Industry: Canon

Before the war German cameras dominated the world market. After the war Japanese cameras began to dominate the world still-camera market. In 1965 the number of Japanese cameras produced exceeded the volume of German products and now the Japanese share of the world camera market is about 30 per cent of the volume and about 66 per cent of the sales. It is expected that this share will increase further in the future, because German camera manufacturers are disappearing from the market. Rollei Werke filed for liquidation in 1981, an action that symbolizes the demise of some of West Germany's most renowned names. In order to meet the competition from Japanese cameras, Rollei decided to move its production to a low-wage area. In 1973 the company opened a 50-million-dollar plant in Singapore with 4800 employees, while the number employed in Germany was decreased from 3800 to 700. However, Rollei could not make a profit at this plant, because the sale of the cameras was far below the planned volume. The management did not realize that competitive power lies in the quality and design and in the production system, not in cheap labour. The Singapore plant had no research and development capability, and has had to be closed. The facilities have been tendered for sale.

What then are the reasons for the strong competitive power of the Japanese camera industry in general, and of Canon in particular?

1. New-product development with the introduction of electronic technology. The old camera was operated by gearwheel mechanisms, but now the camera is an assembly of electronic devices. The electronic eye camera was introduced by Canon in 1960. Besides electronics, a number of improvements were made. The large lens, the range finder, low- and high-speed lens shutter, focal-plane shutter, single-lens reflex camera system and flash system were all fitted to the ordinary low-priced camera. The new camera with these devices was also of reliable quality. In 1980

Canon developed an automatic focusing camera that was immediately successful. Olympus was the first to introduce a half-size camera.

These new-product developments had been supported by strong research and development activity. After the war many optical and mechanical engineers were recruited from the military laboratories. Canon now has a number of laboratories – a future-technology centre, a central product research laboratory and laboratories in two of its divisions; 700 people (excluding designers and drafters) who account for 8 per cent of the total workforce are engaged in research.

2. Large-scale production systems and quality control. Cameras used to be assembled by hand, but Canon and other successful camera manufacturers established mass-production systems with the use of aggressive capital investment. Canon introduced a production-line system in 1960, starting the mass production of Canonett, an electronic eye camera (automatic exposure camera), and sold it at one-third of the price of the equivalent camera at that time (a reduction from 100 dollars to 30 dollars). In 1961 a new factory was completed at Toride and 30 000 cameras were produced per month. This volume itself was an innovative change. Now manufacturing plants were built successively – Toride in 1960, Kanuma in 1963, Tamagawa in 1964, Fukushima in 1969, Taiwan in 1971, Utsunomiya in 1977. These factories are equipped with automatic fabricating machines, automatic assembly systems, automatic lens manufacturing systems and automatic inspection systems. This automation not only improved efficiency but also improved the quality of the products.

The new systems are designed by many competent production engineers. About 20 per cent of Canon employees are university graduates, and they provide a strong force of middle managers and engineers.

To motivate the ordinary employee to improve the quality, small-group activities and suggestion systems are encouraged. On average, ten suggestions per year are presented from each employee.

3. Strong marketing channels. Canon has built surprisingly strong sales channels. Canon Sales Company is engaged in domestic sales of cameras and other products, has thirty-four sales offices, 2000 employees and sells directly to retail stores. For overseas sales, under their international division, there are sales companies in the USA, Amsterdam, Latin America and France, with a total of 4500 employees. The total number employed in sales is 6500, which is 70 per cent of the workforce of Canon Incorporated in Japan (excluding Canon Sales Company). These sales channels are not only engaged in sales pro-

motion, but also in after sales service, which is an important factor in selling durable goods.

German camera manufacturers did develop new products, but the development was relatively slow and they shifted to low-grade cameras. For Japanese camera manufacturers innovation was necessary to survive the domestic competition. There were at one time thirty-six manufacturers but many of them have now disappeared from the market.

7.3 INTENSITY OF COMPETITION

The competitive power of Japanese corporations in the world market originates largely in the severe competition in their home country. In order to survive the competition at home the companies had to improve the quality of their products and had to introduce automated large-scale production to reduce their costs. The size of the market in Japan is sufficiently large that companies who could survive the competition in the home market found that their products were also competitive in world markets. Japanese consumers are very selective and demand high-quality goods, so the companies continually had to improve quality. The quality of cameras and of cars was thus initially improved. It is a misconception that Japanese industries are protected by MITI, and that competition is mitigated under the guidance of MITI.

In order to measure the intensity of competition, we will observe it from the three phases, structure of competition, behaviour and performance (Bain, 1968).

7.3.1 Structure of Competition

The structural determinants of competition are the number of competitors of similar size, amount of fixed cost, exit barriers, product differentiation and others (Porter, 1980). In growth industries in Japan there are many new entries, and the number of competitors is large. In the camera industry there were thirty-six manufacturers in 1950, and now there are only seven. There were forty companies producing electronic calculators in 1960, but now there are only four. As the industry matures, the number of manufacturers decreases, but several companies of similar size survive. Oligopoly, with similar-sized companies, is characteristic of the durable goods industry in Japan. Table 7.1 shows the share of production of the three largest companies in 1965 and in 1979.

TABLE 7.1 Share of production of larger companies in selected industries

Industry	Share of production of the largest three companies		Relative position of the largest (largest ÷ second largest)
	1965 %	*1980* %	*1980*
Shipbuilding	52	38	1.4 times
Cameras	25	62	1.2
Watches	86	92	3.2
Passenger cars	100	73	1.2
Motor-cycles	100	93	1.4
Colour televisions	—	61	1.4
Computers	—	64	1.3
Steel, cold plate	48	68	2.2

Source: Toyo Keizai (1981)*Keizai Tokei Nenkan* (Economic Statistics Year Book).

We can see that among these durable goods industries, the three largest occupy about 60 per cent of the market, and this share in some industries has slightly decreased over fifteen years. The size of share of the three largest is almost the same. Their relative position is measured by the ratio of the sales of the largest company divided by the sales of the second largest. As is seen in Table 7.1, it is about 1.3 times, excluding the watch industry. It is a generally accepted theory that competition in an oligopoly of similar-size companies is the most intensive.

7.3.2 Behaviour

Competition can be classified by behaviour into collusion, incomplete collusion, independent competition and cut-throat competition (Bain, 1968; Caves, 1964; Porter, 1980). Japanese companies are not allowed by anti-monopoly laws to practise collusion: the Anti-monopoly Commission is watchful regarding this behaviour. Japanese companies are strongly competition-oriented. Nakane ascribes this characteristic to organization-mindedness. Employees devote themselves to their organization and co-operate feeling that it will prosper for ever; but they see other organizations in the same business as opponents, because as competitors they stand in the way of survival and growth of their own company (Nakane, 1967).

The acquisition of other companies in the same line is not only restricted by anti-monopoly law, but is not chosen by management. A company is considered to be a community organization of employees who work for their lifetime, so it is not admirable to sell the company, nor it is admirable to buy another company.

7.3.3 Performance

Competition can also be classified into effective competition and ineffective competition by performance. The cost performance ratio is the most important measurement. It has improved in consumer durable goods industries. Taking cameras as an example, before the war the price of a high-quality camera such as Leica or Kontax was almost equivalent to the price of a house, but now the price of the highest-quality Japanese camera is about 200 dollars, and the price of a popular camera is about 30 dollars. The price of an electric calculator was about 1000 dollars in 1965, but a small electronic calculator is now only 20 dollars. The latter drastic price cut was initiated by Casio, whose low-price policy expanded market demand, and drove out competitors who could not establish large-scale production.

In the USA the quality of consumer durable goods is assessed in the *Consumer Report* and Japanese products are ranked highly. This is evidence of the improved performance of Japanese industries. The *Consumer Report*'s evaluation was very advantageous to Japanese manufacturers; it had a much greater effect than their advertisements.

Despite the competititon at home, aluminium, chemical products, paper, laminated wooden board and textile companies are not competitive in the world market. In these industries the factor costs are important and even new facilities could not overcome the disadvantage of higher factor costs.

7.4 PRODUCTION SYSTEMS FOR COMPETITION

The production systems of successful Japanese companies carry very few unprecedented principles; the characteristics for success lie in the over-all implementation of the basic principles.

7.4.1 Production Planning

US companies tend to rely on standard parts, whether they are produced within or bought from outside the company: interchangeable parts and components are used to the greatest extent. Thus the production plan is formulated by assuming that parts and components are prepared by other departments or companies, and there is no linked planning of the two sub-systems. It is then necessary to have enough stocks as a buffer. In the Japanese production system, production planning is more comprehensive; and as in Toyota's system, the sub-systems are linked and parts manufacturers have to synchronize their plans with Toyota's plan so that the right parts are supplied at the right place at the right time. Toyota's inventory level is minimized. This has become possible by the detailed production plannings of three years, six months and one month, and also because the parts manufacturers are members of Kyohokai, a group of quasi-vertically-integrated companies. Toyota's system is one extreme, but its practice is not unusual. Normally the parts have a series of order numbers, the order number being the same for identical products. The parts are manufactured not for stock but for the order. The inventory theory of minimum stock, maximum stock and ordering point is not applicable in this system (for inventory theory, see, for example Whittin, 1957).

Generally speaking, the production planning of successful Japanese corporations is detailed and the sub-systems are all linked. This was shown in the case of shipbuilding. The computer is fully used in drawing up the production plan.

The effect of this planning system can be seen not only in the economy of material costs or in the reduction of other idle costs, but also in that a greater variety of products, to meet the different demands of the consumers, is made possible at low cost.

7.4.2 Large-scale Production

The introduction of large-scale production systems is essential to survive the competition. This was shown in the case of the shipbuilding, camera and steel industries. The custom-built Rolls Royce is not part of the thinking of Japanese manufacturers. The 'round-table-like' workplace at Karuma plant of Volvo was studied but the concept rarely applied to production systems in Japan.

7.4.3 Modernization of Equipment and Automation

Mass production is made possible by new facilities. The successful Japanese companies have been aggressive in modernizing and expanding facilities. The average age of facilities of Japanese steel manufacturers in 1980 was about nine and a half years, while those of US manufacturers in 1979 was seventeen and a half years (survey by MITI, *Nikkei Newspaper*,

TABLE 7.2 Net fixed assets per employee and turnover of fixed assets in selected companies

	Net fixed assets per employee (1000 yen person)	Turnover ratio of fixed assets (sales net fixed assets)
Nippon steel	20 596	1.33
US steel	7 379	1.76
British steel	5 044	1.15
Hitachi	2 625	3.39
GE	1 996	3.76
GEC (UK)	773	4.23
Toyota	7 617	4.51
GM	2 234	5.50
Ford	2 831	4.88
BL Car (UK)	1 015	6.14

Source: MITI, 1980 (exchange rate 1 dollar = 210 yen, 1 pound = 403 yen).

3 November 1981). The level of modernization and automation can be measured indirectly by the ratio of fixed assets per employee. The successful Japanese companies have a higher fixed assets per employee ratio than US companies. According to a MITI survey, the figures are as shown in Table 7.2 (MITI, 1980).

This survey shows that the ratio of fixed assets per employee of Japanese selected companies is more than twice, and up to five times, as high as that of US or European companies. As a result, the turnover ratio of net fixed assets of Japanese companies is lower than that of the counterparts, but the difference is small, and the cost per unit is thus lower.

7.4.4 Quality Control

The method of quality control was imported from the USA, but Japanese corporations have invented some different systems and implemented quality control more thoroughly.

In the USA, quality control is carried out by inspectors at several checking points, and these inspectors are separated from those doing the work. In Japan there are independent inspectors, but, in addition to the formal quality-control system, the responsibility for maintaining or improving quality is vested in the workers and foremen. The identification of workers with their organization is strong, and they feel responsibility for quality. High quality is stressed by business creed and slogan; 'The high quality we make' is one example from a Seiko plant.

Cleanliness on the plant site is very strongly stressed. Cleaning the floor is not the responsibility of the cleaning staff, but of the site workers and foremen. It is not unusual to find the foreman engaged in cleaning. Clean floors are important both for improving quality and for improving morale.

Quality-control group activity or 'QC circle' is popular in most plants. With Honda, QC circle activity goes on throughout all the plants. At Wako Plant there are 152 circles, each circle comprised of seven or eight employees. Approximately 80 per cent of the employees are organized in QC circles. They meet before or after working hours and discuss how to solve selected problems. Overtime allowance is paid for such hours of activity, but not for all hours. Selected successful teams will make presentations at the annual meeting of the company. The QC circle movement not only improves quality, but also enhances morale through participation in the improvement (Nikkan Kogyo, 1980).

The suggestion system is another means for participation in improving quality and efficiency. At one Seiko plant (Takazuka plant), each employee presents fifteen ideas per year on average. The presented ideas are evaluated and a number of points are given. The point numbers of each employee are added up, and those who have a high number of points are awarded prizes – money and certificates of merit. The names of prize winners are listed and displayed.

The method of inspection of purchased materials and components is different from that used in US or European companies. The purchasing company will inspect the method of quality control of selling companies, rather than inspecting the incoming materials and parts. The buying company will work closely with the suppliers on quality-control measures and undergoes training in quality-control method. This system is favourable to both sides. It is made possible because the relationship between the buying and vending company is established on a long-term basis. The Japanese company does not change the relationship for short-term profitability. When the components are important ones for the buyer, the parts manufacturer will become one of the quasi-vertically-integrated companies.

The national prize system for quality control sponsored by one private organization, Nikkagiren (Japan Association of Technology), which is only a small training organization specializing in industrial engineering, gave a great stimulus to the elevation of the quality-control movement among Japanese companies. Companies that have excellent quality-control systems are selected from among many applicants by intensive inspection carried out by a committee of experts, and the prizes are awarded. The awards are published in the newspapers, and published through company advertisements. These prizes have high prestige value, symbolize the high quality of all the products of the company and have a great effect on sales promotion. Companies make efforts for many years in order to win a prize.

7.4.5 Equal Treatment of Workers

There is no differentiation in the company's treatment of blue-collar workers and white-collar workers. From the plant manager to newly hired workers, all wear the same uniform, all use the same dining-room and the same toilet facilities. The wage system, the method of payment, the bonus system and the hours of work are the same. Before the war there was differentiation, but after the war equal treatment became the norm. This change of attitude had several causes, such as the higher level of education and the diffusion of democratic ideas. This equal treatment results in a higher morale among the workers and a higher sense of responsibility – and therefore better-quality products. The above characteristics can be summarized into two features. One is larger systems approach which expands the stage, time and space for integration (sections 7.4.1.–7.4.4). Another is the involvement of ordinary employees for productivity and quality (sections 7.4.4 and 7.4.5).

7.4.6 Reasons Behind the Characteristics of the Production Systems of Successful Japanese Companies

First, the attitude of top management is the most important reason. Top management is growth-oriented and future-oriented; they are aggressive in introducing large-scale production systems and in putting large amounts of money into capital investment. They do this by borrowing money from the banks, at the expense of the equity ratio. The competititon is so intense that positive strategy is required to survive, and if the top management is conservative and sticks to a higher equity ratio, the company will lose its stability in the market.

Second, there are a large number of competent middle managers and engineers. University graduates account for 10–20 per cent of all employees, and they are capable of introducing the new computerized operation systems, and of introducing and designing automated production systems.

Third, the ability level of rank and file workers is high and homogeneous. Even the ordinary workers are uniformly well educated, and are well trained within the company. They can handle automated machines without difficulty. Under the lifetime employment system they are eager to learn all the necessary skills. The lifetime employment system also makes the workers feel that their employment is secure, and makes them co-operate in any modernization of the production system.

Fourth, funds for investment are provided by the banks, and banks support positive investment by manufacturing companies because it increases the demand for loans in the future. The banks have abundant resources for loans since the average savings per household is more than 20 per cent, and it goes to the banks. (Differences between production systems of Japanese and US car manufacturers is partly described in Abernathy, 1981.)

7.5 MARKETING SYSTEMS FOR COMPETITION

Marketing systems vary from industry to industry, and we will concentrate the analysis on consumer durable goods, where 'monopolistic competition' and 'oligopoly with product differentiation' are the dominant competitive structures.

7.5.1 Merchandizing and New-product Development

The successful Japanese companies have developed and improved new products continuously. For example, as we have seen in the camera industry, large lenses with slow shutters were attached to cameras at reasonable prices, and automatic exposure and flash systems were provided with ordinary cameras. These improvements were made possible as a result of research and new production systems. The improvements were equally revolutionary in the watch industry, in colour television and in electronic calculators.

Japanese companies did not follow a policy of selling low-quality products at low prices. The consumer wants quality goods. The cheap camera developed by Kodak was not accepted in Japanese markets, the cheap pin-lever watch did not sell well, the cheap watch mass-produced by Timex was not accepted either. Emphasis on quality was important for competitive strategy in the home market, and this principle worked well in the world market. Imported goods have to have something special.

A delicate sense for product planning is also important. The old Volkswagen was undoubtedly a good car from the viewpoint of the function of the car, but it had far fewer delicate devices than the Carola. The Japanese car has such devices as warning signals for the hand-brake, warning signals for reverse gear, rear windscreen washing and so on, in addition to the basic quality of the car. The improvement of the camera can be seen as a history of the additions of new devices, rather than the omission of unnecessary functions. Japanese products have to be quiet and small. The author lived in Santa Monica and in London and was surprised by the noise and vibration of the US or UK electric old-style washing-machine. The washing-machine, the refrigerator, the electric razor and the car have to be quiet and small since Japanese homes are small and the habitable spaces of the land are narrow. Products have to meet these demands in order to sell in Japan.

7.5.2 Price Policy and Credit Collection

There are two price policies, the cost-plus-profit policy (make-up price) and follow-the-market price policy (going-rate price) (Kotler, 1974). In the early stages of a product's life cycle, the cost-plus-profit policy is followed; in the later stages, follow-the-market policy is followed, and, when the competition is fairly intensive, the market price is based on the costs of the leading company which has the largest share of the market. Eventually the price is based on the cost.

Thus competitiveness of price is largely based on the cost of production, which reflects the level of innovation of the production method. The price of steel from the Nippon Steel Corporation in 1980 was about 90 per cent of the price of US Steel and 80 per cent of the price of ATH (West Germany) steel, and this difference was mostly based on the difference in production technology. The price of a small car from Toyota in Japan is about half the price of European small cars in Europe; this discrepancy too is largely based on the difference in production methods.

Historically the price also changed as the cost of production changed. There are three types of price change. The price of washing-machines went down as the volume of production increased and as the methods of production improved. This is type one. The price of steel sheet made from cold stripmill can be classified under type one, because the volume of production and improved technology could offset price increases in coal and iron ore. Prices of refrigerators and television sets decreased to a lesser extent, because the size and quality changed, although the change of volume of production and the technology changed. This is type two. The price of men's suits went up, because the factor costs

TABLE 7.3 Price differential for each stage of distribution

Stage of distribution	Colour television	Cosmetics (general)
Retail price	100 (%)*	100 (%)
Margin, retailer	22 ⎫	30 ⎫
	⎬ 26	⎬ 35
Discount from maker	4 ⎭	5 ⎭
Wholesale price	78	70
Margin, wholesaler	8 ⎫	15 ⎫
	⎬ 12	⎬ 20
Discount from maker	4 ⎭	5 ⎭
Wholesale price	70	55
Excise tax	8	—
Wholesale price excluding excise tax	62	55
Discount (total)	8	10
Net	54	45
Sales and administrtive expense	10	10
Cost of production	44	35

Note:
* The actual retail price is discounted by 10% or 20% in many cases.

increased and there were no changes of technology. This is the third type. Goods in this third group are losing in world-wide competition.

The price differential at each stage of distribution is another side of price policy. Table 7.3 shows cases of price differential of colour television sets and of cosmetics from cost of production to retail selling price.

It is surprising that the cost of production accounts for only 44 per cent (or 35 per cent) of the retail price, but this low percentage is not peculiar to Japan, it is common in many countries. This low percentage tends to induce the misunderstanding that Japanese manufacturers are dumping the price of export goods because the export price is quoted at 54 per cent, for example, of the retail price in Japan. The percentage of discount from manufacturers is larger in Japan than in the USA or in European competitiveness. Table 7.3 shows that it is 8 per cent (or 10 per cent in cosmetics). Because of this large discount, the retail price tends to be discounted, sometimes up to 20 per cent, because the retailer or wholesaler can make a profit from special discount if they give a large discount to the buyers. The discounts are sometimes equivalent to the ordinary profit margin for them, so the resale prices are the same as the buying price.

The system of special discount from manufacturers is complicated and confidential. The following is typical:

1. Quantity discount. The discount is given on the total sales in one month, not to the size of one lot of order. The percentage may be as much as 6 per cent, and can be even larger to larger buyers. This is not illegal according to the anti-monopoly law.
2. Goal achievement discount. This discount is given when the agreed amount of sales is achieved, the rate being 1–3 per cent.
3. Discount for the size and co-operation of the channel. The large resaler and co-operative resalers are awarded from $\frac{1}{2}$–2 per cent.
4. Cash discount. For example $1\frac{1}{2}$ per cent discount per month for payment within forty days or sixty days.
5. Special promotional discount. During a special sales campaign, $\frac{1}{2}$–1 per cent discount is given.
6. Seasonal discount. To promote the earlier reception of seasonal goods. The earlier the time, the higher the rate.

Among the above discounts, the quantity discount, cash discount and seasonal discount are also popular in the USA, but the rest are peculiar to the Japanese system. The successful company tries to reduce the margin and simplify the rebate by vertical quasi-integration of the sales channel; for example, Toyota and Matsushita both try to do this. By vertical integration the manufacturer can protect himself from a price war in the market, can sustain the list price, assure the profit to the distributors, and reduce the official margin and 'discount' to the necessary minimum.

The collection of sales credit tends to be loose. The salesman may say 'any time you can pay' and leave unordered goods with the store. Trade habits such as 2/10/30 (2 per cent ten days, net thirty days, that is, 2 per cent discount for payment within 10 days, the term of payment is thirty days) are not used. It is not unusual for the collection term to be as long as six months without any interest charge. This is one means of sales promotion. The fiercer the competition, the longer the time allowed for payment tends to be.

One of the reasons for this long term for collection comes from the popular use of the promissory note. This was widely used after the war, and its use does not imply distrust of the payer as is usually the case in the USA. The promissory note is safe, can be discounted (or bought) and paid by the banks before the end of the collection period, so the financial burden is transferred to the banks, at the cost of interest.

The successful companies try to collect payment over a short term, and try to establish clear systems of cash discount. Matsushita is very strict about collection, and tries to enforce cash payments everywhere in the world. This is made possible both by the quasi-integration of its sales channels and the competitive power of its products.

7.5.3 Sales Channel

The large and successful companies have strong sales departments or sales companies; they also have local sales offices, and exclusive sales channels. There are three models of distribution policy – the exclusive distribution channel, the selective channel and extensive distribution channel.

Where durable consumer goods are concerned, an exclusive policy or selective policy is commonly used by large and successful companies. Toyota has an exclusive distribution policy. It has 320 dealers with 2600 selling outlets which sell only Toyota cars. They are legally independent but are controlled by the sales department of Toyota (formerly Toyota Sales Company). They employ 33 000 salesmen in Japan. Nissan also has 2500 exclusive selling stores and 25 000 salesmen.

Matsushita has 120 wholesalers (exclusive), 25 000 quasi-integrated retail stores ('National Shop' whose sales of Matsushita products account for over 80 per cent of all sales), and another 25 000 quasi-integrated retail stores ('National Store', whose sales of Matsushita products are over 50 per cent). In addition, it has nineteen service companies which have 375 service stations. These are the sales channels in Japan. Matsushita has a similar channel policy in the Philippines and Malaysia. In the USA, the quasi-vertical integration of wholesalers and retailers is not so popular, but direct sales are usually made to the retailer or to other industry buyers. The sales policy of Zerox and Coca Cola uses this approach. In Britain, Lex Service Group is the most important distributor of British Leyland cars, but it is an independent dealer and sells Volvo cars also. Usually in these countries the wholesaler and the retailer do not like to be dependent on the manufacturers. But Japanese dealers are rather group-oriented and willingly co-operate with one manufacturer, trying to obtain a regular operation if the manufacturer is strong enough.

The characteristics of quasi-vertical-integration of dealers are as follows. In the case of exclusive distribution channels, only the products of the controlling company are sold, but with a selective distribution policy the products of competitors are sold to a limited extent. A sales territory is allocated to the channel so that responsibility is clear. A number of services are given by the manufacturer to the dealer, namely training of the top manager and employees, display shelves, outdoor advertisements, special discounts, guarantee against debts, and financial aid, among others. The manufacturing company has many training centres for managers and salesmen of the dependent distributors. An association of the dealers is forced and information is disseminated and exchanged through this association.

The merits of quasi-integration for the manufacturer are numerous. The list price is sustained and strong promotion can be expected with lower margins. Overlapping in transport and advertising can be eliminated. Information about new products is passed on well, and after-sales service is good. The advanced methods of management and marketing developed by the large manufacturers are transferred to the dealers. These all result in reduced distribution costs, and this in reduced final prices that are not only beneficial to the consumer but also increase the price-competitive power of large manufacturers.

There are some problems, however. Vertical integration does not reduce the competition between the manufacturers if there are plural dealers in the same area. If this restricts competition, they are subject to the scrutiny of the monopoly commission. But this is still advantageous to large manufacturers.

At the retail level, large independent distributors are increasing their share because they can display many brands and the consumer can compare the brands in one store. This is a serious problem for the integrated retailers, and they too would like to increase the number of brands they can offer to compete with the large-scale independent retailers.

At the wholesale level, these problems are fewer and quasi-integration is advanced to a greater extent. Trading companies like Mitsui and Mitsubishi are very strong independent wholesalers, but they are not used as sales channels by consumer durable goods manufacturers even in overseas markets. They are, however, used by the iron and steel industry and by the textile industry.

7.5.4 Marketing Strategy and Organization Structure

The organizational structure of sales varies depending on the level of diversification. A typical model is summarized as in Table 7.4.

This model is largely modified in Japan. The 'separation of the sales department from the production department' is a basic idea in Japanese organizational structure, and this means that even in diversified

TABLE 7.4

	Specialized company	*Diversified company*
Head office	Strong sales department	No department
Product division	—	Sales department
Export	International department	International department or product division
Local office	Unified local office	Local office for each division

companies sales and production are not integrated in the product division. In Matsushita's case there are strong marketing departments in the head office; each product division will sell the products to wholesalers, but it is controlled by head office. Exporting is operated by an independent subsidiary, Matsushita Trading Company, which has world-wide sales branches for all Matsushita products.

With Canon, the three product divisions do not have a sales department; the sales operation is taken care of by a subsidiary company, Canon Sales Company, and by the international department which has a number of foreign sales companies under its control. It goes without saying that such specialized companies as Toyota, Bridgestone Tire, or Nippon Steel have strong centralized sales departments.

The effects of the functional centralization of marketing departments, even in diversified companies, are as follows. First, it is possible to perform strong marketing operations to cope with an intensive competitive environment. Overlapping sales efforts by many product divisions are eliminated. Second, it is easier to strengthen the vertically integrated sales channels, because the same sales channels can be used commonly by different product divisions. There are disadvantages in this centralization, but many Japanese diversified companies perceive that centralization of marketing functions has greater advantages.

7.6 COMPETITION STRATEGY AND OTHER PRODUCT–MARKET STRATEGIES

7.6.1 Product Mix and Competition Strategy

When the product is technology-intensive, technical improvement and production method are the key factors for success, and when the product is not technology-intensive, then the marketing efforts are the key factors. These statements are self-evident, and can be seen in Table 4.6 on p. 85.

Technological improvement efforts can be measured by research and development expenditure. The percentage of research and development expenditure on sales in technology-related products companies (RMT and RT) is much higher than in other product-mix strategy companies. Marketing efforts can be measured by sales promotion expenditure, and its percentage in marketing-related products companies (RMT and RM) is much higher than in other companies.

7.6.2 Market Share and Product Mix

The market share is important in any product strategy. As seen in Table 4.6, there is no significant difference in share of market among different product–market strategies. This means that even in unrelated diversified companies, it is possible, and necessary, to hold a large share of the market.

7.6.3 Market Share and Multinational Management

For the success of multinational management, the company should have a high share of the market in the home country. According to the survey, there is no difference of share among high multinationals and low multinationals, as Table 6.2 indicates. These survey results do not deny the above statement, nor support it.

7.6.4 Market Share and World-wide Competitive Strength

The competitive strength of the product in the home market is necessary for competitiveness in the world market; this is a necessary condition, but it is not in itself a sufficient condition. There are four groups of products. The first group comprises cameras, cars, steel and motorcycles. The high share of production at home results in high competitive strength in the world. The second group comprises beer, cement and glass products. The high market share is not accompanied by world competitive strength, because of the high cost of transport and because of the lack of technological superiority. The third group is comprised of textiles, paper, petrochemicals and aluminium products. The temporary high share of home production never means world competitive power, because of the high ratio of factor costs. The home market share may become lower.

7.7 MARKET SHARE AND CORPORATE PERFORMANCE

7.7.1 The Share of Market and Rate of Return

A high share of the market is correlated with a high rate of return. (This is also stressed in the USA by PIMS and the growth-share matrix model (*Harvard Business Review*, Mar–Apr 1974, and Jan–Feb 1975; unpublished papers by the Boston Consulting Group).) The simple correlation coefficients between the market share and the rate of return and the growth rate of 102 companies over eighteen years are as shown in Table 7.5.

TABLE 7.5

	ROT *(return of investment)*	*GRT* *(growth rate)*
SHA (share)	0.216	−0.062
RAD (R and D)	0.457	0.209
SPR (sales promotion)	0.350	0.047

The market share has a high correlation with rate of return. Research and development and sales promotion are highly correlated with the rate of return. This indicates that competition strategy affects the profit to a great extent.

The share is not related to the growth rate. This means that the competition was so intensive that it was hard to increase both the market share and growth rate, and further that some companies had experienced a decline in the market share in the process of growth. (The correlation between the share and business growth rate was −0.062.)

7.7.2 The Share, Business Growth Rate and Performance

As stated above, the high market share results in a high rate of return. When the share and business growth rate are considered together, the results are a little different. The empirical analysis of growth-share matrix model (or BCG model or product portfolio model; unpublished papers by the Boston Consulting Group) in Japan has already been stated in Chapter 4.

The findings are as follows. The 'star' has high performance. This differs from the growth-share matrix model which says that the 'star' has only a moderate return and a shortage of cash flow, because of high investment. In Japan, the growth of the economy is high, and wages increase with length of service, so that growth is important to improve the profit, especially where there is no product differentiation.

Where there is product differentiation, even the 'dog' can show high performance; some companies in the confectionery industry, musical-instrument industry and machine-tool industry belong to this group. Because of product differentiation, the increased costs caused by slow growth were probably passed to the consumer in higher prices.

7.8. SUMMARY

Some companies have world-wide competitive strength and some do not. The strong companies have technology-intensive products, and weak companies have low-technology products whose competitive weakness is caused by higher factor costs. This chapter has analysed the companies with strong competitive advantages.

Competition in the Japanese home market is intensive, because the market shares of several top companies are of similar size. The intensive competition in the home market has enforced an improvement in quality and lowered costs, and those companies who can survive the competition find their products are also competitive in world markets. The camera and the car industries are typical examples.

There are four factors important for successful competition, that is, quality (including product design), price (or cost advantage), sales promotion and sales channels. In world markets, the quality and price of products are much more important than the other two factors. The competition is a company-wide all-out war, but according to our analysis the product development system and production system are more important than the marketing system in world-wide competition. The good product sells itself.

No new principles appear in the production systems of successful Japanese companies, but the basic principles have been applied and implemented honestly. Standardization of products, large-scale production with automated production facilities, quality control – these have all been practised in the shipbuilding, camera, steel and motor-car industries. Sophisticated planning systems using computers have helped to utilize the high level of investment. The just-in-time system is a typical planning system.

Middle management and staff are largely composed of capable university graduates who design and operate such systems and equipment. The above features can be summarized as a larger systems approach.

Another important approach is involvement of ordinary workers for productivity and quality. Quality control has been strictly implemented, and expanded to every area of management ('total quality control', TQC), and through the QC circle movement, all workers are motivated to improve quality through their own initiative.

The marketing system of Japanese companies is not as unique as many foreign businessmen maintain. Successful Japanese companies have a strong marketing department in their head office. Even in diversified companies the sales department is separated from product divisions. Marketing departments have given a strong stimulus towards improvement of products and new-product development. Competitive price has been less important than quality advantage, but prices have been reduced as mass production brought down manufacturing costs.

Price differentials at each stage of distribution are complicated by the use of a number of discounts. The collection period tends to be lengthy, and without explicit interest charges.

The sales channels for consumer durable goods are quasi-integrated, and this policy is followed in foreign countries as an important means of competition. Quasi-integration is preferred to direct sales. Although many people say that Japanese marketing channels are complicated, they are not in fact so very complicated; in any country there are wholesalers and retailers. What is different is that the sales channel is quasi-integrated. Yet more different is the trade system, especially the delivery, pricing and collection system.

7.8.1 Problems

7.8.1.1 Transitions in competitive strength

The Japanese cotton fibre and textile industry had a strong competitive position in the world before the war; it was replaced by the rayon industry, and finally by the synthetic fibre industry. Now none of these industries has competitive strength in world markets. The relative competitive positions have changed and other countries have the advantages. Formerly the cotton fibre industry in Japan was strong as a result of positive investment to improve equipment, and because of cheaper labour costs. These advantages have shifted to developing countries.

The Japanese synthetic fibre industry became the second largest producer in the world. This was made possible by improving production methods and by investing aggressively, and by using cheap oil. After the oil crisis, oil prices became higher than the price of natural gas, and the synthetic fibre industry is now losing its advantageous position. Industries in the USA and Canada are going to be more competitive.

In the shipbuilding industry, companies in developing countries are gaining a relative advantage by cheap labour. Japanese industries will specialize in high-technology ships, such as natural gas transporters. In the manufacture of low-class watches, companies in Hong Kong are producing the largest numbers of watches in the world, though many of the components are imported from Japan. Thus relative competitive strength changes as the key success factors change. Japanese industries have to re-evaluate their strength and weakness, and shift to higher technological products – such as computers, super LSI, robots and aircraft.

7.8.1.2 International friction

The total amount of Japanese exports is lower than that of the USA or West Germany. The ratio of export to total gross national product is much lower (13 per cent) than that of European countries. However, the Japanese shipbuilding industry, camera industry and motor-cycle industry have driven the same industries in the UK, West Germany and the USA from the market.

When the exported goods are the products of key industries (such as motor-cars, or micro-electronic products), which employ a large number of workers or which are basic to other industries or to national defence industries, then there is friction. International specialization is necessary to improve the productivity of labour and make the best use of the natural resources of the world, but changes of specialization affect a number of sectors of society, so it must be done gradually.

Some industries will have to continue to operate for national security, without regard to their economic performance. Japan cannot import all her food; rice will have to be produced, whatever the cost. A minimum production of aluminium is another example. In advanced countries, car manufacturing cannot be replaced by imports, but local production by foreign multinational companies may be tolerable.

7.8.1.3 Japan's future competitive strenth

Japanese industry will have to shift to high-technology products, and the problem for Japan lies in whether her companies can get a comparative advantage in these industries in the future. In the past Japanese companies bought licences of original invention, and with applied research and sophisticated production processes were able to manufacture competitive products; for instance automatic focus cameras, crystal quartz watches, colour television sets, computers and LSI. In the future, the purchase of original inventions will become more difficult, and Japanese organization will have to become more creative. This will be studied in Chapter 8.

The competitive strength of successful Japanese companies came from several factors, namely, the aggressive attitude of top management, abundant capital for investment based on the high saving ratio of Japanese households, the large number of engineering graduates, the devoted attitude and high skill of ordinary workers. These are key areas of the resource structure, which all contributed to quality and cost advantage of Japanese products. The problem is whether these advantages will continue in the future.

REFERENCES

Egawa, A. (1980) Canon, Tokyo, Asahi Sonorama.
Kibi, M. (1980) Hitachi, Tokyo, Asahi Sonorama.
Kono, T. (1974) *Keiei Senryaku no Kaimei* (Analysis of Corporate Strategy), Tokyo, Diamond Sha.
Kono, T. (1980) *Senryaku Keiei Keikaku no Tatekata* (Introduction of Strategic Planning), Tokyo, Diamond Sha.
MITI (1978) *Atarashii Keiei-ryoku Shihyo* (New Indices for Corporate Capability), Tokyo, MITI.
MITI (1980) *Sekai Kigyo no Keiei Bunseki* (Financial Analysis of Corporations in the World), Tokyo, Ministry of International Trade and Industry.
Morizumi, Y. (1962) *Dokusen to Kyoso no Hanashi* (Introduction to Competition and Monopoly), Tokyo, Nihon Keizai.
Murata, S. (ed.) (1973) *Gendai Marketing Ron* (Marketing), Tokyo, Yuhikaku.
Nakane, C. (1967) *Tateshakai no Riron* (Vertical Society), Tokyo, Kodansha.
Nikkan Kogyo (1980) *Honda no Sho Shudan Katsudo* (Small Group Activity of Honda), Tokyo, Nikkan Kogyo.

Toyo Keizai (1981) *Keizai Tokei Nenkan* (Economic Statistics Year Book), Tokyo, Toyo Keizai.

Uno, M. and Tajima Y. (ed.) (1970) *Hanbai Keikaku* (Marketing Planning), Tokyo, Yuhikaku.

Yamaguchi, Y. (1980) *Shinnihon Seitetsu* (Nippon Steel), Tokyo, Asahi Sonorama.

Abernathy W. J. *et al.* (1981) 'The New Industrial Competition', *Harvard Business Review*, Sept–Oct.

Bain, J. B. (1968) *Industrial Organization*, New York, John Wiley.

Buzzell, R., Gale, B. and Sultan, R. (1975) 'Market Share, a Key to Profitability', *Harvard Business Review*, Jan–Feb.

Caves, R. (1964) *American Industry, Structure, Conduct, Performance*, New Jersey, Prentice-Hall.

Chamberlin, E. (1946) *The Theory of Monopolistic Competition*, Cambridge, Mass., Harvard University Press.

Engel, J. F., Fiorillo, H. F. and Gayley, M. A. (eds) (1972) *Market Segmentation*, New York, Holt, Rinehart & Winston.

Frohman, A. L. (1982) 'Technology as Competitive Weapon', *Harvard Business Review*, Jan–Feb.

Hall, R. J. and Hitch, J. R. (1939) 'Price Theory and Business Behaviour', *Oxford Economic Papers*.

Hofer, C. W. and Schendel, (1978) *Strategy Formulation, Analytical Concepts*, New York, West Publishing.

Kollat, D. Blackwell, R. and Robeson, J. (1972) *Strategic Marketing*, New York, Holt, Rinehart & Winston.

Kotler, R. (1974) *Marketing Management*, New Jersey, Prentice-Hall.

Porter, M. E. (1980) *Competitive Strategy, Techniques for Analyzing Industries and Competitions*, New York, Free Press.

Robinson, E. A. G. (1931†1958) *The Structure of Competitive Industry* (1958), Cambridge University Press.

Rothchild, W. E. (1976) *Putting It All Together*, New York, American Management Association.

Schoeffler S., Buzzell, R. and Heany, D. (1974) 'Impact of Strategic Planning on Profit Performance', *Harvard Business Review*, Mar–Apr.

Whittin, T. W. (1957) *The Theory of Inventory Management*, Connecticut, Greenwood Press.

8 New-product Development

New-product development is one area of strategic decision-making. This chapter and the next deal with the process of decision-making in Japanese corporations. The analysis in this chapter is based on the detailed analysis of more than fifteen cases and two mail questionnaire surveys conducted in 1980. (The method of survey is explained in Appendix 8.1.)

8.1 NEW-PRODUCT DEVELOPMENT AND PERFORMANCE

Seiko company was the first to develop the crystal quartz watch and came to hold the largest share in the world market. Honda developed a good-quality small motor-cycle and they too soon dominated the world market. Japanese camera manufacturers were sensitive to the change of demand and to the change of technology, and they developed the electrically controlled automatic shutter mechanism, the mini-sized camera, and auto-focus camera, and successfully competed with the German camera manufacturers. In the area of shipbuilding, Japanese shipbuilders found that the new demand was for bulky goods carriers, for instance crude oil carriers, and they made all-out efforts to produce large, standardized, low-priced ships, using innovative production methods. The shipbuilders also diversified into several areas by introducing new products, to override the fluctuating demand for boats. These are the reasons why they too began to dominate the world shipping market.

New-product development enables the company to strengthen its competitive power by introducing an improvement product like the quartz watch. It also changes the product mix by introducing a product with a different use from the present product. It releases the company from the life cycle of one product.

According to our survey in Japan, successful companies developed more new products than the unsuccessful companies did (for definitions,

211

TABLE 8.1 Expenditure for new-product development

	Successful companies (157 co.) %	Unsuccessful companies (4 co.) %
(1) Expenditure for research and development (% on sales)	1.92	1.18
(2) Expenditure for merchandizing (expenditure for market research, designing and marketing) (% on sales)	0.95	0.49
(3) Expenditure for new-market development after sales of new product (excluding capital investment (% on sales)	1.31	0.75
Total	4.18	3.42

see Appendix 8.1). In the case of successful companies, new products developed within the previous five years account for 21 per cent of sales and 23 per cent of profit. Unsuccessful companies in the same industry have a lower ratio, 14 per cent of sales and 19 per cent of profit. These survey results show that even in five years the new products contribute to the growth of sales and improvement of profit. (We should know that the profit rate of successful companies is larger and the percentage is devaluated.) (Average percentage on sales and profit are approximately the same as the survey results in the USA: Pessemier, 1977.)

The resource allocation for new-product development is also related to the performance. According to this survey, the differences were as shown in Table 8.1.

This number does not include the research expenditure for production process, but does include the marketing expenditure, so it is different from the survey on research and development expenditure. It is a resource allocation for the activity of new-product development; it is not the resource allocation for structure, which is studied later.

8.2 CONCEPT AND KEYS FOR SUCCESS

8.2.1 Definition of New Product

A new product is a product with a new brand name, which is added to the company's existing sales. Simple improvement is excluded. A product

TABLE 8.2 Classification of new products

Technology \ Use	Same as the existing products or similar to them	Different use	
		Marketing-related	Marketing-unrelated
Same as the existing products or similar to them	(H) Existing products improvement, complimentary products	(A) Marketing- and technology-related new products	(B) Technology-related new products
Different	(J) Substitutes, Complimentary products	(C) Marketing-related new products	(D) Unrelated new products

TABLE 8.3 Illustration of new products of a camera and film company

Technology \ Use	Same as the existing products or similar to them	Different use	
		Marketing-related	Marketing-unrelated
Same as the existing products or similar to them	(H) (Film and camera) Colour film of ASA 200	(A) Magnetic tape	(B) Industrial chemicals
Different	(J) Video camera	(C) Electronic calculator; copying machine	(D) Housing construction

Note: If companies are diversified, most of the new products are classified as (H) or (J).

already on the market can be a new product because it can still have the effect of releasing the company from the life cycle of its existing products.

The classification of new products is shown in Table 8.2. The reason why the 'use' is used for classification is that when the use is different then the product life cycle is different. (For a similar classification, see Ansoff, 1965; Pessemier, 1977.)

An illustration of new products classification is shown in Table 8.3. The company's major product is camera and film.

The reader will find that the classification in Table 8.2 is similar to the classification of product mix shown in Table 4.2; the principle is the same. There is a difference, however; the product mix is a static situation, the new-product development is a movement, and changes the product mix. The defect of this classification is that if the company is already diversified, then all the new products fall into the (H) or (J) classification.

8.2.2 Distribution of New Products Over the Past Five Years

In 1980 the author conducted two kinds of mail questionnaire survey. One was a survey on the development system and made a comparison between the systems of successful companies and those of unsuccessful companies. The other examined the characteristics of successful products and failure products, by asking a number of questions about the characteristics of the major products developed over the past fifteen years, without disclosing the intention of the questionnaire. (The details of the survey method are explained in Appendix 8.1.)

According to this survey, the distribution of success products and failure products is as shown in Table 8.4. The results show that there had been many improvement products (H), and substitute products (J), especially among successful products. Many failure products were to be found in the area of C (marketing related) and D (unrelated products).

TABLE 8.4 Distribution of new products by classification
Distribution of successful products (S) and failure products (F).

Use Technology	Same as the existing products or similar to them		Different use			
			Marketing-related		Marketing-unrelated	
Same as the existing products or similar to them	(H) %		(A) %		(B) %	
	S 17	F 15	S 14	F 10	S 7	F 10
Different	(J) %		(C) %		(D) %	
	S 30	F 17	S 17	F 22	S 13	F 24

Notes:
[1] Total number of new products was 358. Successful products (S) were 235 and failure products (F) were 123.
[2] Total sum of percentage of S is 100%, and the same in case of F.
[3] Percentage is computed by number of products, not by the number of sales.
[4] For method of survey, see Appendix 8.1.

8.2.3 Ratio of Survival

Few ideas presented survived to be sold in the form of products on the market. 33.1 per cent of the first ideas proceeded to the technical development stage, and 47.1 per cent of those that finished the technical development stage proceeded to commercial development or merchandizing stage, and then 55.9 per cent of that stage advanced to the full-scale production and marketing stage. The total survival ratio is 8.7 per cent $(0.331 \times 0.471 \times 0.559 = 0.087)$.

This is the situation in successful companies; the percentage in unsuccessful companies is a little lower. At first glance we need twelve ideas to yield one successful product – but since one out of three commercialized products (123 out of 358 products) is a failure product, ultimately eighteen ideas are needed in order to arrive at one successful product.

8.2.4 Four Directions of New-product Idea

There are four sources of ideas for new products. The first source is the needs of the market, which accounts for 72 per cent of the number (not the sales amount) of successful products. The second one is from the seeds, or from the technical possibility, which accounted for 25 per cent of successful products. The third is the needs (or policy) of the company and accounts for 6 per cent of successful products. The fourth is imitation, or the success of other companies, which accounts for 22 per cent. (Total percentage is over 100, because of overlapping sources.) (The distribution of sources of ideas for failure products is not very different from that of success products.)

These sources show what kinds of information are needed, and in what direction the company antenna has to be oriented. The information on the needs of the market seems to be the most important (see Appendix 8.2).

8.2.5 Key Success Factors

Key success factors were asked using an unstructured question, and also a structured question. Both answers showed very similar results. Table 8.5 shows the answers to the structured question, and they are arranged so that the success factors and failure factors are contrasted. The failure factors of success products are omitted, and the success factors of failure products are also omitted, because they have low frequency.

It is interesting to discover that the same factors can be important both as success factors and failure factors. We see from Table 8.5 that there are four key factors. The first one is the support of top management. The second one is the organizational structure. Strong research capability and marketing capability are needed. In addition, the fitness of new products with these capabilities; synergy is important. The third factor is market-orientedness. Sufficient marketing research is required for success. The fourth factor is the behaviour of the people involved in development–and the importance of having a strong promoter. The uniqueness of the product may be the result of all the foregoing factors, and intervening variable to the final success.

TABLE 8.5 Key success factors for new-product development

Success factors of success products %		*Failure factors of failure products* %	
1. Support of Top		1. Support of Top	
Support of top management	30	Support of top management	3
2. Structure		2. Structure	
Capable research and development department	54	Weak research and development capability	20
Fitness with the present technology and facilities	36	Insufficient production technology and facilities	15
Good fitness with marketing capability	22	Insufficient marketing capability	24
Strong marketing channel	21	Weak sales channel	18
Good development system	3	Poor development system	7
Abundant fund	2	Insufficient fund	1
3. Market-orientedness		3. Market-orientedness	
Good marketing research to find the needs	26	Insufficient marketing research	34
Right segmentation	23	Unclear segmentation (or error in it)	11
Timing of entry	31	Timing of entry	17
4. Promoter		4. Promoter	
Strong promoter of new product	26	Strong promoter was lacking	10
Atmosphere of the organization was supportive	8	Conflict between development and marketing	3
5. Uniqueness		5. Uniqueness	
Unique products (good cost performance)	40	Not unique products (cost performance was not good)	31

Notes:
[1] The number indicates the percentage of products that had these factors.
[2] For method of survey, see Appendix 8.1.

We will analyse these factors in detail in the following pages. These key factors are much the same as the keys for success in the domestic market. It may be dangerous to extend the analogy to the world market, but we assume that the same factors can in fact be applied to the products that are sold in world markets.

8.3 POSTURE OF TOP MANAGEMENT, AND LONG-RANGE PLANNING

The new product needs to have a new orientation. It is risky, it needs new allocation of resources, and it has a large impact on the performance, and top management has to take a strong initiative. Whether top management takes a short view or a long view, whether it is conservative or aggressive, are all important in the introduction of successful new products. Top management will (i) lay down the basic policy for development of the new product and see that information is collected about new demand and the capability of the company to meet it, (ii) formulate the structure for development, (iii) motivate the inventor, and (iv) evaluate the new product. In other words, top management will 'plan, organize, motivate and control' the new-product development. This would seem to be a matter of course; however, it is not necessarily so, and there are great variations from company to company.

Top management of successful shipbuilding companies were able to foresee the new demand for marine carriers. As a result they decided to produce bulk carriers to introduce new methods of mass production, while top management among British shipbuilders failed to do so.

Toyota and Isuzu were almost the same-size companies and had almost the same level of expertise before the war, but top management of Isuzu could not foresee that there would be greater demand for passenger cars than for freight trucks. Toyota now is five times the size of Isuzu.

Nippon Electric and Oki Electric were also very similar companies, who started to produce telephone equipment in about 1900. However, top management of NEC was more sensitive to new opportunities, and started very early to invest in research and to produce, first, vacuum tubes, followed by microwave communication systems, computers and integrated circuits. Top management of Oki was satisfied with its existing comfortable position as the main supplier for Nippon Telephone and Telegraph company, a monopoly public corporation, which gave it enough profit on a cost-plus-fee contract. The sales of NEC are now more than four times as large as those of Oki.

Top management of Sony and Honda were originally technical inventors, and they themselves invented the transister radio and small motor-cycle. However, they were not only inventors, they were organizers at the same time. In early times, Honda worked with Fujisawa who took charge of organizational management. The two worked to complement each other. When the company introduced their small passenger car in addition to the motor-cycle, and when the company discontinued their best-selling mini car to introduce the new small car CIVIC, and when the company invented a new pollution-free CVCC engine, on each occasion the top management took strong initiatives.

At Sony, Ibuka and Morita co-operated closely. The former was more technology-oriented, the latter more management-oriented. Both were deeply involved with the invention of a new type of colour television, Trinitron, using a new technology different from RCA Technology. Now Sony introduces more than 100 new products in one division in a year, so top management's role is to lay down the basic policy and organize the new-product development.

Simple aggressiveness by itself can be dangerous, however. Top management of Kojin, the pulp and rayon manufacturer, was very aggressive in diversifying into flame-resistant textiles, drugs, housing construction and real estate. It went bankrupt after the oil crisis. Their policy was not based on enough information; there was not enough long range planning to integrate the allocation of resources; the president was too authoritative; the management committee did not work effectively.

All these facts point to the importance of basing policy on adequate information about consumer demand, and on long-range planning.

Then the problem is whether all the ideas put forward are based on long-range planning and related to the policy of the corporation. The practice of successful companies can be seen from the following questions and answers on method of idea generation (Table 8.6).

This survey makes clear that not all ideas are based on a policy or on long-range planning, even in the case of successful companies. (The reader should understand that about 70–80 per cent of large Japanese corporations have long-range planning.) More than 50 per cent of formulation is done outside the long-range planning process. Ideas are being generated all the time and at every level of the hierarchy, so it is natural that more than 50 per cent of ideas are presented by a piecemeal approach.

This is especially the case for very new ideas in the early stages, clear

TABLE 8.6 Method of idea generation

'From which sources are you most likely to obtain ideas for successful new products? (Please select (a) or (b).)'	*Successful companies* %
(a) As a part of comprehensive long-range planning	45
(b) From piecemeal presentation	54
(a) From a policy of research to collection of ideas.	54
(b) From the collection of ideas	45
(a) From aggressive research	61
(b) From ideas brought in from outside	38

Notes:
[1] The number indicates the percentage of companies.
[2] For survey method, see Appendix 8.1.
[3] The distributions are slightly different from Table 9.5, because the subjects are different, but roughly speaking the percentages are similar to those in Table 9.5.

policy for new-product development orientates the direction of information collection and idea generation, and this results in the aggressive search for new opportunities and in the motivation of research and development teams. The survey shows that in more than 50 per cent of cases the policy is formulated first and ideas are generated following the policy. (Long-range planning is useful to build the right policy for new-product development. The other survey shows that the policy of new products are formulated to a great extent in the long-range planning process.)

The aggressiveness of search is asked, and in the majority of successful companies (61 per cent of respondents) aggressive search, rather than waiting for outside sources, is conducted. Aggressive and appropriate policies require top management that is sensitive to new opportunities. This is possible when the company has (i) many top managers with technological backgrounds, and (ii) a team group at the top level. These characteristics of Japanese corporations were studied in Chapter 2.

8.4 ORGANIZATIONAL STRUCTURE FOR DEVELOPMENT AND SYNERGY

New-product development is different from the routine operation of production and sales; it needs to have a special department. Strong research and development departments are relatively new in Japan, but in size and manpower these departments in successful Japanese companies are comparable to corresponding departments in the strongest companies in the world.

The structure of a strategy-generating department, especially its research and development aspects, will be analysed in Chapter 10. Here we will state a few characteristics of the research and development organizations in successful Japanese firms. They are as follows:

1. The scale of such departments is expanding; in particular the percentage of research staff among all employees is higher than the percentage of expenditure. The staff in research and development departments are mostly university graduates, and it is easy to increase the numbers of research staff because of the large supply of university graduates majoring in engineering and science.

2. Project teams are formed frequently, and the joint knowledge and experience from a number of different functions is easily mobilized. Co-operation between a variety of functions is made easier with laboratories centralized under the head office, a structure of organization by function rather than by division. They make it easier to assemble interfunctional project teams and to have transfer of knowledge between the functions.

3. Research worker's motivation is high. They work day and night, they may even bring sleeping-bags to the laboratory. It is generally accepted that the members of the development team work harder than any other employees, and this devoted attitude to their work, rather than the system itself, is the main reason why the period of time for new-

TABLE 8.7 Fitness with existing capability and probability of success

Technology \ Use	Same as the existing products or similar to them	Different use	
		Marketing-related	Marketing-unrelated

Same as the existing products or similar to them	(H) S 0.68
	     F 0.32
		(A) S 0.72
		     F 0.28
			(B) S 0.57
			     F 0.43

Different	(J) S 0.77
	     F 0.23
		(C) S 0.60
		     F 0.40
			(D) S 0.51
			     F 0.49

Notes:
[1] Succesful products (S) were 235, and failure products (F) were 123.
[2] S and F in the cell were added, and the percentage shows the probability of success or failure in the same cell.
[3] For method of survey, see Appendix 8.1.

product developments is said to be shorter in successful Japanese companies than in US or European companies.

The new product should be unique and it should have a good fit not only with the capabilities of the development department but also with those of the marketing and production departments. The new product should have synergy effects with other products and with existing capabilities. Table 8.7 shows that this synergy is an important factor of success. We find that new products in cells H, J and A have a higher probability of success because of synergy with other products. If the new product is similar technologically to existing products then it can utilize the existing development and production capacities and expand them. This is a kind of mass-production effect and is advantageous both for the new product and for existing products. Similarly, if the new product can be marketed in the same way as existing products, it can utilize the existing marketing facilities and can expand them too. If the use of the new product is the same as that of existing products (H and J) then it is obvious that the marketing capability will be the same. Table 8.7 shows that when the new product is related to existing technology, or existing marketing capability, the probability of success is high. We find that in the cells H, J, and A the probability of success is much higher than in B, C and D, which demonstrates that synergy is important for success. (For the concept of synergy, see Ansoff, 1965.)

8.5 INFORMATION FOR NEW-PRODUCT DEVELOPMENT AND EARLY TIMING OF ENTRY

There are several stages in the development of a new product (see Figure 8.1): (1.1) collection of information on general opportunity and threat, (1.2) building basic policy, (1.3) generation of new-product idea, (2) technical development, (3) commercial development, (4) capital investment for mass production and mass sales. Here we are concerned with the information relating to stage (1.3), the information necessary to generate the original idea.

There are two points of debate on the generation of new-product ideas. The first one relates to the different attitudes of the inventing companies, whether they hold that 'the manufacturer knows the consumer's real needs and can teach the consumer', or that 'the consumer is God'. The attitude that the manufacturer knows better than the user is sometimes taken by European manufacturers. Japanese manufacturers tend to put emphasis on the needs of users.

222

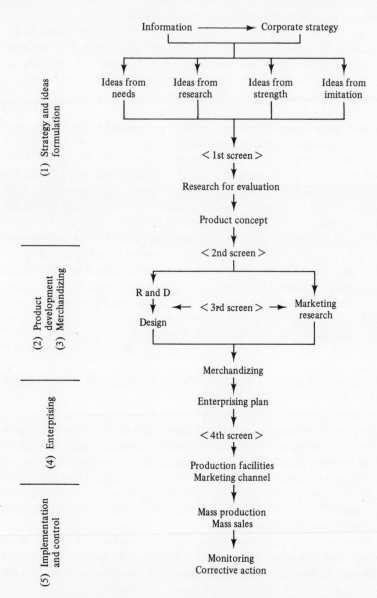

FIGURE 8.1 A model of the process of new-product development

The other point relates to the relative importance of creative intuition or the collection of information. This is concerned with the creative process of invention, about which many research papers have been written. It is also a problem for new-product development. Simply speaking, successful products are the results of a thorough collection of information. To persuade the people involved in the characteristic group decision-making process of Japanese corporations, thorough and sufficient information must be collected beforehand.

These two characteristics have resulted in successful products, and in products with many delicate devices. The 'Walkman' personal stereo cassette player by Sony Corporation is a successful product; around 3 million sets, priced at about 100 dollars, have been sold in a year. It is a unique product: with playing capacity only, it is small, light and produces wonderful stereo sound with small headphones, enjoyable in any place without disturbing other persons.

This was made possible by gathering enough information about the market in addition to technical development. There was a trend for stereo players to become smaller, and personal use of these sets was increasing. The tape as a medium of music was becoming more popular than records. Sony was already selling small-sized tape-recorders, but it was felt there could be a demand for a very small stereo player. If the tape-recording function is excluded, then 40 per cent of space can be saved, and that space can be used for improving the quality of tape playing. All this information pointed towards the possibility of the Walkman. Furthermore, a high-quality small headphone had already been developed at the request of the sales department of the division, and was looking for more use.

It took three years to finish the development after the idea was first put forward. In the course of development, the response from the sales channel was very cold. An expensive small player, without recording capacity, was thought unlikely to compete with the small tape-recorders that were flooding the market. The development team was not confident of success. At that time the president Morita came to see the sample, immediately found that the sound was splendid, and by encouraging the developing team to go ahead gave a great stimulus to the team and to the project as a whole. This story shows, first, that information about market trends was important for success, and second, that a decision at top level played a great part in promoting development.

There are four sources of ideas for new products. A survey was conducted on the kinds of information collected to instigate the successful new product, and the result is shown in Appendix 8.2. The first source is information about consumer needs; the second source is information about successful products that the company can imitate; the third is information about technological needs. The fourth is about the capability of the producing company.

The survey results show that successful Japanese corporations gather information extensively, and regularly – especially a variety of information on consumer needs.

The information collection is classified into regular scanning, and gathering of information after the idea has been put forward. The former is more important because the timing of entry into the market is important for success. The earlier the niche is found, the more time can be spent on development, and the earlier the market entered.

The information listed in Appendix 8.2 is quite different from internal information for control. The company needs to establish a strategic information system, and needs to be outward-looking and future-oriented to be successful.

8.6 FROM WHOM THE NEW IDEA COMES

The ideas for successful new products come from many directions and many departments, as shown in Figure 8.1. The basic strategic policy will be presented by top management and by the planning department. Ideas from consumer needs will be presented by the development department and marketing department. Ideas from needs will also be presented by the development department and the marketing department. Actual practices in idea presentation are shown in Table 8.8. The survey results show two things. First, many successful ideas are presented by top management. According to the author's observation, the first idea for the following successful products were produced from the top down or by an interactive process: Honda CIVIC, Honda CVCC engine (anti-pollution engine), Seiko's crystal quartz watch, Konishi's auto-focus camera, Canon's copying machine, Sumitomo's optical communication fibre, Toray's synthetic leather 'Ultrasuede'. Second, many ideas are presented by specialized development departments. This may be called a bottom-up approach, or an interactive approach. This survey shows the importance of structure – the importance of setting up a development department, planning department and research laboratory.

There are some new products that have been developed privately, as it were, unofficially or developed 'under the table'. It is dangerous to

TABLE 8.8 From whom the idea comes

'Who presented the idea for successful new products?'

	Successful companies (157 co.) %
(1) Top management	53
(2) Development department	70
(3) Planning department	29
(4) Research and development laboratory	44
(5) Production and technical department	58
(6) Sales department	73
(7) Salesmen	15
(8) Sales channel	28
(9) General employees	4
(10) Customer	55
(11) Personnel in overseas office	2
(12) Universities	6
(13) Other research organizations	6
(14) Others	11

Notes:
[1] The number indicates the number of companies responding that this department is important for idea presentation. There are overlappings, so the total number is more than 100%.
[2] For method of survey, see Appendix 8.1.

generalize on this, however, as a typical mode of new-product development in Japan.

8.7 HUMAN SIDE OF DEVELOPMENT PROCESS

The success of new-product development depends on the enthusiastic and dedicated activity of the development team supported by top management. One president of a successful company states that success depends on three factors – the approach, the capability and the enthusiasm. The author wants to emphasize enthusiasm here, because it is the important feature of Japanese corporations.

8.7.1 The Case of the Seiko Quartz Crystal Watch

In 1958 a very large clock, as large as a freight truck, was completed at one of Seiko's plants. This was the first crystal clock, using many vacuum tubes. The top management of Seiko companies were aware that the use of crystal technology was the future key technology.

In 1959 a project team was formed at Suwa Seiko Company to study the crystal watch to be used in the Olympic Games in Tokyo in 1964. The team was led by Mr Nakamura, a 35-year-old engineer, who had been with the company for fifteen years. (Suwa Seiko, a division of Seiko companies, had been recruiting many graduate engineers for a long time.) The team had about ten members, and they analysed not only the crystal watch, but also the tuning-fork mechanism and hourly-correction mechanism by time broadcasting. After comparison, they decided to focus on the crystal watch. Bulova in the USA was using the tuning-fork mechanism in the 1960s.

In addition to the research room, a room floored with tatami, a kind of resilient straw matting, was provided so that the research team could sleep when they worked late. Sometimes they worked overnight. After two years, in 1961, they had succeeded in producing a crystal watch small enough to be held in the palm of the hand.

Then a basic concept was decided by the top management of division. It should (i) be small enough to be used as a wrist-watch, (ii) include an anti-shock mechanism, (iii) use little electric power. In order to achieve these objectives, three technical breakthroughs were necessary – the development of a small motor, invention of a small crystal device and development of small integrated circuits. One group tackled the size of motor, and since a new jump of thought was necessary, they took the existing motor to pieces and re-created an open-type motor. Thus they arrived at the idea of using a stepping motor, more convenient for the watch motion than the conventional motor. These inventions were the result of the enthusiastic day and night activity of the team.

The second problem was how to minimize the size of crystal. The research team arrived at the idea of using the tuning-fork shape for the crystal. By using this shape, they decreased the size and made the crystal shock-proof.

In 1969 the new crystal wrist-watch was announced to the world, and the watch was sold in the market at a price of 450 000 yen (2000 dollars). In 1970 top management decided to go into full-scale production in the near future.

At this time, the third problem, however – how to obtain small integrated circuits – was still unsolved. The company wanted to buy them from outside, but found no company capable of producing such small ICs, so it was again decided to produce them themselves. A thirteen-member team was formed in 1969 and they began the study of

IC from the beginning, under the direction of two professors of engineering, with the special aim of producing small ICs.

In 1971 the small wrist-watch was completed, and full-scale production and mass sales followed. It had taken thirteen years since the first large crystal clock was invented, and eleven years since the project teams were formed. With this quartz crystal watch the Seiko companies greatly increased their share of the world market.

In Switzerland, the manufacturers joined together in 1962 to establish an electronic watch centre to develop a new time-determining device. To begin with, the tuning-fork type was emphasized but latterly they turned to the crystal quartz watch. It was not clear whether the development was successful or not, because Swiss manufacturers could also import the necessary parts from the USA or from Japan. In 1972, Japanese watch manufacturing was one-third of the Swiss production, but by 1980 Japanese watch production was 1.2 times the Swiss watch production.

The reasons for the pioneering success of the Seiko quartz crystal watch are as follows. Top management of the division perceived the possibility of a quartz crystal watch very early and formed project teams to develop it. Seiko developed the crystal watch within their own companies, without any dependence on other manufacturers, which resulted in accelerated development. In Switzerland there are hundreds of parts manufacturers and assemblers, and it proved very difficult to introduce innovations quickly because of conflicts of interest between the companies. Seiko companies had intentionally increased their recruitment of graduates in engineering and natural science in early times, so it was possible to from strong project teams and develop the new products internally. The number of breakthroughs such as the new concept on motors, the use of a stepping motor and the introduction of a tuning-fork shape of crystal were all made possible by looking for new directions, and by switching from conventional viewpoints. Lastly, and not the least important, the teams worked very hard. They did not hesitate to work late at night or overnight, sleeping if necessary in the research room. (For this detailed story, see Uchihashi, 1978.)

8.7.2 Factors of Success of Project Teams

The author stated that the frequent use of project teams is one of the characteristics of new-product development in successful Japanese corporations. Here we will investigate the success factors of project teams.

TABLE 8.9 The key success factor for project team

1.1 Support and encouragement of top management	8 co.
1.2 Clear goals, clear schedule and an adequate budget	21 co.
2.1 Quality of the team members; mixture of experts with necessary skills	27 co.
2.2 Quality of the project leader	26 co.
3.1 Adequate information	6 co.
3.2 Communication and co-operation between related departments	10 co.
4 Enthusiasm of the team member	11 co.

Notes:
[1] The answers of 157-successful companies.
[2] For method of survey, see Appendix 8.1.

Successful development depends on the activity of the team responsible for the development. US corporations put stress on the system of development, and they tend to have standard planning systems, and draw up detailed plans. Japanese corporations emphasize the human side of developing a new product, and their success depends largely on the motivation of the team members. In the survey on new-product development, the author asked about the key success factor for the project team. The answers to the unstructured question were as in Table 8.9.

These factors are very similar to the success factors listed in Table 8.5, but we should understand that here top management, quality of members and availability of information affect the motivation and thus affect the performance of the team. The president of Toray, discussing the factors necessary to motivate the team, says that the first thing is top management support for the development activity;

> There is a risk of failure, so a decisive attitude to support the team is essential. The importance of the project, the mission of the project should be emphasized. Top management should state the goal clearly, but the team members should feel free to select the means. An adequate budget not only allows more experiment, but it makes each team member feel responsible for the activity. If possible, it is desirable that each team member should also have some other future subjects of research, so that he takes a long view. Good co-operation with related departments is necessary, also with outside organizations, not only to get information but also to get stimulus from other research.

This statement supports the above findings relating to key success factors. These factors may be the same in the USA or UK, but the level of motivation and the actual behaviour may be a little different for the following reasons.

In the first place, there are many engineering and natural science graduates at the top level and in the project team. Top management can understand the technical problems of the project and can give practical encouragement to the team. This is the case with Sony and Honda, and in other successful companies. The more advanced the science is, the more difficult it becomes for top management to understand the project, but, comparatively speaking, top management or the higher-level manager from an engineering or science background can understand the problems. Out of many university graduates, it is possible to select good members to form the team, which results in more motivated activity. The centralized organizational structure and less use of division structure also makes it easier to form a strong project team.

Second, the employees work with the same company for life. It is possible to accumulate knowledge and skill in one company: it is possible for the same member to work on the same project for more than ten years. He does not specialize, but has experiences of being moved from one department to another or of working on other projects, so his experience is wider than that of the specialist, and this increases the new product's chance of success.

Communication with related departments is usually good because they know one another through many years of employment together, and this makes it easier to transfer technology from one department to another department or to another team.

These factors mean that the job itself motivates the team members. In Japanese corporations money is seldom used as a reward for accomplishment, and employees are not activated by money. Employees are organization-oriented, and with the above factors to intensify this attitude, each member of the team is willing to work hard – if necessary to work day and night.

Can we explain these success factors by a general theory of motivation, especially by the expectancy theory? (For expectancy theory, see Porter and Lawler, 1968.) The top management involvement and high capability of team members enhance the perception of possibility to attain the accomplishment or result. Because of lifetime employment, the job itself is a motivator, and the successful result is also the direct intrinsic reward. Thus each member of the team can be motivated.

8.8 EVALUATION AND PRIORITY

The new product is evalued several times in the process of its development. It is important to weed out unsuccessful ideas at an early stage so that resources are not wasted, and at the same time not to weed out the hopeful products prematurely. The typical steps of evaluation are shown in Figure 8.1. The first screening is on the original idea. The second screening is on whether or not to allocate resources for development. The third one is done during the technical and commercial development. The last one is done before embarking on full-scale production and marketing.

There are a number of methods of evaluation – subjective judgement, use of rate of return, profitability index, use of probability, or a rating scale with multiple factors. (Pessemier states many methods, see Pessemier, 1977.) Irrespective of the method, Appendix 8.3 shows what items are used in evaluating new products. According to the survey carried out, multiple criteria are used, for instance: (i) the attractiveness of the industry, (ii) possibility of entering, (iii) competitive strength or synergy gain to the new product, (iv) contribution to other products or synergy seen from existing products, (v) the effect on company financial goals. This result shows that, in the early stages, items that indirectly affect the goal, such as industry attractiveness and competitiveness, are considered important, because the effect on the final goals of the corporation cannot clearly be seen. These criteria necessitate a long-term view.

As the project approaches the final stages, the effects on organizational goals are taken as more important criteria. The sales amount, the increase or decrease of sales of other products, are considered important. The number of years it will take to reach the breakeven point is also significant. Three years from the beginning of mass sales to reach the breakeven point, and five years to restore the accumulated loss, are the usual pay-out periods, and this may indicate management's relatively long-term orientation.

In successful companies the evaluation is done by a top level committee of experts. At Mitsui Shipbuilding Company there are two evaluation committees – one technical, including the director of the development department as the chairman and other directors from research, designing and marketing departments – and the other commercial, chaired by the director of the research department, and including directors from the president's office, product divisions and financial department. Honda also has an evaluation committee of top experts. These strong and competent evaluation committees are important not only for weeding out failure products at an early stage, but also to motivate the development team.

8.9 SUMMARY

New-product development is important as a means of improving the company's competitive power by introducing an improved product; it is also important as a means of separating the sales of the company from the product life cycle, when the product introduced has a different use.

Japanese corporations have been successful world-wide in developing new products – in the shipbuilding industry, in cameras, watches, electrical home appliances even in the car industry – although many original patents for the new products have been bought from foreign countries.

The success of new-product development depends on whether the orientation of top management is innovative or not, and whether top management states a clear policy on the new development or not. Top management of successful Japanese companies are long-term oriented, many of them with engineering backgrounds, and thus sensitive to changes in technology. The basic policy is laid down through the long-range planning process.

The organization structure for new-product development is constantly being strengthened. There is a high percentage of university graduates, in science and engineering, so it is possible to build up strong manpower for research. Project teams are frequently used.

The successful company is market-oriented; it collects information for generating and developing new ideas. It is necessary to have adequate information to persuade those taking part in group decision-making – a process that is popular in Japan. The sense of the consumer is delicate, very selective, and it is again necessary to collect information before formulating the idea. This has resulted in the refined design and high quality of, for example, the camera, the watch and the car.

The process of development is characterized by the hard work of the project team. Top management involvement is one stimulus. Under the lifetime employment system, loyalty to the organization is high, and a varied accumulation of knowledge and skill is possible. These are the reasons behind the devotion and motivation of the research team.

The system is weak, however. Japanese corporations tend to rely on the people rather than the system. The US corporation, on the other hand, lays stress on the system.

These characteristics can be seen in the general model of strategic decision-making. The four styles of decision-making are shown in Table 8.10. These styles were formulated taking into consideration the models by Rowe and Boise (1973), Ansoff (1976), Mintzberg (1973) and Nyström (1979). (The styles of Table 8.10 are consistent with the styles of top management in Table 2.4.)

With the innovative analytical mode, the decisions are reached by an interactive process; many ideas are generated by collecting information, and the projects are integrated into a comprehensive plan.

With the innovative intuitive mode, decisions are handed down from the top; the intuitive idea comes before the information is collected, and decisions are made using a piecemeal approach without any integration of projects.

With the conservative analytical mode, a perfect decision is aimed at, safety comes first and no decisions are made until there is enough information, and almost no risk.

With the conservative intuitive mode, safety is the most important feature; decisions are based on past experience, future information is seldom collected, and incremental decisions are only made when problems come to the surface.

The style of new-product development favoured by successful Japanese corporations may be classified as the innovative analytical mode or as the innovative intuitive mode. The trend is towards analytical modes, but where the project is small, the innovative intuitive mode is used, thus different modes are employed depending upon the type of project.

The author estimates that successful US corporations tend more towards the innovative analytical mode, and European companies more towards the conservative analytical mode.

The author is not saying that all Japanese corporations use the same style. On the contrary, a wide variety of approaches are employed depending upon the projects and depending upon the corporations. The author estimates, however, that the successful companies are more inclined to use the innovative analytical mode, but sometimes use the innovative intuitive mode.

TABLE 8.10 Four styles of strategic decision-making

Process \ Models	Innovative analytical (planning mode)	Innovative intuitive (entrepreneurial mode)	Conservative analytical (bureaucratic mode)	Conservative intuitive (reactive mode)
(1) From what level of hierarchy the idea comes	Interactive between top management and staff	Top-down	Bottom-up	(Miscellaneous)
(2) Goals and policies	Clear goals Growth-oriented	Goals are not given Innovation-oriented	Idealism	No clear goal Safety-oriented
(3) Information and idea generation	From information to idea	Intuitive idea	Perfect information required for idea generation	Intuitive idea, based on past experience
(4) Search	Aggressive search Many alternatives	Aggressive search Few alternatives	Not sensitive to opportunity Few alternatives	Search starts when the problem is seen
(5) Time horizon	Long	Long	Short	Short
(6) Evaluation	Deliberate evaluation Consider the worst case	Adventurous	Look at the worst case only	Avoid risk
(7) Integration	Integrate by comprehensive plan	Piecemeal decision	Integrate within the constraint of present resource	Piecemeal decision
Scale of move	Large	Large	Small and incremental	Small and incremental
Fitness	Large project	Small project	—	—

Note: Compare this with Table 2.4.

8.9.1 Problems

8.9.1.1 Originality and expenditure for research

Many original ideas have come from Western countries, and many successful Japanese products are based on licences from US or European companies; for example, transistors from Bell Laboratory, colour television from RCA, computers from IBM and RCA. Sony is a very creative company, but many of its products are based on licensing from US corporations. Aggregating all companies, the ratio of receipts from exported technology to payment for imported technology was 0.10 in 1968 and 0.27 in 1979 in Japan; in the USA the ratio in 1979 was 9.5, in the UK 1.0 in 1975, and in West Germany 0.46 in 1979 (Kagagu Gijitsu Cho. Science Bureau, 1981).

It is becoming more difficult to import technology because the selling company now requests an exchange of patents. Japanese corporations will have to increase their expenditure for basic research, and the government will have to increase its subsidies. The successful Japanese corporations are long-term oriented and, as we have already seen, the successful large corporations have set up large research and development organizations, and the number of personnel engaged in such departments is increasing.

8.9.1.2 Group orientation and creativity

Japanese corporations have been quick to apply basic discoveries to practical goods. When the goal is clear, then the action is quick and the team members can be enthusiastic, but the Japanese scientist is not good at inventions themselves.

It is arguable whether the group orientation of the Japanese or the individualism of Western people gives greater stimulus to creativity. In the early stage of research, individual deliberation may be more workable. In later stages of invention the research is carried out by team activity, so group orientation and the co-operation of team members are more important.

Group orientation is also related to attitudes towards originality. Group orientation tends to lead the individual to disregard his own originality, not to insist on his own idea, and easily follow someone else's idea. Ideas from foreign countries tend to be automatically respected, and tend to be taken up as subjects for group research and development.

8.9.1.3 *Lifetime employment and length of service system*

These two systems encourage innovation to some extent. The lifetime employment system promotes long-range thinking, makes long-term activity for research possible, and does away with any necessity to resist new invention. But it is inconvenient for the creative man to pursue original research that does not coincide with the goal of the company, because he cannot leave the company. It is hard to engage in research in one area and move from organization to organization as a specialist.

It is also difficult to form a research team by recruiting new talent from outside the company. Promotion and wage increase by length of service, with slight differentiation depending upon performance, make the researcher feel secure. There is no short-term feedback of rewards, and this promotes an atmosphere of freedom of research and freedom of failure. This in turn promotes co-operation. The most attractive reward to the creative man is not money, but the achievement itself and the fame. The author believes that it is not the Japanese personnel management system that blocks creativity; the most serious obstacle is the lack of respect for one's own originality.

8.9.1.4 *Weak process system*

The Japanese corporation has much to learn from the system developed by the US corporation. The author once conducted some research on the planning and control systems for large technology-intensive plant construction (such as chemical plant construction) of plant engineering companies, and was surprised by the elaborate system of control in US corporations. The US company tends to depend on the system, and the Japanese company tends to depend on the skill and enthusiasm of its employees. They both must be necessary, but as the project becomes larger, the system plays a more important role.

APPENDIX 8.1: METHOD OF SURVEY BY MAIL

1. The Questionnaires

The questionnaire surveys were designed to assemble the facts and to analyse the current practices on new-product development of Japanese corporations and to find out the success factors. Two kinds of mail surveys were conducted.

    A. Survey on new-product development system.

        This is a comparative analysis between the new-product development

systems of success companies and failure companies. I tried to find out the factors of success using this survey.
B. Survey on success and failure of new-product development.
New products were classified into success products and failure products and factors of success and failure were analysed.

2. Date of Survey

Mail questionnaires were sent out in February 1980.

3. Respondents of the Survey

A. New-product development system
Mail questionnaires were sent to 1044 companies and 227 companies responded (21.7 per cent response ratio) and among 227 companies, 205 were analysed.
B. Survey on success and failure of new-product development
Mail questionnaires were sent to 189 companies and 45 companies responded (23.8 per cent). Among them, 30 companies were analysed.
Distribution of respondents by industry is as in Table 8.11.

TABLE 8.11. Distribution of respondents by industry

Industies	A. New-product Development system		B. Success and Failure of new-product Development
	Success companies	Failure companies	
1. Food and fisheries	14	3	5
2. Fibre, pulp and paper (non-technical)	4	6	0
3. Fibre, pulp and paper (technical)	8	4	2
4. Chemicals	23	4	8
5. Petroleum, rubber, glass and stone	8	3	5
6. Iron, steel and non-ferrous metals	18	13	1
7. Machinery	19	5	7
8. Electrical appliances and precision machine	36	5	8
9. Transportation equipment and machinery	19	1	3
10. Other industries	8	4	0
Total	157	48	39

4. Distribution of Respondents by Sales

TABLE 8.12 Distribution of respondents by sales

Sales in 1978	A. New-product Development system		B. Success and failure of new-product development
	Success companies	*Failure companies*	
Over $10 000 million	0	0	0
$9999–$1000 million	14	0	5
$999–$333 million	25	7	13
$332–$100 million	38	11	13
$99–$33 million	43	17	7
$32–$10 million	35	13	1
Under $10 million	2	0	0
Total	157	48	39

5. Definition of Success Companies and Failure Companies

Success companies should have two of the following three characteristics:
  A. Increase of sales in the eleven years between 1967 and 1978 are more than three times (nominal).
  B. Return on total assets (1967 and 1978) (profit before interest and tax over total assets) is more than 7 per cent on average over two years, or profit after interest and after tax over total assets is more than 2.5 per cent on average over two years.
  C. Equity ratio of 1978 is more than 15 per cent.
Failure companies do not have the two conditions stated above.

6. Definition of Success Products and Failure Products

Products that have a higher profit rate over the sales amount than the other existing products, or sales amount of the new products, are over the planned sales, or leader of the markets, are classified as success products. Failure products have a lower profit rate over sales than the other existing products, or the sales amount of the new products are below the planned sales amount, or they have a very weak position in the market.

238

APPENDIX 8.2: INFORMATION FOR NEW PRODUCTS

TABLE 8.13 Information for new products

'Which of the following items of information were directly important to produce successful new products?'

		(*Successful companies*) %
(1–1)	Survey of the use of related products	75
(1–2)	Claims, customer cards	50
(1–3)	Report of salesman and suggestions	64
(1–4)	Information from sales channel including trading company	68
(1–5)	Interview with consumers	43
(1–6)	Research of growth area	63
(1–7)	Information from monitor	25
(1–8)	Survey on deficiency of present products	58
(1–9)	Information from suppliers	26
(1–10)	Information of important materials	39
(1–11)	Information of substitutes	51
(1–12)	Special market research to find out uncovered needs	52

Needs { (items 1–1 through 1–12)

Imitation	(2–1) Successful products of foreign companies and other companies	69
	(2–2) New-product development trends of competitors	79
	(2–3) Observation of related products in exhibition or in the stores	45
Seeds	(3–1) Information on patents	65
	(3–2) Articles of academic periodicals	44
	(3–3) Papers of academic meetings and conferences	38
	(3–4) Opinions of experts on technology	54
	(3–5) Opinion of experts on the use	53
	(3–6) Trends of research of the competitors	73
Strength	(4–1) Strength and weakness of research capabilities of own company	69
	(4–2) Strength and weakness of marketing of own company	70
	(4–3) Strength and weakness of production of own company	69
General	(5–1) Trends of economy and politics in overseas areas	32
	(5–2) Economic trends of domestic area	39
	(5–3) Trends of policies of the government	39
	(5–4) Trends of important resources	48

Notes:
[1] The percentage shows the number of companies that put emphasis on each item.
[2] For method of survey, see Appendix 8.1.

APPENDIX 8.3: CRITERIA FOR SCREENING

TABLE 8.14 Criteria for screening

'Which of the following items are important to evaluate a new product whether you are using evaluation chart or not?'

Evaluation item	In earlier stage (from idea to technical development) %	In the middle stage (from technical development to merchandizing) %	In the final stage (before production and sales) %
1. Size and stability of the market (industry attractiveness)			
(1) Size of the market	73	38	28
(2) Stage of the life cycle	35	31	13
(3) Competition	49	44	36
(4) Stability of demand	32	40	34
(5) Value for social responsibility	22	21	14
2. Possibility of production and selling (possibility to enter)			
(1) Possibility to obtain the technology	72	21	2
(2) Size of expense for research and market development	48	36	7
(3) Size of capital investment	20	62	25
(4) Possibility to obtain resource	19	40	16

3. Competitive strength (advantage provided by existing capability)			
(1) Capability of research and development	73	19	2
(2) Support of production technology	23	66	11
(3) Cost of production	14	66	37
(4) Sales capability	18	44	38
4. Contribution of new product to present product and future new product			
(1) Contribution to present market	43	27	13
(2) Strengthening of present sales channel	5	37	43
(3) Expansion of research and development capability	48	26	12
(4) Expansion of production technology	11	54	24
(5) Moving to opposite direction to existing product by seasonal or business cycle	15	18	22
(6) Diversification of customer	6	17	27
5. Profitability			
(1) Forecast of sales	31	38	31
(2) Increase or decrease of sales of other products	16	36	28
(3) Profit ratio on sales	16	45	44
(4) Return on investment	18	49	30
(5) How many years to reach the breakeven	13	45	32
(6) Loss in worst case (after capital investment)	9	33	29

Notes:
[1] The number indicates the number of company ÷ total responses.
[2] Responses from 157 successful companies.
[3] For survey method, see Appendix 8.1.

REFERENCES

Egawa, R. (1980) Canon Company, Tokyo, Asahi Sonorama.
Kagagu Gijitsu Cho (1981) *Gagaku Gijutsu Hakusho* (White Paper on Science).
Kibi, M. (1980) Hitachi Company, Tokyo, Asahi Sonorama.
Kono, T. (1974) *Keiei Senryaku no Kaimei* (Analysis of Corporate Strategy), Tokyo, Diamond Sha.
Kono, T. (1980) *Senryaku Keiei Keikaku no Tatekata* (Introduction to Strategic Planning), Tokyo, Diamond Sha.
Shoda, T. (1969) *Seihin Keikaku no Tatekata* (Product Planning), Tokyo, Nihon Keizai.
Uchihashi, K. (1978) *Takumi no Jidai* (Inside Story of New Products Development), I, II, Tokyo, Sanki Shuppan.
Wakayama, F. and Sugimoto, C. (1977) *Toyota no Himitsu* (Secret of Toyota), Tokyo, Ko-Shobo.

American Management Association (ed.) (1964) *New Products, New Profits*, New York, AMA.
Ansoff, H. I. (1965) *Corporate Strategy*, New York, McGraw-Hill.
Ansoff, H. I., Declerck, R. P. and Hayes, R. L. (eds) (1976) *From Strategic Planning to Strategic Management*, London, John Wiley.
Berg, T. L. and Shuchman, A. (eds) (1963) *Product Strategy and Management*, New York, Holt, Rinehart & Winston.
Glueck, W. E. (1976) *Business Policy, Strategy Formulation and Management Action*, New York, McGraw-Hill.
Hilton, P. (1970) *Planning Corporate Growth and Diversification*, New York, McGraw-Hill.
Kollat, D. T., Blackwell, R. D. and Robeson, J. F. (1972) *Strategic Marketing*, New York, Holt, Rinehart & Winston.
Mintzberg, H. (1973) 'Strategy-Making in Three Modes', *California Management Review*, Winter.
Nyström, H. (1979) *Creativity and Innovation*, New York, John Wiley.
Pessemier, E. A. (1966) *New Product Decisions, An Analytical Approach*, New York, McGraw-Hill.
Pessemier, E. A. (1977) *Product Management, Strategy and Organization*, New York, John Wiley.
Porter, L. W. and Lawler, E. E. (1968) *Managerial Attitudes and Performance*, Ill., Richard D. Irwin.
Rogers, E. M. (1962) *Diffusion of Innovations*, New York, Free Press.
Rowe, L. A. and Boise, W. B. (1973) *Organizational and Managerial Innovation*, Calif., Goodyear Publishing.

9 Long-range Planning

Through an analysis of the long-range planning systems of successful Japanese corporations, we can discover how the strategic decisions are arrived at in Japan, and by what means the strategic decision can succeed. Formal long-range planning covers many areas of strategic decisions, so the analysis of the planning process shows the formal behaviour pattern of the organization. As in the previous chapter, we will analyse the formation of goals and policies, organizational process and the features of information processing.

The data for this analysis comes from: (i) Mail questionnaire surveys carried out in 1979 and 1982 in Japan, and in 1981 in the UK and in 1975 in the USA. The details of the survey are stated in Appendices 9.1 and 9.2. (ii) A number of visits to companies and interviews with corporate planners in three countries. (These visits in the UK and in the USA were conducted while the author was a visiting professor at the London Business School in 1980–1, and a Fulbright visiting scholar at the Graduate School of Management, UCLA, 1974–5.) (iii) Published papers of the selected companies.

9.1 DIFFUSION OF LONG-RANGE PLANNING AND LONG-TERM ORIENTATION

A number of studies indicate that approximately 70–80 per cent of large Japanese corporations have some kind of long-range planning systems. MITI's (Ministry of International Trade and Industry) yearly surveys on the corporate capability of about 540 corporations, carried out since 1973 found that 73 per cent in 1974, 71 per cent in 1975, 64 per cent in 1976, 66 per cent in 1977, 67 per cent in 1978, and 74 per cent in 1980 had long-range plans, and the performance of those who had long-range planning was better than that of the non-planners (MITI, 1980).

There are several forces that have contributed to this high spread in Japan. National long-term economic plans have been drawn up since

1956, and are revised approximately every three to five years. These plans gave a stimulus to private business long-range plans.

The attitude of top management has been innovative and long-range oriented. This is a more important factor. Those companies that do not have long-range plans may be long-term oriented or may be short-term oriented, but those that have long-range plans are mostly long-range oriented. The fact that the Japanese corporation is long-term oriented has been already analysed in Chapter 3. Generally speaking, the value of the organization is affected by the stakeholders, by those who have the key resources for the survival of the organization, that is, the power and the values of top management, middle management, general employees, shareholders and the banks. Middle management of Japanese corporations in particular puts strong pressure on top management to look far ahead, because it is in its members' own best interests to have the company grow on a long-term basis, since they themselves will be with the company for the whole of their working lives.

9.2 REASONS FOR LONG-RANGE PLANNING

There are two important objectives for long-range planning: (i) to promote innovation, (ii) to integrate the innovative strategies. The former objective is considered as more important in Japan, and the latter is more important in the UK and in the USA. The perceptions of corporate planners on the objectives were surveyed in Japan and in the UK. According to the result of the mail questionnaire survey, the order of importance is as in Table 9.1.

There are more similarities than differences. In both countries the common reasons are to improve the strategic decisions, by basing them more on reasoned analysis than on intuition.

There are some differences, however. In the UK better allocation of

TABLE 9.1 Reasons for long-range planning

	UK ranking	Japan ranking
(a-1) To examine basic problems	3	2
(a-2) Decisions based on long-range forecasting	4	3
(a-3) To clarify long-range goals	1	1
(b) Better allocation of resources	2	4

resources is considered more important, and in Japan, improvement of decisions. In the other survey conducted in the USA the author found that the integration of strategies and resources allocation are more stressed there also. In the USA and in the UK, the product mix is more diversified, the level of multinational management is higher, and the division structure of organization is more popular. The resource allocation is thus more emphasized.

9.3 TRANSITION OF PLANNING SYSTEM

The long-range planning system has evolved as the environment changed, and as the centre of corporate strategy changed.

9.3.1 Individual Project Planning – Approximately 1950–60

After the Second World War the economy had to be reconstructed. For companies the reconstruction of destroyed factories was the first priority, and they drew up long-range plans for the reconstruction of equipment, but not comprehensive plans.

9.3.2 Quantitative Plan – Approximately 1960–70

After the economy entered a high growth period the government announced an aggressive national economic plan, which gave a great stimulus to the behaviour of management in general, and to business planning systems. Comprehensive long-range planning became widely adopted among large corporations. (See the increase in the response ratio in 1967 in Table 9.2.)

The planning was mostly quantitative, however, because expansion by capital investment was the most important strategy, and in order to attain the balanced achievement of goals it was necessary to integrate capital investment through long-range profit plan. Many specialized companies had forecasting-type plans (A(1) in Table 9.2, 1963, 1967), which made clear the gaps between the needs and the availability of the capacity and the financial results of capital investment. On the other hand, many diversified companies had goal-clarifying-type plans (A(2) in Table 9.2, 1963, 1967). Top management assigned the goals to each department, and each department drew up quantitative plans to implement the goals using a bottom-to-top approach.

TABLE 9.2 Transition of long-range planning system in the past twenty years

Year	1963	1967	1970	1976	1979	1982	UK, 1981 (References)
Number of companies	254	268	160	57	327	110	74
Response ratio (%)	17.9	25.8	25.0	13.8	28.4	45.5	15.0
Characteristics (%)							
A (1) Forecastive	22	23	14	14	19	16	16
(2) Clarifying goals, without details	41	43	23	16	46	47	11
(3) Individual problem-solving	8	2	1	0	3	3	5
(4) Comprehensive, including all of the above	34	32	61	68	30	32	49
(5) Others and NA	–	–	2	–	–	–	18
B (1) Mostly quantitative		53	46	46	41	38	25
(2) Emphasis on projects		3	3	7	10	3	4
(3) Emphasis on projects and also quantitative consolidation		37	46	51	46	53	50
(4) NA		7	6	–	–	7	21
Time horizon (%)							
(1) Over 10 years	1	1	2	2	2	4	1
(2) 10 to 7 years	6	5	4	4	4	6	4
(3) 5 or 6 years	50	59	56	56	34	35	49
(4) 4 years	3	5	2	2	5	6	9
(5) 3 years	30	35	32	32	47	40	19
(6) 2 years	6	6	5	5	5	1	4
(7) NA	11	0	–	–	–	8	13

Note:
Comparison of seven mail questionnaire surveys conducted by the author in the past twenty years. For details of last three surveys, see Appendix 9.1.

9.3.3 Project Emphasis, but Too Many Projects – Approximately 1970–4

The economy continued to grow at a high rate, but the demand structure was changing. Quantitative planning was changed to a type that put emphasis on product–market strategy. In Table 9.2, we notice that A(4), the comprehensive problem-solving type plan, increased in 1970, and B(3) emphasis on projects and also quantitative consolidation increased in 1970. However, many companies took up too many issues, so their priorities were not clear and the resources were not allocated appropriately. The important strategy tended to be built outside the long-range planning process. To overcome the above defects, some companies started to have a two-plan system, the long-range strategic plan and the medium-range plan, and for latter part computer simulation was frequently applied.

9.3.4 Suspension of Long-range Plan and Rationalization Plan, 1974–7

The oil crisis resulted in increased uncertainty, and many companies suspended their long-range planning. The low response ratio in Table 9.2 in 1976 indicates this. The companies that resumed long-range planning laid stress on cost reduction plans. The growth-share matrix model attracted a large amount of attention as a tool of rationalization. The time horizon of the plan became shorter because of uncertainty.

9.3.5 Emphasis on Selected Key Strategies, 1977 to date

When the economy entered a low-growth period, companies began to notice that rationalization planning only was too defensive, and that they needed to take positive action to take advantage of the new emerging opportunities. In Table 9.2, the increase of A(2) goal-clarifying-type plans, and the increase of B(3) emphasis on projects and quantitative-consolidation-type plans in 1979 indicate this awareness. Many successful companies selected five to ten key strategic issues round which they formed their long-range strategy. At the same time they built up medium-range plans to integrate the strategies and to integrate the allocation of resources. Long-range strategies were built using a top-down or interactive approach at the head office.

The above is a simplified account of the transitions in the planning systems of Japanese corporations over the past thirty years. The change of planning system tied in with the changing environment and the resulting change of strategies of the corporations. On the other hand, the accumulation of experience and improvement of technical knowledge was another of the forces for change in the planning systems.

One example of change of planning systems can be seen in Hitachi's case. Their long-range planning started in 1958 as an estimate of customer orders for heavy equipment; and by 1960 capital investment plans and financial plans were major components. In 1967 planning began to emphasize the basic strategy using a top-down approach. During the oil crises their long-range planning was suspended, but in 1975 it was resumed again, and in this planning the emphasis was on basic strategy and strategic policy rather than financial estimates, and using a top-down and interactive process rather than a build-up process. It came to emphasize strategic decisions.

The corporate planner of Hitachi's consumer durable products division says that in old times there was no basic strategy for new products, so product development tended to be done on an *ad hoc* basis. When other companies developed remarkable new products, Hitachi's sales channel salesmen requested the development of similar products, and the company had to develop imitations hurriedly. Without long-range strategy, a company has to be a follower of its competitor in many cases. When there is a basic strategy, the company can go its own way. This case shows how comprehensive long-range planning can improve strategic decisions.

At Matsushita also, the planner in the international department states a similar opinion. Matsushita underwent a number of changes in their planning system. As with Hitachi, planning was suspended after the oil crisis; recently, however, it was revived as a quantitative financial estimate and later it was changed to strategic planning. The planner in the international department states that previously the decisions on multinational investment tended to be done on an *ad hoc* basis, though the company's view was long term. Now in the long-range plan, there is long-range strategy to determine what product is appropriate for production in what area, and what the proportion of foreign production, home country production and export should be. This is another case of integration of strategic decisions into the long-range planning process.

In the following sections, we will investigate the present planning systems in detail.

9.4 PRESENT LONG-RANGE PLANNING SYSTEMS

9.4.1 Components of the Long-range Plan

The subjects of decision can be classified under four headings: goals, product–market strategies, structure and operation. Decisions can be classified according to extent of change into innovative, improvement and maintenance decisions.

By combining two factors, the area of decision is shown in Figure 9.1 as a matrix. The long-range strategic plan covers the innovation of goals, of product–market strategy and of structure. The medium-range plan mostly comprises improvements in product–market strategy (E.G. competition strategy), and change of structure. The annual plan or budgeting covers the maintenance or repetition of operations.

The actual components of long-range plans include some of the processes and a typical model is seen in Figure 9.2. The corporate level strategy corresponds to the strategic plan in Figure 9.1, the division plan plus the corporate functional plan corresponds to the medium-range plan shown in Figure 9.1. (For a number of models, see Steiner, 1969; and Steiner, 1979.)

The mail questionnaire survey on these items is seen in Appendix 9.3. (Long-range strategy roughly corresponds to items from number 6 to 15,

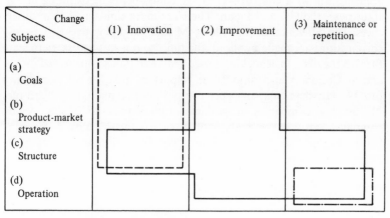

- - - - - area for long-range strategic plan
─────────── area for medium-range planning
─ · ─ · ─ · area for annual plan (budgeting)

FIGURE 9.1 Subjects of decisions

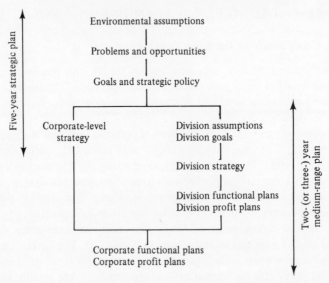

Note:
Functional plan includes marketing, production, research and development, capital investment, personnel. In the case where the company is not divisionalized, 'division' should be replaced by 'product'.

FIGURE 9.2 Typical components of plan

and medium-range planning to items from number 16 to 28.) This appendix shows a comparison of the components of planning in two countries – the UK and Japan. There are more similarities than differences. The differences are as follows. Missions and objectives in Japanese corporations are made public all the time, so it is not necessary to state them in the plan. Instead, long-range goals and policies are stated (nos. 1 and 6). Company acquisition is an important item for UK companies (no. 14). Japanese companies place importance on manpower plans (no. 21), but UK companies stress financial plans (nos. 26, 27, 28). A UK company does a better analysis of its own company (nos. 4, 5) and is better prepared for uncertainty (no. 29). These differences reflect the differences between their goals and strategies.

9.4.2 Time Horizon and Two-plan System

Time horizon of planning depends on three factors: lead time from idea to implementation; how long the impact of a decision continues in the organization or how long a decision binds the organization; and the predictability of the future. The time horizon of planning of Japanese corporations is five or three years (Table 9.2). According to the mail survey and interviews, the majority of US companies and UK companies use five-year plans, but in Japan the three-year plan has a higher frequency than the five-year plan. The environment for Japanese corporations is less certain, and difficult to predict, so the time horizon is not very long. Does this mean that Japanese companies are medium-term oriented and US and UK companies are longer-term oriented? The companies that have long-range plans are long-term oriented. The US and UK companies can make longer time comprehensive plans, because they are in a more stable, less competitive environment.

In Japan two plans with different time horizons are becoming popular. About 20 per cent of the companies surveyed have medium-range plans in addition to long-range strategic plans. In an ideal case, the long-range strategic plan stresses the strategy of the corporation; it decides the area of business and new directions to enter. It is more narrative than quantitative, more conceptual than financially oriented. It lists major projects and gives them priority. It is mostly worked out on a corporate level.

On the other hand, the medium-range plan covers two or three years; it is more quantitative and stresses the allocation of resources. The important items are a detailed schedule of projects, planning by products, capital investments, and financial plans. It is mostly worked out by operating units.

The merits of two-plan systems are: (i) Emphasis on strategic issues becomes possible by separating strategic plans from quantitative plans. (ii) More trust in long-range planning is made possible by shortening the quantitative plan. Financial planning beyond three years is not very meaningful because of uncertainty.

9.5 GOALS OF A LONG-RANGE PLAN

The goals of a long-range plan clarify the implicit objectives that the company aims to attain through the long-range plan. In establishing a long-range plan, the company first hammers out these goals and then proceeds to project planning and formulation of divisional plans.

The goals of a long-range plan are not set intuitively. First the desired levels are determined, then forecasts are made on the assumption that past strategies have been followed to find gaps. Next, strategic policies to fill the gaps are sought, studies are made to find out whether the gaps can be filled, and then the feasible levels of basic goals are set and strategic policies determined. Here, strategic policies mean policies that determine the levels and direction of product–market strategies and company structure.

There is a hierarchy of goals of the long-range plan, that is, basic goals, goals for product–market strategy, goals for structure or resources, goals for productivity. Here, only the basic goals and productivity goals are analysed.

It is generally said that US and UK companies are short-term profit-oriented and Japanese companies are long-term growth-oriented. According to the survey, however, there are more similarities than differences, possibly because the companies in the UK and in the USA who replied to the questionnaire are more long-term growth-oriented than those who did not (see Table 3.2). In all three countries, sales, profit and market share are important.

There are some differences, however. In the UK and in the USA, return on total capital (or total assets), earnings per share and cost reduction are important. Simply speaking, financial goals are given greater emphasis.

In Japan, sales, amount of profit (both as indicators of growth), employee compensation, value added and labour productivity have a higher priority. Simply speaking, growth and employee welfare are considered more important.

What are the reasons for these differences? The UK and the US company is more shareholder-oriented, because of the stronger pressure from shareholders and institutional investors, and because there is the threat of being taken over by some other company if the share price is low. The Japanese company is less shareholder-oriented. Most of the funds come from banks, who take a long-term view, seeking to cultivate customers who borrow money from them. The need for growth is also stronger in order to provide the jobs for their lifetime employees. Japanese middle management puts pressure on top management for growth.

9.6. PLANNING PROCESS IN THE ORGANIZATION

The planning process in Japanese organizations may be classified into bottom-up (decentralized), top-down (centralized) and interactive. This is related to which level of total organizational structure the basic idea is presented from, where the plan is reviewed and where the plan is decided.

Bottom-up approach means that the corporate planning department is small, information is mostly collected by the operating unit, and the goals of the divisions, strategies of the divisions, production plans, functional plans – all are initiated by the operating units. This is a decentralized planning process. The planning department initiates only the format, and co-ordinates the planning activities of the operating units. It should be noted, however, that even in the bottom-up process. within the division the strategic ideas could be presented by the people at the top of the division, as is the case with many US corporations. In this sense, bottom-up here only means that the plan is built up at a lower level of hierarchy; it does not mean that ideas are presented by the rank and file. (The analysis of Table 8.10 is rather on the process within the unit of organization.)

In a top-down approach, basic information, the goals of each department and key strategies are decided at the corporate level, and they are given to the operating units as guidelines, and these units will build up the 'tactical plan'. In this approach the planning department is stronger and plays a more important role. Operating units have less authority to decide the strategy.

The interactive process takes a path between the above two. Ideas are formulated by interaction betwen top management, planning department and operating units. The planning department will collect environmental information and will submit strategic issues to the top. Top management will decide the goals and the broad direction. Strategies are formulated by vertical interaction. In addition, there is a vertical division of labour. Some strategies such as acquisitions, joint ventures and new projects, which are not assignable to any departments, are studied by the corporate planning department of the corporate development department, and are implemented at the corporate level. Operating units will follow the guidelines given from the top, and build a strategy and operational plans specific to the division.

If there is a two-plan system, long-range strategic plans are worked out mostly at corporate level; medium-range plans are worked out by operating units.

A comparative analysis of the results of the survey on the planning process in Japanese corporations and British corporations is shown in Table 9.3. In the UK, there is a greater tendency to build plans by divisions, and in this sense using a bottom-up process. As Table 9.3 shows, the initial plan is more often prepared by the division, or by the division's top management. Usually the general information is collected and guidelines are decided by the planning department at head office. These are shown to the line department and the line department prepares

TABLE 9.3 Planning process

'How is the planning conducted in the organization? Which department prepares, reviews and finally decides the long-range plan? (Please tick as many as necessary.)'

	Preparing UK 174 Co. %	Preparing J 327 Co. %	Reviewing UK %	Reviewing J %	Final decision UK %	Final decision J %
1. Planning department	64	79*	51	11*	4	0
2. Division or line department	54	45	19	7*	3	0
3. Corporate staff department	21	22	14	5	4	0
4. Task force (or project team)†	10	15	0	2	0	0
5. Committee for long-range planning	1	5	8	14	1	0
6. Division's top management(s)	36	–	34	–	12	–
7. Meeting of managing director and department (division) executives	16	1*	41	24*	19	2*
8. Management committee by full-time executives	7	1	25	51*	11	39*
9. Management committee by few top executives	3	1	30	18*	10	13
10. Management director, or president	12	2	28	2*	33	38
11. Board of directors	3	0	18	3*	67	13*
12. Chairman	0	0	11	0	30	2*
13. NA	3	–	3	–	1	–

Notes:
[1] The asterisk (*) indicates level of significance is 10%.
[2] † Question not exactly identical.
[3] For method of survey, see Appendix 9.1.

the initial plan. 'The doer is the planner' is the basic way of thinking in the UK and in the USA.

In the USA also, there is a greater tendency for the planning to be done by the divisions. According to the author's impressions after personal visits to many companies, about two-thirds use a bottom-up process, one-third use an interactive process, and the top-down process was not seen in any company. According to a mail survey (not presented here), plans are prepared in many cases by the operating units, and reviewed by the planning department, staff department and meetings of the chief executive officer with heads of divisions and departments. The final decision is taken mostly by chief executive officers and the board of directors.

In Japan the planning department plays more roles, as Table 9.3 shows. In many cases, especially in specialized companies, plans are prepared in the planning department of the head office with some participation by the line department and staff department. The planning department takes greater initiative; their plan is reviewed by the management committee, and the final decision is made by the management committee and by the president who is the chief executive officer.

Many people have written papers describing the Japanese style of decision-making as bottom-up (Yoshino, 1968). According to our survey, however, this cannot be generalized; the strategic decision-making process is rather a top-down or interactive process. The reason for this is the faster rate of change of environment. Japanese corporations have had to make innovations from the top down. In addition, the Japanese corporation is less diversified and has fewer divisions.

For operational decisions, the situation is different. Operational policy is decided by the staff department, ideas are submitted from the middle, and group decisions are the norm.

In Japan the management committee plays a dominant role in reviewing. It is clear that this is a very important group decision-making body at the top. In Japan final decisions are also made by the management committee or by the managing director (the president). They are seldom submitted to the board of directors.

In the UK the final decisions are made by the board of directors or the managing director or chairman. Management committees do not play a significant role in final decision-making. This UK pattern is very similar to the US pattern (see Kono, 1976), and is significantly different from the Japanese pattern.

In the UK and in the USA the board of directors is expected to play a more important part in the final decision. However, one-third of the board of directors are outside members, and we think that it is dubious whether it is effective to use the board for final strategic decisions, considering not only the capability but also the confidentiality of long-range planning. The reason for the present practice may be that it involves large capital expenditure which affects the interest of the shareholders, and the pressure from shareholders is somewhat stronger than in Japan. There is a possibility that risky projects may be rejected using this kind of organizational process.

In Japan, where similar company law exists, long-range planning is seldom submitted to the board. Most of the board members are inside full-time office-holders, so, after the decision by the management committee, duplication of authorization is not necessary.

9.7 PLANNING PROCESS – MODELS AND CASES

9.7.1 A Model of the Planning Process

This model was arrived at by observing many cases of effective process in successful companies in Japan. (For other models of process, see Ansoff, 1965; Steiner, 1969; Hofer and Schendel, 1978.) There are four phases (Figure 9.3).

Phase (I) – establishing premises

The corporate goals and philosophy are revised by taking into consideration the stakeholders who hold the key resources. Information is collected on general environment, the industry and the competitors, and the future states of the company are forecast. By an analysis of the forecast, opportunities and threats are made clear.

Appraisal of past performance uncovers the problems – information that is useful for forecasting future problems. Comparison with the competitors identifies the strengths and weaknesses of the company.

Phase (II) – clarifying issues

Following the above three premises, levels of aspiration are determined. For example, the growth rate should be more than 10 per cent a year. Then the future performance in the key results area under present policy is forecast and compared with the aspiration level and any gaps are discovered. New strategies are looked for to fill these gaps.

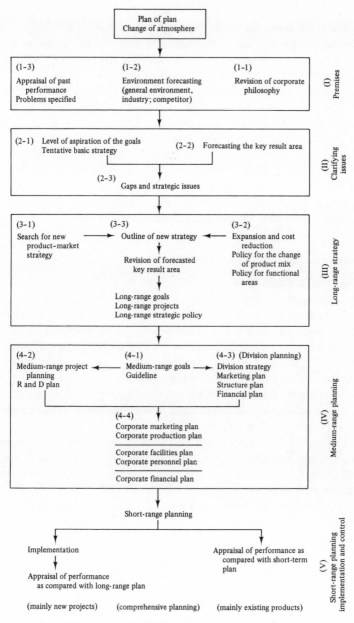

FIGURE 9.3 A model of the long-range planning process

Phase (III) – long-range strategy

In order to close the gaps between forecast and aspiration, new product–market strategies are sought, for example development of new business, vertical integration, multinational management and joint ventures are researched. This is the most important process.

Expansion and cost reduction of existing products are studied; a growth-share matrix model can be used here. Assuming that the above two strategies are carried out, the future performance is forecast, and investigated if the future gap is closed. If the gap is not closed, then the above process is repeated and new research is conducted. If the gap can be closed, then the long-range strategy is established. The long-range strategy comprises three parts. The first is long-range goals, which are supported by long-range strategies; the second is long-range strategic projects; the third is long-range policies in major areas.

Phase (IV) – medium-range planning

Following the decision on long-range strategy, medium-range goals and guidelines are set and medium-range plans are worked out. The medium-range plans also comprise three parts: First, medium-range project planning, which has schedules, and has resources allocated. Second, planning by product groups. The change of product mix and the competition strategy for each product group is an important strategy. The medium-range planning for each product group is conducted by the relevant product division.Third, corporate functional plans, planned by the corporate functional department. It is composed of facilities plans, personnel plans and profit plans.

This model represents a successful planning process in many Japanese corporations. The characteristics of this process are as follows. It makes the gap clear first, and includes measures to close the gaps. The process does not aim at maximizing the performance, but attaining a satisfactory performance. It builds up a long-range strategy first and sets the guidelines for medium-range plans. It proceeds from general decisions to detailed decisions.

9.7.2 The Case of Bridgestone Tire and Rubber Company

The founder and president of Ishibashi was very plan-oriented, and he himself wrote a detailed future blueprint of the company. It was then discussed in management committee, and it was used for actual decisions. As the company grew, more formal planning was adopted and the president's office was established. The first formal plan covered 1967–8 and the second plan 1969–71, but these were quantitative plans, mostly expressed in numbers. They were useful in an expansion period, but top management could hardly set his own plan in the project because the numbers were too coplicated and mutually interdependent. The third plan, covering 1972–5, was changed from a quantitative plan to a more strategic or issues-oriented plan, composed of long-range policy and medium-range financial estimates. There were too many issues, however, and too all-inclusive. A computer simulation was used for the medium-range plan which was tried as a means to integrate the strategy. In this case, there were too many all inclusive issues without any ranking, and the issues lacked detailed analysis. During the planning period, the oil crisis occurred and the plan was modified to stress efforts in cost reduction.

The recent plan started in 1976 has two characteristics. First it stresses five key strategic issues, and second, the issues are initiated and discussed by top management. The planning process is exhibited in Figure 9.4.

The first phase is to collect environmental information. This is mostly carried out by the planning department all the year round. The second phase is the identification of issues. The functional department works for three months to identify the opportunities and threats. Their findings are presented to the management committee; five key issues are found and five committees are set up, chaired by five of the top management including the president (CEO). The five issues are rather broad issues, as shown in Figure 9.4. In the third phase, five strategies and over all strategies are decided by the management committee and checked by simulation. Then the five-year goals, basic strategies and long-range policies are decided. In the fourth phase the medium-range plans are formulated. They are based on long-range strategy, and drawn up by each of the product departments and by the functional departments.

The characteristics of this process are that the long-range strategy focuses on five key issues, that simulation is used to guide the medium-range plan, and that the planning process is relatively centralized.

The older systems were somewhat defective, but still could contribute to the strategy formulation. The strategy of Bridgestone has been to expand the production facilities aggressively, to undertake construction during the depression period, to emphasize research, and new-product development. These strategies were successful largely because of the long-range planning.

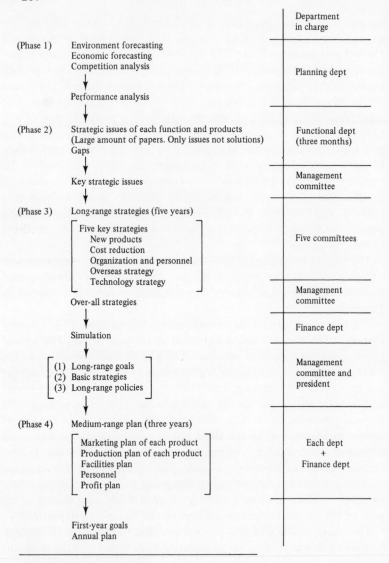

                                                              Department
                                                              in charge

(Phase 1)   Environment forecasting
              Economic forecasting
              Competition analysis   Planning dept

              Performance analysis

(Phase 2)   Strategic issues of each function and products   Functional dept
              (Large amount of papers. Only issues not solutions)   (three months)
              Gaps

              Key strategic issues   Management
                                                              committee

(Phase 3)   Long-range strategies (five years)

                  Five key strategies
                      New products
                      Cost reduction   Five committees
                      Organization and personnel
                      Overseas strategy
                      Technology strategy

              Over-all strategies   Management
                                                              committee

              Simulation   Finance dept

              (1) Long-range goals   Management
              (2) Basic strategies   committee and
              (3) Long-range policies   president

(Phase 4)   Medium-range plan (three years)

                  Marketing plan of each product
                  Production plan of each product   Each dept
                  Facilities plan   +
                  Personnel   Finance dept
                  Profit plan

              First-year goals
              Annual plan

Characteristics of the process:

(1) Long-range strategy is to formulate strategies on five key issues
    during five years to come.

(2) Medium-range planning is based on long-range strategy, and after finding
    satisfying value by simulation, plans of each product and of each
    function are formulated.

(3) Each department participates in finding issues and in formulating
    medium-range plans but, generally speaking, planning is centralized.

FIGURE 9.4 Planning process of Bridgestone Tire and Rubber Company

9.7.3 Case of Hitachi

Unlike Bridgestone, Hitachi is a diversified company, and the planning process is more decentralized. Hitachi started formal long-range planning in 1959, and used it continuously for strategic decisions, the only break being three years after the oil crisis in 1973. Plans in the earlier stages were of the forecasting type, stressed numbers, and were built up using a bottom-up approach, by divisions. Since 1976 top management leadership has been emphasized, and a new style of planning introduced. The new planning system has two characteristics. It emphasizes strategy and policy rather than financial estimates. It emphasizes strategies such as change of product mix, new business areas, new directions for the company, and how to strengthen the capability structure. It introduced two new approaches, the contingency plan and growth-share matrix model. The most important change is that top management now initiates the basic strategy and guideline and that the interactive process is stressed.

The planning process is shown in Figure 9.5. Phase one is to collect environmental information and to analyse one's own company. This is done by the planning department, which is engaged in gathering strategic information all the year round. In the second phase, strategic issues are looked for. Some issues are presented by top management, some are discovered by the planning department through the collection of strategic information, and some are identified through a follow-up of the previous plan. The growth-share matrix model is used here to some extent. In the third phase, corporate goals and business policies are drawn up by the planning department. They include the size of the company, new business, future product mix and other basic policies. Next these goals and policies are discussed by the policy committee which is another name for the management committee, used when it discusses strategic issues. In the guideline, a contingency plan to be incorporated in the division plan is called for. In the fourth phase the division plans are worked out. The contents of the division plan are shown in Table 9.4. We find that the financial estimate is simple, and strategies are emphasized. The planning department consolidates the division plans and identifies the issues. This is the second round of the issue finding, following phase two. Then the plans and issues are presented to the policy committee, and discussed, and a revision of the plan is requested. This revision is co-ordinated by the planning department. In phase five, the corporate plan is drawn up. This includes items similar to those in the division plans; however, it is not just a

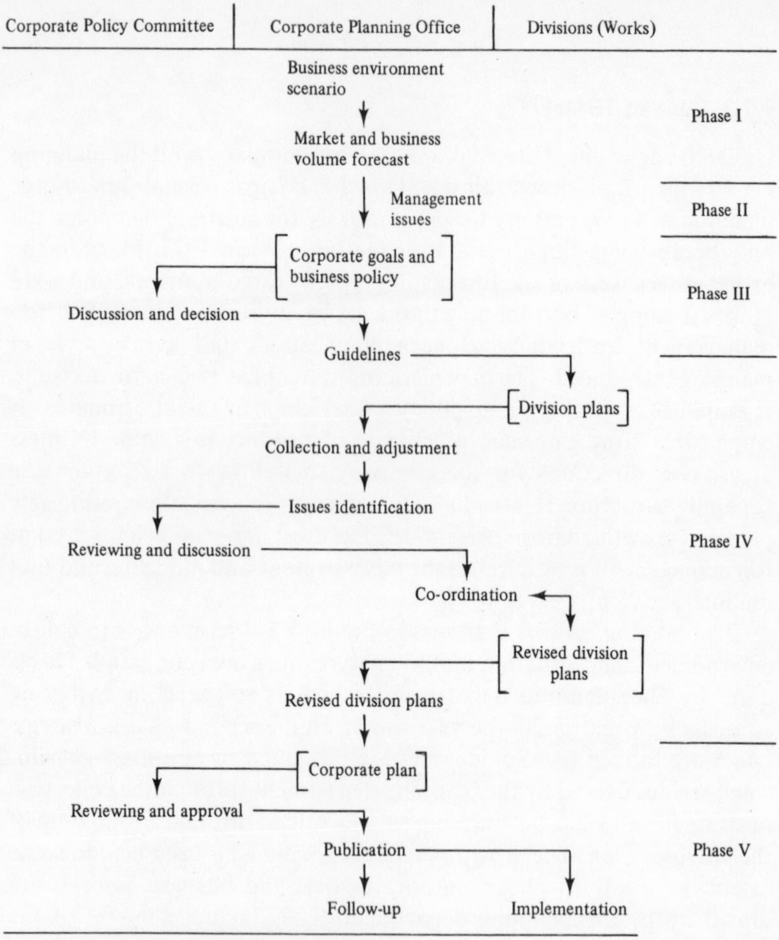

Corporate Policy Committee	Corporate Planning Office	Divisions (Works)

```
                    Business environment
                    scenario                              Phase I
                         ↓
                    Market and business
                    volume forecast
                         ↓    Management                  Phase II
                              issues
                    ┌─────────────────────┐
                    │ Corporate goals and │               Phase III
                    │ business policy     │
                    └─────────────────────┘
    ┌───────────────────┘           ↓
 Discussion and decision ──────── Guidelines ──────────────┐
                                      ↓      ┌─────────────┐│
                                      │      │Division plans│←┘
                                      │      └─────────────┘
                           Collection and adjustment
                                      ↓
    ┌───────────────── Issues identification
 Reviewing and discussion ──────────────────┐
                                            ↓              Phase IV
                                      Co-ordination ←──────┐
                                                 ┌─────────┴────┐
                                                 │Revised division│
                                                 │plans          │
                                      ┌──────────└──────────────┘
                         Revised division plans
                                      ↓
                    ┌───────────────────┐
                    │ Corporate plan    │
                    └───────────────────┘
    ┌───────────────────┘      ↓
 Reviewing and approval ───── Publication ────────────────┐
                                  ↓                        ↓      Phase V
                              Follow-up             Implementation
```

Contents of Long-range plan – Division Plan

(1)   Fundamental plan (five years)

(1-1) Volume of business (five years)
       New order, sales, net income, number of employees
       Investment to equipment and figures connected with these items.

(1-2) Long-range strategies on business activities (five years)
       1. Outline of business environment and important strategies.
       2. Review of products mix.
          a. Important existing markets and new markets.
          b. Important existing products and new products.
          c. Products to be divested.
       3. Methods to strengthen sales ability.
       4. Strategies and tactics about international business.
       5. Other issues to be solved.

(2)   Contingency plan (three years)

(3)   Summary and implementation plan.

FIGURE 9.5 Corporate planning process of Hitachi

262

TABLE 9.4 Business types and planning style

Planning \ Product mix	1. Specialized	2. Diversified
a. Purpose	Formulate the strategy and structure	Integrate the division strategy
b. Idea generation and plan preparation	Centralized	Decentralized
c. Search	Search is narrow and deep, but wide in space, mostly by planning department	Extensive search, mostly by divisions
d. Goals	Order of importance: share of market, growth and profit	Order of importance: profit rate, growth and share of market
e. Key issues	Competition, product improvement and production	New-product development, product mix
f. Time horizon	Long	Long-term strategy plus medium-range plan
g. Uncertainty	Flexible plan	Flexible plan and diversification
h. Control	Direct control	Financial reward is slightly more important

consolidation of the division plan, but also stresses the future strategy that was discussed in phase three. In this case, the sequence of phase is a little different from model. We find that the flow is not straight, but fluctuates. The issues and corporate strategies are found and discussed in the earlier stages and also in the later ones.

9.7.4 Difference of Product Mix and Difference of Planning Process

The above two cases, Bridgestone Tire and Hitachi, show similarities and differences. The similarities are a change from a quantitative plan to a qualitative strategic plan, and from a bottom-up approach to a top-down or interactive process.

There are differences, however, because one company is a specialized company, and the other is a diversified company. Observations of many cases including the above two lead to the following findings. Originally, the strategic decision affects the product mix, but in reverse the product mix affects the strategic decision. The resources have continuity, and the earlier strategy affects the later strategic decisions. For comparison, nine specialized companies and eighteen diversified companies were selected from among 327 companies responding to the survey; the responses were compared, in addition to a number of other direct observations.

9.7.4.1 Purpose of planning

In the specialized company, the purpose of formal planning is to generate a corporate strategy and structure, and in particular to make decisions on capital investment. On the other hand, the main purpose of planning for a diversified company is to integrate the division strategies. The new trend is, however, to emphasize corporate-level strategy so the difference is becoming less.

9.7.4.2 Organizational process of idea generation

It is generally assumed that the strategic ideas in a specialized company come from the top level, because they have the information; while the strategic ideas in a diversified company come from the middle level or from the divisions. In general this assumption is supported. The plan preparation is more centralized in a specialized company, as is shown in Figure 9.4, while it is decentralized in a diversified company, as seen in Hitachi's case in Figure 9.5.

Oversimplification is dangerous, however. The search for strategic issues and the generation of strategic ideas in the early stages of the formal long-range planning process are carried out using a top-down approach or by interaction between top management and the planning staff even in diversified companies. This is seen in Figure 9.5.

On the other hand, many strategic ideas are presented outside the formal planning process, and they are generated by top-down or interactive process, even in diversified companies. The introduction of the computer at Hitachi, and the large investment for super LSI, were both initiated by top management of Hitachi. The strategic decisions at Sony are made by interactive process. The Japanese corporation has centralized authority even in diversified companies.

9.7.4.3 Search

The information collection of specialized companies is narrow and deep, because the product line is narrow, but sometimes the area of research is wider when exporting becomes important. The central planning department plays an important role in the collection of strategic information. Demand forecasting can use sophisticated quantitative approaches – such as econometric models and simulation – to a greater extent.

The diversified company does a more extensive search and this is carried out by the planning department and by the divisions. The information relating to new products is important, because there are more possibilities for new products. For demand forecasting, less sophisticated methods, such as time series extension or logical judgement, are more often used.

9.7.4.4 Corporate goals

It is assumed that the specialized company emphasizes growth and share of the market and the diversified company puts stress on profit. The goals are set by the value system of the controlling power, and the controlling power is held by the key resource holder. If the goal changes, depending on the product mix, then the causal relations will be as follows. Difference of product mix →difference of key resources → difference of managers → difference of the value of the company.

Top managers of the specialized company deal with one major product, and they are involved with its growth and market share. On the other hand, top managers of the diversified company have more variety, and need to have a common measurement, which is profit.

According to the analysis of goals used for long-range planning, the specialized company emphasizes sales (78 per cent of responding companies), growth rate (78 per cent), amount of profit (67 per cent), and share of market (89 per cent). We find that the share of market is particularly stressed. The diversified company emphasizes sales (78 per cent), growth rate (61 per cent), the profit amount (72 per cent), rate of return (56 per cent), return on sales (72 per cent). In this case we find that the two profit rates are stressed (see Table 3.3).

The diversified company sets the division goals. This was also surveyed by different mail questionnaires on organization (addressed to 102 companies in 1982, with responses from 44 companies, 17 diversified companies had division organization structure). The important items for division goals are the sales amount (94 per cent of responding companies), profit (94 per cent), profit rate on sales (59 per cent), and share of market (47 per cent). The growth rate (6 per cent) is not important. These items are almost the same as the corporate goals of the diversified company, excepting the very low importance of growth rate.

9.7.4.5 *Key issues*

Key issues for specialized companies are competition and capital investment, but for diversified companies new-product development and decision on product mix are more important.

9.7.4.6 *Time horizon*

The time horizon for implementing strategic decisions in specialized companies is longer. The time horizon of long-range planning in specialized companies is mostly five years, while that in the diversified company is three years. The two-time horizon system is more useful for diversified companies. The environment of the specialized company is more certain, so longer forecasting is possible. The vulnerability to change of the specialized company also necessitates the longer time horizon.

9.7.4.7 *Coping with uncertainty*

The specialized company has to be more serious and has to be more prepared for risk. Contingency plans and frequent updating are necessary. The diversified company has to be prepared for risks common to all products, such as changes in exchange rate, but to a great extent the stability of the company depends on the difference in the fluctuation of profit among different products which levels down the fluctuations in the total profit of the company.

9.7.4.8 *Control*

The reward for strategic decision and implementation is not in general related to money in Japan, but relatively speaking, financial reward is used to a lesser extent in the specialized company, and to a greater extent in the diversified company. The specialized company uses direct control by top management, and the diversified company uses indirect control by giving financial rewards, though the amount is not large.

9.8 FORMULATION OF INDIVIDUAL STRATEGY

We mentioned previously that strategy formulation is not identical with the long-range planning process. Apart from the comprehensive planning process, we are here concerned with the formulation of individual strategy or project planning.

There are a number of models of strategy formulation. Mintzberg presents three models – entrepreneurial, adaptive and planning modes (Mintzberg, 1973). We stated that there are four models, as is shown in Table 8.10. Here the perceptions of planners on strategic decision-making styles are asked for, and the answers from two countries are shown in Table 9.5.

The answers can be grouped into characteristics of analytical approach and those of intuitive approach. When the decisions are made using an analytical approach, an interactive process is used, adequate information is collected, issues are found by regular scanning, or in the

TABLE 9.5 Style of strategic decisions

'How are the strategic issues, such as new business entry, new-product development, penetration into new markets, found out and initiated? (Please tick one for each six sets.)'

	UK (74 co.) %	Japan (327 co.) %
1. (1) Mostly by top management	35	15*
(2) Mostly by bottom-up	8	32*
(3) Interactive	56	49
(4) NA	1	0
2. (1) Mostly from collection of information	46	79*
(2) Mostly from collection of ideas	46	13*
(3) NA	8	8
3. (1) Mostly in comprehensive planning process	44	21*
(2) Mostly by piecemeal search	51	71*
(3) NA	6	8
4. (1) Mostly from broad policy	71	37*
(2) Mostly by random approach	25	53*
(3) NA	4	10
5. (1) Mostly by agressive search	26	54*
(2) Mostly by ideas submitted from some sources, without agressive search	68	36*
(3) NA	6	10

Notes:
1 The asterisk (*) indicates the level of significance in 10%.
2. For method of survey, see Appendix 9.1.

comprehensive planning process, and a broad policy is set before finding the idea. The intuitive approach uses the other method in Table 9.5. The strategic idea is found intuitively by top management; the idea comes before the information, and is decided by a piecemeal approach.

On the other hand, the innovative or conservative is another category of decision style (see Table 8.10). The innovative style carries out an aggressive search for opportunities, while the conservative style waits until the idea is presented from some source.

The over-all observation of answers in Table 9.5 leads to the impression that the Japanese decision-making style seems to be closer to the innovative and analytical style, and the UK style is closer to the conservative and intuitive style.

The answers for this survey are very subjective; though the same surveys on the same subject in previous years in Japan show similar percentages, they are still not very dependable. It is, however, very important to find out about decision-making styles, and to learn the merits and demerits of each, and which style should be used on which occasions.

We mentioned in previous chapters that the strategic decision-making of successful Japanese companies is rather centralized, using a top-down approach. Table 9.5 shows that, although the bottom-up approach is relatively more frequently used, the interactive process still has the highest percentage. We classify the interactive process into a kind of top-down approach. Also we understand that the bottom-up process in Japan means that many strategic ideas are presented from the heads of departments, so it too is close to the interactive process.

As one example of a strategic decision of a Japanese corporation, we will cite the case where Teijin Company introduced a new product. The introduction of polyester fibre manufactured under licence to ICI, by Teijin Company, one of the largest synthetic-fibre manufacturing corporations in Japan, was a decision that had tremendous impact on the company. The risk involved was very large because large investment was required for the manufacture and because the company was in a bad financial condition.

In 1960 Teijin's sales were one-third of those of Toray and the profit was one-tenth of Toray's. The two companies were the same size until 1953. The choice was whether to stick to rayon and acetate without introducing polyester or acryl, or whether to choose one of the two new synthetic fibres. Teijin had some accumulation of technology on acryl and it was difficult to estimate the future demand for both fibres. The planning department collected a large volume of information and the report favoured polyester, but the research laboratory had more information on acryl. In order to make a decision, the management committee sat and discussed the problem day after day, and finally the president, Oya, was able to get the management committee to make the final decision to introduce polyester from ICI, together with Toray, and produce it under the same brand name. Today the sale of polyester by Teijin accounts for 56 per cent of total sales. This is a typical case of a strategic decision in Japan, following the pattern of Table 9.5.

There are three characteristics in this case. First, top management took a strong initiative. Second, as much information as possible was collected to persuade the decision-makers. The uncertainty remained, however. Third, consensus was considered important, so the management committee sat a number of times in order to arrive at a consensus, although the president had come to the conclusion beforehand.

9.9 DECISION-MAKING UNDER UNCERTAINTY

The difficulty of forecasting the future environment and future results of action taken is the most serious problem in long-range planning. Yet companies have to make a large investment for both research and facilities based on long-term anticipation, because the lead time is long.

When decisions have to be made under uncertain conditions there are several alternative methods of coping. Arranged in order of uncertainty, they are: (1.1) Improvement of information collection and method of forecasting. (1.2) Range forecasting, or three-points forecasting. (2) Sequential decision. (3.1) Early warning system. (3.2) Contingency plan. (4) Diversification of products and markets. (5) Strengthening the power of resistance. (See Table 9.6.)

Increasing the amount of information is the most direct way to cope with uncertainty. It improves the quality of the forecast, and makes it possible to find out the range of the forecast value. Long-range planning itself is a means to increase information.

Range forecasting is predicting a range of sales or profit, usually a three points range of maximum, probable and minimum. One Japanese film company takes into consideration optimistic and pessimistic cases for total national sales, two cases for a share of the imported brands and two cases for the share of the own company among Japanese brands. Two levels of three factors make fifteen combinations, but they are reduced to three points. The most probable case is standard assumption which is used for the standard plan.

TABLE 9.6   Coping with uncertainty

'What is done when forecasting is uncertain? (Please tick as many as necessary.)'

	UK (74 co.) %	Japan (327 co.) %
(1.1) Increase of information in proportion to the effects obtained	21	18
(1.2) Range forecasting, including the worst case	59 ⎱	36*
(1.3) Multiple scenarios	37 ⎰	
(2) Sequential decisions	10	39*
(3.1) Early-warning system	26	8*
(3.2) Contingency plans	47	8*
(4) Diversification of products and markets	21	4*
(5) Basic strength, e.g. strong competitive power, improvement of net worth (equity), or employee morale	23	17

Notes:
[1] The asterisk (*) indicates the level of significance and is 10%.
[2] For method of survey, see Appendix 9.1.

The merits of range forecasting are various. First, it helps to increase the number of strategic options. The company has to be prepared for the pessimistic assumptions, for example. Second, the planner can recognize the real meaning of the expected value of estimation and can avoid building a comprehensive plan on too pessimistic or too optimistic assumptions. Third, the causes of minimum values are identified beforehand, thus it becomes possible to have an early-warning system or to have contingency plans to prevent the performance from going below the expected average. About one-third of Japanese companies use range forecasting.

Sequential decision involves making a partial commitment and collecting information through it, and then making a larger commitment. For example, a new product is sold in a small city as an experiment, and if successful large-scale production goes ahead. It can also mean making a flexible decision first, waiting until enough accurate information is available, and then making detailed decisions later. Two time-span plan is an example of the latter approach, and this is used more often in Japan. In long-range strategy, new directions are decided, important projects are agreed upon and all policy decisions are made with a long-term view; in a medium-range plan a quantitative detailed plan is formulated.

The early-warning system involves finding a key event, and if possible its preceding events, and monitoring both types of events. For example, a Japanese company manufactures textbooks and other educational material for high schools and middle schools; the key factor for change is a change of policy by the Ministry of Education, which is decided at a certain meeting, so the company keeps an eye on the Ministry's meetings. For pharmaceutical companies changes of regulations for medical insurance have a tremendous impact on the demand for their products, so this factor is monitored. This monitoring system is frequently used by Japanese corporations.

The contingency plan system is a recent development. The process of contingency planning is as follows:

1. Identifying key environmental factors of performance. Both the size of impact and the probability of occurrence are measured to select the key factors.
2. Building a standard plan based on the most probable assumption. This constitutes a major part of the comprehensive plan.
3. Selecting several key assumptions other than the most probable situation for each product, and building a separate contingency plan that is not integrated into the comprehensive plan. Not only the worst case, but chance situation too may be taken as an assumption. A contingency plan is not a detailed plan, but it prescribes who should take what action, in what case, and what is expected as the result.
4. A monitoring event is selected, and a trigger point is clearly stated.

Contingency planning brings about several advantages. The company can take quick action in preparation for an adverse situation, and for chance events as well. The company can take better action because it was planned when enough time was available. It increases the usefulness of long-range planning and decreases the distrust of planning. It does not result in too much complexity because the contingency plan is not integrated into the comprehensive plan.

The contingency plan is not yet as widely used in Japan as in the USA and in the UK. The most important reason is that in the UK and in the USA the long-range plan is used by head office to control the divisions, and rewards are related to the accomplishment of the plan, so the plan has to be realistic.

Generally speaking, Japanese corporations are less prepared for uncertainty in their long-range planning, although they are operating in a more uncertain environment. However, we should recognize that the planning itself is a means to reduce the uncertainty, and Japanese corporations make extensive use of long-range planning systems.

9.10 MOTIVATION AND IMPLEMENTATION

People tend to be more concerned with day-to-day jobs and unwilling to foresee an uncertain or ambiguous future or to handle the job with no certainty of results. Motivation is one of the serious problems for formal long-range planning. The more sophisticated the planning system is, the more difficult the motivation and the implementation tends to be.

We asked unstructured questions in two countries about the key success factors for motivation and implementation. We also asked structured questions on the same subject; Table 9.7 shows the result.

The responses to unstructured questions were very similar to the responses to structured questions, so only the latter are shown. According to this response, there are more similarities than differences between the two countries. In both countries, the involvement of top management and line management are emphasized.

In the UK, the involvement and support of top management comes first, the commitment of line management comes next, and a good planning system comes third. In Japan, involvement and support of top management comes first, clear goals and guidelines comes next, and the commitment of line management comes third. Thus the difference is that the system is emphasized in the UK, whereas clear goals are emphasized in Japan. In Japan, the formal planning uses a more top-down approach, so clear goals are more important, but in the UK, for a bottom-up approach from the divisions a good planning system is more important.

According to motivation theory, a man is motivated if the effort is certain to result in performance, if the performance surely affects the reward and if the reward is of value to the man. This is a very pure and general model, but it sheds some light on motivation for strategic decisions. The support of top management is related to the probability of success of performance and probability of rewards. Participation improves the efforts—performance relation, and also changes the value of performance, that is, achievement needs are satisfied. Both guidelines and good planning systems improve the efforts and thus the performance.

TABLE 9.7 Key factors for success (structured question) (related to motivation and implementation)

'What are important factors for motivating planning and for the implementation of it? (Please tick the three most important items.)'

	UK (74 co.) %	Japan (B) (110 co.) %
1. Good planning system	47	24*
2. Understanding and support of top management	90	83
3. Participation of operating department	61	66
4. Appropriate forecasting or assumptions	18	15
5. Appropriate system to cope with uncertainty	10	22
6. Clear goals and guidelines	48	74*
7. Financial rewards for good planning and implementation	11	4
8. NA	1	—

Note: For method of survey, see Appendix 9.1.

A follow-up of the plan is closely related to the motivation. By close follow-up and a clear reflection of the results of performance in the rewards, planners in various departments are motivated to implement the plan. The progress of projects is reviewed once or several times in a year, and the quantitative parts of the plan are reviewed directly, or through the budget.

We then investigated the use of financial rewards for planning and implementation. We asked whether the progress and the performance are related to the financial reward. According to the survey, the Japanese company uses financial rewards to the least extent (see Table 9.8); the US companies put a lot of emphasis on financial rewards; and UK companies' practice comes in between the Japanese and the US practices.

What are the reasons for this difference of reward system? In Japan, the loyalty of the employee to the organization is high since they will work for it for a lifetime. The evaluation of an employee tends to be made on the accumulation of long-term performance. In the USA and in the UK, the manager tends to move from one company to another to obtain better treatment, so the feedback from the performance has to be prompt.

In Japan, however, there is a growing concern for the need of linkage of long-range planning to some kind of reward system in addition to the

TABLE 9.8 Long-range planning and financial rewards

'Is progress and performance related to some kind of financial reward of managers?'

	UK (74 co.) %	Japan (327 co.) %	USA (23 co.) %
1. Not at all	45	57*	30
2. To some extent	50	36*	48
3. To a great extent	4	1	22
4. NA	1	–	–

Notes:
[1] The asterisk (*) indicates level of significance at 10%, comparison is between UK and Japan.
[2] For method of survey, see Appendix 9.1 and 9.2.

four important factors mentioned above. The follow-up of planning by top management is one of the approaches. In one pharmaceutical company, the actual implementation of a long-range plan is translated into numerical points. The level of achievement is expressed by the number of points each department has obtained, and it is made public quarterly. This point is not related to the financial reward of the head of the department, but the publication itself is a strong stimulus to implementation. In order to avoid setting easy-to-implement low targets, the actual results are not only compared with the plan, but also with the performance of the previous year.

9.11 SUMMARY

Long-range planning is a formal system used to improve strategic decisions. With long-range planning the company can collect strategic information, can find long-term opportunities and threats and can prepare for future long-term projects now. By long-range planning, the company can also integrate a number of projects, and can allocate limited resources in the most effective way. In other words, the company can make strategic decisions using the 'innovative and analytical mode' (see Table 8.10).

Long-range planning is widely used among Japanese large corporations, with more than 70 per cent of them having the system. This is evidence that the Japanese corporation is long-term oriented.

The system of long-range planning of Japanese corporations is not necessarily sophisticated. The planning systems of many successful US corporations, such as General Electric, is much more refined. Some Japanese systems consist mostly of numbers, and others consist only of basic strategies. But the trend is from quantitative plan to more strategic plan including both strategies and financial numbers. The author maintains that even if the system is not very sophisticated, long-range planning itself gives a great stimulus to long-term orientation and to strategy orientation.

The planning process of the specialized company is centralized and that of the diversified company is decentralized. Generally speaking, the planning process is centralized, however. This is an organizational characteristic of Japanese corporations. The centralized strategic decisions by top management tend to be innovative.

The goals used in the long-range plan indicate the stated objectives of the corporation. The goals of Japanese corporations emphasize growth and the welfare of employees, whereas the US and UK corporations stress financial goals.

The finding of strategic issues is an important part of the strategic decision process. According to the 'subjective answers' of the survey, the strategic issues arise through an interactive process between top management and the planning staff. Issues derived from collection of information and by a aggressive search. This process is a kind of innovative and analytical approach, as analysed in Chapter 8.

The motivation for long-range orientation and implementation of the long-range plan is an important problem. For this purpose, the involvement of top management, its support and the formulating of clear goals are important. The participation of operating departments is also important. These human elements are much more significant for implementation than the system itself.

9.11.1 Problems

9.11.1.1 *Effectiveness of long-range planning*

A long-range planning system is one means to improve strategic decisions. The MITI survey shows that those companies that have long-range planning show a better performance than non-planners (MITI, 1978). There are a number of surveys in the USA that show that planners outperform the non-planners (Thune and House, 1970; Karger and Malik, 1975), but some surveys show no difference of performance between the planners and non-planners (Hofer and Schendel, 1978). According to the author's observation in Japan over many years, long-range planning is so widely used that it is hard to compare the planners and non-planners, and there is also a variety of performance among the planners. The problem is whether good strategies are incorporated in the plans and whether the plans are implemented. The system of long-range planning of Japanese corporations is not very sophisticated. Plans of many corporations are only quantitative, for example (Table 9.2). The author visited many US companies in 1976 and found that the systems of planning of US corporations – GE, Northrop, LSI, Ameron, Times Mirror and others – are more sophisticated.

There are some doubts as to whether Japanese long-range planning systems, which are not necessarily sophisticated, can be effective. The author thinks that even if the system is not very refined, the long-range planning itself improves the strategic decisions, from intuitive to analytical. At the very least, it is useful in two aspects: to find the right strategic issues; and to integrate the decisions to bring about a better allocation of resources.

The planning system is changing, and improving. The most frequent answers to the question on the recent changes of planning systems show that planning is changing from financial estimation to a greater concentration on the core strategic issues (41 per cent in the 1982 survey).

9.11.1.2 How to cope with uncertainty

As already discussed, there are a number of means to cope with uncertainty, but it is still a problem because the environment is more uncertain in Japan. The competition is severe at home and the exporting market is distant and heterogeneous.

Increasing the amount of information is the most direct approach, but there are limitations, and there remain difficulties in forecasting. As a means of making sequential decisions, the two-plan system – long-range strategy and medium-range planning – is becoming more widely used and annual revision is becoming more popular. Japanese long-range planning used to emphasize the nature of the goal and planning was revised less frequently, but annual revision and updating is now becoming popular (from 47 per cent of companies in 1979 to 67 per cent in 1982). In earlier times, a fixed terminal date with occasional revision was popular (42 per cent in 1979, but 33 per cent in 1982).

9.11.1.3 Follow-up and implementation

If the plan is beautifully drawn up, but not implemented, it is only a useless document. In Japan the follow-up tends to be weak, and some parts of the plan are not implemented. US corporations have a better follow-up, because the long-range plan is used to integrate and control the strategy of many divisions, and because the financial rewards are related to the quality and implementation of the plan. In Japan the top managers tend to trust their subordinate managers, and not to conduct a strict follow-up of plans. The quality and performance is reflected in evaluation over a long period, but it is not reflected in a frequent change of bonus.

Implementation is a problem but, largely speaking, the long-range plan is implemented through budgeting and project plans. The links between the long-range plan and budgeting are improving through the

TABLE 9.9 Distribution of respondents by industry

	Companies with long-range plan			
	UK 1981 Private	Public	Japan 1979	Japan 1982 (Japan (B))
(1) Mining, Construction and Engineering	6	–	25	13
(2) Food, fisheries and tobacco	15	–	12	8
(3) Fibre, pulp and paper	7	–	21	10
(4) Chemicals	7	–	38	16
(5) Petroleum, rubber, soil and stone	7	–	16	3
(6) Iron, steel and non-ferrous metals			24	12
(7) Machinery	6	–	27	14
(8) Electrical appliances and precision machinery	10	–	36	21
(9) Transportation equipment and machinery	(a)	–	27	14
(10) Finance and insurance	10	–	41	–
(11) Commerce, service, real estate	6	–	29	–
(12) Communication, warehousing and transportation	–	7	25	–
(13) Electricity, gas and coal	–	5	6	–
(14) Miscellaneous	–	7	–	2
Total	74	19	327	110

Notes:
[1] (a) Included in machinery.
[2] In the UK 'public' means nationalized industry.

use of medium-range plans, by incorporating the long-range plan into annual guidelines for budgeting, or by incorporating the structure plan (capital budgeting and personnel plan) into the budget. The projects are implemented by the use of project teams which are used frequently in successful Japanese corporations.

APPENDIX 9.1 METHOD OF SURVEY BY MAIL

1. In Japan, questionnaires were sent out in July 1979 by mail to 1607 companies, of which 402 companies responded (response ratio 25 per cent), and 327 companies with long-range plans were analysed. In April 1982 additional questionnaires were sent to 327 companies, and 110 usable responses were obtained. 'Japan (B)' indicates this survey.

   In the UK, questionnaires were sent out in February 1981 by mail to 838 companies, of which 122 companies responded (response ratio 15 per cent) and 93 companies with long-range plans were analysed.
2. For this paper, only private companies were analysed.
3. Distribution of respondents by industry is as in Table 9.9.
4. Distribution of respondents by sales is as in Table 9.10.
5. In the UK, Professor J. Stopford of the London Graduate School of Business co-operated with me for designing and analysing the survey. The Society for Strategic and Long Range Planning in London also helped me in many ways for implementing the survey.

TABLE 9.10 Distribution of respondents by sales

	UK 1981			Japan 1979	Japan 1982 (Japan (B))
	Private	*Public**	*Total*		
Over $10 000 million	2	0	2	8	0
$9 999–$1 000 million	27	8	35	54	17
$999–$333 million	17	4	21	69	26
$332–$100 million	15	3	18	95	43
$99–$33 million	7	0	7	67	15
$32–$10 million	3	1	4	29	9
Under $10 million	3	3	6	3	0
NA	0	0	0	2	0
Total	74	19	93	327	110

Note:
* Public companies operating in the non-market sector were allocated to the size ranges on the basis of their total employment, using a capital–labour ratio in the nearest equivalent private-sector concern.

APPENDIX 9.2   METHOD OF SURVEY BY MAIL – USA

1. In the USA, questionnaires were sent out in May 1975 to 152 companies in the southern California area, to which 26 companies responded (response ratio 17 per cent), and 23 companies with long-range plans were analysed excepting question 1.
2. Distribution of respondents by industry is as in Table 9.11.
3. This survey was carried out with the co-operation of Los Angeles Chapter, Planning Executives Institute.

TABLE 9.11

	USA	
	Companies responded	Companies with long-range plan
(1) Mining and construction	3	3
(2) Food and fisheries	1	1
(3) Fibre, pulp and paper		
(4) Chemicals	1	
(5) Petroleum, rubber, soil and stone	2	2
(6) Iron, steel and non-ferrous metals		
(7) Machinery		
(8) Electrical appliances and precision machinery	5	5
(9) Transportation equipment and machinery	3	3
(10) Finance and insurance	5	4
(11) Commerce, service, real estate, communication, warehousing and transportation	5	4
(12) Electricity and gas	1	1
Total	26	23

3. Distribution of respondents by assets is an in Table 9.12.

TABLE 9.12

| | USA | |
	Companies responded	Companies with long-range plan
Over $10 000 million	1	1
$9 999–$1 000 ,,	10	9
$999–333 ,,	5	5
$332–100 ,,	5	5
$99–33 ,,		
$32–10 ,,	5	3
Under $10 ,,		
	26	23

APPENDIX 9.3   CONTENTS OF LONG-RANGE PLAN

TABLE 9.13 Contents of long-range plan

'What are the contents of the long-range plan? (Please tick important items.)'

	UK (74 co.) %	Japan (327 co.) %
1. Missions and objectives of the company as a whole	73	31*
2. Environement forecasting and competitive analysis	71	60
3. Analysis of the company strength and weakness	58	58
4. Forecasting future of own company under present policy	60	37*
5. Problems and opportunities of the company	66	43*
6. Goals and policies of company as a whole	69	91*
7. Vertical integration	10	2
8. New-product development	67	50*
9. New-market development	63	32*
10. Multinational management	25	27
11. Strengthening the marketing competitive power	32	43
12. Cost reduction plan	41	57*
13. Information system	16	16
14. Company acquisition	45	1*
15. Research and development	38	34
16. Marketing plan	57	60
17. Production plan	42	49
18. Capital investment	73	72
19. Investment for subsidiaries	37	38
20. Material plan	18	18
21. Manpower plan	54	77*
22. Education and management development	27	32
23. Employee welfare	11	12
24. Industrial relations	15	–
25. Planning or organization	36	24
26. Estimated profit and loss statement	79	63*
27. Estimated flow of funds	74	67
28. Estimated balance sheet	71	40*
29. Contingency plans for adverse situations	37	8*

Notes:
[1] Asterisks (*) indicate level of significance is 10%.
[2] For details of survey, see Appendix 9.1.

REFERENCES

Imai, K. (1980) *Keiei Senryaku Nyumon* (Introduction to Strategic Planning), Tokyo, Management Sha.

Kansai Productivity Centre (1976) *Keiei Soshiki no Shindoko* (New Trends on Business Organizations), Tokyo, Kansai Productivity Centre.

Kobayashi, Y. (1967) *Keieikeikaku* (Business Planning), Tokyo, Kinbara Shuppan.

Kono, T. (1975) *Choki Keieikeikaku no Tankyu* (Analysis of Long-range Planning), Tokyo, Diamond Sha.

Kono, T. (1978) *Choki Keieikeikaku no Jitsurei* (New Cases of Long-range Planning), Tokyo, Dobunkan.

Kono, T. (1980) *Senryaku Keieikeikaku no Tatekata* (Introduction to Strategic Planning), Tokyo, Diamond Sha.

MITI (1973–80) *Keiei Ryoku Hyoka* (Measurement of Corporate Capability), Tokyo, MITI.

Ackoff, Russell (1970) *A Concept of Corporate Planning*, New York, John Wiley.

Al-Bazzaz, S. and Grinyer, P. M. (1980) 'How Planning Works in Practice – A Survey of 48 UK Companies', *Long Range Planning*, Aug.

Andrews, Kenneth (197?) *The Concept of Corporate Strategy*, Homewood, Ill., Dow Jones-Irwin.

Ang, J. S. and Chua, J. H. (1979) 'Long Range Planning in Large US Corporations – A Survey', *Long Range Planning*, Apr.

Ansoff, H. I. (1965) *Corporate Strategy: An Analytic Approach to Business Policy for Growth and Expansion*, New York, McGraw-Hill.

Ansoff, H. I., Avener, J., Brandenburg, R. G., Portner, F. E. and Radosevich, R. (1971) *Acquisition Behavior of US Manufacturing Firms*, Nashville, Tennessee, Vanderbilt University Press.

Davies, A. H. (1981) 'Strategic Planning in the Thomas Cook Group', *Long Range Planning*, Oct.

Fildes, R., Jalland, M. and Wood, D. (1978) 'Forecasting in Conditions of Uncertainty', *Long Range Planning*, Aug.

Galbraith, J. and Nathanson, D. (1978) *Strategy Implementation: The Role of Structure and Process*, St Paul, West Publishing.

Glueck, W. (1976) *Business Policy, Strategy Formation and Management Action*, New York, McGraw-Hill.

Godiwalla, Y. M., Meinhart, W. A. and Warde, W. D. (1978) 'Corporate Planning – A Functional Approach', *Long Range Planning*, Oct.

Henry, H. W. (1977) 'Formal Planning in Major US Corporations', *Long Range Planning*, Oct.

Hofer, C. W. and Schendel, D. (1978) *Strategy Formulation, Analytical Concepts*, Minnesota, West Publishing.

Hussey, E. E. (1974) *Corporate Planning, Theory and Practice*, Oxford, Pergamon Press.

Karger, D. W. and Malik, Z. A. (1975) 'Long Range Planning and Organizational Performance', *Long Range Planning*, Dec.

Katz, A. (1978) 'Planning in the IBM Corp.', *Long Range Planning*, June.

Kono, T. (1976) 'Long Range Planning – Japan–USA, A Comparative Study', *Long Range Planning*, Oct.

Lenz, R. T. and Lyles, M. A. (1981) 'Tackling the Human Problems in Planning', *Long Range Planning*, Apr.

MacMillan, I. (1978) *Strategy Formulation: Political Concepts*, St Paul, West Publishing.

Mann, C. W. (1978) 'The Use of a Model in Long Term Planning – A Case History', *Long Range Planning*, Oct.

Mintzberg, H. (1973) 'Strategy-making in Three Mode', *California Management Review*, Winter.

Murakami, T. (1978) 'Recent Changes in Long Range Corporate Planning in Japan', *Long Range Planning*, Apr.

Naor, J. (1978) 'A New Approach to Corporate Planning', *Long Range Planning*, Apr.

Nazel, A. (1981) 'Strategy Formulation for Smaller Firm', *Long Range Planning*, Aug.

Richards, M. (1978) *Organizational Goal Structures*, St Paul, West Publishing.

Steiner, G. A. (1969) *Top Management Planning*, New York, Macmillan.

Steiner, G. A. (1979) *Strategic Planning*, New York, Free Press.

Steiner, G. A. and Miner, J. B. (1977) *Management Policy and Strategy: Text, Readings and Cases*, New York, Macmillan.

Taylor, B. (1975) 'Strategic for Planning', *Long Range Planning*, Aug.

Taylor, B. and Hawkins, K. (ed.) (1972) *Handbook of Strategic Planning*, London, Longman.

Thompson, J. D. (1967) *Organization in Action*, New York, McGraw-Hill.

Thune, S. and House, R. (1970) 'Where Long Range Planning Pays Off', *Business Horizons*, Aug.

Töpfer, A. (1978) 'Corporate Planning and Control in German Industry', *Long Range Planning*, Feb.

Warren, E. K. (1966) *Long Range Planning*, New York, Prentice-Hall.

Yoshino, M. Y. (1968) *Japan's Managerial System, Tradition and Innovation*, Mass. MIT Press.

10 Organizational Structure and Resource Structure

10.1 CONCEPT

The organizational structure of a company is the way that company groups its jobs and defines the line of authority to integrate the jobs. Organizational structure has three dimensions, as illustrated in Figure 10.1. From the similarity of goals, the sub-units are grouped under products. The diversified company takes this grouping as the first stage; it uses the product division structure. From the similarity of required knowledge, the jobs are grouped under strategic planning, development, production and marketing. This is a functional grouping. The specialized company uses functional organization as its first stage of grouping.

The company's capability has three resource elements: the system, the human resources (and atmosphere) and the facilities. These elements specify the contents and quality of the capability. If there is a balance between each element, and if the level of key capabilities is high, then the strategy will be well generated and well implemented and the company's performance will be high.

10.2 BALANCED CHANGE OF STRATEGY AND STRUCTURE

The structure needs to fit the strategy. As the strategy changes, the structure has to be changed, and there should be a dynamic matching between the two. There is a good deal of support for this view (Chandler, 1962; Scott, 1971; Channon, 1973; Galbraith and Nathanson, 1978). The author finds that it is true for successful Japanese enterprises, but with some modification. We should differentiate the strategy-generating department from the strategy-implementing department; the former is more important than the latter. The process of balanced change is then as follows.

284

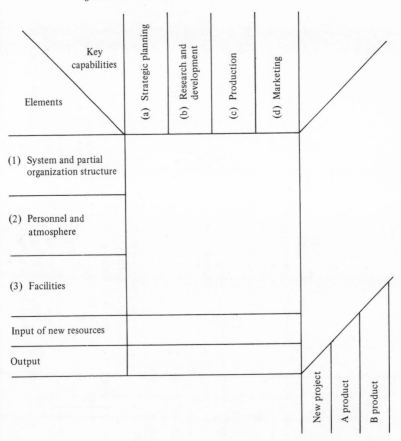

FIGURE 10.1 Three dimensions of organizational and capability structure

The perception of opportunity and threat by the top management → strengthening of the strategy-generating department → high-level strategy → the strategy-implementing capability → operation → performance

The problems of functional departmentation or product division are frequently discussed in relation to the strategy (Rumelt, 1974, for example), but they are mainly concerned with the implementation of strategy, and have little relation to strategy generation. Strategy generation should have separate departments.

The successful Japanese companies first tried to strengthen their

TABLE 10.1 Change of product mix and changes of capability structure of Canon Company

Period	1937–55	1955–65	1965–75	1975–
Product mix	Camera	Camera Optical products	Camera Optical products Office equipment	Camera Optical product Copier Electronics products
New products — Camera	High-quality camera	Medium-quality camera Single-lens reflex		Auto-focus camera
New products — Optical	X-ray camera	TV lens	Eequipment to produce semi-conductor	Medical optics
New products — Office equipments		Microfilming system	Electrocalculator Copiers	Office computer Facsimile Razor beam printer
(a) New capacity for development	Optical technolocy Fine mechanical		Electronics Physics Chemical Fine optical technology	Software technolocy Element materials technology Communication technology

	One plant	Three plants	Multinational production	Six plants in Japan and three plants overseas
(b) Production				
(c) Marketing channel	Wholesaler	Exclusive wholesaler	Exclusive wholesaler	Strong exclusive channels Direct sales network in overseas countries
(1) Organizational structure	Functional	Functional	Product division	Product division
(2) Personnel (home country)		(1960) 4 600	New wage system (status system)	(1980) 9 000
Sales (million yen)	(1950) 378	(1960) 4 190	(1970) 44 790	(1980) 240 800

strategy-generating departments and next strengthened the key implementing capabilities. Table 10.1 shows the changes in strategy and structure in Canon Company.

Over the last thirty years, Canon has developed a number of new products. The product mix has changed, and the capability for product development has expanded. The company diversified from cameras to optical instruments and to office equipment. To develop these new products the company added new capability, in the fields of electronics and semi-conductor technology, in addition to optical and mechanical technology.

The new products need the new capacity, because the existing capability was a limiting factor. It is one of its key success factors that the company has been able adequately to expand its capability to meet the need for new-product development. Canon had two strokes of luck in this connection. After the war, the company was able freely to recruit many competent optical and mechanical engineers from the dissolved army laboratory, which enhanced its capability tremendously. In 1960 Canon developed a kind of electronic disc recorder and recruited many electrical engineers. The product itself was a failure but this early addition of electronic skills put the company in a favourable position to develop the electronic camera and office equipment, this time successfully.

It should be noted that Canon's strategy-generating department was to some extent already strong in 1955 before diversification. Top management was a management committee; there was already a planning department; and when their sales were still only 4 billion yen (15 million dollars), Canon had three kinds of research and development departments. In 1962 it started long-range planning to integrate the strategic decisions.

In order to implement the strategy, it built a succession of new manufacturing plants – five large factories in twenty years, all of which incorporated new production technology. The sales capabilities were added afterwards.

Production and sales increased, but it is surprising that the number of employees did not increase very much. Whereas the sales have increased sixty times in nominal terms and fifteen times in fixed price during the past twenty years, the number of employees has barely doubled, from 4600 to 9000. It shows that by introducing new technology, the optimum combination of labour and facilities changed, and balance of resources was attained.

Bridgestone Tyre and Rubber Company, which became one of the three strongest tyre manufacturers in the world, built up strong development capabilities and they were followed with aggressive capital investment. In 1965, when the Tokyo plant was built, it included a strong technical centre incorporating a research laboratory, new-product development department and a tyre development department. The company was the first to introduce the nylon cord tyre, polyester cord tyre and steel-radial tyre, the last being one of the company's key success factors in recent years. The company now has a strong technical centre with 1100 employees (6 per cent of all employees) and spends 4 per cent of sales on research and development. In addition to the four plants in 1960, it has built nine large manufacturing plants in Japan and four in foreign countries over the last twenty years. The timing of investment was carefully selected so that the construction would be carried out during depression periods. The sales increased from 37 billion yen in 1960 to 500 billion yen in 1980 (thirteen times in nominal terms and 3.25 times in real terms), but the number of employees only went up from 9370 to 17 800. Although two of the foreign plants (Iran and Singapore) proved to be failures, the aggressive capital investment for plant expansion was one of the company's success factors. To integrate a balanced increase of the various capabilities, the president initially drew up a detailed long-range plan, and after 1967 the company adopted a formal long-range planning system.

The successful companies have been able to achieve this balanced growth in key areas. As stated before, their top management is long-range oriented and growth-oriented, supported by a competent middle management employed for life; they are aggressive in expanding and improving their capability structure. The high percentage of university graduates on the staff makes it possible for the company to plan highly technological facilities; the standard of the ordinary workers is also uniformly high, and they can immediately operate the new machines. There is a plentiful supply of capital in the form of loans from the banks, who are supported by the high savings rate of the average Japanese household (over 20 per cent). The successful companies have been able to avoid over-capacity by the use of long-range planning to integrate the decisions.

Some companies failed because they could not build a balanced capability structure. Van Jacket Company was a high-growth company. It was established in Tokyo in 1958, and by 1974 the sales had increased to 45 billion yen (0.2 billion dollars). In 1978 it went bankrupt. Van Jacket company was a manufacturer of young men's fashion suits. The president was a famous designer. However, the company did not have a planning rtment, could not analyse changes in demand, and did not have ˌ ˌugh product mix to offset the decline of one product. It did not have any production facilities, the manufacturing being ordered from whichever outside manufacturer offered the lowest price. It did not train its sales force, and did not have enough information on the dead stock. Nor did it have the necessary accounting and control systems. The equity ratio was only 1 per cent. This is one of the failure cases where balanced capabilities were not developed.

Another failure case, Fuji Sashi Company (an aluminium window-frame manufacturer), was also a rapid-growth company with sales of 78 billion yen in 1976, but it went bankrupt in 1978. The founder was a strong, authoritative leader, without any assisting planning staff; the company lacked an open and appropriate financial control system. There were a number of reasons for its failure, but one is important: the imbalance of its sales capability and production capability. Because of a comparatively weak sales force, its share of the market fell continuously from 33 per cent to 15 per cent in ten years. The total sales of aluminium frames were increasing, so the company continued to expand its production facilities, and after the oil crisis found itself with over-capacity. To strengthen its sales capability, it hurriedly built thirty direct sales channels, which became a financial burden on the company. Thus the imbalance between sales and production and the over-capacity of production were the most important reasons for the failure of Fuji Sashi Company.

From the above cases, we can generalize on the principles for success. A strategy-generating capability should be built up before the strategy is formulated, and then the strategy-implementing capability is changed as necessary.

A balanced change of capabilities is important. A partial weakness, if in a key capability, inpairs the whole.

No one capability should have over-capacity; there should be a complementary balance between capabilities for efficient operation, a synergic relationship.

10.3 LESS USE OF ACQUISITION AND MERGER

Capability can be changed by any of the following methods: (i) internal growth, (ii) internal growth through licensing, (iii) joint venture by contract, (iv) joint-venture company, (v) purchase of assets, (vi) acquisition and merger (Kono, 1974).

Acquisition is a quick means of augmenting the capability but

Japanese companies seldom acquire other companies for diversification, preferring to use internal development or joint venture by contract. This is easily evidenced by looking at the history of large corporations, or by looking at the statistics.

It is true that there were many acquisitions before the war. For example, from 1935 to 1940 there were a lot of acquisitions by Hitachi and Mitsubishi Heavy Industries. This was, however, an unusual period. Companies acquired other companies to diversify in order to meet military demands. Many of these acquired companies had to be sold after the war, to comply with orders under the anti-monopoly law.

Toyota and Matsushita Electric's growth after the war was due to internal development with few acquisitions. If this strategy is compared with the strategy of US and UK companies there is a sharp contrast. When we read Moody's manual we find that the history of the US company is the history of acquisitions.

Growth by acquisition tends to have several problems. Easy entry into the market using acquisition may result in diversification without synergy, with eventual failure. Weak companies that should be driven out of the market might be kept alive by acquisition with the result that resources are wasted.

Less use of acquisition, and more use of internal development, tend to make management pay more careful attention to the effects of synergy, with the result of good concentration of the company's strength. It has also resulted in severe competition and in the application of the 'survival of the fittest' principle.

Another reason is that there was a technology gap between Japan on the one hand and the USA and European countries on the other. It was more profitable to buy the patents than to acquire other companies in Japan.

More important reasons are sociological ones. Even in low-technology industries there are no acquisitions. It is considered shameful behaviour to sell one's own company. Japanese people are group-oriented, and members of the company have a deep sense of identification with their company and find it difficult to integrate as members of other companies. Wages and promotions are determined by length of service to a great extent, so wages of the same profession in different companies are not necessarily the same. The labour unions are organized on a company-wide basis, so unions tend to be against acquisitions. Since companies guarantee lifetime employment, it is not easy to decrease the number of employees after acquisition. These are important reasons for the lower use of acquisitions in Japan.

Joint venture by contract and establishment of joint-venture companies are more frequently used as growth strategies. In cases where one partner is a foreign company, the technical knowledge is provided by the foreign partner and production and marketing capabilities are provided by Japanese companies. In cases where both partners are Japanese companies, each one offers its stronger capabilities, which form a complementary relationship, so that each company can attain a much better performance than when the project is carried out by one company. This is one synergy effect. A typical example is the case of joint venture on 'Crestin', an anti-cancer drug. A chemical company called Kureha Kagaku Company developed this drug and through a joint-venture agreement it was sold by Sankyo Company, a large pharmaceutical company that has strong marketing channels. The joint venture did indeed have a synergic effect, and it proved to be a surprising success – a sales figure of 30 billion yen per year which brought handsome profit to both companies.

Through the joint venture the partners can remain independent, and can keep their own identities, which is important for both management and employees. In addition, the Japanese company is willing to co-operate with complementary organizations, as was stated in Chapter 1. In the USA, the joint venture is a cause of frustration in many cases; both parties want to be more independent, so the acquire-and-control policy is necessary. (For joint venture, see Kono, 1974.)

10.4 STRATEGY-GENERATION DEPARTMENT

The generation of new products and other new strategies is different from the routine operation of production and sales. It needs to have special departments. Here we will study the planning department and the research and development department.

10.4.1 The Planning Department and Top Management

Top management plays the most important part in finding strategic issues and promoting the strategies. The planning department supports top management in generating the strategy.

The establishment of planning departments is of recent development, but it is remarkable that almost all large companies have had a planning department from early times. Long-range planning became popular in the 1960s, and the planning departments appeared along with this system.

The total number of personnel in planning departments is about 9.4 (6.8 planning staff and 2.6 assistants), according to my survey on the long-range planning of 327 companies in 1979.

There are four major responsibilities for the planning department. The first one is to promote strategic thinking. It is important to let top management recognize that strategic decisions are different from operational ones. It is also important to let the line managers support the new strategy. The second responsibility is to collect strategic information. Indications of future political changes, general economic trends, changes of society, general business trends and information about competitors are sought by the planning department. There is no other department that collects such strategic information. The research and development department collects information on future trends in technology.

The third responsibility is to recommend the new strategies. The planning department will recommend any new business that is not related to the present line departments. It also prepares the basic plans for improving the existing products. The concept of growth-share matrix (Hofer and Schendel, 1978) is sometimes used here. The preparation of basic goals and guidelines for long-range planning is very important.

The fourth responsibility is to integrate the divisional strategic plans and to control their implementation. This is a very important job for the diversified companies.

It is surprising that such a small department plays such an important role; in Japan top management relies on their planning departments to collect strategic information and generate strategic ideas.

A case in point is the planning department at Hitachi. This department has twelve planning staff plus two assistants, and all the members are university graduates. This can be compared with one planner at GEC in the UK, and thirty-six planners at GE in the USA (fifteen for economic research, fifteen for strategic planning, six for co-ordination, in 1978).

The responsibilities of the corporate planners at Hitachi are as follows: (i) To help the top management formulate its long-range plans and to collect related strategic information. (ii) To plan changes in the present product mix. (iii) To plan new products and new business. These are the products that are expected to have a large impact and a wider span than the divisions' products, or else a different nature from them.

Project teams are organized for this purpose. (iv) To make a two-year estimate of demand by the macro approach. (v) To plan special projects ordered by the president. This is one example of a planning department that is an active rather than a co-ordinative type.

10.4.2 Research and Development Department

For technology-intensive manufacturing industries the capability of their research and development departments is the key capability. There are two characteristics of Japanese companies' research and development departments. The first is that the laboratories are centralized even when the products are diversified. The second one is that the expenditure and the number of personnel employed have been increasing in recent years.

Mitsubishi Heavy Industries is a very diversified company, producing ships, heavy equipment and aeroplanes. It has seven divisions, but the research laboratories are centralized. Five laboratories are under the direct control of the technical department of the head office, employing 1400 research staff and assistants (2.5 per cent of total number of employees). By concentrating the laboratories the research effort can be more efficient. Hitachi has one central laboratory and five specialized laboratories under the head office, and two laboratories in the home appliance division. There are also development departments in twenty-four plants. The total number of personnel in research and development is about 7500 people, or 10 per cent of all employees. It spends about 100 billion yen, or 5.5 per cent of its sales. This percentage is slightly lower than that of GE or Siemens, but in Japan the research funded by government is negligible, while in the cases of GE and Siemens, more than half of their research is paid for by their respective governments.

Canon has three kinds of research organizations. The first one is the Future Technology Centre, having about six members of staff. It forecasts the likely technological development in the five or ten years ahead, and studies the future direction of new products for Canon. The second one is the Central Research and Development Laboratory with about 200 staff. It does basic and applied research, and develops new products three to five years in advance. The Central Production Technology Centre, with a staff of 300, is responsible for developing new-production technology. The third type of research organization is the development departments of the three product divisions, with about 600 employees over all. They deal with the improvement of products, and also the design of the new products transferred from the central laboratory. The total number of people employed in the new-product development and production technology department is approximately 1000. If 300 drafters and designers are excluded, the remaining 700 comes to about 9 per cent of all employees.

Strong organizations for research and development have only recently emerged, but now the size and manpower of these departments in successful companies are comparable to those of the strongest companies in the world.

The percentage of research expenditure of the 102 manufacturing companies is as shown in Table 4.6. The average is 1.97 per cent of sales, but the technology-related diversifiers have a higher percentage (2.83 per cent for RMT and 2.61 per cent for RT). This is a kind of fit between the strategies.

Other surveys show that the technology-intensive industries spend more than the sum shown in the author's survey. The survey by the Bureau of Statistics shows rates of research and development in 1976 and in 1980 (Table 10.2).

This percentage is comparable to that of the US or German companies. It is characteristic that the percentage of research personnel is higher than the percentage of research expenditure. The large number of staff employed in research is the strength of successful Japanese corporations.

Toyota has one research laboratory and two technical centres, employs 2500 people in research and development (5 per cent of all

TABLE 10.2 Ratio of research expenditure on sales and research staff in total employees

	Ratio of research expenditure on sales		Ratio of research staff to total employees	
	(1976) %	(1980) %	(1976) %	(1980) %
Electrical equipment	3.66	3.72	4.95	5.55
Fine mechanical equipment	2.37	3.02	3.26	4.06
Chemical	2.39	2.55	4.72	5.67
Transportation equipment	2.08	2.34	1.77	2.57
Machine	1.79	1.90	2.31	3.09
Iron and steel	1.02	1.14	1.03	1.28

Source: Statistic Bureau, Survey of Research and Development, 1981.

employees) and spends 100 billion yen (in 1978, 400 million dollars, if one dollar is 250 yen), or 4 per cent of sales, on research and development.

10.5 DEPARTMENTAL ORGANIZATIONAL STRUCTURE – FUNCTIONAL AND DIVISIONAL STRUCTURE

The specialized company has a functional structure, and the diversified company has a divisional structure; this is the general principle. There is less diffusion of division structure in Japan. Kansai Productivity Centre survey shows that 38 per cent of 491 companies have division structure (Kansai Productivity Centre, 1976). There are a number of surveys on the organizational structure in the USA and they show that about 80 per cent of large US companies have product division or geographical division structure (for example, Conference Board, 1973; Rumelt, 1974; Kagono *et al.*, 1981).

In the case of the 102 companies we are investigating, the relationship between the strategy and the organizational structure is shown in Table 4.2. When we compare the organizational structure with that of businesses in other countries, we find that in Japan the divisional structure is used to a much lesser extent. Table 4.11 shows that there is a large difference in diffusion of division structure. Although the percentage of diversified companies is only somewhat lower in Japan, the percentage of division structure in Japanese corporations is much lower, and there is little trend towards change.

Even the companies that have product division structure and where the product division is the profit centre, seldom integrate both their marketing and production function into one division, the marketing department being a centralized functional department in many cases. In the case of Matsushita Electric the manufacturing plant, which is the product division, is the profit centre, and it sells the product to the wholesaler at the market price. The product division contains the marketing department. This is the normal product division. There is, however, a strong central marketing staff department that does the planning and promoting effort, and the local sales office is under this department. In addition, exporting is carried out by the independent export company, a 100 per cent owned subsidiary.

In the case of Hitachi, the manufacturing plant is the profit centre. It sells the product to the centralized marketing department or to the product group's marketing department at the market price. The international department takes care of the exporting. Here we can see the case where marketing function is separated from production function.

What are the effects of the deformed product division structure, and much lower use of division structure in Japanese manufacturing corporations?

Functional departmentation can result in a centralized, strong marketing and production function. The product division system scatters these functions and weakens them. To cope with the severe competition in the Japanese market, it is necessary to have a strong marketing and production function, and to have specialized staff in these fields. The centralization of the marketing function is more important.

The Japanese manufacturing companies use wholesalers instead of direct sales forces. These wholesalers are the sole agencies for sales, the exclusive distribution channel of the company. These exclusive channels are commonly used by many divisions. The centralization of the marketing function is necessary in this system.

Where products are technically related even in diversified companies, then functional departmentation is more appropriate than product division. Product division is especially inappropriate when the new product is a large-system product, and has to make use of the technical skill of several existing products. It is easier to form a project team comprised of a variety of disciplines under the functional organization. In the strict product division structure with a research laboratory for each division, it is not easy to establish a large project team with members selected from product divisions, because it weakens the capability of divisions.

The goal of the product division is the profit, and this tends to make the product division shortsighted and conservative. It is difficult for the profit centre to expend large amounts on research and capital investment. By centralizing the research, marketing and production functions, it is easier to make large, innovative decisions.

The author does not overlook the advantage of the product division system. The strength of Matsushita and Hitachi comes from the tremendous efforts of line managers to improve the efficiency of the profit centre, and to attain a better divisional performance. The profit competition within the company is the greatest advantage of division structure. (Concerning the problems of division structure in Japanese corporations, see Kansai Productivity Centre, 1976.)

There is a hybrid organizational structure: the functional structure for major product and division structure for minor product'. It is closer to functional organization. Our survey finds that one-third of functional organizations belong to this type, which is found in both specialized companies (S & D) and diversified companies (R), and it is increasing as time passes. This trend is seen as a shift towards divisions structure.

10.6 CENTRALIZATION OF AUTHORITY AND LARGE HEAD OFFICE

The level of centralization is measured by (i) the level from which the idea is presented, (ii) level on which the final decision is made, and (iii) how the decision is directed by rules and guidelines.

Generally speaking, the strategic decision is centralized, the operational decision is decentralized and the administrative decision lies between the two (Kono, 1980; Anthony, 1965). The larger the company is, the more decentralized it is (Pugh *et al.*, 1969), and the more uncertain the environment is, the more decentralized the company (Lawrence and Lorsch, 1967; Burns and Stalker, 1961; Kono, 1980 (opposite opinion); Woodward, 1965 (the automated process matches the centralized structure). With these general principles in mind, we are here concerned with the characteristics of Japanese organizations.

It is a misconception that the Japanese organization has a decentralized authority structure, and that the bottom-to-top approach is popularly used. Table 10.3 shows the findings of a number of international comparisons of organizational characteristics.

Azumi's two surveys were conducted at plant level, and are concerned with the operational decisions. Kagono's survey is more related to the administrative and strategic decisions. These surveys both show that Japanese organization has a more centralized structure.

The author finds that the Japanese organization does have centralized authority, but within the sub-systems participation is popular, and consensus is commonly used to arrive at decisions.

We will focus on the strategic decisions now. It is the author's opinion that the top management of successful Japanese companies is future-oriented and aggressive, and ready to take the initiative in making strategic decisions. These decisions are arrived at by a top-down or interactive approach. In this sense, the authority is centralized. The evidence of centralization is as follows.

Long-range planning is a means to integrate the strategy. Long-range planning systems are widely used in Japan; more than 70 per cent of

TABLE 10.3 International comparison of organizational characteristics

Name of researcher	Method of research	Countries compared	Findings			Source
			(1) Centralization	*(2)* Formalization	*(3)* Specialization	
Azumi *et al.* (1978)	Objective questions (twelve plants for each country)	Japan Britain Sweden	Same (leve of decisions)	Same (number of rules and reports)	Same (specialized personnel are allocated)	*Organizational Science*, Tokyo, Winter 1978
Azumi *et al.* (1979)	Subjective questions (twelve plants)	Japan Britain Sweden	Perceived as higher (asking the boss)	Perceived as harder (rules are important)	Perceived as specialized (job is repetitive)	Same as above (Winter 1979)
Kagono *et al.* (1981)	Mail questionnaires (291 companies in Japan and 227 companies in the USA)	Japan USA	Higher (high level is influential	Softer (less rules}	Lower (consensus is important)	Same as above (Autumn 1981)
Hofstede	Mail questionnaires (forty companies)	Forty countries	Medium (do not oppose to the boss)	—	—	Same as above (Winter 1979)

Notes:
¹ 'Same' or 'higher' means Japanese organization is the same as, or higher than, the organizations of other countries.
² Words in the parentheses indicate the questions or measurement.

large companies have such a system. To build long-range plans, the planning department plays an important role in preparing the goals and basic strategies. It interacts frequently with top management. (The roles of the planning department and top management can be seen in Table 9.3.) The preparation is done by planning departments to a greater extent in Japan than in the USA or UK, where long-range planning is used for integrating and co-ordinating the division strategies.

In Japan many important projects are initiated by top management or by the heads of departments. The introduction of polyster by Teijin was promoted by the president, Oya. NKK's (Nippon Kokan) huge investment of 4 billion dollars in the Ogishima steel plant was initiated by the planning director, and was promoted by the president. Canon's copying machine was also initiated by the planning department. These are interactive processes.

The organization structure is centralized:

1. There is less use of division structure and more use of functional structure, as is shown in Table 4.11.
2. There is a large staff at the head office even if the company uses a division structure.
3. The research laboratory is centralized even in diversified companies.
4. There is a strong production and marketing staff, and the sales channels are under the direct control of the marketing department.

These organizational characteristics interrelate and overlap.

Head office includes top management, planning and control staff, special staff (examples; personnel, purchasing and accounting production staff and marketing staff) and service staff (examples: computing purchasing). It does not include the research laboratory nor the sales channel. The approximate number of employees in the head office is as follows: Toyota – 4000; Matsushita – 2000; Hitachi – 2000; Canon – 1500. According to my observation on visits to many US companies, the number of personnel in head offices of US or UK companies is usually smaller. The head offices of ICI and GEC of the UK accommodate about 100 persons. GE, Lockheed, and Northrop of the USA may have less than 300 people in the head office. Specialized companies such as Shell or Union Oil, however, have larger head office staffs.

Other surveys in the USA show that specialized companies have large head offices and diversified companies, especially conglomerates, have small head offices (Berg, 1965; Lorsch and Allen, 1973). The results of a survey of forty-four Japanese manufacturing companies (selected from 102 companies), carried out by the author in 1982, is shown in Table 4.10. The survey shows that the average number employed at head office is approximately 1000 persons, and the average percentage of the total number of employees is about 9 per cent. There is no difference between the specialized company and the diversified company.

The strong head office of Japanese companies means not only that strategic decisions are centralized, but also the administrative and the operational decisions. The effects of the centralization may be as follows.

Innovative adaptation to environmental change is made possibe by centralization. Small adaptations to an uncertain environment, or operational decisions, may be more effectively carried out with decentralized management. The advocates of decentralization mostly deal with operational decisions. The saleswoman cannot ask the boss everything. However, the billion-dollar capital investment, large expenditure for new-product development, the closing down of old plant, planned decreases in personnel – such strategic decisions cannot be delegated. General Electric in the USA recently centralized their strategic decision-making to cope with the current uncertainty. Japanese enterprises developed in a more quickly changing environment, and were only able to adapt and innovate by centralizing.

The competition is severe in Japan, and many successful companies could only survive the competition by having a centralized marketing and production staff; for instance, cost reduction was guided by the central production staff (Hitachi). The exclusive sales channel is an important weapon, and it can be strengthened by a centralized marketing department. In Japan, functional strength and functional integration are more important than integration of the activities for the product or for the geographical area.

Decentralization, on the other hand, motivates people more effectively. This is one of the important reasons for decentralization, especially in the USA and in the UK where the organization is more decentralized and the responsibilities are clear. This is important to motivate the more individualistic employee. It is also necessary to give quick rewards for performance, otherwise the employee may leave the organization. The Japanese employee is more organization-oriented, and there is less need for the kind of motivation provided by decentralization. Within the group, however, the decisions are made by consensus and by participation.

A comparative survey by Nakahashi on the bonus system of division managers shows that the bonus of Japanese division managers is related to the division profit to a much lesser extent than the bonus of US managers. Out of seventeen companies, seven do not relate the division manager's bonus to the profit of the division; seven companies relate the bonus to profit to some extent; and only three companies relate it to profit to a great extent (Nakahashi, 1981). This is different from the results of Vancil's survey showing that in 83 per cent of the cases surveyed (total 282 persons), the bonus is solely or greatly related to the profit of the division (Vancil, 1979).

In the USA, financial reward and sometimes the threat of dismissal are necessary to motivate the division manager; in this case the responsibility has to be clearly delegated to make the performance clear. In Japan, financial reward plays a less important role and the division manager cannot be discharged, so in this case the authority has to be centralized.

The strong functional departments in the head office exercise functional control over product divisions, manufacturing plants and sales offices. The Japanese organization may have some of the traits of a matrix organization. However, the concept of matrix organization is not fixed yet, so it is not safe to describe Japanese organization in these terms.

10.7 SOFT ORGANIZATION (OR ORGANISMIC ORGANIZATION)

Burns and Stalker classified the organizations into organismic and mechanistic. (Burns and Stalker, 1961). Japanese corporations have many characteristics of the organismic (or soft) organization.

1. Job delineation is ambiguous. Japanese organizations are comparable to the natural stone walls which are seen in many Japanese castles. The shape of the stones are all different but they are combined so as to complement one another. Western organizations are comparable to brick walls, which are composed of standardized square bricks. In Japanese organizations, jobs are ambiguous. The characteristics are as follows:

(a) jobs are roughly defined, or not well defined, and employees are required to do any related jobs;
(b) job contents change all the time;
(c) employees are expected to present ideas to improve the jobs;
(d) there are less rules and those that do exist are sometimes ignored.

The opposite model, or bureaucratic model, is as follows:

(a) jobs are clearly defined by contract;
(b) change of job is a serious matter, especially if the wage changes or the membership of the union has to change;
(c) it is not necessary to do any work other than the specified job;
(d) there are many rules.

It is true that jobs are less defined and less divided in the UK than in the USA, but at the plant site employees of different jobs wear different colour uniforms. They usually belong to different unions. Operators of machines cannot repair the machines.

The Japanese managers of Japanese subsidiaries in the UK and in the USA complain that people there will only perform the specified jobs, and are not willing to do any related tasks.

In Japanese organizations, sometimes job names are not clear, and wages are paid by formal status, by performance and by length of service. In this situation employees will perform other duties if required. There is no problem of job demarcation, and there is only one company-wide union. In the office, people work together in a large room. They work as a team. Even the head of department is located in one corner of the large room. This system is quite different from the UK or US office layout where each staff has his individual room and perhaps has a secretary.

Job flexibility is closely connected with job classification. In Japan, in many cases, operational jobs on the plant site and administrative jobs are graded by job content, but in other areas people are graded by capability without any relation to job content. Under this system, jobs need not be well defined.

Thus the reasons for this Japanese ambiguity spring from several sources. Wages are related to the job to a lesser extent; they are also related to capability and length of service; the union is organized on a company basis, and the sense of involvement of the employee is high.

The effects of this system are to make it easy to change one's job, and easy to introduce new technology. This system tends to increase the productivity of labour by mutual help.

2. Group decision and participation. Group decision-making and participation are popular. Meetings within the section, and meetings of the heads of sections, are held frequently. This decision style is different from the system where the responsibility of each person is clear, and each manager does his job in his own room with the help of a secretary.

This decision style has many similarities with the decision-making style of system IV by Likert (Likert, 1961). Group decision-making is called decision by consensus. (This is not identical with the Ringi system using many stamps.)

On the plant site, participation is limited, but group meetings are frequently held and each employee is encouraged to present his ideas. In the office, people work together in a large room, and group decisions are more popular.

A suggestion system is another means of participation, and in many cases each employee might present more than ten suggestions a year. Matsushita Electric has to deal with 460 000 suggestions a year; Japanese workers are willing to present their ideas. In the UK, ten suggestions a month in the whole of one plant is about average.

The reasons for favouring group decision or participative decision-making may be that the employees have equal capability and should be allowed to participate, and that people are willing to participate because of a high sense of involvement.

The effects of this Japanese style group decision-making can be stated as follows. Decisions tend to be slow but implementation is quick, because everybody concerned knows the issue in detail. Decisions are good ones and there are fewer errors because a lot of information and ideas are collected. Morale is high because of participation.

3. Better communication, horizontally and vertically. Communication from individual to individual tends to be better. This is rather hard to prove, but many Japanese managers of subsidiary companies in foreign countries comment that foreigners do not communicate well with one another.

In the UK and in the USA written memos are used frequently, but in Japan oral communication is more often used. For individual-to-individual relations, a Japanese will communicate better with his colleagues and someone in authority will teach his subordinates. If he does not communicate with his colleagues well beforehand, he will be criticized during conferences. 'Nemawashi' (lobbying or log rolling) is required before any group decision can be reached.

Under the length of service system, people are not so competitive with one another, so it is easier to have a good communication system. Also, there is less fear of being out-promoted by a subordinate.

On the plant site, everybody wears the same uniform, from plant manager to operator, so it is easy for the managers to walk through the plant and to talk with everybody on the site. In the UK, office workers never wear uniform, and they are provided with a separate lunch-room from that of blue-collar workers. In this setting communication tends to be poor.

The above features are similar to the concept of organismic organization put forward by Burns and Stalker. However, there are some differences. In the Japanese style, strategic decisions are made using a top-down or interactive approach, because strategic information is held by those at the top level. Authority is not distributed equally in this respect.

Knowledge of the operation of a particular organization is emphasized rather than knowledge of specific professional skills. There is rarely an occupation recognized as a professional one, knowledge of which is transferable from company to company. Unlike the original concept of organismic organization, people are not loyal to the occupation, but instead to the organization.

The softness of organization provides a favourable climate for innovation. When the job is clearly defined, and the wage is determined by the job, a change of job as a result of innovation will be resisted by the worker. When there are different unions for different jobs, as is the case with the UK, change will be resisted more strongly.

The softness is also favourable to the generation of new ideas. The development of new products cannot be done successfully by hard organization. The members of successful project teams will do any related job and in addition they are prepared to work any hour of the day and night. The cases of the development of the crystal quartz watch and the auto-focus camera are good examples.

10.8 HUMAN RESOURCE AND FACILITIES

10.8.1 Human Resources

The quality of personnel is an important element of organizational capability. The competitive power of Japanese products largely originates in the quality of the personnel.

10.8.1.1 *University graduates*

The percentage of university graduates among all employees is high. In the case of Canon, it is about 20 per cent, and this is one of the reasons why Canon was able to develop new cameras and install large-scale production systems. It is doubtful if German camera companies have such a high percentage of university graduates.

In 1980 Canon (total number of employees, 9000) newly employed 196 high-school graduates and 424 university graduates, out of which 191 were graduates from engineering and the natural sciences. We should notice that the number of university graduates who are newly recruited is more than the number of new recruits from among high-school students. In the same year, Hitachi (total number of employees, 71 000) recruited 1440 high-school students and 565 university graduates, out of which 464 graduates were from engineering and the natural sciences. We should notice that the majority of university graduates are from the engineering and science faculties. This is a popular policy of recruitment among technology-intensive corporations in Japan.

In the Musashi Plant of Hitachi (3600 employees), which produces super LSI, 28 per cent of its staff are university graduates, and 100 university graduates out of the total 564 recruits from all universities go to this plant in one year. This is a heavy allocation of human resources to this plant producing key-technology products.

Companies with attractive performances, such as Hitachi and Canon, can attract good students from good universities.

The total volume of new employment is shown in Table 10.4. It shows that the percentage of college and university graduates is very high.

These large numbers of university graduates are supplied from 446 universities that hold 2 million students; and they make up a strong corps of middle managers and key technicians in successful Japanese companies. These middle managers are the resources of the functional

TABLE 10.4 Total new employment according to educational background (1970 and 1980, thousands)

Educational establishment	1970 %	1980 %	Total (1000)	Male (1000)	Female (1000)
Junior high school	16	6	62	36	26
Senior high school	59	57	597	278	319
Two year college	25	12	122	8	114
University		25	261	205	56
Total	100	100	1 042	527	515

Notes:
[1] Ministry of Education, *Survey on New Employment From Schools* (1980).
[2] New employment is part of total graduates.

capabilities of the head office, the resources of the research laboratory, the resources of the plant site as middle managers.

The success of the Japanese management system is largely due to these competent middle managers. The European companies lack this large number of proficient middle managers, though a small number of upper managers are very competent. In Japan university graduates are placed in the manual-working sector when they enter the company, and are trained there for some months. They are willing to be located on the plant site as engineers. Usually all the members of the plant, from the head of the plant to the sweepers, wear the same uniform; it does not matter that the key technicians come to the plant site from the development room, or are located in the manual-working sector. Thus communication between the research department and the plant engineer is easily made, which is essential in developing a successful new product or a new production system.

The competitive power of the camera industry comes from the development of new products, and this was made possible by the large number of university graduates, which German camera companies did not have.

The author asked the corporate planner of Nippon Kokan, one of the largest steel manufacturers, about the future competitive power of NKK as against the US steel manufacturers. He answered that the present newest facilities may become older, but the quality and volume of middle managers and engineers is superior to their US counterparts, and that he is confident about their future competitive power.

It is said that indirect departments of Japanese corporations are overstaffed, and the productivity of these departments is low. For example, there are 71 000 employees at Hitachi, and the approximate numbers of employees in indirect departments are as follows:

Head office – 2000; central research laboratories – 3700; plant research departments – 4000; sales department – 7000; salesmen in divisions – 3000 (estimate); administrative departments of divisions and manufacturing plants – 5000 (estimate). Total 24 700.

This means that more than one-third of the employees are in indirect departments. The author believes that this large staff in the indirect department is the strenght of Hitachi. The productivity of all employees at Hitachi is not low. The sales per employee at Hitachi was 21 250 thousand yen in 1978, but the same at GE is only 10 314 thousand yen. (We should take into consideration that the level of vertical integration of GE is probably higher than that of Hitachi.)

10.8.1.2 Blue-collar workers

The ordinary workers in Japanese manufacturing companies are a homogeneous group and the level of skill is high. This homogeneity is a favourable condition for team building, and for good communication between workers.

They are all well educated. After finishing the compulsory course of nine years, 90 per cent go on to a three-year senior high-school course, and 40 per cent of them go to university. The new recruits for blue-collars are mostly senior high-school graduates. The successful companies can attract good pupils from the high schools, which results in the high level of skill of the lowest echelon. The less capable pupils and students go to service industries that are not competing in world markets.

The average age of employees in 102 manufacturing companies is 35.8 years for male employees and 26.9 years for female employees, the total average being 34.1 years. Males account for 85 per cent and females for the remainder. The average age of Japanese people between 20 and 60 years is 39.0 years for males and 40.2 years for female. The average age of the female workers in the above 102 companies is much lower than the national average. This is a result of the early retirement of female workers to marry. Women are also organization-oriented; they select one organization and devote themselves to it. After marriage, they devote themselves to the family organization. Thus the company can have younger employees, despite the lifetime employment system.

10.8.1.3 Planned decrease of employees

Successful Japanese companies have been trying to increase the productivity of labour, to reduce their costs, to have flexibility of costs and to improve wages. During the last twenty years the sales of Hitachi have increased from 128 billion yen in 1960 to 1950 billion yen in 1980, more than fifteen times in nominal terms and 4.2 times in real terms, but the number of employees has only increased from 60 800 in 1960 to 83 500 in 1980 to 72 300, only 1.2 times the number in 1960.

Many successful Japanese manufacturing companies have a higher productivity of labour than that of other countries. Table 10.5 is the comparison of the productivity of three car-manufacturing companies. Toyota has a higher labour—equipment ratio, and the physical productivity of labour is much higher; value added per employee is also slightly higher.

TABLE 10.5 Productivity of labour of three companies (1978)

	GM	Ford	Toyota
Number of cars produced (1000)	6876	3790	2929
Number of employees (1000)	839	507	52
Fixed assets per employee (1000 yen)	2234	2831	7619
Cars produced per employee per year	8.2	7.5	48.0
Value added sales (%)	44.4	34.79	16.3
Value added employee (1000 yen)	7038	6184	9464

Source: Nikko Research Centre, *Analysis of Industries* (1980); MITI, *Analysis of World Enterprises* (1980].

After the oil crisis in 1973, many companies decreased the number of their employees. Under the lifetime employment system, decreasing the number of employees has to be done on a planned basis. The methods used are as follows: suspension of new recruiting and decrease by natural retirement; transfer of employees to subsidiaries who in turn decrease their numbers by shortening the retirement age which is usually older than in the parent company; offering a higher retirement allowance which is usually one month's pay for one year's service; temporary staying at home with pay. This can reduce the labour costs by reducing the overhead costs. The forced discharge is seldom used, but it is used on a planned basis if necessary.

Where do the redundant workers go in the economy as a whole? The real growth rate of the Japanese economy was around 5 per cent even after the oil crisis, and the growing sector could absorb the new supply of labour. At the same time the service sector that employs 55 per cent of the total workforce provides abundant opportunity for employment, and the labour productivity there is very low.

10.8.2 Equipment

Until the oil crisis the expansion of production facilities was one of the most important strategic decisions, and many successful Japanese companies were aggressive in their capital investment, by borrowing money from banks. As a result, Japanese companies came to be equipped with the newest facilities, and had a high fixed asset per labour ratio and a low equity ratio. Some industries failed, but many succeeded. The petrochemical industry and aluminium industry could not harvest their investment because of the high price of raw materials, but in the motor-car industry, the steel industry and the shipbuilding industry, the capital investment created key capabilities for competition. After the oil crisis the growth rate declined; management became more careful about investment; the percentage for rationalization increased. That is, investment for new products, for saving energy consumption, for cost reduction, for replacement of equipment and for pollution control increased. The management of successful companies pursued these rationalizations aggressively, rather than waiting for a decrease of capital cost by using depreciated facilities.

One of the dramatic stories of replacement investment is the 1000-billion-yen (4-billion-dollar) steel plant investment at Keihin (Ogishima), near Tokyo, by NKK steel (Nippon Kokan Company). The 16-million-ton steel plant at Fukuyama, the largest steel plant in the world, was being completed in 1968. The Keihin plant was old and pollution control was a problem. When the president was satisfied with the near completion of the world's largest plant at Fukuyama, the director of corporate planning visited the president, and strongly insisted on the immediate replacement of the plant at Keihin in parallel with the completion of Fukuyama, because the old plant was too old and its costs were not competitive. They were losing their share of the market by holding on to this old facility. The president hesitated because another huge investment would worsen the financial ratio. The equity ratio in 1968 was only 14 per cent. Next day the president visited the president of Fuji Bank, the bank in the same Yasuda group, about the new investment. The president of the bank strongly recommended the new investment for replacement to improve the competitive position of the company, and promised that the bank would make every effort to support the new construction. The construction started in 1968 by creating new land on the shore by reclamation work and constructed the new facilities with a computerized control system. The designing was done by the engineering department of the company. The replacement investment was completed in 1979 by investing 1000 billion yen (4 billion dollars). This plant has the following features.

The replacement was done by building a completely new plant on a new island, the layout is on a straight line and is fully automated. The process is continuously controlled by two central computers and twenty-five local computers, as a total system. With this control system, the quality has been improved, and the amount of labour required was cut by half. There is a total energy control system, and the gas from the furnace is fully utilized which has resulted in low energy costs.

The production capacity stayed almost the same as the 6 million tons a year from the old plant, but the number of employees went down from

18 000 to 9 000, and the productivity of labour was doubled. This decrease was carried out by suspending new recruitment, by moving the employees to the Fukuyama plant whose capacity was enlarged, and by soliciting voluntary retirement by increasing the retirement allowance. The transfer of employees within the plant was on a large scale. This is one example of ways of decreasing the number of employees under the lifetime employment system.

This huge replacement investment of NKK contrasts with the case of US Steel which acquired a resource company instead of replacing the old plant. US Steel is probably more concerned with short-range profit.

This case symbolizes such characteristics. Huge investment is carried out for replacement, rather than waiting for the decrease of capital cost of old facilities. The decision is made from the top down or by an interactive process. The bank supports the long-range plan. Manpower is curtailed if necessary under the lifetime employment system.

The successful Japanese companies have been aggressive in expanding and modernizing their plant. During the last twenty years, NKK Steel increased its factories from two major plants to five, Toyota from two plants to ten, Bridgestone Tire and Rubber from four to thirteen. Bridgestone intentionaly selected the depression years for construction, because the construction costs were lower. Mitsui Shipbuilding increased the number of its plants from three to four, and Canon from one to six. These new facilities incorporated large-scale production systems, so the number of employees did not increase, and the production was almost tripled. The change in the number of employees was as follows: Toyota from 15 000 to 52 000; Bridgestone from 9370 to 17 800; NKK Steel from 38 300 to 34 200; Mitsui Shipbuilding form 7400 to 12 200. Some companies went bankrupt by the failure of capital investment, however. Fuji Sashi Company was one such case.

The decision to make large capital investments is arrived at by strategic evaluation, and Table 10.6 shows how the large investment decision is evaluated.

Japanese companies put more emphasis on the future prospects of the market and on the competitive consideration than on the financial effect. The DCF method is not popularly used for economic evaluation. Table 10.6 shows that pay-out period and rate of return using accounting methods are more important measurements. These measurements reflect the fact that the investment is implemented by borrowing from the banks, so the pay-out period is important, and that the strategic evaluation is more important than the analysis of future rate of return.

Comprehensive long-range planning plays an important role in

TABLE 10.6 Evaluation of capital investment
(a) Over-all evaluation

'How do you evaluate the strategic investment (or large capital investment)? (Please tick one).'

	UK %	Japan %
1. Mostly by future prospect of market, rather than financial effects.	8	15
2. Mostly by competitive consideration, rather than financial effects.	3	12
3. Mostly from financial effects, such as rate of return or contribution to the increase of sales volumes.	20	18
4. By multiple criteria, including the above.	68	55
5. NA	1	–

Note:
Method of survey: mail questionnaires on long-range planning, seventy-four private companies in the UK in 1981, and 110 manufacturing companies in Japan in 1982. This is a part of the survey on long-range planning.

(b) Method of economic evaluation

	Japan %
Pay-out period	81.2
Rate of return by accounting method	33.7
Net present value	16.1
Internal rate of return	16.5
Others	2.4
Not using	9.4

Source: Japan Productivity Centre, *Mail Survey on Budgeting, 255 Companies,* 1981.

evaluating the capital investment, for allocating the funds for investment, and for ensuring that the company's financial health is not impaired by large investment. The successful companies have used long-range planning continuously. Many bankrupt companies have not used any long-range planning system, however, the investments being made on the intuitive decisions of top management who expected that money would flow in if they had good facilities.

The characteristics of capital investment can be summarized as in Table 10.7.

TABLE 10.7 Characteristics of successful capital investment

	Successful Japanese companies	*Other models*
Attitude for capital investment	Aggressive expansion and replacement	Conservative
Orientation	Long-range growth	Short-range EPS
Source of fund	Internal fund plus loan capital	Mostly internally ploughed-back funds
Co-operation of the union	Co-operative for modernization	Not necessarily co-operative for labour-saving investment
Means of integration	Long-range planning	(various)

The successful companies have tried to achieve the following causal relations, new investment for expansion and replacement →increased labour–capital ratio →high total productivity →high rate of return → more fund for capital investment.

10.9 SUMMARY

The successful companies have changed the product mix and the quality level of their products during the past twenty years by introducing new products and by changing production methods. This was made possible by strengthening their development capabilities.

The high calibre of their human resources, especially the large number of university graduates, was invaluable in setting up their development capabilities. Once this was done, they implemented their strategy, by changing their production and marketing capabilities. There was aggressive capital investment on the one hand; on the other, excessive capacities were weeded out. Thus a high level of capacity, balanced strengthening of capabilities and high productivity of resources were aimed at.

This balanced change of capability structure is seen in Canon's case. Canon strengthened its development capability first and then the implementation capability was changed. The companies who failed could not build such balanced capability structures. The reasons for the failure of Fuji Sashi (window frame company) were its weak planning department, including its top management, its weak marketing capability and over-capacity at plant level.

Japanese companies rarely used the acquisition of other companies as their growth strategy; instead, they developed their own capability. They frequently used licensing agreements and joint ventures to introduce new technology, and in this way organizations could continue to hold on to their identity, which is important for the employee. Less frequent use of acquisition means that companies do not become unrelatedly diversified or conglomerates.

The research and development departments have been strengthened recently, but compared with large successful US companies the accumulation of technological knowledge is not yet very large. Creative invention is something to be expected in the future.

As the companies diversified, more companies used the product division structure, although compared with the US or UK practice, the division structure is much less used. The organization is more centralized. The head office has a large staff, though there are some problems with the productivity of indirect personnel. The strong middle managers and staff are the strength of Japanese enterprises. Companies that have weak middle power cannot become strongly innovative or competitive. If a strong head office is filled by competent middle managers, this is a strength for the whole company.

The system, human resources and facilities are three important elements of the capability structure.

The facilities of successful companies are relatively new, because new construction has continued in the growth economy. Recently, replacement and modernization investment has occupied the greater part of investment. NKK Steel Company shows how replacement investment can be positively implemented. The average age of facilities of the Japanese steel industry was 9.5 years in 1980, but 17.5 years in 1979 for the US steel industry (Survey by Japanese Association of Iron and Steel, *Nikkei Newspaper*, November 1981).

During the growth period of these companies, the number of employees was not increased – if necessary it was decreased. The combination of manpower and facilities have changed over the last twenty years, with the resulting higher productivity of labour and higher wages. The successful companies thus deliberately avoided over-capacity, but some companies failed by over-expansion of plant capacities.

The Japanese organization is soft and organismic, although the softness varies depending on the repetitiveness of the job; the more repetitive the job is, the less soft the organization structure is, and vice versa. Generally speaking, there are fewer rules, job demarcation is rare, and the employee is willing to do any job. The softness of organization has been useful for generating strategy and, to a greater extent, in implementing new strategy. The numerous suggestions presented as a result of the suggestion system created an atmosphere where change is welcome. There is less friction in changing production methods by introducing new technology in Japan.

The organization is centralized not only for making strategic decisions, but also for making operational decisions; but within the units of organization, participation and consensus are popularly used to arrive at the decision.

10.9.1 Problems

1. Creativeness of the Japanese organization. This problem has already been raised in Chapter 8.

2. Balance of centralization and decentralization. Strategic decisions should be centralized and operational decisions should be delegated, but in both areas the balance of centralization and decentralization is a problem. As the educational level of the employee becomes higher, the delegation of authority may become more necessary.

3. The slow growth rate and ageing of employees and of facilities. When the growth rate of the company goes down as the growth rate of the economy slows down, the average age of the employees increases because less young people are recruited. At the same time, the age of retirement is extended from 55 years to 60 years to match the longer life expectancy. However, for the most part the female employee quits the company after marriage, and this habit mitigates the problem. Wage increase and promotion by length of service is a typical system, and this system does not work well when the average age of the employees rises. A bicycle falls down when the speed is too slow. The labour cost will go up with a length-of-service wage system. To cope with this problem, the wage system is being changed to slow down the average wage increase by length of service, and the job content is being given more weight in deciding differentials in the wage structure.

The average age of the facilities will rise if equipment is not replaced on a planned basis. The lower average age of facilities at Toyota is due to the rapid expansion of business. The same can be said of the equipment at Bridgestone Tire Company, and of Nippon Steel and NKK Steel. The situation will change in a slow-growth economy. For example, it is estimated that the average age of equipment in the steel industry will rise from 9.5 years in 1980 to 13.9 years in 1990, even if the present rate of replacement continues.

REFERENCES

Furukawa, E. (1973) *Nihon no Kigyo Seicho* (The Growth of Japanese Corporations), Tokyo, Chuo Keizai Sha.

Japan Recruit Centre (1980) *Survey on Recruit*, Tokyo, Japan Recruit Centre.

Kagono, T. *et al.* (1981) *Nihon Kigyo no Senryaku to Soshiki* (Strategy and Structure of Japanese Business), Tokyo, Organization Science. Summer.

Kansai Productivity Centre, *Keiei Soshiki no Shin Doko* (New Trend of Business Organizations), Osaka, Kansai Productivity Centre.

Kono, T. (1974) *Keiei Senryaku no Kaimei* (Analysis of Corporate Strategy), Tokyo, Diamond Sha.

Kono, T. (1977) *Keieigaku Genron* (Principles of Management), Tokyo, Hakuto Shobo.

Kono, T. (1980) *Senryaku Keieikeikaku no Tatekata* (Strategic Planning), Tokyo.

Ministry of International Trade and Industry (1980) *Keiei Ryoku Shihyo* (The Index of Corporate Capabilities), Tokyo, MITI.

Morimoto, M. (1975) *Keiei Soshiki Ron* (Business Organizations), Tokyo, Moriyama Shoten.

Muramatsu, S. (1979) *Takakuka Kigyo Ron* (Business Diversification), Tokyo, Maki Shoten.

Nakahashi, K. (1981) *Jigyobusei Kigyo ni okeru Soshiki Sekkei* (Organizational Design of Division Structure Companies), Otaru, Shogaku Tokyu, Mar.

Takamiya, S. (1961) *Keiei Soshiki Ron* (Business Organizations), Tokyo, Diamond Sha.

Urabe, K. (1967) *Jigyobusei to Rieki Kanri* (Division Structure and Profit Management), Tokyo, Hakuto Shobo.

Urabe, K. (1971) *Gendai Keiei Soshiki Ron* (Principles of Business Organization), Tokyo, Hakuto Shobo.

Ansoff, I. *et al.* (1971) *Acquisition Behavior of US Manufacturing Firms 1946–1965*, Tenn., Vanderbilt University Press.

Anthony, R. N. (1965) *Planning and Control Systems*, Boston, Harvard University Press.

Berg, N. A. (1965) 'Strategic Planning in Conglomerate Companies', *Harvard Business Review*, May–June, vol. 43.

Bower, J. (1970) *The Resource Allocation Process*, Boston, Harvard Business School Division of Research.

Brown, J. K. and O'Connor, R. (1974) *Planning and the Corporate Planning Director*, New York, Conference Board.

Burns, T. and Stalker, G. M. (1961) *The Management of Innovation*, London, Tavistock Publications.

Chandler, A. D. (1962) *Strategy and Structure*, Cambridge, Mass., MIT Press.

Channon, D. (1973) *The Strategy and Structure of British Enterprise*, London, Macmillan.

Conference Board (1973) *Corporate Organization Structure, Manufacturing*, New York, The Conference Board.

Dale, E. (1952) *Planning and Developing the Company Organization Structure*, New York, AMA.

Dessler, G. (1980) *Organization Theory*, New Jersey, Prentice-Hall.

Dore, R. (1973) *British Factory – Japanese Factory. The Origins of National Diversity in Industrial Relations*, Calif, University of California Press.

Galbraith, J. R. and Nathanson, D. A. (1978) *Strategy Implementation, The Role of Structure and Process*, Minnesota, West Publishing.

Greiner, L. (1967) 'Patterns of Organizational Change', *Harvard Business Review*, May–June.

Hofstede, G. (1978) *Organization-related Value Systems in Forty Countries*, paper presented at the Ninth World Congress of Sociology, Uppsala, Sweden.

Hofer, C. W. and Schendel, D. (1978) *Strategy Formulation, Analytical Concept*, New York, West Publishing.

Lawrence, P. and Lorsch, J. (1967) *Organization and Environment*, Boston, Division of Research, Harvard Business School.

Likert, R. (1961) *New Patterns of Management*, New York, McGraw-Hill.

Lorsch, J. and Allen, S. (1973) *Managing Diversity and Interdependence*, Boston, Harvard Business School.

Lorsch, J. and Morse, J. (1974) *Organizations and Their Members*, New York, Harper & Row.

Miles, R. and Snow, C. (1978) *Environmental Strategy and Organization Structure*, New York, McGraw-Hill.

Nakane, C. (1970) *Japanese Society*, Calif., University of California Press.

Penrose, E. T. (1966) *The Theory of The Growth of the Firm*, London, Basil Blackwell.

Perrow, C. (1967) 'A Framework for the Comparative Analysis of Organization', *American Sociological Review*, vol. 32.

Pugh, D. S., Hickson, D. J., Hinings, C. R. and Turner, C. (1969) 'The Context of Organizational, Structures', *Administrative Science Quarterly*, vol. 14, Mar.

Rumelt, R. (1974) *Strategy, Structure and Economic Performance*, Boston, Division of Research, Harvard Business School.

Scott, B. R. (1971) *Stages of Corporate Development*, 9–371–294, BP 998, Intercollegiate Case Clearinghouse, Harvard Business School.

Stopford, J. and Wells, L. (1972) *Management, the Multinational Enterprise*, London, Longman.

Thompson, J. D. (1967) *Organizations in Action*, New York, McGraw-Hill.

Woodward, J. (1965) *Industrial Organization, Theory and Practice*, London, Oxford University Press.

Yoshino, M. Y. (1968) *Japan's Managerial System, Tradition and Innovation*, Boston, MIT Press.

Vancil, R. F. (1979) *Decentralization, Managerial Ambiguity by Design*, Ill., Dow Jones-Irwin.

11 Personnel Management System

The feature of personnel management systems of successful Japanese corporations can be explained by the concept of *Gemeinschaft*, or community organization, as opposed to *Gesellschaft* (association) – concepts first put forward by Tönnies (Tönnies, 1887). *Gemeinschaft* is like a family or a church where members are combined by mutual love. Getting together is itself a source of joy. People love, help, trust and understand one another, and share bad luck as well as good.

Gesellschaft, on the other hand, is like a pure profit-making economic organization. Unless there is a reward, people will not work. There is no spiritual unity. People are combined by contract, but they are apart, and in a state of tension. They work by division of labour, within the strict limits of the job, and each one becomes merely one of the atoms of the organization.

Japanese organization is somewhat similar to *Gemeinschaft*, because the company respects the welfare of employees and gives more equal treatment on a length-of-service system; in turn, the employees devote themselves willingly to the organization.

11.1 LIFETIME EMPLOYMENT

Once a person enters the organization, he will devote himself to it for his lifetime and stay until retirement age at 55 or 60. He will not move around from organization to organization. The organization will take care of the employee for his lifetime, and will not discontinue his employment lightly. For the employee, leaving or discharge causes serious damage to his career.

Because of the lifetime employment system, recruiting is usually done in April from among new graduates from high schools and universities. Companies seldom recruit by advertising vacancies throughout the year.

318

There are several misconceptions about lifetime employment. It is not a contract. It is a way of thinking on both sides – by the employer and by the employee. Women employees do not stay for life. They leave the company when they get married, since married women will devote themselves to the family. This is another sort of organization orientation. In the case of small-sized companies, however, and in service industries, mobility is much higher than in larger manufacturing companies. Until some years ago there were a certain number of temporary employees as a buffer for lifetime employment, but after the period of worker shortage during the late 1960s, they almost disappeared, and now, if any, there are very few.

When its profit declines, the company will take all kinds of measures to decrease its costs, and will curtail dividends, but the employees will be kept on as far as is possible. US corporations might lay off employees and keep the rate of dividend.

The lifetime employment system does not mean, however, that the number of employees cannot be reduced. There are various methods to cope with decreased demand for man-hours. Overtime is cut first. Workers are transferred from the departments with slack jobs to other departments with busier jobs, sometimes to sales offices and to subsidiaries. Suspension of new recruiting, early retirement with an increased rate of retirement allowance (flexible retirement system), temporary 'going back to country home' with pay, are all frequently used. Voluntary retirement is solicited from older workers. The last resort is to decrease the number in employment. In this case older people will be asked to go first and younger people will stay on. After the oil crisis, many companies in fact decreased the number of their employees, but these reductions were done on a planned basis, not by sudden declarations of redundancy nor by sudden lay-offs.

The lifetime employment system originates from the traditional Japanese way of thinking that devotion to an organization is a value, and this system was further reinforced afrer the war, because it has merits on both sides. Before the war, companies had little idea of respecting their workforce. Young female workers and unskilled workers from farmers' families were considered as only so many interchangeable parts, and labour turnover was high. However, in the heavy industries, such as shipbuilding, railways, chemical industries and mechanical industries, the company needed skilled workers, and it was important to hold on to them. These industries needed a lifetime employment system (Yoshino, 1968; Nakagawa, 1977).

After the war, the structure of industry changed: technology-intensive heavy industries increased production as compared with light industries such as textiles. Moreover, the unions were becoming organized and they requested stable employment. Democratic ideas became prevalent, and encouraged respect for people working in the organization. These forces all contributed to the establishment of the lifetime employment system after the war.

11.2 EMPHASIS ON TRAINING

Under the lifetime employment system, training within the company is not only necessary, it also pays. The employees ae promoted within the company and their jobs change as the product and the technology change, so education is necessary. This thought is expressed at Hitachi in the following phrase: 'the essence of enterprise is people'. At Matsushita a similar phrase is used: 'Matsushita produces capable people before it produces products'. We should understand that the people means not only the higher echelons but also the rank and file workers. Recently, as the product and its production process have become more technology-intensive, and as the company activity has become more international, the training within the industry has become even more important. The need for training comes from the necessity of the company, but it also derives from the idea of respect for people. US and European companies tend to think that the necessary human resources can be bought from outside by money.

Trainees can be classified under three headings: (i) the newly hired employees, (ii) general employees, and (iii) managers.

The new employee is trained mostly by lectures and on-the-job training. The indoctrination of company philosophy and teaching of technical skills are the important subjects. The length of training varies from company to company, but it is usually from three to eight months. In Matsushita, the orientation and training of new employees from universities (about 800 persons) are centralized in the head office and the training is conducted as follows: lectures in the head office, three weeks; training in retail stores, three months; training in the works, one month; lectures on cost accounting, one month; lectures on marketing, two months. After this eight-month training new graduates are distributed to various departments and subsidiaries.

General employees are trained in functional technical skills and also in human skills, and for this purpose they undergo (i) on-the-job training, (ii) self development, and (iii) off-the-job training. On-the-job training is the most emphasized, and this is done with planned instruction by the supervisors. Under the promotion by length of service system the employees are not in competition with one another and the supervisors are willing to pass on the necessary skills.

Job rotation is another means and this is one of the characteristics of training in Japanese corporations. In the USA or in Europe, people will move from company to company in the same profession, but in Japan people will move from department to department doing similar jobs in the same company. Honda has a planned rotation programme for the first ten years; Toyota's policy is to rotate employees once every three years; Canon has a policy of choosing the head of the section from among those members of staff who have served in at least three different departments. Since there are company-wide unions, as opposed to trade unions, there is no problem of job demarcation, and there are few obstacles in the way of rotation.

Self-development is another important aspect of training, and opportunities for frequent promotion and wage increases stimulate the desire for self-development. The company encourages this by distributing reading materials, and lists of recommended books, and subsidizing the cost of buying books. Group activities such as QC circle are widely used, and in successful companies more than 80 per cent of the employees participate, the company paying overtime for group activities.

Off-the-job training is conducted in company training centres and in outside institutions and consists of, for example, technical training classes, other functional training classes and language classes. Such training is sponsored both by the divisions and by the head offices. Hitachi has six training centres in addition to a number of training rooms at plant sites.

Manager training consists mostly of off-the-job training in the company's training centres and its purpose is to improve conceptual skills and human skills.

The amount of money spent on training is not clear: one survey shows the cost at about 60 dollars (15 000 yen) per employee per year (Takamiya, 1976). This does not include the cost for on-the-job training. At Hitachi about 2.2 days are spent in training each university graduate employee in technical skills every year. This does not include on-the-job training either.

11.3 FREQUENT PROMOTION AND FREQUENT WAGE INCREASE BY LENGTH OF SERVICE AND BY ABILITY

11.3.1 Two Ladders of Promotion

In many cases there are two ladders of promotion, one is the hierarchy of job gradings, the other is the hierarchy of status gradings, with the result that there are many opportunities for promotion. At Hitachi the promotion policy is, 'any person can be promoted to the First Grade of eight grades in the formal status grading system by the age of 53 at the latest'. The simplified promotion scheme at Hitachi is exhibited in Table 11.1. Employees are promoted on the job grade. Operational jobs are graded by the formal job evaluation method. This system is the same as the US system, but differs from the UK system where grading is almost completely lacking for operational jobs. If the job does not change, there is no promotion on the job grading.

Employees are also promoted on the formal status grade according to length of service and merit. There is a minimum number of years for staying in the same status grade, and beyond the maximum number of years the employee is automatically promoted to the higher grade.

Promotion, however, by no means takes place automatically. The job contents (and the job grade), ability and efforts are taken into consideration for promotion. This means that there are matchings between the job grades and status grades to some extent, but an employee can be promoted on the status grades by merit even if he is working in the same job.

At Hitachi, two-thirds of the wage is determined by status grade and one-third is by the job grade for operational jobs.

In the higher echelons all staff are located in the status grade, but many are not titled in the job grade, particularly those in 'junior manager status', because the number of positions for heads of sections and departments are limited. Some are graded by specialist title. The salary is totally determined by the status grade at this level.

The promotion system in Hitachi is a typical model. There are three models, however.

1. Two-ladder system as at Hitachi.
2. Job grade for operational jobs and status grade for clerical and technical jobs, but two ladders for higher echelons (Matsushita).
3. Only status grades, but for higher echelons a two-grade system (Toyota, Canon).

323

TABLE 11.1 An example of status grade and job grade (simplified)

	Status grade	Job grade	Professional status
Administrative level	Director class	Head of plant	Chief engineer
	Senior manager (1)	Head of department	Vice chief engineer
	Senior manager (2)		
	Junior manager	Head of section	Senior engineer
Supervisory level	Senior leader	Head of group	Junior engineer
	Junior leader (1)	Foreman	
	Junior leader (2)	Head of small group	
General		Class 9	
	B 1	,, 8	
	B 2	,, 7	
	B 3	,, 6	
	B 4	,, 5	
	B 5	,, 4	
	B 6	,, 3	
	B 7	,, 2	
	B 8	,, 1	

Notes:
[1] At the general level and at the supervisory level, wages are determined by status grade (two-thirds) and by job grade (one-third), but above supervisory level wages are determined by status grade.
[2] Actual grading is more complicated.

The two-ladder system, especially the formal status grade system, increases the opportunities for promotion, gives everyone hope of climbing to the middle ranks and increases the sense of loyalty and dedication to the organization. Lifetime employment is necessary to increase the opportunities within the company.

Promotion reflects ability and effort and there are differences in the speed of promotion, so this system provides an incentive to work harder. There is no special fast track for the very capable, but there is a difference of promotion depending on ability, although the difference is not too large. Employees in the lower echelons are appraised for promotion by the rating-scale method or the classification method. In the middle ranks, tests and presentation of papers are used in addition to the above two methods. In the higher echelons over-all rating is used.

For favourable appraisal, the short-term contribution to profit is not so important as technical skill, co-operation with colleagues and quality of performance. This evaluation might be considered subjective, but frequent evaluations make it more objective. The evaluation of one employee is also checked by multiple evaluations; for example, three supervisors at the three successive levels above one employee do the evaluation of him and these three are compared to one another. At Toyota, six persons will evaluate a candidate to decide on his promotion to manager. Frequent evaluations also result in a long-term accumulation of evaluations of performance.

11.3.2 Wage Increase by Length of Service and Merit

As already mentioned in discussing the Hitachi system, one-third of the wage is determined by the job grade. This is a single-rate system, that is, one rate for one job grade. Two-thirds of the wage is determined by the status grade. Wages are increased by an annual wage progression system. The average amount of annual wage progression differs according to the status grade – the higher the status grade, the larger the average amount. Thus the higher the status grade, the higher the standard line of wage progression by length of service (or age).

In other cases where the wage is solely determined by the job grade, the number of grade is about five or six for ordinary employees, and the rate range is very wide. The wage is increased every year as an annual wage progression. The average amount of progression is different depending upon the level of grade.

The same principle applies to the wage scheme where wage is determined solely by the status grade.

The amount of annual wage progression for each employee differs depending upon the capability and effort even in the same status grade; the differential of annual wage increase thus reflects the merit. This is a strong incentive to work harder. The differential is small, but it is given every year, so the accumulated amount can be large – although it is not very large in the same status grade. Again, since the differential occurs every year the feedback is relatively quick, and the accumulated wage also reflects the long-term performance of an employee.

In the higher echelons, the salaries are totally determined by the status grade, so those who are capable and are performing important jobs but are not in the position of heads of sections or departments can receive appropriate salaries.

Generally speaking, there are three types of wage system.

1. Two wage components for the lower ranks of employees, that is, wage component by status grade plus wage component by job grade like Hitachi's system.
2. Wage by job grade for those on operational jobs. For clerical and technical job staff and for those in the higher echelon, the wage is determined by status grade (Matsushita).
3. Wages solely determined by status grade for all ranks of employees (Canon).

In every case the rate range in each grade is large. In many cases there is no maximum rate, so wages are increased every year, reflecting the grade and merit. Annual wage progression is a kind of wage system that reflects length of service.

There are three occasions for wage changes: (i) promotion on job grade or status grade, (ii) annual wage progression, and (iii) over-all wage increase that changes the total rate scale. This is explained in Figure 11.1.

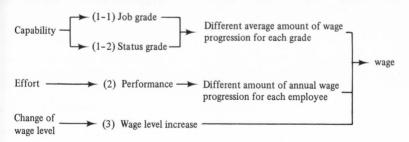

FIGURE 11.1 Wage determination

The method of payment is the same for every level of hierarchy: the wages and salaries are paid every month. There is no difference in the method of payment between blue-collar workers and white-collar workers.

A large amount of bonus is paid twice a year – about two month's wages in summer and about three months' wages in December. The bonus is related to the profit of the company only to the slightest extent; it is almost a fixed amount. The bonus is usually paid as a straight multiple of monthly wage, without any reflection of merit. It is thus only a pattern of payment method.

Before the war there was a large difference in the amount of bonus paid to managers and to rank and file workers. Blue-collar workers received a very small bonus. Also before the war, the wage system was largely based on jobs and job grades. The annual wage progression was popular, but the amount was small and there was a maximum rate for the job. There was almost no status system at this time.

There is insufficient space here to describe the historical development of the promotion and wage system in Japanese enterprises, but we should recognize that the present unique promotion and wage system were shaped after the war as a result of much rational thinking, although respect for people was also important.

We can locate the promotion and wage systems in Figure 11.2. The horizontal axis shows the extent of importance of job capability for promotion and wage increase. The vertical axis shows the extent of equal treatment, whether it is equal or discriminated. The merit system

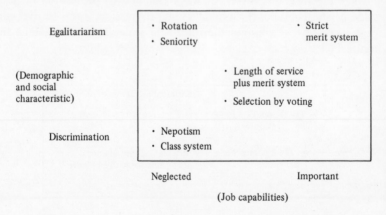

FIGURE 11.2 Various models on promotion and wage determination

emphasizes job capability and rapid promotion of the capable, and firing and demotion of the incapable. From the viewpoint of the employee it is not a stable system. The opposite is nepotism or the class system, where job capability is neglected and only those from a certain family or a higher social class (or caste) are promoted. Abilities are not taken into consideration. The 'length of service and merit' system goes between the two. It is fair and also has some stability for the participant. The US personnel system is close to the merit system; the UK personnel system uses two systems: for the higher echelons the merit system, and for the lower echelons the class system. The length of service and merit system is a blend of the merit system and egalitarianism.

11.4 RESPECT FOR PEOPLE

As members of a community organization, employees are considered partners of the company. They are not regarded as interchangeable components. Respect for people is the original force behind lifetime employment, emphasis on training, promotion and wage increase by length of service. Here we will describe some other systems following the same philosophy.

11.4.1 Detailed Personal Records and Self-statement System

Personal records are mainly comprised of personal career and merit-rating records. Records are kept even for the blue-collar workers; there is no distinction between blue- and white-collar workers. These records supply information for reviews for promotion and wage increases.

Self-statement is a statement of personal annual goals, self-appraisal, necessary skills to be developed, extent of use of ability, desirable other jobs where ability may be used to a fuller extent. This is sometimes accompanied by an observation sheet from a supervisor, which states the job content, qualifications, training given, capability in present job, need for promotion or transfer, training needed, characteristics of personality, etc.

These personal records are numerous and detailed in content. Such records are not found in the personnel record systems of US or UK enterprises. (For example, see Famularo, 1982.)

11.4.2 Equal Treatment and Participation

There is no difference in the treatment of blue-collar and white-collar workers. The promotion system and wage system are the same, the bonus system is the same, hours of work are the same. Both types of workers wear the same uniform at the plant site.

Nor is there any basic difference in treatment between the higher echelons and the lower ones. At the plant they wear the same uniform, use the same dining-room, use the same toilet. The office workers work together in large rooms.

Participation is much encouraged. Group decision is popular, and working together in a large room facilitates communication and participation.

Group activitity is common on most of the plant sites. The subjects of the activity are selected by the group. They mary be quality control, cost reduction, production method, or improvement of machines and materials. A group is formed usually within the formal organization, and thus a group activity is an informal organization within the formal group. The group leader is selected by the group members. Group meetings are usually held during the lunch hour or after working hours, and overtime is paid for some part of the activity. Group activity is a kind of job participation. It not only helps to improve the quality of the products, but also enhances the employee's sense of identification with the company.

Suggestion systems are nothing new, but they are implemented well as a means of participation. In Toyota and Matsushita Electric, each employee presents ten to fifteen ideas a year on average, so the total number is about 450 000 and 900 000 a year. In UK companies, ten suggestions a month for a whole plant is usually the norm.

11.4.3 Welfare System

Housing provided by the company and resort houses are very popular. Toyota, for example, provided houses for 4200 families and dormitories for 17 200 single men. There are seven resort houses. It also has a hospital and several recreational grounds.

Loans for home ownership, stock ownership with partial aid from the company, and company savings accounts with high rates of interest are provided by many companies

Recreation meetings are frequently held. There are a number of recreation groups, such as tennis clubs, skiing clubs, baseball clubs,

Japanese chess (Go) clubs and so forth which are partly subsidized by the company. Athletic meetings are held in spring and autumn; and the occasional group outing is popular. These simple group meetings are not only a pleasure in themselves, but also promote a group spirit and loyalty to the organization.

11.5 EFFECTS OF THE JAPANESE STYLE OF MANAGEMENT

The characteristics of the Japanese style of personnel management can be expressed as those of a community organization, so the satisfaction of the employees should be high. The complicated problems of subjective judgements on job satisfaction will be analysed later. Objective evidence of satisfaction can be seen in the figures for labour turnover and absenteeism. The turnover ratio of successful manufacturing companies, excluding retirement at 55 or 60 years old, is about 5–7 per cent per year for male workers (usually a higher percentage in the first five years of new employment, and a lower percentage after that year until retirement age) and about 20 per cent per year for female workers. The absence ratio is usually less than 3 per cent, including paid vacation, and less than 1 per cent excluding paid vacation (Ministry of Labour, 1982).

The economic performance of this system is best measured by the quality and cost of the products of successful Japanese manufacturing companies. The increase in labour productivity in Japanese manufacturing industries in the past ten years has been much higher than that of the USA and the UK, and a little higher than West Germany (Japan Productivity Centre, 1981).

The causal relationship is shown in Figure 11.3. Respect for people is the original source of all the other characteristics. Lifetime employment engenders the sense of all being together in the same boat, and the employees perceive that their hard work brings benefits to themselves. There are many opportunities for promotion and wage increases, and with little differentiation between workers, so they also estimate that hard work is profitable. On the other hand, emphasis on training and greater opportunity for participation improve the understanding of the job. These two intervening variables result in high productivity, willingness to accept innovation, and eventually competitive power in the world market.

These causal relationships can be explained by the expectancy theory. (For expectancy theory, see Porter and Lawler, 1968.) This theory assumes such relationships as effort–performance–rewards–value of

330

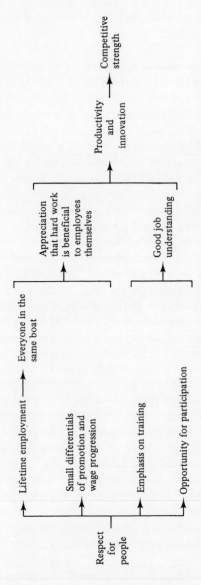

FIGURE 11.3 Effects of Japanese style of personnel management on productivity and innovation

rewards, and it assumes that the effort is determined by (i) the probability that performance depends on effort, (ii) the probability that reward depends upon performance, (iii) the value of reward. The sense of being in the same boat increases the perceived probability of performance–rewards relationships; the small differentials in promotion and wage progression increase the probability of effort–performance–reward relationships; the good personal records make certain the effort–performance relationships. Good training and participation increase performance for the same effort. Identification with the organization under the Japanese style of management increases the value of intrinsic rewards.

What are the effects on other strategies and strategic decisions? Lifetime employment influences strategic decisions, since the company tends to orient to long-range growth and to greater use of long-range planning. The lifetime employment and length of service system affect the type of diversification. In the past they facilitated the accumulation of knowledge in the company, which in turn led to the successful development of technology-intensive products. One result of this is the popularity of related diversification as a company strategy. On the other hand, the acquisition of other companies is not widely practised, so the conglomerate company is not common.

The lifetime employment and length of service system also affect vertical integration. Quasi-vertical integration is popular because the long-term association between the companies is advantageous to both sides.

The success of multinational management of Japanese subsidiaries is partly the result of the successful transplanting of the philosophy of respect for people.

The strategy also affects the personnel management style. Technology advanced rapidly after the Second World War, and the demands for technology-intensive products – such as cars and electronic products – also increased rapidly. Technology-intensive production needed and benefited from long-term services such as lifetime employment, and the emphasis on training. Company strategy and personnel management had such interdependent relationships. In the service industries, where such conditions are lacking, labour turnover is high.

11.6 SUMMARY

The Japanese company is like a community organization. It respects people. Employees are considered as partners in the organization and they have a high sense of loyalty and dedication to the organization.

They stay in the organization for their lifetime. The organization provides many opportunities for promotion, and wage increases with small differentials, which operates as incentives. Training within the company is very much stressed, and it pays under the lifetime employment system. Respect for people welcomes staff participation in decision-making at every level of the hierarchy.

This Japanese style of personnel management can be contrasted with other styles, as shown in Table 11.2.

TABLE 11.2 Two styles of personnel management

(Japanese style – Gemeinschaft)	*(Other model – Gesellschaft)*
Respect for people	Employee is one of the factors of production.
Lifetime employment	Open organization.
	Employment by contract, freedom of lay-off.
Emphasis on training	Human resources can be bought from outside the company.
Frequent promotion and wage increases	Severe merit system or class system.

11.6.1 Problems

11.6.1.1 The least satisfied workers in the world

There are a number of surveys showing the international comparison of employee satisfaction. Table 11.3 is the result of a survey conducted by the Prime Minister's Office on job satisfaction. The survey shows that Japanese workers are the least satisfied (Prime Minister's Office, 1979). Other surveys show similar results (Prime Minister's Office, 1972, 1978). This is surprising and shows that respect for people and stable employment do not apparently result in higher job satisfaction. Reasons for the dissatisfaction were requested, but there are no significant differences between countries.

There are two interpretations. One is that Japanese workers are compelled to work hard under strong pressure from the company and from their colleagues, and since they cannot escape from such pressure under the lifetime employment system, they are dissatisfied.

Another explanation is that the high level of education, and the egalitarian tendency in society and in business, enhance the aspiration

TABLE 11.3 Job satisfaction – an international survey
"Are you satisfied with the place you work or not?"

	Japan	USA	UK
1. Yes. satisfied			
Young	8%	32%	32%
Adult	15	49	42
2. More or less satisfied			
Young	51	51	55
Adult	56	40	49
3. More or less dissatisfied			
Young	28	10	10
Adult	21	7	7
4. No, dissatisfied			
Young	11	6	4
Adult	5	4	3

Note:
[1] The number indicates the percentage of respondent who selected each item.
[2] The age of the young is between 18 and 24, the age of adults is over 35.
[3] Survey by Prime Minister's office, 1978, samples are about 1500 young and adult
   workers in Japan, in the USA and in the UK.
[4] Prime Minister's Office: The Attitude of Young Workers in the Organization, 1978.

level of the employee, thus leading to dissatisfaction with the job and
pay. The author takes the latter view. Supporting evidence for this view
is that the long-term labour productivity of Japanese workers in the
manufacturing industries has been high. (Short term productivity is not
necessarily related to job satisfaction. See, for example, Likert, 1968;
Porter and Lawler, 1968.)

11.6.1.2 Lack of labour mobility between the organizations

Under a lifetime employment system it is hard, though not impossible,
to increase the necessary human resources quickly. Sony and Pioneer
have recruited many mature scientists and engineers from other
companies, but these are rather exceptional cases. (At the same time,
these companies do not easily separate or lay off their employees.) If a
person who cannot find in one organization the appropriate job in which
he can extend his ability is not able to move to another company, this is
inconvenient for both the company and the employee. The company
does not fire the incompetent even if they are useless to the company.

11.6.1.3 *Average age increase*

A problem already mentioned in Chapter 10 – the average age of the employees – is increasing. Fewer young people are being recruited as the result of the slow down in the growth rate of companies, and the age of retirement has been extended from 55 to 60 years old to match the longer life expectancy. A system of promotion and wage increase by length of service brings about two problems under these circumstances: too many employees are promoted to higher grades in the status system, and too many get higher wages that result in higher labour costs. To cope with this problem, companies have to put more emphasis on ability and merit for promotion and for wage progression. There is, however, a conflict between the needs of the company and the needs of the employees. The older the employee, the more the needs for promotion by status grade, but to control the increase in labour costs the greater the company need to emphasize merit.

REFERENCES

Fujita, C. (1981) *Gendai Jinji Romu Kanriron* (Personnel Management), Tokyo, Hakuto Shobo.

Japan Productivity Centre (1981) *Katsuyo Rodo Tokei* (Statistics on Labour), Tokyo, Japan Productivity Centre.

Ministry of Labour (1982) *Maitsuki Kinro Tokei (Monthly Labour Statistics)*, Jan–Dec.

Nakagawa, K. (ed.) (1977) *Nihonteki Keiei* (Japanese Management), Tokyo, Nihonkeizai.

Nakane, C. (1967) *Tateshakai no Ningenkankei* (Human Relations in Vertical Society), Tokyo, Kodansha.

Nikkeiren (1973) *Shokumu Shokuno Kanri no Hoko to Jissai* (Practice on Job and Wage Administration), Tokyo, Nikkeiren.

Prime Minister's Office (1972 and 1978) *Nihon no Seinen* (Japanese Young Workers), Tokyo, Prime Minister's Office.

Prime Minister's Office (1979) *Soshiki de Hataraku Seshonen no Ishiki* (The Attitude of young Workers in the Organization), Tokyo, Prime Minister's Office.

Takamiya, S. (ed.) (1976) *Nihon no Keiei Kyoiku eno Teigen* (Recommendation on Business Training in Japan), Tokyo, Sangyonoritsu Tandai.

Dore, R. (1973) *British Factory–Japanese Factory*, Calif, University of California Press.

Famularo, J. J. (1982) *Handbook of Personnel Forms, Records and Reports*, New York, McGraw-Hill.

French, W. (1974) *The Personnel Management Process*, Boston, Houghton Miffin.

Gibbs, R. (1980) *Industrial Policy in More Successful Economies* – Japan, London, NEDO.

Hunt, J. (1979) *Managing People at Work*, London, McGraw-Hill.

Likert, R. (1968) *The Human Organization*, New York, McGraw-Hill.

Macrae, N. (1980) 'Must Japan slow?' *Economist*, Feb.

Ouchi, W. (1981) *Theory Z*, Calif, Addison-Wesley.

Pascale, R. T. and Athos, A. G. (1981) *The Art of Japanese Management*, New York, Simon & Schuster.

Porter, L. W. and Lawler, E. E. (1968) *Managerial Attitude and Performance*, Ill., Richard D. Irwin.

Tönnies, F. (1887) *Gemeinschaft and Gesellschaft.*

Vogel, E. F. (1979) *Japan As Number One*, Cambridge, Mass., Harvard University Press.

Yoshino, Y. (1968) *Japan's Managerial System; Tradition and Innovation*, Cambridge, Mass., MIT Press.

Appendix A
Organization Chart
of Hitachi Ltd (1982)

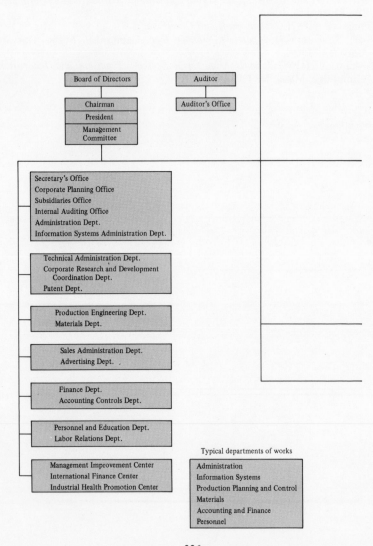

Board of Directors

Auditor

Chairman
President
Management
Committee

Auditor's Office

Secretary's Office
Corporate Planning Office
Subsidiaries Office
Internal Auditing Office
Administration Dept.
Information Systems Administration Dept.

Technical Administration Dept.
Corporate Research and Development
Coordination Dept.
Patent Dept.

Production Engineering Dept.
Materials Dept.

Sales Administration Dept.
Advertising Dept.

Finance Dept.
Accounting Controls Dept.

Personnel and Education Dept.
Labor Relations Dept.

Management Improvement Center
International Finance Center
Industrial Health Promotion Center

Typical departments of works

Administration
Information Systems
Production Planning and Control
Materials
Accounting and Finance
Personnel

Research Laboratories	Operating Groups / Divisions	Works / Offices
Central Research Laboratory Hitachi Research Laboratory Mechanical Engineering Research Laboratory Energy Research Laboratory Production Engineering Research Laboratory Systems Development Laboratory	Power Generation and Transmission Group	Power Generation and Transmission Div. Nuclear Power Generation Div. Hitachi Works Kokubu Works Omika Works
	Industrial Process Group	Tsuchiura Works Mito Works Kasado Works
	Castings and Forgings Div.	Katsuta Works
	Industrial Components and Equipment Group	Shimizu Works Yanai Works Nakajo Works Narashino Works Domestic Sales Offices
	Automobiles Appliances Div.	Sawa Works Sales Dept.
	Consumer Products Group	Design Center Consumer Products Research Center
	Home Appliances Div.	Taga Works Tochigi Works Ome Works
	Television, Audio and Video Products Div.	Yokohama Works Tokai Works Toyokawa Works
		Totsuka Works Sales Dept.
	Telephone Systems Sales Div.	
Hitachi Institute of Technology Hitachi Institute of Supervisory and Technical Training Technical Colleges (Ibaraki and Keihin)	Computer Group	Device Development Center Kanagawa Works Odawara Works Software Works Asahi Works Sales Dept.
	Office Systems Div.	
	Electronic Devices Group	
Odaira Memorial Tokyo Hitachi Hospital Ibaraki Hospital Center	Electron Tube Div.	Mobara Works
	Semiconductor and IC Div.	Musashi Works Takasaki Works Sales Dept.
	Measuring Instrument Div.	Naka Works
	Systems Engineering Div.	
	2 Sales Divisions (Power generation and industrial process)	District Offices
	3 Sales Companies (Consumer products and measuring instruments (2))	
	International Operations Group	International Sales Div. I International Sales Div. II China Business Div. Overseas License and Business Support Div. Overseas Offices
	Project Teams	

Appendix B
List of 102
Manufacturing Companies

MNM...Multi-national management level, EXP...Export ratio
ROT...Return on total investment, DEV...Standard deviation
of ROT, GRT...Growth rate of sales, EQU...Equity ratio

Company number	Company	Product mix (1980) (%)	Sales (SAL) (bilion yen) 1980	Diversification pattern 1967	Diversification pattern 1980	Organization structure 1967	Organization structure 1980	MNM (%) 1978~1980	EXP (%) 1967~1980	ROT (%) 1962~1980	DEV (%) 1962~1980	GRT (%) 1962~1980	EQU (%) 1967~1980
101	Kirin Brewery	beer(91), soft drinks(7), others(1)	786	S	D	F	F	0.7	0.5	10.91	1.95	11.9	37.9
102	Sapporo Breweries	beer(92), soft drinks(6), others(2)	244	S	D	F	F	0.0	0.0	8.34	2.46	8.2	29.1
103	Asahi Breweries	Beer(75), soft drinks(25)	184	D	D	F	F	0.0	0.0	7.76	2.17	5.3	32.2
201	Morinaga Milk Industry	milk(43), dairy products(21), others(36)	245	D	RMT	F	F	0.0	0.5	6.91	3.08	11.1	19.6
202	Meiji Milk Products	milk(46), dairy products(15), icecream(14), others(25)	284	D	RMT	F	F	0.0	1.5	7.27	2.29	11.7	23.5
203	Snow Brand Milk Products	milk(33), dried milk(14), butter & cheese(15), icecream(12), others(26)	417	RMT	RMT	DIV	F	0.0	0.0	6.23	1.40	12.6	20.8
301	Morinaga & Co.	confectionery(71), foodstuffs(28), others(1)	116	D	D	F	F	1.1	1.0	6.40	2.96	7.1	33.4
302	Meiji Seika	foodstuffs & confectionery(58), pharmaceutical(40), others(2)	175	RT	RT	DIV	DIV	1.5	4.0	11.17	3.25	10.1	41.1
303	Ezaki Glico	confectionery(95), foodstuffs(5)	101	D	D	F	F	0.6	0.0	12.23	4.12	12.5	41.5
304	Fujiya Confectionery	confectionery(56), restaurant(42), others(2)	106	RM	RM	F	F	0.0	0.0	7.37	3.13	10.1	34.1
305	Ajinomoto	seasonings(27), oil & fat(23), foodstuffs(33), amino acids(10), others(8)	340	RT	RT	F	F	20.0	7.5	9.73	1.99	13.0	36.6
401	Kanebo	cotton(9), nylon(13), polyester(17), cosmetics(25), wool(14), acrylic(9), others(14)	360	RM	RM	DIV	F	14.0	20.3	7.43	1.39	7.2	16.6
402	Toyobo	cotton(20), wool(6), synthetic fibers(65), others(9)	212	RM	RM	F	DIV	14.4	19.1	6.48	1.46	7.9	19.4
403	Unitika	nylon(27), polyester(28), cotton(10), wool(6), others(30)	181	RM	RM	DIV	DIV	9.1	12.1	7.03	1.85	5.0	20.6
404	Toray Industry	polyester(37), nylon(24), plastics(17), acrylic(8), chemical products(6), others(8)	404	D	RMT	F	DIV	36.4	29.0	8.90	3.80	8.1	37.3

Company	Product Mix (%)	SAL (billion yen)	PME	PML	OGE	OGL	MNM (%)	EXP (%)	ROT (%)	DEV (%)	GRT (%)	EQU (%)
405 Teijin	polyester(54), nylon(13), chemical products(29), others(4)	337	D	D	F	F	26.8	21.5	8.29	2.58	8.6	27.4
406 Asahi Chemical Industry	textiles(39), chemical products(31), plastics(13), construction stuffs (14), others(4)	425	D	RT	DIV	DIV	8.5	16.3	8.23	2.01	13.6	24.3
407 Kuraray	rayon(12), vinylon(16), polyester(47), non-fiber(25)	165	D	D	DIV	F	6.4	22.5	7.14	1.70	10.1	17.8
408 Mitsubishi Rayon	vonnel(24), soluna(34), pylen(3), synthetic resins(36), others(3)	147	D	RMT	F	DIV	16.6	17.0	7.18	2.50	11.5	17.5
501 Jujo Paper	printing paper(37), newsprints(28), other papers(4), converted paper(11) pulp(7), processed product(10), others(3)	228	D	RMT	F	F	0.0	4.5	6.39	0.75	12.9	15.5
502 Oji Paper	newsprints(32), printing papers(40), wrapping papers(8), lumber(6), others(14)	214	D	RMT	F	F	6.0	3.0	7.91	1.68	14.7	23.0
503 Daishowa Paper Mfg.	Papers(70), paperboards(26), pulps & others(4)	150	RMT	RMT	F	F	3.4	3.0	7.40	1.07	11.8	10.2
504 Honshu Paper	paperboard(28), papers(29), converted products(27), lumber & others(16)	179	RMT	RMT	F	DIV	10.4	5.5	7.23	1.31	13.0	11.9
601 Sumitomo Chemical	industrial chemicals & fertilizers (56), plastics & rubbers(21), fine chemicals(11), pharmaceuticals(4), farm chemicals(8)	435	RT	RT	DIV	DIV	0.1	9.0	7.05	1.11	14.7	21.2
602 Showa Denko	chemical products(69), furnace products(24), developments(7)	280	U	RT	F	DIV	4.1	9.5	7.08	1.21	14.0	15.5
603 Mitsubishi Chemical Industries	petrochemicals(48), carbon products(27), farm materials(12), others(13)	514	U	RT	DIV	DIV	3.4	11.5	6.92	0.68	16.9	17.9
604 Mitsui Toatsu Chemicals	industrial chemicals(40), synthetic resins(26), fertilizers(11), fine chemicals(13), others(10)	305	RT	RT	DIV	DIV	2.7	8.5	6.70	1.30	12.1	13.3
605 Mitsubishi Petrochemical	ethylene products(50), propylene products(24), automatic compounds(3), others(23)	254	S	S	F	F	0.0	7.0	6.46	1.81	20.5	21.2
606 Ube Industries	synthetic resins(10), fertilizers(6), nylon raw materials(11), cement(23) ready mixed concrete(7), machinery (23), others(20)	296	U	U	DIV	DIV	0.0	17.5	7.70	0.96	13.2	16.8
607 Dainippon Ink & Chemicals	synthetic resins(27), printing ink (19), chemicals(13), plastics(12), petrochemicals(12), others(17)	261	RT	RT	F	DIV	17.7	5.0	8.08	0.65	17.1	17.4
701 Kao Soap	soap & cleanser(83), industrial chemicals(17)	214	D	D	F	F	0.0	2.5	10.58	3.29	14.8	32.0
702 Takeda Chemical Industries	pharmaceuticals(58), foodstuffs(15), industrial & chemical products(14), others(14)	373	RMT	RT	DIV	DIV	3.9	5.5	12.43	3.99	12.0	38.4

Company	Product Mix (%)	SAL (billion yen)	PME	PML	OGE	OGL	MNM (%)	EXP (%)	ROT (%)	DEV (%)	GRT (%)	EQU (%)
703 Sankyo	pharmaceuticals(87), farm chemicals(8), others(5)	131	RMT	RMT	Fr	Fr	0.7	1.5	12.86	4.41	12.6	34.9
704 Shionogi & Co.	antibiotics(47), nervous system agents(11), hormones(5), agents for epidermis & sensory organs(9), others(28)	119	RMT	RMT	Fr	Fr	0.7	2.0	14.55	1.29	11.9	47.2
705 Tanabe Seiyaku	circulatory & respiratory(35), nutrient drugs & alteratives(12), nervous system agents(16), hormones(9), others(28)	94	RMT	RMT	Fr	Fr	1.8	6.0	9.39	2.61	12.9	17.8
706 Fuji Photo Film	photo films(39), cameras(8), products for medical use(14), graphic arts(18), others(21)	279	RT	RT	Fr	Fr	0.0	23.0	11.71	2.10	16.7	37.5
707 Shiseido	cosmetics(87), soaps(7), sundry goods(6)	266	D	D	Fr	Fr	1.1	3.0	14.96	2.26	14.7	40.4
708 Konishi-Roku Photo Industry	photo films(36), printing papers(17), cameras(15), dry-process copies(23), others(9)	132	RM	RM	Fr	DIV	11.1	32.5	9.00	3.14	15.8	27.6
709 Lion Corp.	dentifrices & toothbrushers(26), detergents(35), house hold goods(14), toiletries & others(25)	74	RM	RM	DIV	DIV	3.6	3.0	12.66	4.72	22.5	34.2
801 Maruzen Oil	gasoline(33), fuel oil(33), kerosene & gas oil(14), lubricating oil(2), others(11)	880	S	S	Fr	Fr	0.0	5.0	6.24	1.32	18.6	8.1
802 Nippon Oil	petrochemical products(2), others(16), gasoline(32), fuel oil(37), kerosene & gas oil(15), lubricating oil(3)	1612	S	S	Fr	Fr	0.0	2.5	6.64	3.30	14.2	12.9
803 Mitsubishi Oil	gasoline & naphtha(36), fuel oil(34), kerosene & gas oil(16), others(14)	679	S	S	Fr	Fr	0.0	1.8	5.85	3.16	18.6	10.3
804 Toa Nenryo Kogyo	gasoline & naphtha(39), fuel oil(30), kerosene & gas oil(22), lubricating oil & others(9)	533	S	S	Fr	Fr	0.0	1.5	11.74	2.64	19.7	28.1
901 Bridgestone Tire	auto tires & tubes(85), chemical products(15)	370	D	D	Fr	Fr	11.4	22.0	14.47	1.84	13.2	40.6
902 Yokohama Rubber	auto tires(82), industrial products(15), auto parts(2)	150	D	D	DIV	Fr	0.0	18.5	6.93	2.04	11.5	15.9
1001 Asahi Glass	glass(57), chemical products(37), ceramics(4), others(2)	325	RT	RT	Fr	Fr	6.8	5.8	10.84	2.04	14.5	42.2
1002 Nippon Sheet Glass	sheet glass & figured glass(17), float glass(57), sashes & others(26)	96	S	D	Fr	Fr	8.3	5.8	9.19	2.43	12.5	30.7
1003 Central Glass	glass(47), chemical products(31), chemical fertilizers(20), others(2)	116	U	U	Fr	Fr	11.2	12.0	5.25	2.43	17.6	10.0
1101 Onoda Cement	cement(81), limestone & others(19)	201	S	S	Fr	Fr	9.2	7.0	7.86	1.87	10.5	18.2
1102 Nihon Cement	cement(80), others(20)	131	S	S	Fr	Fr	0.6	5.0	8.09	1.66	10.3	21.4
1103 Mitsubishi Mining & Cement	cement(52), ready mixed concrete(4), petroleum(33), construction materials(8), others(3)	181	U	U	Fr	Fr	0.4	4.5	9.78	1.17	18.0	15.8

Company	Product Mix (%)	SAL (billion yen)	PME	PML	OGE	OGL	MNM (%)	EXP (%)	ROT (%)	DEV (%)	GRT (%)	EQU (%)
1201 Nippon Steel	steel products(91), engineering & others(9)	2412	S	S	F	F	0.5	27.0	7.74	1.58	12.6	23.2
1202 Nippon Kokan	iron & steel(86), engineering, construction & shipbuilding(14)	1115	RT	D	F	DIV	1.4	25.5	7.29	1.31	13.3	16.3
1203 Sumitomo Metal Industries	steel pipes(34), steel plater(40), steel wires(9), rollingstock parts(17)	1029	D	D	F	F	0.9	32.0	7.86	1.78	15.7	19.3
1204 Kawasaki Steel	plates & sheets(66), rods, bars & shapes(10), pipes(14), engineering works & others(10)	961	S	S	F	F	4.5	28.0	8.29	1.86	14.4	23.6
1205 Kobe Steel	iron, steel & welding rods(60), machinery(23), aluminum & copper(17)	884	RMT	U	DIV	DIV	0.9	19.0	7.90	1.34	15.5	18.9
1206 Nisshin Steel	steel products(60), stainless steel (31), others(9)	294	RMT	RMT	F	F	0.0	16.5	8.12	1.60	11.6	19.9
1301 Nippon Mining	copper(13), petroleum(69), metal fabricating products(5), zinc(2), others(11)	491	U	D	DIV	DIV	6.2	4.5	7.53	1.31	17.0	12.8
1302 Mitsubishi Metal	copper(38), zinc(6), lead(3), gold & silver(23), acid(2), processed metal products(26), others(2)	203	RT	RT	F	DIV	3.8	9.0	7.44	1.10	13.4	17.5
1303 Mitsui Mining & Smelting	copper(23), zinc(13), Processed metal products(22), lead(3), other metals(2), chemical goods(12), others(4)	178	RT	RT	F	DIV	5.6	5.5	6.94	1.27	12.3	18.8
1304 Furukawa Electric	cables & wires(52), rolled copper products(14), light metal products(25), others(9)	305	D	RT	DIV	DIV	15.3	12.8	7.38	1.01	12.0	16.5
1305 Sumitomo Electric Industries	cables(61), special steel wires(8), powdered alloys(10), brakes(5), other(16)	311	S	RT	DIV	DIV	2.9	14.3	8.51	1.24	13.3	25.7
1401 Niigata Engineering	chemical plants & other equipment(38), diesel engines(24), shipbuilding(8), others(30)	144	U	U	DIV	DIV	0.4	26.5	6.75	0.99	14.4	19.3
1402 Komatsu	construction machinery(89), industrial machinery(7), steel casting & others(5)	397	D	D	F	F	3.5	28.0	9.48	1.48	12.9	27.9
1403 Sumitomo Heavy Industries	general machinery(51), standardized machinery(31), shipbuilding & offshore (18)	192	RT	RT	DIV	DIV	1.7	26.5	6.91	3.03	16.0	19.6
1404 Ebara Corp.	pumps & blowers(80), refrigerators & boilers(9), oil-hydraulic machinery(3) plants(8)	103	RT	RT	F	F	0.4	12.5	9.92	1.72	12.4	33.6
1405 Toyoda Automatic Loom Works	textile machinery(14), automobiles(28), industrial vehicles(34), others(24)	174	RT	RT	DIV	DIV	0.0	20.0	10.53	2.79	15.2	45.0
1406 Kubota	farm machinery(43), machinery(9), pipes (26), building materials & housing(9), molding(9), others(4)	464	U	U	DIV	DIV	3.1	7.5	11.94	1.77	12.6	43.4
1407 Koyo Seiko	ball roller bearings(74), other machinery parts(26)	85	S	S	F	F	3.9	24.5	7.41	3.86	12.6	28.0
1408 Nippon Seiko	bearings(68), machinery parts(32)	124	S	S	F	F	16.0	13.0	9.66	2.64	14.5	30.2

Company	Product Mix (%)	SAL (billion yen)	PME	PML	OGE	OGL	MNM (%)	EXP (%)	ROT (%)	DEV (%)	GRT (%)	EQU (%)
1501 Hitachi	electrical equipment(25), consumer goods(23), communications & electronics(27), industrial machinery(12), transportation equipment(13)	1509	RT	RT	DIV	DIV	5.1	18.5	8.34	1.41	11.1	27.6
1502 Toshiba Corp.	home electric appliances(39), heavy electric machinery(35), communications & electronic machinery(26)	1240	RT	RT	DIV	DIV	5.9	16.5	6.35	1.48	10.9	24.0
1503 Mitsubishi Electric	heavy electric machinery(26), standardized electric machinery(17), home electric appliances(26), electronic industrial machinery(31)	935	RT	RT	DIV	DIV	4.1	13.0	6.74	1.28	12.3	21.0
1504 Matsushita Electric Industrial	wireless equipment(47), home appliances(34), batteries(5), lamps & tubes(4), others(10)	1598	RMT	RMT	DIV	DIV	15.9	17.3	15.37	3.15	14.6	45.1
1505 Nippon Electric	communications equipment(24), radio equipment(15), computers(25), electron devices(27), others(9)	615	RT	RT	DIV	DIV	6.3	21.0	8.02	1.71	16.9	21.4
1506 Sanyo Electric	consumer electronics(51), electrical household(34), commercial electrical equipment(11), others(4)	528	RMT	RMT	DIV	DIV	37.1	36.0	9.55	2.36	14.1	37.2
1507 Oki Electric Industry	communications equipments(31), data processing units(43), electronic parts(13), others(13)	137	D	RT	DIV	DIV	7.1	9.0	7.52	2.80	12.8	18.4
1508 Fujitsu	computers(65), telephone exchangers & sets(9), radio equipment(12), others(14)	441	D	D	DIV	DIV	8.0	10.0	10.23	2.35	19.6	28.3
1509 Sony Corp.	TVs(25), tape recorders & radios(19), VTRs(28), audio equipment(10), others(18)	414	RMT	RMT	DIV	DIV	25.1	59.5	14.11	3.22	20.2	39.9
1510 Victor Company of Japan	audios(31), TVs(13), electronic instruments(4), phonograph records(3), VTRs(49)	187	RMT	RMT	DIV	DIV	1.9	40.0	11.47	4.64	15.4	36.4
1511 Matsushita Electric Works	plastics(8), construction materials(25), electric fixture materials(25), lighting apparatus(33), electric appliances(9)	388	RT	RMT	DIV	DIV	1.5	3.5	16.03	3.48	19.0	38.5
1601 Nissan Motor	automobiles(89), auto parts & others(11)	2307	S	S	F	F	2.9	36.0	11.43	2.64	18.2	35.8
1602 Isuzu Motors	large trucks & buses(29), small trucks(36), passenger cars(13), engines & parts(22)	572	RMT	D	F	F	5.3	24.5	6.58	2.50	12.1	20.4
1603 Toyota Motor	passenger cars(59), trucks & buses(22), others(19)	2617	S	S	F	F	2.4	33.0	17.60	3.90	18.8	51.7
1604 Hino Motors	diesel trucks(50), diesel buses(8), pickup trucks(26), parts(16)	329	D	D	F	F	3.8	16.5	7.85	1.13	13.6	23.1
1605 Tokokogyo	passenger cars(57), trucks(26), auto parts(8), others(8)	686	S	S	F	F	8.7	38.5	8.19	2.96	14.9	21.5

Company	Product Mix (%)	SAL (billion yen)	PME	PML	OGE	OGL	INM (%)	EXP (%)	ROT (%)	DEV (%)	GRT (%)	EQU (%)
1606 Honda Motor	motorcycles(29), automobiles(59), farm machinery & others(12)	922	RMT	RMT	F	F	6.3	52.0	10.12	2.30	18.3	36.8
1607 Fuji Heavy Industries	automobiles(80), bus bodies(5), rollingstock(7), aircrafts(3), industrial machinery(5)	327	D	D	DIV	DIV	0.3	26.5	7.68	2.28	16.2	22.8
1608 Suzuki Motor	automobiles(48), motorcycles(39), out-board motors(4), parts & others(9)	272	D	RMT	F	F	4.9	33.5	9.43	3.34	18.9	20.7
1701 Mitsubishi Heavy Industries	shipbuilding & ship repairing(23), chemical plants(4), machinery(19), special vehicle(25), others(9)	1275	U	RT	DIV	DIV	5.0	24.0	5.32	1.27	13.4	13.1
1702 Ishikawajima-Harima Heavy Industries	shipbuilding & ship repairing(23), industrial machinery & plants(77)	698	RT	RT	DIV	DIV	10.4	36.5	5.24	0.93	12.9	9.7
1703 Hitachi Shipbuilding & Engineering	shipbuilding(35), ship repairing(20), machinery(13), others(32)	258	RT	RT	DIV	F	3.6	40.5	5.09	0.90	11.4	12.8
1704 Kawasaki Heavy Industries	shipbuilding(14), rollingstock(6), air-craft(4), plant engineering(31), machinery(21), engine & motorcycle(23)	501	RT	RT	DIV	DIV	5.8	41.0	5.45	1.07	18.0	13.4
1705 Mitsui Engineering & Shipbuilding	shipbuilding(35), ship repairing(11), ocean development products(4), prime movers(17), industrial plants(13), steel structures(6), others(14)	255	RT	RT	DIV	DIV	0.0	47.5	5.12	1.64	14.3	15.1
1801 Hattori & Co.	watches(78), clocks(12), jewels & others(4), measuring instruments(3), others(3)	280	D	D	F	F	8.6	30.5	13.55	3.21	15.0	27.9
1802 Citizen Watch	wrist watches(89), office equipment(3), machine tools(4), others(4)	83	D	D	F	F	14.3	41.0	12.44	3.38	14.7	43.4
1803 Canon Inc.	cameras(51), electoronic calculators(12), copiers(27), others(10)	137	D	RMT	F	DIV	7.5	61.0	11.23	3.44	19.1	39.6
1804 Ricoh	copier(64), sensitized papers(21), data processing equipments(10), photographic equipment(5)	197	RMT	RMT	F	DIV	7.0	22.5	10.89	3.67	18.6	19.4
1805 Nippon Kogaku	cameras(66), microscopes(7), spectacle linses(16), optical measuring instruments (5), telescopes(4), others(3)	84	RT	RT	DIV	DIV	0.0	48.5	10.78	4.46	17.8	29.5
1806 Olympus Optical	cameras(53), medical instruments(27), microscopes(16), micro taperecorders(4)	67	RT	RT	DIV	F&D	1.1	50.5	13.98	4.66	19.2	45.0
1901 Nippon Gakki	pianos(30), electronic organs(22), stereo(7), audio equipments(18), home utensils & others(23)	276	D	RMT	F	F	3.3	15.0	14.81	3.42	12.9	48.4
1902 Kawai Musical Instrument Mfg.	pianos(53), electronic organs(22), other musical instruments(12), others(22)	65	D	D	F	F	0.0	13.0	12.67	7.70	12.5	37.1
Average		445					5.56	17.22	9.04	2.29	13.91	26.10
Standard Deviation		486					7.25	14.67	2.76	1.13	3.37	10.63

(note) For definition of abbreviation, see Appendix 4-1, in Chapter 4.

Index